Hedge Fund Governance

Evaluating Oversight, Independence, and Conflicts

Hedge Fund Governance
Evaluating Oversight, Independence, and Conflicts

Jason Scharfman
Managing Partner, Corgentum Consulting, LLC

ELSEVIER

AMSTERDAM • BOSTON • HEIDELBERG • LONDON
NEW YORK • OXFORD • PARIS • SAN DIEGO
SAN FRANCISCO • SINGAPORE • SYDNEY • TOKYO

Academic Press is an Imprint of Elsevier

Academic Press is an imprint of Elsevier
525 B Street, Suite 1800, San Diego, CA 92101-4495, USA
225 Wyman Street, Waltham, MA 02451, USA
The Boulevard, Langford Lane, Kidlington, Oxford OX5 1GB, UK

British Library Cataloguing-in-Publication Data
A catalogue record for this book is available from the British Library

Library of Congress Cataloging-in-Publication Data
A catalog record for this book is available from the Library of Congress

ISBN: 978-0-12-801412-7

For information on all Academic Press publications
visit our website at http://store.elsevier.com/

Typeset by Thomson Digital

Printed and bound in the United States

Dedication

This book is dedicated to my wife and family for their continued inspiration and support.

Contents

3.   Regulatory Governance of Hedge Funds

11. Good Governance in Bad Situations: Understanding Governance During Fund Turmoil and Liquidations

12. Trends and Future Developments

Biography

Jason Scharfman, Esq., CFE, CRISC—Managing Partner, Corgentum Consulting, LLC

Jason Scharfman is the Managing Partner of Corgentum Consulting, LLC. Corgentum is a specialist consulting firm that provides the industry's most comprehensive operational due diligence reviews and background investigations of fund managers including hedge funds, private equity, real estate, and traditional funds. Mr. Scharfman is recognized as one of the leading experts in the field of operational due diligence and is the author of *Hedge Fund Operational Due Diligence: Understanding the Risks* (John Wiley & Sons, 2008) and *Private Equity Operational Due Diligence: Tools to Evaluate Liquidity, Valuation and Documentation* (John Wiley & Sons, 2012).

Before founding Corgentum, he previously oversaw the operational due diligence function for a $6 billion alternative investment allocation group called Graystone Research at Morgan Stanley. Prior to joining Morgan Stanley, he held positions that primarily focused on due diligence and risk management at Lazard Asset Management, SPARX Investments and Research, and Thomson Financial.

Mr. Scharfman received a B.S. in finance with an additional major in Japanese from Carnegie Mellon University, an M.B.A. in finance from Baruch College's Zicklin School of Business, and a J.D. from St. John's School of Law. He is admitted to the practice of law in New York and New Jersey. Additionally, he holds the Certified Fraud Examiner (CFE) and Certified in Risk and Information Systems Control (CRISC) credentials. He has consulted with the US House Judiciary Committee on the subject of hedge fund regulation. Additionally, he has provided training to financial regulators on the subject of hedge fund due diligence. Mr. Scharfman has served as a consultant and testified as an expert in hedge fund litigation, and has lectured on the subject of hedge fund operations and operational risk as an adjunct professor at New York University. He has written extensively on the subject of operational due diligence and travels and speaks worldwide on hedge fund operational risks.

Preface

Investors don't trust hedge funds. This might seem counterintuitive because they place billions of dollars with them, but they still don't necessarily trust them. Don't feel too bad for hedge funds; the feeling is mutual. With this mistrust, why then do the two continue to do business?

For starters, investors can utilize hedge funds to add real value to their overall portfolios. This is especially true for the increasingly large number of underfunded pension systems who are increasingly turning to funds to generate returns. After the 2008 financial crisis, multiple large-scale frauds, and more recent insider trading scandals, however, the blind trust investors used to place with investment consultants and hedge funds was shaken to say the least.

It's not as if the hedge funds were the only ones to blame; during the post-2008 financial crisis many investors simply couldn't wait to redeem their capital from funds. Hedge funds, facing decreasing valuations and illiquidity, didn't necessarily want to be forced into liquidation and employed a number of techniques such as lowering their gates and utilizing side pockets to slow the pace of capital outflows. These were the rules of hedge fund investing that investors had willingly signed up for, and now investors were complaining and even suing. You could see how this could make some hedge funds a bit gun shy of giving investors too much flexibility going forward.

Despite these tensions the two groups continue to coexist. The rules of hedge fund investing, however, have changed significantly. Investors are increasingly conscious of the fact that when allocating to hedge funds they have to consider more than just a fund's potential for profits. More than just trading desks, it is now widely accepted that hedge funds are complex organizations that need to be managed properly from both an operational and an investment perspective in order to be successful. Increasingly investors have accepted that a key element to this success is something called governance, but what exactly does that mean? The goal of this book is to attempt to answer that question.

To start off we will frame governance in a historical context to arrive at a modern working definition of the term. This book will outline how the definition of governance has evolved and broadened over time. To do this we will focus on the expanding definition of governance including regulatory governance of hedge funds, internal hedge fund governance mechanisms, service provider governance, and governance in valuations and fund liquidations.

This book will also highlight a key player in the world of hedge fund governance, the board of directors. Investors generally fall into three camps when it comes to talking about fund boards: they love them, hate them, or dismiss them. Much of this criticism comes from a lack of clarity with regards to the roles of directors as well as a lack of in-depth director due diligence. In an attempt to reconcile the different sides of the arguments for and against directors, we will discuss the role of fund boards and provide perspectives on board-related considerations ranging from the delegation of duties and director liability to capacity considerations, and the ways that they work with other service providers. To provide recent perspectives on the role of directors and governance this book also features exclusive interviews with directors, regulators, and operational due diligence analysts.

Once you have developed a detailed understanding of governance, we will then show you how to put it into practice in the real world. To do this we will introduce techniques that investors can use to conduct initial and ongoing assessments of governance. We will also cover historical examples of governance failures. Finally this book will outline trends in the space with regards to governance practices in general and the board of directors specifically.

Governance does not live in a vacuum and is not centralized within any one part of a hedge fund such as compliance. Nor is it the sole domain of any single service provider such as the board of directors. Instead, governance can be thought of as a living system that controls the operational and investment functions of funds. It does not refer to the actual functions that are in place, but oversees them to ensure they are running efficiently and effectively. It is the glue that binds the disparate functions of a hedge fund together. Without proper oversight the system will eventually fail; hedge funds will go out of business and investors will lose money. Investors who take measures to evaluate the quality of the governance framework in place at a hedge fund through deep-dive due diligence can avoid these risks and ultimately make more informed investment decisions.

A strong governance infrastructure can help rebuild the broken confidence between hedge fund and investors. It is up to both parties to trust but verify that controls and oversight not only are put in place but also stay in place to prevent the next crisis of confidence.

Jason Scharfman
July 2014

Chapter 1

Introduction to Hedge Fund Governance

Chapter Outline Head

INTRODUCTION TO THE CONCEPT OF GOVERNANCE

What exactly does the term "governance" mean? Many investors are perhaps more familiar with the term governance when it is paired up with the term "corporate." Ok, so what then does the term "corporate governance" mean exactly? Does this definition vary based on the context of what type of corporate governance you are talking about? Can there be other types of governance besides "corporate?" Does the definition of this perhaps change when applied to hedge funds?

As an investor in equities, bonds, private equity, real estate, or certainly hedge funds you may have never really given this much thought. Frankly, why should you? Who cares what governance is as long as a hedge fund's net asset value ("NAV") beats its benchmark? In this chapter we will provide a working definition of hedge fund governance and outline its historical perspective. Before addressing these issues, we should address the issue of why investors should care about this important subject to begin with.

WHY SHOULD INVESTORS CARE ABOUT HEDGE FUND GOVERNANCE?

Hedge fund investing is complicated enough. There are lots of strategy and fund options. Depending on the year several of them may seem quite attractive. It can be difficult enough for investors to select a fund manager who can generate a sustainable profit year-over-year; who has the time to worry about anything else? At its core the goal of investing is to generate a profit, and things outside of that direct goal aren't necessarily always a primary concern to investors. Of course, the investments have to be made in a legal way, but outside of these basic principles does anything else really matter to an investor's bottom line? Especially seemingly vague notions such as governance?

It could be argued after all that governance, whatever that means, isn't even necessary for a hedge fund to function or be profitable. Some have attempted to write off governance as being entirely unnecessary to hedge funds. To continue that analogy, a boat can successfully navigate the ocean without life preservers, can't it? Of course it can. It isn't necessarily a good idea for the passengers, but that doesn't mean the propellers won't spin. It could be argued that governance functions in the same way as the life preservers; it's not functionally required for a fund to make investments but it's a bad idea to proceed without it. Is this line of reasoning correct? Could it be that governance is indeed operating in the background of seemingly basic operational functions, even though it may not be readily apparent? This book will address these questions about governance.

If you are reading this book, it means you are most likely fall into one of two camps. The first group is people who are perhaps unfamiliar with hedge funds and want to learn more and the subject with a particular focus on governance. This book will certainly equip you with knowledge about hedge fund governance, but it is not meant to be a primer on the hedge fund industry. This is best left for other books, and there are a number of other introductory resources in this area (Anson, 2006). The other group of people reading this book are those who are familiar with the hedge fund industry. You are likely a direct investor in hedge funds (i.e., high-net-worth individual or family office), represent a large hedge fund allocator (i.e., corporate or public pension plan, fund of hedge funds, endowment, foundation, bank, insurance company, etc.), or work in some capacity in the hedge fund industry [i.e., an operational due diligence (ODD) analyst at a fund of hedge funds].

Regardless of your level of sophistication with the hedge fund industry, understanding the role of governance is more critical today than ever before.

Governance has influence across all aspects of the hedge fund industry ranging from the managers themselves and their investments to their service providers and investors. By learning about what hedge fund governance is and trends in the space you will, hopefully, be able to promote better governance practices in your respective corner of the hedge fund world.

Analyzing, implementing, and monitoring governance in hedge funds, as this book will hopefully convince you, is a critical element of hedge fund investing. It not only relates to the implementation of checks and balances, and adherence to technical policies and procedures, but can also influence the nature of a hedge fund's investments and ultimately affect the fund's overall profitability. Before seeking to analyze the role of governance, however, we must return to our original question seeking to define what governance actually is.

GOVERNANCE: A VAGUE CONCEPT?

The use of the word "governance" has grown in popularity in recent years in the hedge fund industry. Beyond being the latest hedge fund buzzword, what does it actually mean? Originally the term in a hedge fund context was tied to hedge fund activist investors seeking to promote good governance in the companies in which they invested. We will address this concept later in the chapter.

One of the more recent applications of the term has been with regards to promoting good governance not within the companies that the hedge funds invest in, but in the hedge funds themselves. This increased attention has come about for a number of reasons including regulatory changes, historical frauds, and increased investor demands for transparency to name a few. But, returning to our original question, what exactly does this application of governance mean?

Pinning down the concept and actual definition of governance in the hedge fund industry has presented a bit of a challenge for many investors and hedge fund managers alike. Unlike many parts of the hedge fund, governance is not a heavily quantitative subject. There are no carried interest calculations, VaR analysis, turnover ratios, or leverage calculations. Instead governance is more of a qualitative subject that relates to notions of ethics, conflicts of interest, and even, depending on your perspective, things such as being a good corporate citizen.

The qualitative nature of this subject perhaps is one of the reasons that has created a definitional challenge to the term governance, in the traditionally more quantitative hedge fund industry. It's not because people in the hedge fund industry aren't smart. Indeed, many have argued that hedge funds house some of the financial industries' best intellectual capital (*Bloomberg*, 2003). It's just harder for most people, particularly in a quantitative slanted industry, to digest more qualitative learning concepts such as governance. Also contributing to the problem is that there is no consistent market or legal definition of what governance in the hedge fund industry actually means. Further contributing to the confusion is the fact that there is a mixed consensus on who is actually responsible for governance. But perhaps we are getting ahead of ourselves; before we can begin to talk about gauging if a hedge fund has good or bad governance we must first attempt to define the concept in a hedge fund framework.

HOW SHOULD INVESTORS THINK ABOUT HEDGE FUND GOVERNANCE?

What is the appropriate way to think about hedge fund governance? This might seem like an odd question at first, but discussing it will help us better frame a definition of what exactly hedge fund governance itself is. At its core, what this question is really asking is first, "how should investors classify hedge funds?" The second question is, "once we've made a decision about what a hedge fund is, how should we think about governance in that class of funds?"

Let us try to tackle the first part of this question. We could take the easy way out and say a hedge fund is just that, a class unto itself of hedge funds. Continuing this line of reasoning we could say that private equity funds are their own class, and so are mutual funds, index funds, etc. This may be true, and depending on your perspective hedge funds may be in such a unique asset class unto themselves. Others may argue that this certainly may be even too much of a generalization. Under the broad category of hedge funds there are numerous subcategories differentiated by numerous categories including location, assets under management, and investment strategy. From a regulatory perspective some have suggested that certain hedge fund strategies could be compared with closed-ended US mutual funds while others suggest that they should be viewed more as private partnerships (Lehmann, 2006).

Prior to the most recent waves of enhanced hedge funds' regulatory requirements, including that hedge fund become registered with regulatory entities such as the US Securities and Exchange Commission (SEC), some investors thought of hedge funds as merely one option in a series of largely unregulated, or exempt from regulation, investments. Further complicating the issue, the nature of many hedge fund investments has become blurred with other asset classes such as private equity. A good example of this was in the aftermath of the 2008 financial crisis. During that time many hedge funds opted to side pocket illiquid or distressed positions. For reference, for the purpose of our discussion here a side pocket can be thought of as a separate fund where illiquid assets are placed. We will address side pockets in more detail in Chapter 11. These side pockets often exhibit private equity–like characteristics and unfortunately for many investors further lengthened payout and recovery timetables. Considering it from another angle, many other types of investments have sought to take on hedge fund–like approaches and some in the academic community have suggested that hedge funds themselves are effectively not providing the alpha they promise and instead investors are really adding hedge fund beta to their portfolios when allocating to hedge funds (Jaeger, 2005; Kat and Palaro, 2005).

Unfortunately for us, therefore, there seems to be no real consensus on whether or not hedge funds are a unique asset class unto themselves. This is not very good for our attempt to answer the second part of the question of how we should think about governance. If we were able to answer the first question, our approach would have then been to look at the likely body of research on governance within that particular asset class and then use that to inform our opinion of how we should think about hedge fund governance. Fortunately for us, however, we are not stuck. This exercise was merely meant to demonstrate that the issue of classification of hedge funds has been one that is debated in the industry.

For the purposes of our discussion, we are attempting to define governance in a hedge fund context. As such, despite debatable notions to the contrary, we will follow the assumption that hedge funds are a unique asset class unto themselves. This does not mean that they do not share common characteristics with other types of investments, both traditional and alternative. Rather when discussing fund governance for the purpose of this book, we will look for similarities within the hedge fund space itself, instead of seeking to overly borrow from governance concepts for other asset classes. Stated another way, to put together a working definition of hedge fund governance, we cannot simply say that it is effectively the same as governance in other funds in its class. Private equity governance is not the same as hedge fund governance that is not the same as mutual fund governance. Certain characteristics of governance across these types of funds and asset classes may be similar, but ultimately they are not identical from a governance perspective as hedge funds themselves pose unique governance challenges.

WHAT HEDGE FUND ENTITIES ARE INVESTORS LOOKING AT TO PROMOTE GOOD GOVERNANCE?

In developing a definition of hedge fund governance, this text will also seek to provide an overview of methodologies and techniques that are employed in hedge fund governance. Often times, hedge fund investors are the ones driving the governance process. As part of this process they are looking to implement *good governance*, a term which we will discuss in more detail below, in the hedge funds in which they invest. To clarify a bit of terminology the term hedge fund, as with many terms that we will encounter in this book, is a bit of a misnomer. To get technical about it, the term "hedge fund" is a catch-all term that can mean a number of different things depending on the context. For starters, a hedge fund may be referring to the management company of a hedge fund. This is the central legal entity that usually coordinates the firm's business activities. For example, the employees of hedge fund organizations are usually employed by the management company.

When investors allocate to a hedge fund though, they are not typically referring to an investment in the management company. While this is possible, under perhaps a construct such as a seeding arrangement, it is not typically what is implied. Instead, investors for the large part are making investments into a hedge fund investment vehicle, which is also sometimes called a fund. These investment vehicles come in a variety of flavors. Two of the more common vehicles are based around the jurisdiction of the particular funds. The first is an onshore vehicle, which is also referred to as a domestic vehicle or fund. Taken from the perspective of a United States–based investor, an example of this type of vehicle would be a Delaware-domiciled fund. The other common vehicle type is an offshore vehicle. From the perspective of a US-based investor this would be a non–US-domiciled fund, such as a hedge fund vehicle registered in the Cayman Islands. Each of these vehicles may then have other associated funds and entities including a master fund, a General Partner, and an Investment Manager.

Returning to our original question, when investors state that they want to promote good governance at a hedge fund, in which of these entities are they referring to? The typical answer, and the approach we will take in this book, is all of them.

There are two primary reasons we make this assumption. First, beginning with the hedge fund vehicle level, many different hedge fund vehicles across the same strategy complex are typically managed in materially the same manner. In hedge fund speak, this is sometimes referred to as in a pari passu manner (Scharfman, 2008). Investors, however, generally invest in one particular vehicle within the same hedge fund strategy. This is done for a variety of reasons including the tax consequences of investing in one type of vehicle over another. There are also legitimate concerns that within the same fund complex, investors in one fund vehicle could be disadvantaged at the expense of another. Examples of this could include certain opportunities being allocated on a non–pro rata basis or not at all to an onshore vehicle instead of an offshore one. It could also be the case that there are related party transactions among the funds that negatively impact one over the other. Another example of the risks posed by related party transactions among fund vehicles would be the allegations brought by the US SEC against Martin Currie (US Securities and Exchange Commission, 2012).

To play devil's advocate for a moment, while there are legitimate concerns of intervehicle fund risks, among vehicles in the same strategy, it could be argued that on a vehicle level an investor should primarily be concerned only with what happens in the particular vehicle they are invested in. Such an approach, however, only works when your vehicle is on the winning side of any conduct, which is disadvantageous to the other vehicle(s) in the fund complex. Furthermore, there is always the overarching risk of the potential for a claw back of profits from one vehicle to another if it is shown that a particular vehicle profited unjustly from actions that hurt investors in another vehicle.

A good corollary to this example comes from the world of hedge fund ODD. When conducting an ODD review of a particular hedge fund vehicle's audited financial statements, it is considered best practice to review all of the financial statements from affiliated vehicles within the hedge fund's strategy complex. This practice has developed because of an increasing acknowledgment from investors of the risks that information about other vehicles in which an investor might not be directly invested can still be valuable in conducting an overall assessment of the vehicle into which an investor is allocating capital as well as the hedge fund itself. Following up on this point, as we will discuss shortly, by focusing on the specific governance aspects of only the specific vehicle in which an investor is invested in, an investor is forgoing learning about some of the good governance aspects at the management company level.

We can next turn to the second primary reason this book will assume that investors want to promote governance across all the hedge fund vehicles and related entities. As we have stated earlier in this section, the management company of a hedge fund is the central legal entity where the firm's business is conducted. As the saying goes leadership starts at the top. If a hedge fund has bad governance at the management company level, then it is likely that these poor practices will also translate down to the fund level.

As we outlined earlier, however, investors are not allocating their capital directly to the hedge fund management company. Once again, the narrow view of the governance relationships would be to play the cynic and take the approach, "Who cares what else happens outside of the specific fund I am invested in?" As intimated above, and as will be outlined throughout this book, there are significant implications for the fund vehicles based on what happens at the management company level. If investors are truly interested in promoting good governance and making more informed hedge fund investment decisions, then a holistic approach to governance is what is required. To clarify this does not mean that there should be an exclusive focus on the bigger management company entities at the expense of vehicle-level governance. Rather, promoting good governance at a hedge fund requires promoting total governance across all of the aspects of the firm.

DISTINGUISHING BETWEEN GOVERNANCE AND DUE DILIGENCE

So far we have provided some general background on governance and introduced the concept of good governance. As we continue our discussion in developing a definition of governance it is important to address its relationship with due diligence.

Particularly, as we have just touched upon the concept of due diligence, it is worth clarifying the difference between the two concepts. The terms due diligence and governance are sometimes confused. To be fair, the two concepts are related, but markedly different in their meaning and application.

Further complicating the issue is that the term due diligence is in itself somewhat difficult to define. The first problem that typically arises when attempting to define due diligence, as it relates to hedge funds, is that in fact it is a broad umbrella term that encompasses a number of smaller concepts. As a result, the term due diligence can often mean different things to different investors. This is not to say that there are not common understood market norms used among investors as to what is meant by the term due diligence, but rather that there is some wide variety as to what is meant by due diligence. For example, some investors or even large allocation organizations such as fund of hedge funds may refer to due diligence as primarily encompassing a review of a fund's investment merits. Other investors may encompass reviews of other concepts such as a fund manager's personal backgrounds or a fund's back-office procedures within the term due diligence. In its most basic form hedge fund due diligence can be thought of as including investment due diligence and ODD (Scharfman, 2012).

In general investment due diligence involves evaluating the investment merits of a particular hedge fund. ODD involves focusing on the other purely non–investment-related risks of hedge fund investing. For a reference on hedge fund ODD you can refer to my other book on this subject (Scharfman, 2008). ODD has evolved from analyzing traditional back-office procedures of hedge funds to include a wide array of other risks ranging from fund service providers to counterparty risk.

As it relates to the concept of the role of fund directors, to be addressed in more detail in Chapter 2, governance is typically reviewed as part of an ODD review. Indeed, as noted above, some investors, and particularly ODD analysts, may feel that fund governance is exclusively in the domain of ODD.

With this background on due diligence we can now focus on governance. Are the subjects all that different? Both aspects of investment due diligence and ODD relate to governance, but due diligence itself cannot be equated directly with governance. Instead, due diligence is the process by which investors gather information to learn about, diagnose, and evaluate a number of factors including the governance in place at the hedge fund. That being said, as we will outline in more detail in Chapter 6, due diligence alone when performed without governance in mind may not encompass all the factors relevant to conduct a thorough governance evaluation. Therefore, while many times the result of the due diligence process helps investors to promote good governance at funds, it is a diagnostic tool in the process and not the solution to governance itself.

IS GOVERNANCE CONTROLLED BY THE HEDGE FUND BOARD OF DIRECTORS?

In considering a definition of hedge fund governance, we must also address the role of a common governance mechanism, fund boards. If you talk to hedge fund investors or even hedge fund managers themselves, about the concept of hedge fund governance, not too far into the conversation you are likely to come to the subject of the role of the board of directors. This is particularly true when discussing hedge funds that employ common offshore fund structures. While we will address the roles of affiliated and unaffiliated board members in Chapter 2, for the purposes of our discussion here we will focus on the board of directors of offshore hedge funds. These unaffiliated offshore directors are typically based in a variety of jurisdictions with one of the most popular hedge fund director locations being the Cayman Islands.

In fact, many people believe that the fund governance and the role of the offshore board are synonymous. Many board of directors themselves would likely support this assertion as well. While the role of the board is certainly critical to the hedge fund's governance, the board is not the end of hedge fund governance. Rather it is a good starting point from which we can begin our discussion of governance.

To pause for a moment and to highlight why hedge fund governance does not start and stop with the board of directors, let us consider a hedge fund that only has a domestic (i.e., US-domiciled) hedge fund. Let us further assume that, as is usually the case, unlike many popular offshore jurisdictions, the United States–based fund is not subject to any legal requirement that outlines that it must have an independent board. Does this mean that because this fund is not required to have a board, and has opted not to have one, the investors in this fund don't have to worry about governance?

When the question is posed this way, most investors would agree that the lack of a board does not remove the need for the hedge fund to practice good governance. Assuming that is the case, the next question is, besides the board of directors of the offshore hedge fund vehicle what else does fund governance entail?

Although we will touch upon the role of the board throughout this book, we will first begin to address this question by developing a definition of governance. Once we have defined what hedge fund industry governance means, we will work to outline some of the central elements of governance. Through this process we will then start to develop a framework by which investors can begin to evaluate governance and incorporate board-level reviews into this analysis. Before proceeding to develop this definition of governance in a hedge fund context, it will be useful if we first understand the origins of governance and its development in the modern financial system.

GOVERNANCE OUTSIDE OF HEDGE FUNDS

As a starting point to develop a definition of hedge fund governance, we can look outside of the hedge fund space for definitions. The core concepts of governance are not only applicable to hedge funds. Within the realm of finance, governance concepts similar to those we will discuss in the hedge fund space are shared by those with similar fund structures. Examples of this include private equity funds or real estate funds. Although, as we have outlined above, the particulars of the ways in which governance is implemented in these fund types vary; they are still closely related to hedge funds governance at least from a fund structuring perspective for the purposes of our discussion here.

Outside of the purely financial world, the concepts of governance are also applied to many different industries in business. There are many other bodies of literature dedicated to analyzing corporate governance within the context of publicly traded companies. Considerations related to the quality of public company governance are also frequently the subject of much analysis during the investment process. Additionally many academic studies have been done with regards to corporate governance in public firms. These studies have analyzed governance from many different perspectives ranging from board compensation and monitoring conflicts of interest to even evaluating the size of CEO's homes and swimming pools using aerial photos as governance indicators (Liu and Yermack, 2007). Governance concepts also have a wide variety of applications in social science, political science, and public policy. There are also dedicated areas of study within the field of governance seeking to examine how different types of governance structures interact with one another. An example of this would be multilevel governance (Enderlein, 2010).

THE ORIGINS OF HEDGE FUND GOVERNANCE LIE IN CORPORATE GOVERNANCE

The modern development and current incarnation of hedge funds governance is firmly rooted in traditional corporate governance. Corporate governance has traditionally referred to notions relating to corporate boards of directors, executive compensation oversight, and conflicts of interest monitoring. This repackaging of the term into "corporate governance" in this context includes many of the common characteristics of the core issues governance tries to address including promoting oversight and independence.

From an etymology perspective, the word governance has its roots from the Greek word *kybernao* to steer something (Clarke, 2007). Plato used the word in book VI of his book titled *Republic*, who was borrowing from Aeschylus's *Seven Against Thebes*, to analogize the running of the government of a city to the steering of a ship, and coined the well-known phrase "Ship of State" (Pappas, 2013). The *Oxford English Dictionary* defines governance as "the action or manner of governing" (Oxford, 2014). While this provides us with a good starting point, it does little to inform our perspective of what governance practically is. As a more concise definition it has been suggested that "corporate governance is about the exercise of power over corporate entities" (Tricker, 2012).

Perhaps clarifying what is meant by the term "power" in the previous definition, governance in a more political context has also been defined as "the act or manner of governing, of exercising control or authority over the actions of subject" (Vyas-Doorgapersad et al., 2013). This definition emphasizes he control of a central authority over its members. To pause for a moment you might be asking yourself, "What does Plato and concepts of power have to do with hedge funds?" Well, if we think of the hedge fund as the central authority to which all its investors (i.e., members) allocate capital to, then, using this definition, it is the hedge fund that is the driver or governance, and not the investors. But is this hedge fund–centric approach the best way to define governance?

We will provide examples of these types of issues and address these questions in more detail throughout the book. For now let us simply suggest the notion that depending from what perspective you approach the issue of fund governance, there may be well-reasoned disagreement over who the market considers to be the driver of governance and what the market considers to be best practice governance. To further our understanding of governance in building our definition in a hedge fund context it will be useful to consider additional historical perspectives in this area. With the background we have laid out so far on the subject, as you read through this historical background on governance, if you keep the question "How do these concepts relate to modern hedge funds?" in the back of your mind, you might find yourself coming up with some new perspective on these issues.

HISTORICAL PERSPECTIVES ON CORPORATE GOVERNANCE

In a more modern financial context, the roots of corporate governance can be classified into two basic areas. One area that has historically driven governance is the law and regulation. The other is market- or investor-driven governance. We will analyze the regulatory roots of financial governance in more detail in Chapter 3. An analysis of the recent history of market or investor governance will provide some perspective on highlights in the growth of interest in corporate governance, which we can then apply to hedge funds. More detailed discussions on the historical growth of corporate governance systems outside of the financial markets are better left for other texts (Morck, 2005).

INVESTOR-DRIVEN GOVERNANCE

Governance in the Prewar Period

Outside of the political arena, the subject of governance has been largely developed in the boardrooms of corporations. It may come as no surprise that these corporations were not always focused on governance as a key element of their overall operations. Just the opposite, governance was not even on the corporate radar for a long time. Not to place all the blame on the corporations, shareholders weren't overly focused on governance either.

This was largely the case in part before World War II. Indeed even before World War II, trends of a lack of focus on corporate governance were largely consistent globally. In Japan, for example, there were large corporate conglomerates called *zaibatsu*, which were controlled by individuals or families as the major stockholders. The interdealings of the zaibatsu-affiliated entities often epitomized the definition of what we would classify as conflicts of interest when viewed under a modern lens (Mallin, 2009). Likely furthering these potential conflicts was a practice in Japan known as *amakudari* where public officials would "step down" from public service to join private corporations at age 55. It was no secret that these former public officials continued to hold a great deal of influence in the public sphere and would secure preferable treatment for their new private corporate employers. Oh, and let's not forget that when they were in public service, these civil servants were likely made very aware of the fact that in order to secure a lucrative postretirement corporate position it would be in everyone's best interest not to make life too difficult for the corporations they were supposed to be overseeing.

In prewar Germany similar conglomerates with a handful of corporate influential shareholders existed. Similarly, during this period in the United Kingdom it was not uncommon for influential families to control businesses and collusion among the business was also permitted (Dingham and Galanis, 2009). As an aside, unfortunately the notion of a regulator having close ties to those they regulate isn't a phenomenon solely relegated to the past. As noted above, we will address this issue in more detail in Chapter 3 that addresses regulatory governance of hedge funds.

In the United States, as compared with Europe and Asia, there was more of a separation between ownership and control of companies with the use of equity markets and stock ownership being more common. This separation of control and ownership still did little to promote any material distinction in US corporate governance. Some have also argued that the American interest in democracy was tied to a more progressive US view of democratizing the corporate boardroom as well in prewar America (Dine and Koutsias, 2013). While the roots of the American interest in corporate governance may have been tied to promotion of the ideals of democracy, it was not until many years after the war that any real changes came about in the boardroom. Much the opposite, in prewar America anything resembling the ideals of modern corporate governance was virtually unheard of. Instead, the lack of US corporate governance was more likely tied to the old robber baron style system where corporate boards were often shared with large investment bankers to facilitate their agreeing to provide financing to these companies (Musacchio, 2009).

The Postwar Era of Governance From the 1960s

It has been said that a rising tide lifts all boats, and when people are making money, they tend to have different priorities than when they are losing it. As part of this when corporations are profitable, there tends to be less of an interest among shareholders and corporations alike to focus on governance. Instead the concentration tends to be more heavily focused on profitability and sustained growth. This was the case in the post–World War II era, when the United States was experiencing an economic recovery. During this recovery in corporate America, and indeed through most of the developed world, there was little to any emphasis placed on governance and shareholders' rights. The 1960s were defined by a general market acceptance of weak shareholders as compared with strong corporations (Jackson, 2010).

Focus on Insider Trading in the United States

The somewhat hostile political and business climate toward governance reforms began to thaw in the late 1960s. In general, this increased acceptance of governance was not magnanimously volunteered by these corporations. Rather, the initiators of much of this change have been driven by shareholders. From the perspective of the market, as opposed to the regulatory perspective, the key drivers in this area have included a continued focus on transparency, accountability, and profitability. From a financial regulatory perspective some notable examples of this include an increased focus by the US SEC on insider trading with the appointment of William Carey in 1961 as the new chair of the SEC. One of the seminal cases in this area occurred in the 1961 case of *In re Cady, Roberts & Co.* (40 S.E.C. 907, 1961).

This case dealt with the uses of material nonpublic information, also sometimes called insider information. Specifically, in that case it was alleged that a stockbroker received a tip from the director of a corporation that it was going to reduce its quarterly dividend (Ferrara et al., 2013). The broker then sold shares in that company for his clients before the information was announced to the public. For the first time the SEC ruled that taking such activities in the public equity markets was a violation of securities rules, Rule 10(b)-5 specifically, and imposed a so-called "disclose or abstain" rule. This rule effectively outlines that if an individual, such as the broker in the Cady Roberts case, comes into possession of what is known as material nonpublic information, then they must either disclose it before trading or decline to trade if disclosure is not feasible (Bainbridge, 2012).

Decisions such as Cady Roberts began to create a precedent in the 1960s that sought to for the first time actively penalize insider trading. They also overturned long-standing court decisions, such as the 1933 case of *Goodwin v. Aggasiz*, which had not penalized insider trading that was conducted on an exchange (Donald, 1999).

The fact that the SEC was now actively pursuing insider trading was a core element that sought to build the foundation for corporate governance reforms that were to come. Another notable case that cemented the SEC's intentions to crack down on insider trading in this area was the 1968 case of the *SEC v. Texas Sulphur Co.* (401 F.2d 833, 848 (2d Cir.), 1968). That case dealt with several issues relating to material nonpublic information concerning an ore discovery including the impact of a misleading press release on stock price (Rosenfeld, 1973). One of the central issues related to the SEC's allegations was that insiders at the Texas Sulphur company had traded on advance knowledge of a significant ore discovery.

To pause for a moment you may be questioning what this history leeson has to do with hedge fund governance. Well, all one has to do is look at the recent modern string of insider trading allegations and convictions in the hedge fund world to realize that in the over 50 years after Cady Roberts, insider trading still represents a material risk to both the integrity of the overall financial system and the controls and policies in place to promote governance at hedge funds. Anecdotally, most investors and hedge fund managers would likely agree that when a hedge fund manager such as Raj Rajaratnam's Galleon Group is convicted of insider trading, there is likely an absence of governance in place.

Rise of the Class Action Lawsuit

Another notable example of the increased interest in corporate transparency in the United States is related to the birth of the modern class action lawsuit. For those who are unfamiliar, a class action lawsuit can be defined as "a lawsuit in which the court authorizes a single person or a small group of people to represent the interest of a larger group" (Garner, 2004). Effectively class action lawsuits came about because there was some allegation of damage to a large number of people, some of which may be unidentifiable. Proponents of the class action lawsuit saw it as a mechanism to attempt to effectively compensate the largest number of people while bringing the item to some sort of resolution for those alleged to have done the damage.

Although this is not a legal textbook, to understand what happened during this period and how it influenced class action lawsuits, it would likely be helpful to provide some additional brief legal context here. Today, class action suits, which are sometimes called representative suits, are used for a wide number of reasons ranging from consumer products litigation to securities fraud and environmental litigation. Across the 50 states of the United States of America and in the federal system as well, there are a number of legal requirements that govern class actions including outlining how a class is defined and who can be in a class.

Additionally, under US law there is something known as the Federal Rules of Civil Procedure ("FRCP"). The FRCP are the rules that govern civil (i.e., noncriminal) actions in US district courts (Garner, 2004). Class actions fall under the umbrella of the FRCP. In particular, Rule 23 of the FRCP is central to class actions. In 1966, a major revision occurred to Rule 23. Specifically, the rule changed the law to add a so-called opt-out requirement (Wilson, 2012). This meant that if you could have been a party to the class and didn't opt out, you are automatically part of it. For history buffs this modern version of the class actions comes out of the English equitable doctrine of virtual representation. This change in 1966 was a major revision to the old class action framework that didn't necessarily bind absent parties to the class action.

So what do class actions have to do with corporate governance? Well, quite a lot actually. The revision to the class action laws opened the flood gates for securities cases to be brought under the class action mechanism (Vernon

Patrick, 1974). These class action cases later started to become more frequent into the early 1970s as we will outline more in the next section.

1970s: The Decade of Governance

It wasn't until the 1970s that the modern era of corporate governance in the United States first came about through the increasing popularity of the term itself at that time (Cheffins, 2013).

At that time there were already groundswells of interest in increased accountability for corporations. In the United States, in part, this interest was driven by elements of the civil right movement, and increased consumer and political activism, which sought to review the power wielded by large corporations (DeMott, 1977). The literature of the time also reflected an increased desire for corporate accountability with books published such as *Taming the Giant Corporation* (Nader, 1977).

The reforms made to the class action rules in the mid-1960s were also slowly starting to bear fruit for shareholders in the 1970s. During this time some initial class action lawsuits were brought by shareholders' attorneys seeking compensation after a stock had declined (Gershman, 2014). These cases typically alleged that the declines were tied to fraud in one form or another. Two examples include a 1970 case where proxy-fraud was alleged during the merger of two companies (*Percodani v. Riker-Maxson Corp.*, 1970) and a 1971 case that involved allegations of prospectus statement fraud (*Feit v. Leasco Data Processing Equipment Corp.*, 1971).

We will address the relationship between fraud and governance in more detail in Chapter 8, but for now will suffice to say that when a fraud occurs there is not exactly best practice governance employed at the corporate level. Underpinning much of this litigation was a desire to increase the transparency in the corporate boardroom and to eliminate many conflicts of interest that were more common at the time.

Also during the 1970s there were increased efforts to focus on the social responsibility of corporations that fueled corporate governance efforts. Those seeking social change also used the courts to promote their interest in increasing corporate accountability and transparency. An example of such a case is the *Medical Committee for Human Rights v. SEC*. In that case, the Medical Committee was interested in stopping the Dow Chemical Company from producing napalm that was being used by the Department of Defense in Vietnam (Pinto and Branson, 2009). At first the Medical Committee attempted to resolve the issue by petitioning the board of Dow; however, this was rejected. With increased use of the regulatory process and courts for governance reasons in the securities area, the Medical Committee decided to contact the SEC to see if they would intervene and force Dow to include the Medical Committee proposals to stop producing napalm in Dow's proxy statements. The SEC effectively sided with Dow prohibiting the inclusion of the Medical Committee's proposal in the proxy materials (Choper et al., 2004). The Medical Committee then decided to sue the SEC, and eventually Dow did include the proposal in the shareholder proxy statement.

Cases like this represent a marked shift in the promotion of governance and transparency in corporations that was unheard of just 20 years prior. Increasingly during the 1970s political activists and investors began to exert increased pressure, both in the public discourse and through the courts, to promote enhanced corporate responsibility, accountability, and overall better governance.

Not everyone was a supporter of these reforms. Nobel Prize–winning economist Milton Friedman wrote a book in 1962 called *Capitalism and Freedom*. In it he referred to social responsibility as a, "fundamentally subversive doctrine." He echoed this sentiment eight years later in a 1970 *New York Magazine* article, in which he stated that the corporation should have only one objective, which is to generate profits in a legal way (Friedman, 1970).

Rise of Agency Theory

Throughout the latter half of the 1970s and into the 1980s there was a slow continued interest in corporate governance and transparency. Although many major reforms in corporate governance were still to come, during this period in particular there was a renewed interest in an economic theory called agency theory. Specifically, the works of Michael Jensen and William Mecklin in 1976 and later of Nobel laureate Eugene Fama in the 1980s are examples of the rising interest in this area (Farazmand, 2002).

Agency theory is a branch of neoclassical economics that has been applied to the management of corporations (Lawrence, 2010). In an agency relationship there are two groups of parties. One party is the owners or principals of an organization, and in a corporate context these would be the shareholders. The other party is the agents or managers of the organizations.

One of the central tenants of agency theory relates to the so-called agency problem or the principal–agent problem. Agents need principals and vice versa. As a general rule, shareholders do not possess the requisite skills to run corporations and principals need shareholders' investments to run the corporation (Schroeder et al., 2010). Despite this symbiotic relationship, a problem persists that presents a continued risk to the shareholders. Their agents, the management, may possess inherently different goals than the shareholders. Specifically, shareholders are generally interested in a firm's overall profitability. In the academic literature of corporate governance this is sometimes referred to as shareholder value theory (Stelios, 2012). Managers may, in economic speak, seek to maximize their own utility. This translates to making certain choices that may be in the management's best interest, but not in the best interest of the shareholders.

Not everyone has been a fan of agency theory. Similar to those who have levied criticism on the links between governance and social responsibility, others have argued that agency theory does not necessarily reflect the realities of corporate governance. Some of these criticisms include that the analytical models of the principal–agent relationship are too simplistic as compared with the real-world challenges of implementing such relationships in practice (Predergast, 1999). Others have criticized what are known as the adverse selection problems that arise in agency theory due to the control and access to asymmetrical information among the principals and the agents (Iris, 2006). Certainly such criticisms have direct corollaries to the imperfect flow of information among hedge funds, their directors, and investors, among others, in the hedge fund food chain. We will revisit the link between these agency theory criticisms and hedge fund governance with a particular focus on the board of directors in more detail in Chapter 2; however, for now simply note that this is an example of the link between the roots of traditional corporate governance and hedge fund governance.

Regardless of whether you believe in the benefits of agency theory or not, the rise in popularity of agency theory also played a critical role in shareholders' push for enhanced corporate governance reforms to come throughout the 1980s and into the 1990s.

1980s Onward—The Growth of Modern Corporate Governance Reforms

Due to a flurry of M&A activity many have referred to the 1980s as the deal decade (Blair and Uppal, 1993). Not all of the takeover activity during this time period could be called friendly and indeed many corporate takeovers of the period were hostile. This led to the use of various takeover prevention techniques including greenmail and poison pills to name a few.

At the same time in the 1980s institutional investors markedly increased their ownership in US public companies (Useem, 1996). Although shareholders were rarely successful in preventing these defensive takeover tactics in court, the increased interest in these activities alone was enough to promote a further interest in corporate governance. One example of this effort during this time period was the launch of the Council of Institutional Investors ("CII") in 1985 by entities including the California Public Employees' Retirement System ("CalPERS") (Cheffins, 2013).

The early efforts toward the institutional focus on corporate governance began to bear fruit in the 1990s and beyond. In the United States the result of all of these efforts ultimately led to an increased acquiescence by corporations to diversify the independence of their boards. Research has shown that between 1950 and 2005, the composition of public company boards shifted from only 20% being independent in 1950 to over 75% in 2005 (Gordon, 2006, 2007).

A Growth in Governance Failures and Frauds at Large Corporations

Fueling the modern interest in corporate governance was a series of financial crises and corporate scandals and failures. Certainly, one of the major drivers of corporate reform has always been reforms made in the aftermath of these scandals. While it could be argued that any such reforms are better late than never, the steady drum beat of corporate governance failures and outright fraud shows us that instead perhaps an ounce of prevention is indeed worth a pound of cure. In particular, during the 1990s and into the 2000s and onward there were an unfortunate number of large corporate scandals that had governance issues, including outright fraud, at their heart. A summary of these scandals across the world is contained in Exhibit 1.1.

Unfortunately, the list contained in Exhibit 1.1 is by no means comprehensive. We could have also included a whole host of other well-known corporate failures that had major corporate governance issues at their core. Examples of others on the list in the United States could have been Tyco, Adelphia, Refco, Global Crossing, ZZZZ Best, National Student Marketing, and Equity Funding to name a few. As Exhibit 1.1 shows, this was not solely a US phenomenon and other non-US examples of corporate governance failures often resulting in the major issues of large corporations include Polly Peck (the United Kingdom), Satyam (India), and Allied Irish Bank (Ireland) (Monks and Minow, 2011). Still other more recent examples of public company governance failures outside the United States include the Olympus scandal in Japan and Northern Rock in the United Kingdom to name a few.

In the hedge fund world, historical frauds have also been recent drivers of governance reforms. In Chapter 8, we analyze in more detail the historical influence of these frauds on changes in hedge fund governance, but for right now it is sufficient for the reader to merely keep in the back of their minds that governance problems and frauds at large corporations pose a direct corollary to similar issues of governance in the hedge fund space. The mistake should not be made of simply classifying leesons learned from historical corporate governance failures as being limited solely to the public company arena. Such thinking is frankly shortsighted and provides an escape hatch for investors and hedge funds alike to excuse poor governance practices. Just the opposite, these historical failures provide valuable leesons, which are directly applicable toward promoting better governance practices in hedge funds.

DEFINING HEDGE FUND GOVERNANCE

Now that we have outlined the historical background of market-driven governance reforms, we can now proceed toward developing a definition of hedge fund governance. Perhaps a good starting point in this regards is with a gentleman named Alfred Winslow Jones. Beginning in 1949 Mr. Jones ran a long/short style fund, which was one of the first, if not the first, of its kind. Incidentally, later in life Jones applied his long/short philosophy in an attempt to combat poverty (Landua, 1968).

EXHIBIT 1.1 Examples of Major Corporate Collapses from Mid-1990s Onward

Company name	Countries where occurred	Year occurred	Summary
Barings Bank	Singapore, the United Kingdom	1995	Rogue trader Nick Leeson's unauthorized derivative bets and overall governance failures at the bank caused losses of over £800 million that ultimately caused the over 200-year-old UK bank to collapse. To learn more about the Barings Bank fraud you could watch the 1999 Ewan McGregor movie called *Rogue Trader* or you could read Nick Leeson's 1996 book, also called *Rogue Trader*
Enron	The United States	2001	American energy company that engaged in aggressive accounting practices and special-purpose entities that ultimately led the $63.4 billion company to file for bankruptcy. This also led to the failure of Enron's auditor Arthur Anderson. After Enron failed one of the key governance failures reported on was the firm's Audit Committee that consisted of, among others, committee chair Robert Jaedicke (a former accounting professor and former dean of Stanford Business School) and Wendy Gramm (former chairman of the Commodity Futures Trading Commission) (Steven, 2011). In their wisdom, this committee suspended Enron's conflict of interest policy in mid-1999 so Enron's CFO could engage in outside partnerships
HIH Insurance	Australia	2001	HIH was Australia's second largest insurance company. HIH's series of failed expansion plans and misstatement of its financial position resulted in the company not properly providing for future claims. This is generally a problem for a company whose primary business is insurance. With losses of over $5.3 billion, this was the largest corporate collapse in Australia's history. The company's CEO, Ray Williams, served over four years in jail based on charges related to the case

(Continued)

EXHIBIT 1.1 Examples of Major Corporate Collapses from Mid-1990s Onward (*cont.*)

Company name	Countries where occurred	Year occurred	Summary
Royal Ahold	The Netherlands	2003	A grocery chain based in the Netherlands was charged with improper accounting practices including fraudulently recognizing promotional allowances and improperly consolidating joint ventures (Zach, 2012)
Parmalat	Italy	2003	Italian-based dairy producer orchestrated a widespread collusive fraud for over 10 years that involved the invention of assets valued at over $11 billion in offshore sham companies to offset parent company liabilities. Banks and auditors, among others, were also alleged to have been involved in perpetrating the fraud. Also somewhat unusual was that only 8 out of 160 Italian pension funds were invested in Parmalat at the time, with the remainder being American (Ramage, 2006)
China Aviation Oil	China, Singapore	2004	Jet fuel purchasing corporation suffered over $500 million in losses after violating internal risk management policies and losing on bearish options bets in the oil market (Jackson, 2008). Several of the firm's executives were fined and sentenced to jail time in Singapore including CEO Chen Jiulin. After being released from jail Mr. Jiulin, a Chinese native, became a senior official at a state-owned construction firm CGGC International Company Ltd. (Nanlan, 2010)
WorldCom	The United States	2002	WorldCom was one of the largest US telephone and communications companies. Multiple failures of corporate governance ranging from accounting fraud to mismanaged loans to corporate insiders and earnings manipulations caused the firm to collapse. It was estimated that the company inflated its assets by approximately $11 billion (Beresford et al., 2003). The filing of bankruptcy by WorldCom was the largest US bankruptcy at the time and CEO Bernard Ebbers was sentenced to 25 years in federal prison

As we have outlined above, during the heyday of the Jones fund, the implementation of what we would deem today to be robust corporate governance was not en vogue. Although most of us were not personally there at the time, it is safe to say that the hedge fund industry as a whole, including the Jones fund, was no exception to this larger corporate trend of lax governance at best.

Therefore, if we are to take 1949 as a starting point, we are effectively starting from a period of no governance. Of course, there were legal obligations in place with regards to subscribing to a hedge fund at the time, but this could hardly be considered to be governance. Furthermore, as most modern hedge fund investors would likely agree, the rights of hedge fund investors as dictated by the offering memorandum of any hedge fund they are likely to have invested in are, from a legal perspective, meager at best. Rather, from a legal perspective the odds are more heavily stacked in the favor of the manager. So it seems in this perspective perhaps little has changed. For right now, however, we will table a discussion of governance in hedge fund legal documents and rather focus on governance practices with the goal of developing a definition of governance.

Diving right in, we should first look at the question of how broad a definition it is appropriate to develop. Is a definition that applies to all hedge funds appropriate, or perhaps one that instead is strategy specific?

A UNIVERSAL DEFINITION OF GOVERNANCE?

The following question could be posed: is there a single universal definition of governance in hedge funds? What this question is seeking to highlight is that perhaps there are really different types of definitions of governance for hedge funds. The first would be a universal definition that seeks to address what governance is regardless of whether you are a hedge fund manager, investor, regulator, or service provider. The next series of definitions would then build upon this universal definition based on the perspective related to your role in the hedge fund industry.

To clarify this is not meant to imply that governance should be thought of as a floating standard, customizable to each different hedge fund industry participant at their discretion. Rather this book will argue that there are certain universal elements of hedge fund governance that most hedge fund industry participants, regardless of their role, would agree to constitute so-called good governance. Similarly, there would be another separate group of practices that could generally be thought of to promote bad governance. Beyond this basic universal definition, however, there may be disagreement among the different industry groups as to whether or not a particular practice is good, bad, or otherwise as it relates to governance. The reason for this can be simply that while both hedge funds and investors are seeking to make money, there can be numerous competing interests and goals at play in accomplishing this goal. The same of course can be said for service providers to hedge funds, including boards of directors.

IS GOVERNANCE DEFINED BY PERSPECTIVE?

As you can see, penning down an exact definition of governance in a hedge fund context can present a challenge. Depending on what your interaction is with the hedge fund industry, governance is a term that can be interpreted differently. An investor in hedge funds might define governance via broad terms such as "oversight," "control," or "processes." On the other hand, a hedge fund manager may take the approach that governance means adhering to their particular investment strategy. A hedge fund administrator may take yet another approach and think that effective governance means that a hedge fund will adhere to the terms of their offering memorandum.

On the other hand, the perspective could be taken that it is not the hedge funds but investors who are responsible for implementing governance. Still others may take the approach that it is not the sole responsibility of hedge funds or investors to implement governance but the role of service providers as well.

WHO IS RESPONSIBLE FOR HEDGE FUND GOVERNANCE?

In seeking to define hedge fund governance, another question related to perspective is: ultimately who is responsible for governance? One approach that some investors have taken traditionally is that when they allocate capital to a hedge fund, isn't it up to that fund to handle not only the investments but also everything else that an investor doesn't need to worry about? As part of that responsibility shouldn't it be up to the hedge fund manager to be responsible for governance?

The answer to this question helps us to distinguish some of the finer points in developing a definition of hedge fund governance. Ultimately, hedge fund managers are the ones who implement governance changes but typically it is hedge fund investors who influence it. As will be discussed in more detail in Chapters 3 and 4 other groups such as regulators and service providers also play a role in governance.

This book will take the position that governance is not the single responsibility of any one group such as the board of directors. Instead, governance is a system of controls, policies, and procedures for which investors, hedge funds, regulators, and service providers have responsibility. Exhibit 1.2 outlines some of the key players responsible for hedge fund governance.

IS GOVERNANCE PRIMARILY AN INVESTMENT-RELATED CONCEPT?

Now that we have provided some perspective on governance in general and responsibilities for overseeing governance, we can better approach developing a definition. However, before attempting to define hedge fund governance

EXHIBIT 1.2 Key Players in Hedge Fund Governance

Investors including the following groups:	Hedge fund employees including those responsible for the following functions:
Individual investors such as high-net-worth/ultra-high-net-worth	Investments
Family offices/multifamily offices	Risk management
Pension plans (corporate, public)	Operations
Fund of hedge funds	Compliance
Endowment/foundations	Technology
Banks	
Insurance companies	
Service providers:	Regulators:
Board of directors	Financial regulators
Administrator	
Auditor	
Prime broker	
Legal counsel	
Information technology consultant	
Custodian	
Fund bank	

perhaps we can narrow down the definition by outlining what it is not. As we have outlined above, governance does not typically refer to the ability or quality of the firm to make money.

That being said some investors may outline governance to include guidelines around the nature and type of a hedge fund's investments. One example of this would be socially responsible investing ("SRI"), sometimes referred to as ethical investing. Under an SRI approach, investment goals are combined with certain ethical or environmental goals (Sparkes, 2002). In a hedge fund context this would mean that a manager would adhere to a policy of making investments, or avoiding others, with certain goals such as preserving the environment. Some have questioned whether it is possible for a hedge fund to function as a true alpha generation entity while still balancing SRI goals. Proponents of hedge fund SRI counter that SRI funds can be profitable and effectively hedge funds seeking to adhere to SRI principals are merely faced with the compliance issue of making sure that these hedge funds do not violate SRI (Hedge Funds Review Editorial, 2013). If, as an investor, your goal is to invest in a hedge fund that adheres to certain SRI principles, then you would also likely agree that the violation of such principals would be representative of poor governance.

A related concept would also be when investment-related governance would be so-called environmental, social, and governance ("ESG") investing. Depending on which investors you talk to, in some cases it may be purely a matter of semantics as to whether a certain investment program is categorized as SRI or ESG. Highlighting this is the fact that in practice many institutional investors link both SRI and ESG investing with the United Nations Principles for Responsible Investment, which is commonly referred to as the UNPRI. For reference, we will address ESG, SRI, and related concepts in more detail in Chapter 7.

Instead of focusing on profitability of a particular fund governance framework, in this book, the focus of governance will be on the nature of the environment at the hedge fund from a noninvestment perspective.

Incidentally, before we proceed toward developing our definition of hedge fund governance, it is worth pausing for a moment to distinguish between the noninvestment or operational governance we will be focusing on in this book and another governance-related concept that is often used to focus on the nature and style of a hedge fund manager's investments, which is referred to as activist investing.

DISTINGUISHING BETWEEN GOVERNANCE AND HEDGE FUND ACTIVISTS

If you searched for the words "hedge funds" and "governance" on a search engine such as Google, you would find that the majority of the results are articles related to the concepts of activist investing. As it relates to governance, these references to activist investing often relate to hedge funds seeking to promote what they deem to be good governance at the companies in which they invest. Often they feel that this promotion of good governance will result in the company making certain changes or pursuing policies that will increase the company's share price. In many cases these so-called good governance changes relate to changing the board of a company or spinning off certain divisions.

The companies that are the subject of this activism are not always initially amenable to the hedge fund–suggested changes and these activist activities can often turn contentious. Other hedge fund managers have taken on various levels of activism. This includes some managers who seek to develop more amicable working relationships with companies including hedge fund manager Larry Robbins, who describes the approach of his Glenview Capital Management as "suggestivist" (Arvedlund, 2013).

In recent years as there has been an increase in the media attention paid to hedge fund activist investors many corporate boards have become more responsive to activist feedback (Green and Jinks, 2014). One example of a well-known activist hedge fund manager is Carl Icahn's Icahn Capital Management, which has pushed for governance changes in firms such as Apple and eBay (McSherry and Williams-Grut, 2014). Other activist managers that have received a notable press include the following:

Firm name	Well-known founder	Notable companies in which activist positions have been taken by the hedge fund
Third Point LLC	Daniel Loeb	Sony (De La Merced, 2013), Yahoo! (Adams, 2012), Dow Chemical, and Sotheby's (Fontevecchia, 2014)
Greenlight Capital	David Einhorn	Apple (Ablan and Gupta, 2013), Lehman Brothers (Summers, 2013), Green Mountain Coffee Roasters (Allison, 2014), and Microsoft (Ahmed, 2011)
Pershing Square Capital Management, LP	William Ackman	Herbalife (Copeland and Benoit, 2014), J.C. Penny (Yousuf, 2013), Proctor and Gamble (Chang, 2013)
Trian Fund Management, LP	Nelson Peltz	Mondelez (Egan, 2014), H.J. Heinz Company (Weiss, 2013), and PepsiCo (Cavale, 2014)

While hedge fund activism is certainly an interesting, and sometimes controversial, topic, as noted above, this type of governance is focused on implementing change at the target companies being invested in, and not within the hedge fund complex itself.

This background on activism helps us flesh out an important point in our definition of hedge fund governance. Namely, it draws out an interesting point between the focus of activism and governance. Activism focuses externally on the companies that a hedge fund invests in. The focus of governance, on the other hand, for the purposes of our discussion is not external to the hedge fund itself, but focused internally. This might not seem somewhat overly intuitive particularly when you consider the historical investor focus on the role of external hedge fund service providers such as fund directors in implementing governance. However, although these service providers are not directly members of the hedge funds, their work is largely focused on the internal working of the fund itself.

As such our definition of governance will focus on the operations, policies, and procedures in place within the hedge fund as opposed to externally. As noted above, while the role of entities such as the board of directors certainly has an influence on this, they are not in and of themselves, the end of governance. In practice, this is not really much of a new revelation. Indeed, while certain investors may struggle to seek to define governance as more than the board, increasingly directors and hedge fund managers accept that governance is much more of a broad concept that flows through the entire hedge fund system.

HEDGE FUND GOVERNANCE: A WORKING DEFINITION

Let's take stock of where we are in developing our definition of hedge fund governance. So far we have shown that governance in hedge funds has its roots in the evolving history of traditional corporate governance. We have made some headway in outlining who the key players are in hedge fund governance, discussing governance responsibilities, and distinguishing hedge fund governance from other investment-related terms. So far so good, but we still don't really have a neat workable definition of what hedge fund governance is.

As a final step in developing this working definition, it is worth discussing a series of related concepts known as GRC or governance, risk, and compliance. The concepts of GRC are certainly not unique to the hedge fund space. Most recently renewed interest in GRC in the corporate world came about largely due to financial regulatory reforms. One of the more notable prompters of this was Sarbanes-Oxley, often called SOX legislation, which placed the requirement on firms to install and monitor enhanced governance oversight controls. As a result of this GRC focus, many publicly listed companies have sought to utilize technology to assist in GRC monitoring and compliance. Indeed, much of the literature relating to GRC these days relates to GRC tools for enterprise risk management, referred to sometimes as "ERM" solutions.

Concepts of GRC certainly can be applied to hedge fund governance. Once again this is often a shortcut of self-definition that certain investors and funds themselves attempt to take in defining hedge fund governance. By this we mean that in seeking to define hedge fund governance, this approach simply says it is what it is. So effectively, when we say GRC equals hedge fund governance, it's kind of the same as saying being rich is the presence of richness. While perhaps technically correct, it does little to further our understanding of the subject. Furthermore, by seeking to define hedge fund governance as being only the GRC principles we are effectively attempting to define governance as a list of the sum of its part rather than define what it actually is.

Making matters worse GRC in and of itself, it can be argued is an incomplete list of subcomponents of hedge fund governance. So, for example, consider the concept of information security. Information security focuses primarily on how a hedge fund protects information. Right now it doesn't matter what type of information we are speaking about, but let's just assume all information for right now. Which category of GRC does this fit into? Governance? As we have, hopefully, made it clear already this is an umbrella term, many elements of which can often be open to interpretation depending on who you ask the question to. Risk management? Well, certainly the prevention of data loss can fall into some category of risk management, but which category of risk management are we referring to? Traditionally, risk management has referred to investment-related risks. For risk management related to noninvestment risks, such as perhaps the theft of data, this is commonly qualified under a category such as operational risk management.

Is this what most in the hedge fund space are referring to when they reference the "R" in GRC? Not necessarily. How about compliance? Well, the security of certain types of data is certainly related to elements of compliance; however, information security is generally not a critical element within the wheelhouse of traditional compliance functions. Perhaps making sure that certain data are organized or set aside to prevent conflicts through information barriers commonly referred to as Chinese walls falls within the ambit of compliance. Protecting data integrity, however, is generally more of an information technology function than compliance in many cases. Does this mean that a hedge fund that does not maintain a robust information security program still satisfies all the GRC elements of governance? As this example demonstrates, you can see perhaps how even going beyond the somewhat traditional constructs of equating hedge fund governance to the board of directors and venturing into broader concepts such as GRC can still leave areas uncovered, which many would argue lead not only to a well-functional hedge fund but also to one with good governance.

Instead, based on our analysis we can come to the conclusion that governance is best defined by a broad working definition. Something to the effect of the following: governance in hedge funds can be defined as an interconnected system of controls and procedures that seek to promote independence, transparency, and oversight through the hedge fund ecosystem. Now based on the criticisms, I have lobbed at other attempts to define hedge fund governance above, you might be scratching your head a bit. Isn't this definition too vague to be practical? Well, not really when you put it in context.

Let's return to the GRC notion above. Well, let's lose the "G" since that seeks to define governance as itself, and just keep the "RC." Risk management, whatever kind of risk management in hedge funds you are talking about such as investment or operational, is a system of oversight and control, isn't it? What about compliance? Sort of the same thing. And the board of directors? Definitely they provide some sort of oversight, don't they? Well, you may argue that they don't, and that's fine; we will address both sides of the issue in the next chapter. Regardless, are you noticing where we are going here? At this point rather than define governance as specific items such as best practice compliance and cash management, we will define it more generally here.

This allows the definition of governance to evolve and be somewhat flexible. This does not mean that there are not certain key elements that are universally agreed upon by the majority of those in the hedge fund space to be elements of best practice governance. Instead, as we discuss the many aspects of governance in hedge funds throughout this book, you will hopefully see that it is a multifaceted subject. Certainly, effective risk management and compliance are elements of good governance, but they cannot function in isolation. That is the "interconnected" part of the definition. A great risk management function alone will not result in good governance throughout a hedge fund.

Additionally, while there are certain universal good governance elements in hedge fund strategies and firms, beyond those basic universal minimum good governance elements, there may be a great deal of flexibility based on this uniqueness. Depending on the peculiarities of each hedge fund, certain controls and oversight are likely in the opinion of most investors required for a manager to meet an acceptable standard of governance. For example, consider an event-driven manager who holds illiquid or more thinly traded positions. Let's further assume that the manager utilizes a third-party administrator; however, for these illiquid positions the manager values the positions himself or herself and simply provides his or her own valuation support to the administrator. Is this the same level of independent valuation oversight that would be appropriate to facilitate good governance, for example, with a long/short hedge fund manager who holds a completely liquid portfolio? Most investors would probably say no. This example demonstrates the dangers of establishing too rigid of a framework to define governance by its elements rather than the general goal of what a good governance system seeks to accomplish. The specifics of how these good governance goals are achieved are certainly important, the forest should not be sacrificed for the trees, and the broader governance goals such as independence and oversight should be kept in mind.

Another point about the definition of hedge fund governance that has been outlined above is that governance is intertwined. Governance is a critical element to the overall health of the hedge fund ecosystem. It is a system that flows through all the players and entities that interact with the hedge fund. It is not the exclusive domain of the board of directors, despite certain hagiographic works by these groups to the contrary. Instead, investors, the hedge funds themselves, and service providers, among others, all play key roles in developing and implementing a good governance system at a hedge fund. As we will discuss in more detail in Chapter 6, investors seeking to develop a framework to evaluate governance need to take this fact into account.

Now that we have established a working definition of hedge fund governance, where do we go from here? The next step is to understand the different component parts that make up hedge fund governance. As a starting point we will begin by analyzing the role of the board of directors in the next chapter.

REFERENCES

40 S.E.C. 907 (1961).

401 F.2d 833, 848 (2d Cir.) (1968).

Adams, S., 2012. Why Daniel Loab is trying to get Yahoo's CEO fired. *Forbes*, 4 May. Available at: http://www.forbes.com/sites/susanadams/2012/05/04/why-daniel-loeb-is-trying-to-get-yahoos-ceo-fired.

Ahmed, A., 2011. Ballmer must go, Einhorn says. *NY Times DealBook*, 25 May. Available at: http://dealbook.nytimes.com/2011/05/25/ballmer-must-go-einhorn-says/.

Allison, K., 2014. Coke and Einhorn take opposite sides of Green Mountain bet. *NY Times DealBook*. 7 February. Available at: http://dealbook.nytimes.com/2014/02/07/coke-and-einhorn-take-opposite-sides-of-green-mountain-bet/?_php=true&_type=blogs&_r=0.

Anson, M., 2006. Handbook of Alternative Assets, first ed. Wiley Finance, s.l.

Arvedlund, E.E., 2013. Barron's. Available at: http://online.barrons.com/article/SB5000142405274 87047553045786215400368305674.html#articleTabs_article%3D1.

Aspen Publishers, 2004. Casenote Legal Briefs, Business Organizations/Corporations. Aspen Publishers, s.l.

Bainbridge, S.M., 2012. An overview of insider trading law and policy: an introduction to the insider trading handbook. In: Bainbridge, S.M. (Ed.), Research Handbook on Insider Trading. Edward Elgar Publishing Ltd., s.l.

Beresford, D.R., Nicholas, deB.K., Rogers Jr., C.B., 2003. Report of Investigation by The Special Investigative Committee of the Board of Directors of Worldcom, Inc. Available at: http://www.sec.gov/Archives/edgar/data/723527/000093176303001862/dex991.htm.

Blair, M.M., Uppal, G., 1993. The Deal Decade Handbook. Brookings Institution Press, s.l.

Bloomberg, 2003. Hedge funds draw traders, bankers in Wall Street 'brain drain'. *Bloomberg*, September 30.

Cavale, S., 2014. Nelson Peltz revives campaign to split up PepsiCo. *Reuters*, 20 February. Available at: http://www.reuters.com/article/2014/02/20/us-peltz-pepsico-idUSBREA1J0B720140220.

Chang, S., 2013. Pershing Square's Ackman pushes change at P&G. *MarketWatch*, 1 October. Available at: http://www.marketwatch.com/story/pershing-squares-ackman-pushes-change-at-pg-2012-10-01.

Cheffins, B.R., 2013. The history of corporate governance. In: Wright, M., Siegel, D., Keasey, K., Filatotchev, I., (Eds.), The Oxford Handbook of Corporate Governance. Oxford University Press, s.l.

Clarke, T., 2007. International Corporate Governance: A Comparative Approach. Routledge, s.l.

De La Merced, M.J., 2013. George Clooney rebuts Loeb's critique of Sony. *The New York Times*, 2 August. Available at: http://www.cnbc.com/id/100935927.

DeMott, D.A., 1977. The impact of the SEC on corporate governance. In: Reweaving the Corporate Veil. Law and Contemporary Problems, Vol. 41, Number 3. School of Law, Duke University.

Dine, J., Koutsias, M., 2013. The Nature of Corporate Governance: The Significance of National Cultural Identity. Edward Elgar Publishing Ltd., s.l.

Dingham, A., Galanis, M., 2009. The Globalization of Corporate Governance. Ashgate Publishing Limited, s.l.

Donald, C.L., 1999. Rereading Cady, Roberts: the ideology and practice of insider trading regulation. Columbia Law Rev. 99 (5), 1319–1343.

Egan, M., 2014. Proxy war averted: Mondelez adds activist Nelson Peltz to board. *Fox Business*, 21 January. Available at: http://www.foxbusiness.com/investing/2014/01/21/proxy-war-averted-mondelez-adds-activist-nelson-peltz-to-board/.

Enderlein, H., 2010. Handbook of Multi-Level Governance. Edward Elgar Publishing Limited, s.l.

Farazmand, A., 2002. Organization theory: from pre-classical to contemporary and critical theories—an overview and appraisal. In: Modern Organizations: Theory and Practice. Praeger Publishers, s.l.

Feit v. Leasco Data Processing Equipment Corp., 332 F. Supp. 544 (E.D.N.Y.) (1971).

Ferrara, R.C., Nagy, D.M., Thomas, H., 2013. Ferrara on insider trading and the wall. *Law Journal Press*, November 28.

Fontevecchia, A., 2014. Under pressure by Dan Loeb, Sotheby's to return $325M to shareholders. *Forbes*, 29 January. Available at: http://www.forbes.com/sites/afontevecchia/2014/01/29/under-pressure-by-dan-loeb-sothebys-to-return-325m-to-shareholders-marcato-asks-for-.

Friedman, M., 1970. The social responsibility of business is to increase its profits. *New York Times Magazine*, 13 September.

Garner, B. A., 2004. Black's Law Dictionary. Thomson West, s.l.

Gershman, J., 2014. Securities lawsuits are on the rise. *The Wall Street Journal*, 26 January.

Gordon, J.N., 2006. The rise of independent directors in the United States, 1950–2005: of shareholder value and stock market prices. ECGI—Law Working Paper, No. 74, August.

Gordon, J.N., 2007. Columbia law and economics working paper. Stanford Law Rev. 59 (301), 1465.

Green, J., Jinks, B., 2014. Icahn's EBAY talks show boards listening to activists. *Bloomberg*, 23 January.

Hedge Funds Review Editorial, 2013. Hedge funds face dilemma of implementing socially responsible investing. *Hedge Funds Review*, March 20.

Iris, A.H., 2006. Effective and Efficient Organisations?: Government Export Promotion in Germany and the UK from an Organisational Economics Perspective (Contributions to Economics). Physica, s.l.

Jackson, K.T., 2008. The China aviation oil scandal. In: Matulich, S., Currie, D.M. (Eds.), Handbook of Frauds, Scams and Swindles: Failures of Ethics in Leadership. CRC Press, s.l.

Jackson, G., 2010. Understanding corporate governance in the United States. Arbeitspapier, vol. 223. Hans-Böckler-Stiftung, Düsseldorf, Germany.

Jaeger, L.A., 2005. Factor Modelling and Benchmarking of Hedge Funds: Can Passive Investments in Hedge Fund Strategies Deliver? SSRN. Available at: http://ssrn.com/abstract=811185 or http://dx.doi.org/10.2139/ssrn.811185.

Kat, H.M., Palaro, H.P., 2005. Who needs hedge funds? A copula-based approach to hedge fund return replication alternative investment. Research Centre Working Paper No. 27, Cass Business School Research Paper. Available at: http://ssrn.com/abstract=855424 or http://dx.doi.org/10.2139/ssrn.855424.

Landua, P., 1968. Alfred Winslow Jones: the long and short of the founding father. *The Institutional Investor*, August.

Lawrence, P., 2010. Driven to Lead: Good, Bad, and Misguided Leadership. Jossey-Bass, s.l.

Lehmann, B.N., 2006. Corporate governance and hedge fund management. *Economic Review*, Federal Reserve Bank of Atlanta. Available at: http://www.frbatlanta.org/filelegacydocs/erq406_lehmann.pdf (accessed June 1, 2014).

Liu, C.H., Yermack, D., 2007. Where are the shareholders' mansions? CEOs' home purchases, stock sales, and subsequent company performance. In: Boubaker, S., Nguyen B.D., Nguyen, D.K. (Eds.), Corporate Governance: Recent Developments and New Trends. s.l.: s.n.

Mallin, C., 2009. Corporate Governance, third ed. Oxford University Press, s.l.

McSherry, M., Williams-Grut, O., 2014. Raider Carl Icahn tell eBay to spin-off its Paypal business. *EDX*, 22 January.

Moore, H., 2013. Einhorn sues Apple, marks biggest investor challenge in years. *Reuters*, 7 February. Available at: http://www.theguardian.com/technology/2013/mar/01/david-einhorn-apple-iprefs-lawsuit.

Monks, R.A.G., Minow, N., 2011. Corporate Governance. Wiley, s.l.

Morck, R., 2005. A History of Corporate Governance Around the World. NBER, Chicago.

Musacchio, A., 2009. Experiments in Financial Democracy, Corporate Governance and Financial Development in Brazil, 1882–1950. Cambridge University Press, s.l.

Nader, R., 1977. Taming the Giant Corporation. W.W. Norton & Company, s.l.

Nanlan, W., 2010. Jailed Oil Exec Chen Jiulin Fills Top SOE Post. Available at: http://www.china.org.cn/business/2010-06/23/content_20328859.htm (accessed June 15, 2014).

Oxford, 2014. Oxford Dictionaries. Available at: http://www.oxforddictionaries.com/us/definition/american_english/governance (accessed June 1, 2014).

Pappas, N., 2013. The Routledge Guide to Plato's Republic. Routledge, s.l.

Percodani v. Riker-Maxson Corp., 1970. 50 F.R.D. 473 (S.D.N.Y.).

Pinto A.R., Branson, D.M., 2009. Understanding Corporate Law, third ed. LexisNexis, s.l.

Predergast, C., 1999. The provision of incentives in firms. J. Econ. Lit. XXXVII, 7–63.

Ramage, S., 2006. A Comparative Analysis of Corporate Fraud: Fraud Law, fourth ed. Universe, Inc., s.l.

Rosenfeld, M., 1973. The impact of class actions on corporate and securities law. Duke Law J. 1972 (6), 1167–1191.

Scharfman, J., 2008. Hedge Fund Operational Due Diligence: Understanding the Risks. Wiley Finance, s.l.

Scharfman, J., 2012. Private Equity Operational Due Diligence: Tools to Evaluate Liquidity, Valuation and Documentation. Wiley Finance, s.l.

Schroeder, R., Clark, M., Cathey, J., 2010. Financial Accounting Theory and Analysis: Text and Cases, 10th ed. Westford, s.l.

Sparkes, R., 2002. Socially Responsible Investment: A Global Revolution. John Wiley & Sons Ltd., s.l.

Stelios, A., 2012. Enlightened shareholder value: is it the new modus operandi for modern companies? In: Boubaker, S., Nguyen, B.D., Nguyen, D.K. (Eds.), Corporate Governance: Recent Developments and New Trends. Springer, s.l.

Steven, M.D., 2011. Out of the ruins where directors landed. *The New York Times*, 2 August.

Summers, N., 2013. When David Einhorn talks, markets listen—usually. *Business Week*, 21 March. Available at: http://www.businessweek.com/articles/2013-03-21/when-david-einhorn-talks-markets-listen-usually.

Tricker, B., 2012. Corporate Governance: Principles, Policies and Practice. Oxford University Press, s.l.

US Securities and Exchange Commission, 2012. SEC Charges Scotland-Based Firm for Improperly Boosting Hedge Fund Client at Expense of U.S. Fund Investors. Available at: http://www.sec.gov/News/PressRelease/Detail/PressRelease/1365171489060#.UxYj74VRb-p.

Useem, M., 1996. Investor Capitalism: How Money Managers are Changing the Face of Corporate America. Basic Books, New York.

Vernon Patrick Jr., J., 1974. The securities class action for damages comes of age (1966–1974). 29 Bus. Law. 159, s.l.

Vyas-Doorgapersad, S., Tshombe, L.-M., Ababio, E.P., 2013. Public Administration in Africa: Performance and Challenges. CRC Press, s.l.

Weiss, M., 2013. Peltz helped spur Heinz turnaround setting stage for bid. *Bloomberg*, 12 February. Available at: http://www.bloomberg.com/news/2013-02-14/peltz-helped-spur-heinz-turn around-setting-stage-for-bid.htm.

Wilson, S.H., 2012. The U.S. Justice System: An Encyclopedia. ABC-CLIO, s.l.

Yousuf, H., 2013. Bill Ackman's Herbalife bet drops. *The Wall Street Journal*, 20 February. Available at: http://money.cnn.com/2013/08/26/investing/bill-ackman-sells-jcpenney/.

Yousuf, H., 2013. Bill Ackman takes huge loss on J.C. Penney. *CNNMoney*, 26 August. Available at: http://money.cnn.com/2013/08/26/investing/bill-ackman-sells-jcpenney/.

Zach, G., 2012. Financial Statement Fraud: Strategies for Detection and Investigation. John Wiley & Sons, s.l.

Chapter 2

Hedge Fund Board of Directors: A Governance Proxy?

Chapter Outline Head

INTRODUCTION TO THE HEDGE FUND BOARD OF DIRECTORS

It's not an exaggeration to say some people hate hedge fund directors. To provide some perspectives on this matter we will outline some of the common rhetoric raised by critics.

Some people argue that they effectively function as useless rubber stamps. The critics continue that hedge funds could function perfectly fine without them. After all, they claim, it's not like they perform a crucial function like a prime broker, bank, or auditor. In fact, they claim directors just slow things up at the fund and further complicate the process. Some people think they're like weeds. Once they get into the fund, they are hard to remove and keep spreading into areas that they are not supposed to get into.

And don't get them started on the reasons for directors. Some pundits argue the reason for boards of directors at hedge funds is because offshore jurisdictions, or tax havens as they might say need a way to boost the local economy. They base their belief that isn't the whole concept of directors just an unnecessary effective tax on hedge funds and their investors? They further argue that while directors talk a big game and tell everyone they have true oversight of funds and work on behalf of investors, we all know that in reality all they do is collect fees for little to no work.

Their logic continues that at the end of the day, won't they always simply side with the hedge fund manager over investors? Hedge funds after all select and hire them, determine their remuneration, and can fire them if they want. Isn't this whole relationship a little too cozy to not make anyone concerned about conflicts?

Turning to the issue of delegation the critics become even more riled up. Their thinking continues that directors outsource, or to be polite delegate, a lot of their responsibilities to others in a never-ending shell game of passing the buck of liability while still claiming to be accountable enough to do their job. After all, they continue, being a director can't be that much work, right? If it is, then why can they sit on multiple boards?

The criticisms continue with regards to issues of director capacity. Questions critics raise include what's the big deal with telling me how many boards they sit on? Are they trying to hide something? Even those who admit how many boards they sit on act like they are doing everyone a favor or making some big revelation. Who cares? They further continue that the numbers are still too high to be meaningful or really make anyone believe that they have the best interest of investors at heart. The critics then focus on the whole issue of directors seeking to reduce their numbers by grouping multiple individual fund boards by relationship, as opposed to providing detail on the actual numbers, just to show they have more capacity. They perhaps rightly raise the question if directors honestly think they are fooling anyone?

Turning to the issue of director qualifications, the critics raise questions as to what even qualifies them to be directors. They continue that many of them are semiretired expat accountants, lawyers, operations people, and the like who have no formal training in some of the key areas they govern. Furthermore, the critics raise the point that many of them have never run a hedge fund, much less invested in one, and therefore raise the question as to what makes them think they are qualified to tell hedge funds what they should and shouldn't be doing.

Some have argued that these directors are simply a smoke screen and represent a fantastical offshore oasis claiming to promote governance and oversight while instead just going through the motions. Those who are critical of the directorship industry even go so far as to suggest that we should get rid of all directors and let hedge funds and investors work it out themselves and if there is a problem that can't be worked out, then the courts can handle it. A common question raised by critics in this area is: after all won't investors and the invisible hand of market dictate what is good governance and what isn't?

The director criticism continues then to expand beyond this point to focus on offshore regulators. Certain critics raise questions relating to their conflicted interests and argue that they certainly wouldn't kill the so-called golden goose directorship industry that is the life blood of many of their offshore economies. The critics continue that even if they spotted a problem, the directors themselves wouldn't dare be critical of the regulators in these offshore jurisdictions and after all, why would they complain for more scrutiny when investors for a long time in many jurisdictions have instead accepted voluntary self-regulation by the directors themselves through industry associations.

Some critics raise points along the lines of, "Really don't these financial regulators instead provide just enough oversight so nobody complains. And once people do complain they take so long to make any changes that after the consultation period and surveys, they are way behind the curve. They are not as well equipped or resourced to handle real financial problems."

Furthermore, to support their argument some critics point to allegations of corruption in offshore jurisdictions. For support in this area they look to Alan Stanford's experience in Antigua and Barbuda and the corruption-related charges brought against the former Premier of the Cayman Islands McKeeva Bush (Britell, 2013a, 2013b). The charges against Mr. Bush, as announced by the Royal Cayman Police Service, included abuse of trust and theft related to the misuse of a government credit card in an American casino.

But maybe its investors who are the biggest joke of them all because they put up with it?

ARE VITRIOLIC DIRECTOR CRITICISMS MERITED? CLARIFYING A MODEST PROPOSAL

Whether you agree with the criticisms outlined above, it is important to note hedge fund directors come in all shapes and sizes, both good and bad. The role of directors, indeed even their necessity as you may have guessed, is one of the most contentious and hotly debated issues within the world of hedge funds. This is particularly true when you discuss the director's role in overall hedge fund governance. Indeed, as we outlined in Chapter 1, many in the hedge fund space simply equate the concept of hedge fund governance to the board of directors themselves.

A Lack of Uniform Opinion About the Directorship Industry

Complicating matters further is the fact that there is not necessarily uniformity of opinions about the directorship industry among the different players in the overall hedge fund complex. To clarify here at this point we are talking about criticisms of the directorship industry as a whole. Although the concepts are related, this is not the same as criticizing a particular director or directorship firm. We will address this later issue in more detail shortly.

With this point clarified we can now return to our discussion of opinions regarding the concept of the directorship industry as a whole. It's not as if it can be said with absolute certainty that the majority of investors dislike the concept of directors. Can we? A 2014 Corgentum Consulting survey of investors and operational due diligence professionals showed that over 73% of those surveyed felt directors did not serve a useful function (Corgentum Consulting, LLC, 2014). While this was based only on a limited sample set, is a lack of belief in director utility the same thing as disliking a whole industry?

The same line of thinking can likely be applied to hedge funds. Some hedge funds likely feel that the directorship industry is a good thing. They have another source of third-party guidance in the directors. Additionally, some investors may feel that directors do a good job in providing oversight and this can take some heat off of the hedge fund managers with regards to investors' governance concerns. On the other hand, some hedge fund managers may dislike the directorship industry. One reason may be that they view it as another cost center in an increasingly competitive and expensive hedge fund environment. Additionally, who knows how to run their businesses better than them? What can directors practically do to improve things that lawyers, for example, can't?

The same can also be said of other hedge fund service providers, investor consultants, hedge fund third-party marketers, and the like. Depending on who you talk to, opinions vary greatly within each group from admiration of director's important function or passive acceptance to ambivalent dismissal or outright criticism.

Institutional Investor Directorship Industry Objections

As we have noted with our example criticism above, some groups such as large institutional investors are very passionate about the issue. Or at least they have become increasingly focused on the role of directors since the 2011 Cayman Weavering decision (Lindsay, 2014). For reference more details on the facts surrounding the Weavering case can be found in Chapter 8.

This passionate criticism typically comes from disagreements on matters of principle. This includes arguments, for example, relating to: how many directorships are too many? How much directors should be paid? Whether directors truly are beneficial to investors? Do directors facilitate oversight and promoting governance?

Such criticisms may certainly be merited. The goal here is not to defend one side of the argument or the other, but rather to highlight and provide perspective on the issues. After all, these are issues of largely ideological debate to which there is really no correct answer. Perhaps it is best left for the market to determine, for example, how much directors should be paid. Those investors who feel directors are being paid too much or too little have every right in the world to complain about it.

What's a bit different is when this criticism, or admiration, of the directorship industry as a whole becomes automatically translated to the conclusions about a specific director sitting on the board of a specific hedge fund.

Wholesale Director Dismissal—Throwing the Baby Out With the Bathwater?

In Chapter 6 we will discuss techniques by which investors can analyze governance in place at hedge funds. This includes not only an analysis of internal hedge fund governance mechanisms but the roles played by their service providers as well. This includes of course hedge fund directors. If investors, however, do not perform research on the directors' role and instead immediately extend the above-mentioned criticisms of the directorship industry to the directors at funds under review, then there is a real risk that good directors will be unnecessarily chastised along with the bad ones. But is the risk of throwing the baby out with the bathwater so to speak a real one? Aren't investors devoting enough time to vetting directorship roles? Let's provide a bit more perspective on this matter.

Perhaps somewhat counterintuitively, one of the contributing issues in this area is that investors are doing more due diligence on hedge funds than ever before. Shouldn't this be a good thing? Yes, it is. The problem is that this increased scope of due diligence has not necessarily come with commensurate resources. This is a particular problem in the area of operational due diligence.

To frame the discussion in modern hedge fund times, even before the Madoff scandal came to light in 2008, investors were increasing their focus on reviewing operational risks in hedge funds. After Madoff, this focus increased exponentially. When you add the increasing web of global compliance regulations, you can see how investors have increasingly full plates with regards to operational risks. For larger allocators who may employ in-house operational due diligence personnel they haven't necessarily gone on hiring sprees however to bulk up ODD teams. In many cases, it doesn't make financial sense to build up the in-house teams. As such there has been a growth in the use of operational due diligence consultants such as my firm, Corgentum Consulting, to support in-house ODD teams.

Now add the topic of governance and directors to an already full roster of ODD work and you can see how it could be overwhelming. This doesn't of course mean that they should be excused for not necessarily getting around to the issue properly; it just becomes less of a priority, particularly if they feel they are wasting their precious time with what they might mistakenly classify as a useless service provider.

Some things fall through the crack or indeed become under-researched, and directors and governance can be one of them. On the whole, despite the increased attention paid to governance and the directors of late, this area continues to be one that is under-researched. Some evidence for this is found in the above-referenced 2014 Corgentum Consulting survey, which showed that only 39% of investors and operational due diligence professionals surveyed indicated that they conduct interviews with fund directors as part of their due diligence process. Furthermore, a much smaller segment (18%) performs background investigation on these directors.

This results in under-resourced investors and larger allocators with overworked operational due diligence groups not dedicating the appropriate level of review to these issues. As such, some investors and ODD professionals take the above-referenced default position that they are going to focus their efforts on the hedge fund and what they deem to be its key service providers and devote less efforts to directors. Shockingly, some ODD professionals, at large allocators, have expressed the sentiment that outside of checking who the directors are, they effectively ignore the function entirely because of their perceived lack of authority and ineffectiveness. This all translates into a situation where those who haven't spent much time researching the specifics of a fund director relationship at a particular hedge fund become overly critical of it.

For those who do make the time to engage with directors, you could see how it could perhaps be frustrating when they may be a bit inherently skeptical of some of what they are told. The biggest leap of faith for many investors and operational due diligence analysts may be believing that the directors actually protect investors' interests over those of hedge funds or their own. While one can look to the courts for examples of cases that bolster either side of the argument, it still may be a difficult bill of goods to sell to certain people. This is particularly true among ODD people who are paid to be professional skeptics.

To be clear, I would like to reiterate that I take the perspective that investors and ODD professionals should definitely have the right, if not the obligation, to be critical of the director function. This is particularly true when, as noted above, there are legitimate concerns in place unique to the facts and circumstances of each directorship position. These criticisms may also be well founded when focusing not on the relationship between the director and the hedge fund itself, but rather on the directors themselves. For example, an investor or ODD professional may have concerns regarding a director's background, their qualifications, or the fact that they feel that the directors may be overcommitted to too many boards. The problem, however, is that investors and ODD professionals may be casting wide strokes with such criticisms based on ideological objections against the industry as a whole. Although related, for the purposes of analyzing the circumstances of a particular directorship under review the two positions should in large part be separated. Of course, hedge fund investors and operational due diligence analysts are not robots, nor should they be. If an investor is negative on the concept of hedge fund directors, then they should approach the review of a particular directorship position with enhanced skepticism and scrutiny. The point, though, is that they should not let such negative opinions about the industry completely blind them to conducting analysis of the specific directorship position at hand. As noted above, the risk is that many investors, so clouded by rage or ambivalence in this area, simply don't bother to dig deep into the role at all and that is a mistake.

UNDERSTANDING HEDGE FUND BOARD STRUCTURES

As we have outlined in our definition of hedge fund governance in Chapter 1, governance consists of a lot more than simply the board. This is not to minimize the role that the board plays in governance; just the opposite, often times the board can be one of the key drivers in governance at the fund. The goal of this chapter is to focus on the role of the board directors. Before delving into directors more deeply, it is useful to take a step back and outline exactly the different types of hedge fund boards they can serve on.

OFFSHORE VERSUS ONSHORE HEDGE FUNDS

The concept of offshore hedge funds versus onshore hedge funds is really all about your perspective. We addressed this issue in Chapter 1; however, in case you are reading this book out of order, we will summarize this concept again as it is critical to our discussion of boards here. The term onshore typically refers to a hedge fund in the same jurisdiction that you, the investor, are from. For example, from the perspective of a United States–based investor a hedge fund domiciled in Delaware would be considered to be an *onshore fund*. Similarly, a hedge fund domiciled outside the United States, such as in Jersey or Malta, would be an *offshore fund*. To clarify the onshore and offshore funds would typically be managed by the same hedge fund manager and follow effectively the same investment strategy. This is commonly referred to as a pari passu arrangement. The purpose of the same hedge fund manager running these two strategies is primarily for tax reasons. Investors from one jurisdiction, depending on a number of factors including the type of entity they are, might realize better tax benefits by investing an offshore vehicle as opposed to an onshore one.

It should also be noted that this onshore and offshore terminology could be reversed if the perspectives were reversed. As a practical matter, however, the terms typically do not need to be reversed because offshore vehicles are typically in jurisdictions where not many direct hedge fund investors come from such various Caribbean jurisdictions as Bermuda and the Cayman Islands.

DIFFERENT TYPES OF HEDGE FUND BOARDS

Now that we have some of the basic terminology out of the way we can begin to outline the structural ways in which hedge fund boards come about. To do this it will also be helpful to discuss a common hedge fund structure known as the *master–feeder structure*.

The master–feeder structure, or master–feeder fund complex as it is sometimes called, is an arrangement whereby there are two tiers of funds in place. Before understanding how hedge fund boards interact with this structure we must cover some of the basics relating to the different component vehicles and legal entities involved in the fund.

Starting from the perspective of an investor, the first tier in the structure is the feeder funds. These are the different investment vehicles into which investors allocate capital. Each of them is a separate legal entity. Onshore funds are typically structured as a type of company known as a limited partnership. A limited partnership is composed of general partners ("GPs") and limited partners ("LPs"). The LPs are the investors in the fund. From a technical perspective a GP can be defined as, "one or more persons [or entities] who control the business and are personally liable for the partnerships debts." GPs can serve an accounting purpose, such as by acting as the legal repository entity where the onshore fund incentive allocation (also sometimes called performance fee) is collected. Just to add another entity to the mix, GPs are typically wholly owned by a hedge fund's affiliated legal entity. These GP ownership companies are generally organized as limited liability companies ("LLC") and typically share the same jurisdiction as the onshore fund.

Here is as an example of how this all works in context:

- The onshore fund in a complex is a Delaware limited partnership called Jason Alpha Fund I, LP.
- The GP of the onshore fund would also be a separate legal entity but also registered in Delaware and established as a LLC. The GP is named Jason Alpha GP Holdings, LLC.

For the purposes of our discussion effectively GPs are simply a purely legal entity in the overall master–feeder fund complex.

As we have outlined above, from the perspective of a US investor, non-US jurisdictions such as the Cayman Islands would be considered offshore jurisdictions. By association, funds domiciled there, from the perspective of a US investor, would be considered offshore funds. Offshore funds are typically organized under limited company structure, which ends with the "Ltd." abbreviation at the end of the fund name. For illustrative purposes an example of a name of a Cayman offshore fund would be Jason Alpha Fund I Ltd.

Just to put a spanner in the works, there are exceptions to the general rules we have outlined above. One example, continuing our focus on the Cayman Islands, is that there can be limited partnerships in the Cayman Islands. A further wrinkle is that in the Caymans in particular there are regular limited partnerships and exempted limited partnerships. For hedge fund investors and fund managers, the traditional Cayman LP structure has traditionally posed a number of burdensome restrictions for hedge fund investors seeking to benefit from the traditional liability limitations afforded by the limited partnership structure. These limitations on the traditional or ordinary limited partnership include:

- The limited partnership's registration had to be published in an official Cayman publication known as the *Cayman Islands Gazette* that is available online at http://www.gazettes.gov.ky. The *Cayman Islands Gazette*, sometimes just referred to as *The Gazette*, today typically includes details of the legal notices of summaries of fund liquidations among other legal notices. You can search the *Cayman Islands Gazette* archives yourself for information about hedge funds.
- LPs could not take any active role in the business of the fund, sometimes referred to as a Partnership.
- LPs' profit-sharing ability was ostensibly limited to fixed payments taken only out of profits of the fund.
- LPs also ostensibly had ongoing liability to contribute capital in the event of fund insolvency. This was even the case after they had redeemed.

One reference for more information on the difference between limited partnerships and exempted limited partnerships in the Cayman Islands is *Guide to Exempted Limited Partnerships* (Appleby, 2014).

As a result a structure known as an exempted limited partnership has increased in popularity. The exempted LP structure, which has subsequently been amended many times including recent 2012 and 2013 revisions, remedies many of the problems with the ordinary LP structure.

As the purpose of this book is not to be a legal textbook but rather to focus on governance we will not delve into intricacies of all of these structures in this text.

To recap, we should now be clear on what the terms onshore and offshore mean as well as having covered some ground on basic structures in each instance. Up until this point we have addressed the feeder parts of the master–feeder structure. Feeder funds are essentially onshore and offshore legal entities (i.e., funds) that allocate capital to a central fund, which sits above them in the overall fund complex hierarchy. This fund that they allocate to is called a master fund. The underlying funds are called feeders because they are effectively feeding the master fund with capital. The master funds are typically the entities that are actually making the investments.

Master funds are typically domiciled in the same jurisdiction as the offshore feeder fund. Additionally, they typically follow the same legal structure as offshore funds under a limited company structure. So continuing our naming conventions an example of a master fund would be Jason Alpha Master Fund Ltd. Now that we understand all the players in the master–feeder complex we can now address how the master board plays into the complex.

Just like a corporation, hedge funds can have boards of directors. Continuing our master–feeder complex structure example, a good way to think about each individual hedge fund vehicle is like a corporation. In our case, the corporations have to be affiliates. Some of the hedge fund corporations have their own board and others have not. It depends on whether they are legally required to have one or simply if they want to. Also just like corporations each of these boards has different rights, obligations, members, and responsibilities. As such, when we compare the different boards of directors of hedge funds, just like corporate boards they can all be different.

In master–feeder structures typically only the offshore and master funds have boards. While the onshore fund could also have a board traditionally, it has been less common since it is not often required by the jurisdictions, such as Delaware, where the onshore funds are domiciled.

To pause for a moment, you might be asking yourself a simple question. If hedge fund complexes have more than one board, why does the offshore fund receive all the attention? To answer this question we should analyze the ways in which these boards interact and the makeup of these boards. Let us first start with the board of the master fund, but before we do that we need to clarify one more point of terminology.

CLARIFYING DIRECTOR TERMINOLOGY

At its most basic level there are two types of hedge fund directors. The first group comprises those who are in some way directly affiliated with the hedge fund. In more traditional corporate governance jargon these individuals might be referred to as *interested directors*, *in-house directors*, or *affiliated directors*. These are individuals who are employees of the hedge fund management company such as the founder of the firm or a portfolio manager.

The other type of hedge fund director is a nonaffiliated director. Once again borrowing from the traditional corporate governance world these types of directors might be called *nonexecutive directors*. These are individuals who are not direct employees of the hedge fund. Under this construct, these nonaffiliated members would include board members from professional directorship firms or stand-alone sole proprietor directorship firms consisting of a single individual. These types of directors are effectively directors for hire and as such another common term for these individuals is *professional directors*.

Now as noted above, it is of course a bone of contention for many investors as to whether or not despite their nonaffiliated title, these directors are closely aligned with the hedge funds they are supposed to provide oversight of. Furthermore, it may be even more contentious to refer to them as *independent directors*, another common term. We will address the potential conflicts surrounding directorship relationships later in this chapter, but for now it is simply helpful to classify these nonaffiliated directors as not being direct employees of the hedge fund manager. Now that we have some basic terminology out of the way we can return to the question of why the offshore boards have received the bulk of investors' attentions in recent years.

A BRIEF HISTORY OF HEDGE FUND DIRECTORS

The first widely publicized hedge fund is thought to have been started in 1949 by an individual named Alfred Winslow Jones. In Jones' days hedge funds didn't really have so-called professional directors. Even if they did, they were likely merely filing the role of legal technicality and no one really cared about them. Instead, the individuals who ran the hedge fund, and any associated management companies, were likely also required board members of the fund. In Winslow's time, and as we outlined in Chapter 1, representative of the corporate governance mindset at the time, it was likely that governance at a hedge fund was one of the furthest things from everyone's mind. As long as it was all legal, they were most likely happy. They were equally likely not concerned about who any fund directors were or what they did. The focus among investors and hedge funds was primarily focused solely on profitability.

Also in Winslow's time the use of offshore tax havens wasn't nearly as popular or accessible as it is today. Of course, the ultrawealthy had access to places such as Switzerland to place capital outside of the reach of many tax authorities, but in general many investment partnerships didn't make extensive use of the tax benefits of such offshore centers by modern standards. It was not until many years later beginning in the late 1970s and into the 1980s that increased acceptance of the use of offshore jurisdictions in the financial sector began to take hold. This, coupled with the growth in popularity of hedge funds, resulted in an eventual alignment of interests between hedge funds and the use of offshore jurisdictions. During the early days of the hedge funds' use of offshore centers, hedge funds enjoyed the tax reduction benefits and often lax regulatory environments in place. Similarly, investors continued to encourage hedge funds in the direction of offshore centers to facilitate tax-efficient structures in their investments in hedge funds as well.

This increased use of offshore centers was a boom for the local economies of many of these countries. This included places in the Caribbean in particular such as Curacao, the Cayman Islands, and the British Virgin Islands, and domiciles in Europe such as Ireland and, to a lesser extent, jurisdictions such as Luxembourg. While they appreciated the business, eventually many of these offshore jurisdictions no longer wanted to be seen as simply places where people could go to avoid taxes with no real oversight. As a result, many jurisdictions began to enact some sort of legislation to provide enhanced regulations, to facilitate oversight, on paper at least anyways, of the funds that were established there.

Also, many of these offshore jurisdictions wanted to further leverage off of the use of their jurisdictions to promote the local economies. This involved promoting the establishment of offshore financial centers to encourage companies to set up operations in these jurisdictions. We can see the results of this today with many hedge fund service providers such as administrators maintaining offices in these popular offshore jurisdictions such as Ireland and the Cayman Islands.

To make a long story short, and perhaps oversimplify the issue a bit for the purposes of our discussion here, as part of the combined effort to increase regulatory oversight as well as promote increased business in these offshore centers for their residents, this resulted in eventual requirements in many offshore centers for offshore hedge funds to have directors on the boards of those funds. As we noted earlier in this discussion, such board directorship requirements are not in place for the majority of onshore funds in master–feeder complexes. As such, when investors began to focus on issues related to governance, practically the only unaffiliated directors around were on the offshore board. This led to the increased focus on offshore boards.

THE FORGOTTEN MASTER FUND BOARD

To take stock of where we are in our discussion, we have some basic terminology out of the way regarding directors, both affiliated and unaffiliated. We have also covered some background information on offshore boards, as well as why they have traditionally received investor attention. You may remember earlier in our discussion we mentioned that in addition to the offshore fund in a master-fund complex having a board, the master fund may also commonly have a board. But who sits on that board and what does it do?

Legal Fiction or Effective Board?

For a long time the board of the master fund effectively functioned as a legal fiction. Much like the separation of the different hedge fund vehicles in the master–feeder complex itself, in reality the board of the master fund served little to no purpose with regards to the practical realities of running a hedge fund. Are we being too critical in our dismissive attitude toward this board, surely it must do something? After all, if it truly did nothing, then why create it?

In the early days of the hedge fund industry, and indeed in many instances unfortunately still today, the board of the master fund consisted of a single member. It generally could have been more than one individually, but typically only one. Perhaps the fact that the board of the master fund typically had only one member was a less than disguised tacit admission that no one really cared, particularly investors, who sat on this board.

Who was this lone individual tasked with being the master board bastion of governance? In smaller hedge funds, this person was typically the founder of the firm who was also the Lead Portfolio Manager and Chief Investment Officer. In larger hedge funds that perhaps managed multiple strategies, it could be the Lead Portfolio Manager of the particular strategy to which the fund was related, as opposed to the Chief Investment Officer of the entire hedge fund firm. To clarify the selection of who sat in this board was primarily in the sole discretion of the hedge fund itself, and there were, and still aren't, typically firm legal requirements as to who sits on this board. The fund simply designated this individual and, bam, they were the entire board. As we noted above, regardless of whether it was one, two, or multiple individuals they were all likely affiliated with the hedge fund manager. Under either scenario, there was a distinct lack of independence in the relationship. As a result, because the board of the master fund was effectively simply just the hedge fund itself, investors just didn't bother with it because of this conflict and instead, as we noted earlier in this chapter, focused their board to review efforts around the offshore board.

At this point, you may be asking yourself why investors would permit such a seemingly conflicted arrangement like this to persist. After all isn't the master board, which sits on top of the whole master–feeder complex, seemingly the most important fund in the whole structure. Shouldn't investors put equal, if not more, emphasis on independence at this level as compared with the offshore fund?

Unmasking the Master Board Members

Perhaps one of the reasons for the lack of attention historically paid by investors to the board of the master fund is that the master fund is not typically offered for direct investment to investors. Rather it is a vehicle that facilitates the trading activities of the feeders.

As a result of the fact that the master funds are not offered to investors often times, they do not have similar legal documentation, such as an offering memorandum, limited partnership agreements, or articles of association produced as compared with their onshore and offshore counterparts. When investors do not have a document to collect and review, the onus is often on them to remember to separately inquire about this issue, and they may not.

Unfortunately, further aggravating the problem hedge funds may not be anxious to volunteer information that they believe some investors may view as stymieing independent oversight, and this may be an example of such an issue. Of course, this is a generalized statement that implies that only the most sleuth investors could determine the identity of the member(s) of the master board. In reality, depending on the quality, read disclosure level, of the hedge fund offering memorandum for the particular hedge fund vehicle (i.e., offshore or onshore) being offered for investment, this information may be disclosed in the fund's documentation, or simply hiding in plain sight as it were. Of course, such disclosures were and continue to be effectively at the discretion of the magnanimous hedge fund manager. Said another way, there is typically no requirement, legal or otherwise, for the legal documentation including the offering memorandum of a feeder fund to disclose who may be on the board of the master fund.

Of course, such disclosures may be in the best interest of investors governance due diligence, and frankly if a fund doesn't make such a disclosure, an investor might rightly scratch their head and wonder what else might this fund not be so forthcoming with, but certainly it is not illegal. As is the usual cop-out for many managers when pressed on why or why not certain disclosures such as the identity of the master board may or may not have been disclosed in the PPM of a fund, they will often use the convenient, albeit often high-priced, scapegoat to the effect of, "Oh our lawyers advised us to write the document that way ...." But that is neither here nor there.

We should also note that even if the identity of the board members of the master board is not disclosed in the legal documentation for an offshore feeder fund, that is not to say it may be nowhere else. As anyone who has ever performed any sort of due diligence, operational or otherwise, on a hedge fund will tell you, there is no shortage of documentation often produced by these managers. The identity of the individual(s) on the board of the master fund may be somewhere else. The legal documentation is simply the most likely suspect in the lineup. Examples of other documentation that may contain this information could include the firm's due diligence questionnaire (often called a DDQ) or marketing presentation (commonly called a pitch book). Additionally, the notes to the audited financial statements of the master fund may also provide disclosures regarding the board that may be helpful in identifying who is on the board.

Ignoring the Master Board—Fool's Paradise or Blissful Ignorance?

What's the big deal about this? Why is the mere identity of who is on the master board treated like a national secret? Well, it isn't so much that hedge funds are interested in protecting the identity of the individual(s) sitting on the master board; it's more that as we intimated above, there has traditionally been a lack of interest in this subject.

To be frank, even if many investors were told that the board of the master fund consisted of only a single member who was affiliated with the hedge fund manager, this might not have raised any concerns historically. In fact, I would wager that, to play devil's advocate, even if this information had been brought to certain investors' attention historically, they may have plainly stated, "So what?" or "Who cares?" when presented with such information.

You also have to remember another point that relates in part to the historical context of the analysis of master boards. The traditional bias against ignoring master boards comes about in part because of who was tasked with typically evaluating this information. Historically, for large institutional investment allocators such as corporate pensions, endowments, and foundations, often times reviewing items such as governance and boards, which remember weren't necessarily a key area of focus several years ago, was the task of the operational due diligence group. Indeed this is still the case today. However, in the early days of operational due diligence, and in particular hedge fund investing, the term "operational due diligence group," should be taken with a grain of salt. I use this term loosely, because at many institutional investors who were affiliated, for example, with large banks or fund of funds, these groups were not groups at all but instead individuals with other full-time jobs.

It was not at all uncommon, for example, at a midsized pension fund who made some direct hedge fund investments to call upon someone from operations, traditionally with an accounting background such as a Fund Accountant, Controller, or Chief Financial Officer, to conduct operational due diligence. There is nothing wrong with this type of approach except that this person doesn't necessarily have the background, legal or otherwise, to necessarily know that master boards have directors. Even if they did, they further might not know why they should care who sits on this board or have any game plan as to how to make an assessment as to whether this person, affiliated or otherwise, is positioned in the best interest of the feeder fund to which they are likely investing.

This is not to criticize the traditionally important role of fund accountants conducting operational due diligence. Further it is not to say that ODD professionals with fund accounting personnel can't analyze master boards. Rather, this is just not what was traditionally done by people in those situations. Furthermore, as noted above, these individuals typically had full-time jobs and very limited time and resources to conduct entire operational due diligence reviews. Therefore, this resulted in even less time to devote to thinking about governance and boards. As an aside, somewhat unbelievable, you will still find surprisingly large investment plans that follow operational due diligence personnel models similar to the one described above. The primary difference is the increased acceptance by these plans of the need to augment this function with the use of additional internal resources and specialist operational due diligence consultants such as my employer Corgentum Consulting.

Returning to the question of investor apathy toward the master board, we are still presented with the issue of why investors should care. To once again put on my devil's advocate hat, after all it wouldn't be in the hedge fund manager's best interests to utilize this arguably legacy master board arrangement to hurt investors. Isn't it just basically accepted that the master board is, as we have outlined above, the governance nom de guerre of the Chief Investment Officer? Or to take it a step further, some may even argue that if the industry as a whole hasn't objected to this practice, as they have, for example, against the hedge funds' self-administration of funds, then why should individual investors even bother to bat an eyelash?

As we have outlined above, today many investors still unfortunately take this position, even if passively. Such a seemingly anemic response may not be as ostensibly anodyne as it seems. Just the opposite, at least in today's world of increasing due diligence a lack of complaining about a particular operational practice can suggest one of three likely things. First, it could be suggested that no one is complaining because everyone is comfortable enough with the risks and potential conflicts of the practice at play to make it acceptable. As we questioned above, to play the scenario out to the fullest we could say that if a hedge fund is utilizing this master board issue to somehow pull one over on investors, there are likely bigger issues at play that investors would likely complain about and, therefore, it's not a big enough issue to require an industry-wide paradigm shift.

Second, it could be suggested that despite general enhanced investor due diligence compared with several years ago, there are a series of issues, the board of the master fund being one of them, that investors aren't too aware of or don't overly focus on. Could such a series of so-called underground operational issues exist? These issues might not be as absurd as it sounds. For example, how many investors are familiar with common practices in certain operational areas such as audit holdbacks, fund reserves (which directors have a say in creating), and the level of valuation bandwidth discretion among administrators and hedge funds. It's not to say that an investor may never have heard of these things, but rather how informed about them they are.

The same could be said for the board of the master fund. Yes, investors today may know that a fund is part of a master–feeder complex. They may even become familiar with not only who sits on the master board but also the name and documentation of the master fund itself, but they still might not focus on it. This is not to say that investors are inept by any means; rather that they are just not fully informed about the gamut of risks and structures relating to master boards. To be clear it's not just investors; even some operational due diligence analysts may not realize or pay much attention to the fact that the master fund has a board. Once again, it might not be due to a lack of hedge fund industry experience, but rather it deals with a lack of an individual background in this area and familiarity of practices in this regard.

Finally, it could be that investors are aware of the issue but they don't fully understand the risks involved, or they don't care, and instead choose to focus their attention around what they feel to be higher areas of traditional fund operational risk, such as valuations or cash management. That is not to say that cash management is not important, but it does not mean that an analysis of the cash management function should be sacrificed for analyzing governance practices.

Why Investors Should Care About Master Boards

Although the board of directors of the offshore fund has many duties and responsibilities, very similar in many cases to the GP of an onshore fund, as we have outlined above, the master fund sits on top of both of these funds. During the operational due diligence process, investors run the very real risk of being so focused on the board of directors of the offshore fund that they neglect to inquire about the board of the master fund. Indeed, even if investors did think of it, they may not have had a good reason to ask about the master board during due diligence because they were too focused on other items they may have felt were more important. But ultimately why should they care?

From an investor's perspective, there are two primary reasons why inquiring about the board of the master fund matters. First, from a due diligence perspective it can provide useful insights for investors to learn who is actually on the board of the master fund. If it consists of entirely affiliated members, perhaps this is a signal that the hedge fund doesn't really take the board of the master fund seriously.

This could be a signal about the general attitude the fund has toward governance practices as a whole. Or perhaps the fund has been in business for awhile and this is the way they've always done it. Sometimes hedge funds don't make certain changes, even if they think it might be a good idea, because they don't want to rock the boat with sometimes finicky investors. If investors proactively look into issues such as this and investigate it, the hedge fund might take these inquiries as an opportunity to engage in dialogues with investors about such issues and make positive changes.

Second, and arguable more important, depending on a number of factors including the legal structure of the master–feeder complex, and the way in which the legal documents are written, the master fund's board may have the ability to effectively trump any decisions made by the board of directors of the offshore fund.

This is a point worth repeating. Yes, that's correct; despite the makeup of the offshore board and the rigorousness of their oversight, the master board may be able to render some of the work of the offshore directors as effectively moot point and utterly meaningless. This may surprise many hedge fund investors, but it's true. Indeed many hedge funds might concede this point if you raise it with them, but they will not likely volunteer this piece of information. Or they haven't even thought about it. Why not? Well, you see, by acknowledging this it renders as lame the impliedly ferocious independent oversight of the directors that many hedge funds may tout when asked about it by investors. Additionally, directors may not be likely to highlight this point as well for similar reasons. After all, you don't have much power if all your decisions can ultimately be nullified by someone else with higher authority.

Now while from a technical legal perspective the master board may be able to trump the offshore board, in practice there is often an implied understanding among hedge funds and directors that such trumping won't occur. It's often similar to the understanding between hedge funds and their administrators. While hedge funds do technically have the ability to override an administrator's valuations in many situations, doing so too often may damage the relationship. But that's not to say it doesn't happen. Similarly, hedge funds and directors may not always agree. Furthermore, investors may not always be privy to the details of such discussions. Indeed, they may not even know that any disagreements occur.

In conclusion, as part of a governance evaluation the master board should not be ignored out of hand with the focus shifted to the offshore feeder fund directors. Many valuable insights can be gained from an analysis of the master fund board. The information learned by researching the membership and authority of the master board during the due diligence process can provide valuable insights that inform the overall directorship evaluation.

For a further discussion of the potentially negative governance implications of the master board rendering the oversight role of offshore boards moot, please refer to the interviews contained in Chapter 10.

WHO ARE THESE BOARD MEMBERS?

So far we have discussed the types of boards directors commonly sit on. We also just covered that an individual affiliated with the hedge fund typically served on the board of the master fund. But who are these individuals who serve on offshore fund boards?

To take a step back for a moment, before discussing who commonly sits on offshore boards, we should further clarify some of the terminology we used earlier in this chapter regarding the distinction between professional directorship firms and stand-alone directors. As noted above stand-alone directorship firms were usually sole proprietorships. These directors were effectively entrepreneurs who had set up one-man shops to offer their services. While they still exist today, the more common arrangement is for hedge funds to engage with directorship firms. These are often fully fledged companies with multiple directors in multiple jurisdictions. To provide some clarification on who these one-man band directors actually were it may be helpful to understand how the situation of how a hedge fund manager would go about and hire directors would typically work by way of a hypothetical example.

In the early days of the offshore hedge fund industry, hedge fund directors were mostly freelance stand-alone directors. If you were a United States–based hedge fund and you were starting an offshore fund, you had a bit of a problem. Your lawyers would tell you that to set up the fund offshore, let's continue to use the Cayman Islands as an example, you would need to hire fund directors. Ok you can spend money and hire someone, so it's a solvable problem, right?

Well, it's a bit more complicated than that. Continuing our example, you see you are in New York. You've never been to the Cayman Islands. You don't know anyone down there and certainly you don't know who would be qualified to hire as a director. Sure you could take the wife and kids on a trip down there and try to meet some directors, but that's complicated and expensive. Besides you've already paid the deposit on your place in the Hamptons for the summer, so this just won't do. Now what?

You ask your lawyer if he knows anyone down there. Lucky for you he has a solution. Does it even matter to you at this point what the rest of the story is? It's a fund expense after all, isn't it? Even the conversations with your lawyer about the problem is a fund expense, so who really cares what the solution is, right? It's not as if these directors are going to do anything anyways; you're the one running the fund. You'll be the one doing all of the actual decision making for the fund and all you need is a name to put on piece of paper and fill out any local paperwork, right? In the interest of completeness, even though our fictional hedge fund manager in our example no longer cares, we'll continue. Your lawyer's solution was likely one of two options.

The first option could be that his firm, or their Cayman branch, could just fill the board position. End of conversation. Well, that was easy. While such solutions effectively no longer exist, in the good old days, lawyers from the hedge fund's counsel would serve as directors. Due to the obvious conflicts associated with these relationships, many investors raised concerns surrounding such relationships. As such, those law firms today that still offer directorship services have typically segregated the role of individuals who serve on fund boards into distinct areas that focus on this.

The second option would be that your attorney just happens to have a relationship with a different Cayman Islands–based law firm. Or maybe instead his firm just happened to have an office in the Caymans—even easier. The Cayman firm, or affiliate of the US firm, has a handful of local semiretired standalone freelance people on the island that they typically work with and will recommend some of them to sit on your fund. Oh and don't worry your lawyer tells you, "they all know the drill, which forms to sign and even the right things to say if investors come calling." Great, you would think, and go back about your business never even meeting them. Of course, this is a bit of an exaggerated situation outlined for example purposes, but it's likely not that far off from the truth of the way things used to work. The Caymans was simply used as an example here, but the same scenario was likely applicable in other jurisdictions as well.

Now to return to our original question, who exactly are these people? They could generally be either locals from the particular island where the hedge fund had domiciled the offshore vehicle or expats who are now living on the island. Many of these expat directors were typically American, Canadian, British, or Irish fund accountants who had moved to the islands for previous work. In the 1990s into the early 2000s as we noted earlier in this chapter, many fund administrators and accounting firms, coupled with the boom of assets into the hedge fund industry, focused on building up their offshore presence. This included building up the number of staff in offshore centers. As part of this process, these firms hired a number of locals who had either grown up with the hedge fund industry or themselves worked overseas to gain hedge fund industry experience and since returned to the offshore center. Additionally, many firms brought in individuals from Europe and the United States to work in those offices. When the hedge fund industry continued to grow, certain of these experienced expats and locals decided to go into business for themselves and offer their services to funds as directors. Logically, they had a good sales pitch. They knew the hedge fund industry, had spent time in the islands, and knew the local lay of the land. Also, their services were in demand because there were a small number of directors who were on a relatively small Caribbean island.

To be frank, most directors at the time also knew where their bread was buttered. Without hedge fund managers there would be no directorship business. The focus in the early days of the directorship business was not necessarily on having directors oversee hedge fund governance practices in the fund, but more to fulfilling the local requirements of having an offshore board. It was sort of a disconnect between the realities of the situation and the facade that was in place.

If you asked any hedge fund manager about their offshore board at the time, you would most likely get one of two responses. The first would be that the board fulfills a regulatory requirement and that's basically it. On more than one occasion when performing operational due diligence I had hedge fund personnel perform double takes when I asked them who was on their offshore board. Once we moved past the inquisitive look of, "Why would anyone care about that?" and I was provided with the answer, it was often followed up by something to the effect of, "Look, who cares, these are just some people in the Caribbean who serve in a purely check the box statutory function and nothing more." At the time, this likely would be the more truthful answer. The other response would be something along the lines of the standard party line that the hedge fund employs independent board members and is heavily focused on governance and oversight. In the early days of the directorship industry, many directors were simply focused on gathering hedge fund clients to add to their fiefdoms as opposed to providing any real oversight. How else could we practically explain the widely reported legacy situations of long-time directors sitting on literally hundreds of boards (Ahmed, 2012)? Today as investors' and hedge funds focus has shifted in this area, and the potential risks to directors have risen after decisions such as that in the Weavering case, standards of practice in this area have greatly risen as well.

THE EXPANDING DIRECTOR TALENT POOL—A BLESSING AND A CURSE?

The director talent pool has expanded in recent years. This pressure has come from two sides. First, investors have continually scrutinized the number of board memberships directors hold. This has put downward pressure on the number of hedge fund boards individual directors will sit on. Indeed, some directors as marketing tools have opted for self imposed caps in the number of directorships.

The second source of expansion in the director talent pool has come from an ever-growing number of expats in the Caribbean. These individuals have seen the lucrative businesses being built by professional directorship firms and rather then leave the islands, they want to a piece of the business. This coupled with an increasing investor sentiment against large big box hedge fund directorship firms has allowed certain smaller directorship shops and individual directors to carve out niches. Also contributing to increasing pressure on directors are enhanced regulatory requirements, discussed in Chapter 3, as well as increased demands on directors' time by hedge funds. This relationship is summarized in Exhibit 2.1.

In some cases, these smaller players are able to compete by lowering directorship fees to hedge funds, which may be attractive to smaller and start-up funds. While such smaller-scale options may indeed offer more hands-on service at a more affordable price point, as we will cover in more detail throughout this book, as a cautionary note about directorships you often get what you pay for. Besides the actual liability recovery issues of an independent director versus a larger firm, there are also considerations of appropriate insurance coverage and scalability to consider among others. Larger firms may charge more, but may also offer more assurance in these other areas.

EXHIBIT 2.1 Representation of Increased Director Challenges

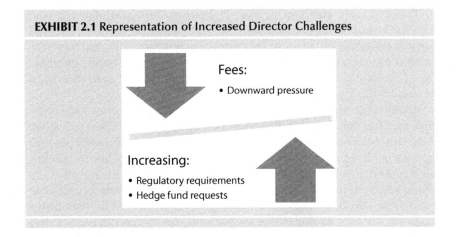

Fees:
• Downward pressure

Increasing:
• Regulatory requirements
• Hedge fund requests

As outlined above, whether a directorship firm is large or small, in addition to reviewing the quality of directorship firms as a whole, investors are increasingly focusing on the individual directors themselves, their qualifications and capacity.

WHO DECIDES WHO GETS TO BE ON THE BOARD?

Now that we have an understanding of who these directors are, another question is who picks directors? It's just in the hedge fund manager's sole discretion, right? Does this model promote governance?

When you think about it for a minute, the way hedge fund board members get hired is actually quite interesting. In traditional corporate America, board members are elected by the shareholders of the public company. They might not know much about who they are actually electing, or care for that matter, but the point is that they have a vote. Surely hedge funds must follow a similar democratic process. It would make sense that they should, shouldn't it?

Not so fast. Hedge fund boards are not elected; they are appointed. Appointed by whom, you ask? Well, as we highlighted above, the hedge fund of course. Since this is the way it has always been, most hedge fund investors simply take for granted the fact that this is the way it is supposed to be. Wouldn't it add more independence to the governance oversight process if these directors were elected by investors in the fund? Probably, but unfortunately such a change is not likely to happen anytime soon. Why not?

Some hedge fund investors frankly don't want this level of engagement with their managers. Certain investors take a very laissez faire attitude. They just want to allocate capital to a fund and as long as it's making them a good return and they are not reading the hedge fund's name in the newspapers, all is well.

They don't care who is on the board of directors. Sure others may care who is on the board, but they dismiss the oversight role of the board. Or they did initial due diligence on the hedge fund management organization, and they were satisfied that they knew what they were doing, including selecting directors. Therefore, they feel the board doesn't add much value, so the exact makeup of the board doesn't necessarily matter to them either.

Additionally, while many investors might gripe about the current board of the fund, they feel they have a limited pool of candidates from which to pick from. In the Caribbean islands, for example, the directors often need to have a physical presence on the island in which the hedge fund is domiciled. While the director talent pool has expanded in recent years, as we outlined above, it is still relatively limited based on continued hedge fund demand for directors. Furthermore, some investors are simply ok with a herd mentality that lands many of the same hedge funds with the same handful of directorship firms. For reference, we refer to this as the *good guy problem*, which is discussed in more detail in Chapter 7.

Returning to our discussion, as a result of these mindsets many investors ultimately end up putting their hands up and just moving on. The same is unfortunately even truer of the aforementioned membership of the master fund board of directors. Until there is enough investor momentum to push forward a proposal such as investor-nominated hedge fund directors or investor-elected directors, we are left with the current model of hedge fund manager–selected boards. Of course, there has already been some movement in this area as investors have become increasingly vocal in sharing their criticisms of certain board members, or directorship firms, but ultimately still it is at the manager's discretion. The fact that the hedge fund managers themselves retain control in this area raises the importance even higher of investors taking measures to analyze what type of due diligence, if any, a hedge fund manager has done before selecting directors. For reference, this issue is addressed from the perspective of funds and directors in Chapters 5 and 6.

YOU'RE NOT WHO I HIRED!—THE "ASSOCIATE DIRECTOR" BAIT AND SWITCH?

In our discussion of who directors have traditionally been and who has selected them, we overlooked an important unsung heroes who are often left out of such discussions—the so-called *associate directors*. Sometimes also called *junior directors* or *supporting directors*, investors will likely have not come across the names of these individuals as being referenced anywhere in a hedge fund documentation. Indeed if investors asked their hedge funds themselves who the associate directors are who may be working on their funds, they likely would have no names to provide you with.

Associate directors are not the individuals who are typically touted as being the fund directors in places such as the offshore fund's private placement memorandum. Instead the individuals listed in those documents, for the purposes of our discussion here, could perhaps be called the formal or official directors.

This doesn't mean that they are the ones doing all of the heavy lifting. Instead, particularly at larger directorship firms, there are armies of associate directors who handle the more menial director tasks. Oh and if the so-called official director is not available to conduct director meetings, no problem; the associate director can always step in to pinch hit on their behalf. There's nothing wrong with that, right? "Not so fast!," some investors and hedge funds may say.

It is not as if this is some big secret. If hedge funds bothered to conduct due diligence on the directorship firms before hiring them, they would likely know that this is a common practice in the business. Additionally, this discussion should not be read as to imply that directors are trying to pull the wool over the eyes of investors and hedge funds. Of course, they may not volunteer this information outright, but most will undoubtedly provide details regarding these associated directors if prodded enough.

Some hedge funds, however, don't bother to focus on the specifics of these relationships. Furthermore, as we noted above, the perspective could be taken that who cares whether it is the official director who is doing the work, or it is done in coordination with a group of associate directors, as long as the job gets done properly. Isn't it better to have more people involved anyway to provide more access to skill sets and diversity of the relationship to reduce key person risk with any single director? These are some valid points to consider.

On the other hand, some investors may raise concerns relating to the official director's involvement in the process at all. As we have already referenced, and will discuss in more detail throughout this book, director capacity is an ongoing concern. Investors are understandably concerned that official directors will in many cases simply become figureheads, and the associate directors will be doing all the real work. Often times, little to no scrutiny is applied by either hedge funds or investors to these associate directors. Furthermore, many of these associate directors may be less qualified and experienced than the figurehead directors.

Which side of the argument is more correct? As with all of the issues we have highlighted in this chapter, further arguments could be made to support each side. Our goal here is not to decide this issue once and for all. Rather, the goal of this discussion here is two-fold: first, to raise awareness to the reader of the role of associate directors and their interaction with hedge funds and official directors; second, to once again reiterate that investors should factor in the considerations outlined above, and apply them to reviewing the specific facts and circumstances of a particular hedge fund directorship engagement. For example, one hedge fund may engage with a smaller directorship firm in which no associate directors are utilized to support the official directors. Another hedge fund may hire a larger directorship firm that makes extensive use of associate directors. Is one better than the other? Not necessarily. The only way to answer that question is for investors to vet the detail of each different directorship arrangement through due diligence. Otherwise, they are simply making an uninformed guess about the relationship.

DIRECTOR COMPENSATION—A DOUBLE STANDARD?

So far we have discussed the role of directors at great length, but we haven't addressed the issue of director compensation. Nonaffiliated directors after all aren't employees of the hedge fund and they don't work for free. The range of directors' fees can vary widely depending on the specific directors or director-ship firms engaged, and the level of services provided. To provide some very general perspective on such issues, two directors serving on all the relevant boards in a master–feeder complex could charge around US$10,000–15,000. To clarify, as we outlined in our fictional hedge fund manager example earlier, these are traditionally fund expenses and not management company expenses. For those unfamiliar with the difference, fund expenses are ultimately paid by investors in the fund. In some cases certain expenses may be capped depend-ing on the unique terms of different hedge funds. Examples of other fund-level expenses include audit fees and legal bills. Management company expenses are not paid by the funds, and therefore not directly paid by investors in the funds. A traditional example of a management company expense is the compensation of the hedge fund manager's employees. For reference a common focus of many investor due diligence reviews related to expenses is to determine whether a manager is appropriately separating fund-level and management company ex-penses. The fear is that in certain instances, managers may try to sneak in cer-tain traditionally management company expenses as fund-level expenses, and therefore offload the cost to investors.

Returning to our discussion of directors' fees, in regards to the fee range pro-vided above, of course if you are analyzing a hedge fund and find out that a hedge fund's directors charge more or less than this range, this isn't necessarily an im-mediate red flag that there is a problem. The additional fees, or reductions, may be perfectly justified. These ranges are simply a guide to provide perspective on the matter. Now that being said, if a directorship firm was charging $1,000 or $50,000 for plain vanilla directorship services, then that would be suspicious. Further-more, to clarify as we will outline in more detail below directorship firms have begun to offer hedge funds additional services in addition to traditional director-ships to funds, and as such the total amount paid to these directorship firms by funds that take advantage of these additional services would also likely increase.

While a generally flat director fee, as typically described in the fund docu-ments, may sound perfectly reasonable and in the best interest of investors, it is worth pausing for a moment to consider whether this relationship is truly in the best interest of fund governance. Let's put this in some context via an example outside of the board of directors.

Consider, for example, a hedge fund administrator. We will discuss what an administrator does in more detail in Chapter 4, but for now let's focus on the way administrators are compensated. They are typically paid by hedge funds based on a portion of assets under management of the hedge fund. These compensa-tion arrangements are typically based on a sliding scale such that as the assets of the hedge fund increase at certain breakpoints, the percentage of assets that the administrator's fee is made up of declines. There are two key elements of this relationship that are worth mentioning for the purposes of our discussion here.

First, the hedge fund hires and pays the administrator. Yes, the money to pay the fees comes from the fund itself, so effectively this is an expense passed along to the fund investors. Furthermore, it can be also argued that depending on the voting mechanisms in place at the fund, the investors could have an influence on hiring or firing an administrator, but in practice such decisions are left with the manager. Therefore, there is an incentive for the administrator to keep the entity that hires them, the hedge fund, happy. The second point worth noting here is that the administrator's compensation arrangement is tied to the overall performance and fund-raising abilities of the fund. This aligns the interest of the hedge fund manager with the administrator.

One of the problems with this compensation arrangement, however, is that administrators are typically represented as being investor watchdogs who put the interests of investors over those of fund managers. As we have just shown, however, the structure of the compensation relationship does not necessarily promote such lofty investor-focused goals. Many investors know of the flaws in such relationships, yet they still consider the administrator to play a crucial role in the overall hedge fund governance process, warts and all.

Now let us consider director compensation. If directors were paid on a sliding scale based on a hedge fund's assets under management, similar to administrators, investors would similarly shrug their shoulders in apathy? Not to put words in anyone's mouth, but based on the bile spewed from certain investors' mouths regarding the conflicts of interests directors themselves pose, it is likely that further tying the interest of hedge funds and directors together would do much to quell concerns. On the other hand, wouldn't such a compensation arrangement actually better align directors with the interests of investors and hedge funds by giving them more skin in the game?

After all, a director would want the hedge fund to succeed because this would allow the fund to raise more capital and, therefore, the director would earn higher fees. Additionally, directors ideally would work to promote better governance because they would want to keep investors happy so that they would keep their capital with the hedge funds, which would similarly increase director fees based on assets under management. Too good to be true? Perhaps this takes a bit of a rose-colored view of the world, but as compared with the administrator compensation arrangements, is it all that crazy?

Why does this double standard therefore exist between groups such as administrators and boards of directors? Is it because administrators may be more established than boards of directors? In the context of analyzing independence in compensation arrangements, the seeming discrimination between the two groups becomes even more apparent. As noted above, directors of hedge funds often charge the fund an initial flat fee. Their compensation is not, therefore, overly aligned with the performance of the fund itself. Yet still many cast aspersions on the independence of these directors.

The goal of our discussion here is not to necessarily defend director compensation arrangements, but rather to show that double standards are employed when directors are compared with other service providers in the hedge fund complex. Furthermore, simply ignoring or dismissing hedge fund directors by attacking compensation arrangements, because you don't agree with the concept of them or question the independence of the function, ultimately results in less-informed hedge fund investing. If you are considering investing with a hedge fund manager who you like and you believe will be very profitable, yet you despise the concept of directors, it doesn't mean you should ignore them or how much they are paid. Like it or not, you're footing part of the bill through your investment, and they may influence the way your hedge fund operates.

WHAT DO DIRECTORS ACTUALLY DO?

We've been talking a great deal about fund directors by now, so it might seem like a bit of silly question at this point, but what is it that directors actually do?

For reference Chapter 10 contains interviews with, among other people, hedge fund directors. As part of these conversations a more expansive discussion of the key duties of directors is provided. For reference here we will summarize some of the more common director duties as well.

One of the primary function duties carried out by directors is to conduct board meetings for the funds that they sit on. As described above this is typically the offshore fund's board. The frequency of these meetings can vary based on a number of factors including the offshore jurisdiction where the fund is domiciled. Most jurisdictions have general requirements that such meetings take place annually. In some cases, some hedge funds have required more frequent board meetings. In other cases, the directorship firms themselves have pushed for enhanced meeting frequency such as quarterly. To clarify just because we are using the term meeting here, it doesn't mean that all the board members physically get in the same room together. On the contrary, these meetings can take place via other methods, such as telephonically, as well.

The next question you may be asking is what actually happens at these meetings. There is no single answer. At a minimum, typically at annual meetings directors will review and approve the financial statements. What they actually do to "review" such statements prior to the meeting, as well as any discussions related to the financials during the meeting, is an entirely different question altogether. To promote a more lively discussion surrounding the financials many directors commonly will opine that they welcome any additional commentary from the fund auditors and administrator during this review.

To put on my operational due diligence skeptic hat momentarily, it's a bit difficult to imagine a situation where an auditor would raise their hand and tell a director that the audit went poorly and the proposed hedge fund's audited financial statements have problems. If this was the case, then wouldn't the auditor note this in their disclosures in the financial statements? Issues of course could arise such as when a hedge fund manager and the auditor or administrator, for example, disagree over the valuation of a position, and the director could be asked to opine one way or another to lend support to an argument. This could of course flow down through to the financial statements of a fund, but these would be specific circumstances that would need to be considered in each case.

It should also be noted that directors typically have discretion over many items outlined in fund offering documents. Often this discretion is very similar, if not identical, to the rights of the GP of a fund in an onshore fund. For reference, examples of the items the board of directors of the offshore fund have say over include such things as:

- Determining the terms of any new share classes
- Converting an investor's holdings from one share class of the fund to another
- In regards to subscriptions:
  - (i) Discretion over accepting minimum subscription amounts for initial and additional subscriptions below state minimums (this may be subject to absolute minimum limits in certain jurisdictions)
  - (ii) Discretion over accepting subscriptions in kind from investors
  - (iii) Discretion with regards to the timing of the acceptance of new subscriptions outside of predefined general timelines
  - (iv) Discretion over determining or enforcing interest charges for off-cycle or late redemptions
- With regards to redemption of capital including:
  - (i) Permitting off-cycle redemptions
  - (ii) Permitting a redemption notice to be revoked when normally this wouldn't be allowed
  - (iii) Enforcing redemption gates
  - (iv) Raising or lowering the amount of predetermined gate percentages
  - (v) Allowing redemptions in kind
  - (vi) Suspending redemptions or forcing compulsory redemptions of certain investors
- Discretion over investors' ability to sell, assign, or transfer shares
- A host of other issues including granting the fund manager (i.e., investment manager) the authority to establish reserves and holdbacks, for example, to meet certain redemption requests or for extraordinary expenses

Additionally, directors may also be called upon on a more frequent basis, outside of regularly scheduled meetings, to provide perspective or comment on other issues that may arise. In addition to issues related to valuation as outlined in the example above, other examples of these issues could include litigation potentially affecting the fund, monitoring fund performance, holdings and capital flows, providing perspective on future fund plans, and discussing how a fund may adapt to new regulatory changes.

As noted above, some directorship firms have also sought to follow the lead of many other service providers and expand their relationships with hedge funds through additional service offerings. One example of a recent offering in this area has been an increased focus on seeking to gain business by working with hedge funds in complying with the Foreign Account Tax Compliance Act, commonly known as FATCA. Of course, these directors are competing with the hedge funds of other service providers such as law firms and administrators that have traditionally provided assistance with these types of compliance-related matters. Under this new expanded directorship services model, it is interesting to consider how a directorship firm on the one hand may, as noted above, seek an administrator's perspective on certain issues while on the other hand compete with that same administrator for the hedge fund's business in other areas. Investors should be conscious in monitoring these potential conflicts across all service providers when evaluating governance.

DIRECTOR LIABILITY—A FEW WORDS ABOUT INDEMNIFICATION

Another common hot button issue for many investors and hedge funds when discussing directors relates to the liability of directors, or lack thereof.

To highlight this let's consider the following scenario. I decide to move to the Cayman Islands. After getting settled I set up the Jason Directorship Agency. I then call upon every hedge fund I can think of and one of them hires me to sit on the board of their offshore fund. Unfortunately, let's say as a director, I don't do a great job. Of course, I read whatever they send me and sign where told to. I even occasionally go beyond the call of duty and ask for some additional information sometimes but that's it. One day out of the blue it turns out that the hedge fund manager starts investing in the private debt of a hot new clean tech company that makes widgets. The problem was that the manager was supposed to be running a long/short equity fund and private debt wasn't necessarily within their mandate. Let's also say that it didn't take very long for the widget company to go bust and within a few weeks of making the investment, which was a large portion of the fund, the widget company files for bankruptcy. The investment is now worth a lot less than it originally was and is highly illiquid. Understandably upset the fund's investors sue everyone. This includes unfortunately me as the fund director.

Well, shouldn't I be somewhat liable as the fund director? After all, I didn't really do anything to stop the manager from making this investment. Forget about stopping him, let's say I didn't even know it happened until I received notice of the lawsuit. Sounds like I wasn't doing my job. I should hang my head in shame out of embarrassment and dereliction of duty. I should own up to my share of the fault and help make it right for investors. This sounds like the honorable thing to do. Even if I'm not that honorable, wouldn't I have a legal obligation to the fund's investors to do so? In the realities of most people's worlds yes, but in the hedge fund world, of course not!

Let me explain. To understand why I wouldn't necessarily owe anyone anything you need to understand the concept of indemnification. Indemnification is a legal concept that effectively allows one party to shift risk to another party. It is a common mechanism contained in hedge fund offering memorandum. Before discussing this concept further, it may be useful to review an example of the use of an indemnification clause as outlined below:

> *Every director and officer of the Fund, and the Master Fund, their heirs, execu-tors, administrators, and personal representatives (each, an "Indemnified Par-ty") of the Fund, and the Master Fund shall be indemnified by the Fund, and the Master Fund from and against all actions, proceedings, costs, charges, losses, damages and expenses which they or any of them may incur or sustain by reason of any act done or omitted in or about the execution of their duty except (if any) as they would incur or sustain by or through their own willful negligence, gross negligence, fraud, dishonesty or bad faith and no such Fund and Master Fund Indemnitee will be answerable for the acts, receipts, neglects of any other Fund and Master Fund Indemnitee or for joining in any receipt for the sake of confor-mity or for the solvency or honesty of any banker or other persons with whom any monies belonging to the Fund, or the Master Fund may be lodged or deposited for safe custody or for any insufficiency of any security upon which any monies of the Fund, or the Master Fund may be invested or for any other loss or damage that may happen in or about the execution of his office unless the same shall happen through the willful negligence, gross negligence, fraud, dishonesty or bad faith of such Fund and Master Fund Indemnitee.*

Is this perfectly clear now? Not likely. Even for those readers of this book who have legal backgrounds, indemnity clauses such as this can be a bit confusing. Of course, we have only included a sample of such a clause here and a reading of it within the context of a larger private placement memorandum may make inter-preting it easier.

Although this book is not meant to be a legal textbook, understanding the spirit of such clauses, as opposed to every word, is critical to understanding director liability. Effectively what clauses such as this outline is that directors are only liable when bad things happen, such as they did in our example above, in certain specific situations. Using our sample clause those situations would be in instances of the directors' own "willful negligence, gross negligence, fraud, dishonesty or bad faith." Other than those specific situations the directors are indemnified (i.e., not responsible). The risk is shifted by this indemnification clause to the so-called indemnitee. In our example, this is the "Fund and Master Fund Indemnitee." So effectively the risk is transferred from the directors to the fund and by association to investors in those funds. Ok now that this back-ground is out of the way let's return to our example.

In this hypothetical, as the director of the example hedge fund that went bust, would you think most investors would think I acted with "willful negli-gence, gross negligence, fraud, dishonesty or bad faith." Let's say the fund's investors say I did in their lawsuit against everyone and I say I didn't. Do I have a leg to stand on as a director?

Well, my lawyer would likely argue that I wasn't willfully negligent; after all I tried to monitor the situation. If I wasn't willfully negligent, how then could I be grossly negligent? Besides, my lawyer would be able to muddy the water a bit by picking out old cases, which showed that in cases of even worse alleged director behavior willful negligence and gross negligence were still not found. Furthermore, the cases would also likely show that courts have different interpretations over the exact definitions of such terms in the past. Can anyone say with certainty where exactly the line is drawn between negligence and willful negligence? My lawyer would then continue that I didn't act with any sort of fraud, dishonesty, or bad faith in mind. If there was any fraud involved, it was the fault of the manager. He pulled the wool over everyone's eyes. Yes I, the poor director, am a victim too.

Oh and by the way I have a good lawyer. He's so good in fact that if you are not convinced by the first argument, he'll give you another one. Let's say that the court doesn't buy the argument that it wasn't really only the hedge fund manager's fault, and as a director I should have known about his diversion into widget trading and said or done something that would have possibly protected investors' interests. No problem, then we'll find a different scapegoat. We'll plead in the alternative that while it could have been my responsibility, I'm still not responsible. How does that work, you may ask? Well, to understand how this argument can hold water you need to understand a bit more about directors' duties.

DIRECTOR DELEGATION

As we highlighted earlier in this chapter, hedge fund directors are sometimes referred to as nonexecutive directors. This nonexecutive terminology is representative of the fact that as part of the arrangement it is understood that directors will outsource a portion of their responsibilities and by association the implied need for ongoing executive oversight, say, on a daily, weekly, or even monthly basis.

To clarify how this works in practice, let us analyze a sample director delegation clause as outlined below:

> *The Board of Directors and the board of directors of the Master Fund have delegated day-to-day responsibility for the management of the Fund's, and the Master Fund's assets to the Investment Manager, and have delegated day-to-day responsibility for the administration of the Fund, and the Master Fund to the Administrator, in each case subject to the supervision of the Board of Directors and the board of directors of the Master Fund.*

This clause outlines fairly clearly that the directors are not responsible for day-to-day management and administration of the fund. I should clarify that this doesn't mean that they are necessarily off the hook should something go awry in any one of these areas that they outsource their more frequent oversight duties to. On the contrary, the directors would also likely have a finger pointed at them, as I hypothetically did in the directorship example. Rather, directors as fiduciaries are responsible for taking measures to ensure that they have appropriately reviewed and monitor these other parties to which they delegate duties. That is to say that they cannot necessarily blindly rely on them, but have taken measures to gain a level of comfort that not only the firm is capable of performing the services required but they are also actually meeting this standard. A good analogy perhaps is to both the initial and ongoing due diligence that investors would perform on hedge funds, or indeed on directors themselves.

Now of course we are speaking in generalities here. The different requirements of a standard as to what level of rigor is appropriate for a director to have sufficiently vetted fund managers and service provider competencies may not be universal in nature. Indeed depending on the laws of different jurisdictions this test as to what constitutes an appropriately level of review may vary. The regulations in many popular hedge fund jurisdictions predictably don't get into this level of detail.

Instead, most lawyers and directors would likely tell you that the heart of any guidance from the law is really that which would be applied to the standard of a fiduciary. Once again, this is not a legal textbook, but common legal standards applied in such cases relate to the so-called prudent man standard. To perhaps overly simplify the concept, that is to say what would an average prudent person have under the same circumstances? Furthermore, it could be argued that as part of their responsibility the director could reasonably rely on representations made by others, such as the hedge fund manager, in vetting the other service providers relied on, such as the fund administrator. The actual nuts and bolts of whether such specific tests or director's reliance on others holds water would likely ultimately be a matter for the courts should issues turn to litigation for resolution. However, the point is that while it is important to remember that directors can rightly delegate some of these responsibilities, the actual test as to the level of vetting required may be unique to the facts and circumstances of each fund engagement.

It should also be noted that due to liability concerns many directors may not even want to receive information more frequently. It's effectively the same concept as an old adage in investor due diligence. For example, let's say an investor who manages capital on behalf of others such as a fund of funds receives a piece of information from a hedge fund during the due diligence process, but never reads it and throws into their files. Fast forward to the same hedge fund blowing up and litigation ensuing. If there is documentation in the file regarding certain red flags that the fund of hedge funds should have investigated further but simply never read, from a liability perspective the fund of funds may have been better off never having the document in their files to begin with. Of course, this is not at all best practice from a due diligence perspective, where they should have collected it, read it, and followed up on the document. Rather here, we are simply discussing some of the potential liability implications of collecting the additional information versus not collecting it. Similar to the fund of funds in our example, some directors feel they are more insulated from risk by not having the information to begin with. Nor are they necessarily required to have such information.

As we noted above, they have the ability in many instances to rightly delegate a great deal of this day-to-day oversight to others. Furthermore, they are not keeping it a secret, as it's typically disclosed in the fund offering documents. Now, of course, there are arguments whether such practices should be permitted altogether. This is similar to many of the principle and policy arguments we have outlined above. If enough hedge fund investors object to such practices, then the practices of hedge funds and directors in this regards will have to change. As it relates to liability this would likely include changes in the laws as well through pressure on regulators in offshore jurisdictions. However, such regulators are often cautious to impose additional liability on these thriving local directorship businesses that benefit the local economies of these jurisdictions.

Returning to our example, now that we have explained the common practice of director delegation of duties we can see how it would be possible to make the argument that it wasn't really my responsibility as a director to catch the problem here; perhaps that duty was properly, or at least legally implied to be, delegated to, say, the administrator of the fund. When you combine that with the indemnification standards we previously discussed, you see how the case against my hypothetical bad directorship isn't exactly an open and closed one.

It's also worth considering that the investors whose interests I was, depending on who you talk to, supposed to represent have been stuck this whole time. Not only can they not redeem what little capital they have left in the fund due to the illiquidity of the positions and ensuing litigation, but they also now have to front the bill for large legal bills that can quickly add up.

As a director by the way, I may have one or two other cards up my sleeve. In regards to litigation costs, depending on how the fund and my directorship are structured I might be able to have the fund advance me money to cover litigation costs. I might ultimately have to pay the fund, and therefore by association the investors back, if I lose in court but that's certainly a big up-front advantage to have. Furthermore, even if I lose, I might have insurance, such as directors' and liability insurance, which would cover potential litigation costs and the money I am found to end up owing to people. As perhaps the final nail in the coffin, in some cases the fund itself may be the one who paid for this insurance policy to begin with. Oh and if I lose, I can always appeal anyways.

This is merely an example scenario and it may seem, from the perspective of investors at least, that directors have all the cards in such situations. While directors do have many rights, as we have outlined above, so do investors. Additionally, it is the responsibility of investors through detailed due diligence to understand the playing field in which they are operating. The peculiarities of each hedge fund situation are different. By taking the time to perform appropriate due diligence up front, they will end up not only being more informed about the role of their directors but having more confidence in them as well.

REFERENCES

Ahmed, A., 2012. In Caymans, it's simple to fill a hedge fund board. *The New York Times DealBook*, July 1.

Appleby, 2014. Guide to Exempted Limited Partnerships. Available at: http://www.applebyglobal. com/publication-pdf-versions/guides/guide-to-exempted-limited-partnerships.pdf.

Britell, A., 2013a. Former Cayman Premier McKeeva Bush formally charged with corruption. *Caribbean Journal*, March 21; Britell, A., 2013b. Treasure islands in trouble. *The Economist*, May 25.

Corgentum Consulting, LLC, 2014. Hedge Fund Investors Continue to Question Offshore Director Independence and Credibility, According to Corgentum Consulting's Survey, March 6.

Lindsay, M., 2014. USS IM cajoles hedge funds to behave better. *Hedge Funds Review*, June 13.

Chapter 3

Regulatory Governance of Hedge Funds

Chapter Outline Head

INTRODUCTION TO REGULATORY GOVERNANCE

Despite their sometimes Wild West reputation, hedge funds do operate in highly regulated environments. These regulations directly influence multiple aspects of the hedge fund world, including fund governance structures and approaches.

This chapter will focus on the way in which regulations influence hedge fund governance. We will start by providing you with an overview of the key regulations that have influenced hedge fund governance structures. We will then address the ways in which some of these regulations have also influenced the creation and structuring of fund boards. These discussions will center on several popular hedge fund jurisdictions. Finally, we will proceed with a discussion of some of the ways in which governance, and the directorship industry in general, has attempted self-regulation.

A FEW WORDS ON WHAT THIS CHAPTER DOESN'T COVER

Now that we have outlined what we will cover in this chapter we should also clarify what we're leaving out. The topic of hedge fund regulation is a broad one. The last few years in particular have witnessed an explosion in the number of new laws and regulations that affect hedge funds. In particular as they relate to the globally oriented world of hedge funds, these changes should not be viewed in isolation as being important in only the particular countries in which you may reside or invest. Rather, many of these new laws and regulations influence multiple aspects of the hedge fund industry across multiple jurisdictions.

If you are a United States–based hedge fund investor, the changes in US securities laws as a result of Dodd–Frank legislation, for example, are not the only ones you need to worry about. Changes in laws in places such as the Cayman Islands and Europe may also have a direct impact on a number of activities including operations, investing, and fund-raising activities for United States–based hedge funds in which you invest.

Although this chapter will provide an introduction to key hedge fund regulations influencing governance globally, in the interest of focusing our conversation, this chapter will not address every jurisdiction in which hedge funds do business. These include places such as Australia, Luxembourg, Gibraltar, and Liechtenstein. This is not to minimize the importance of regulations in these jurisdictions, but rather to focus instead on the primary ones in which hedge funds operate. On a related note, although an interesting topic certainly relating to regulation, we are omitting the investment activities that hedge funds undertake in certain offshore jurisdiction due to lax regulatory environments to instead focus our discussion on fund-level governance implications on regulations. An example of what we are talking about would be the increasing establishment of Bermuda-based reinsurance companies (Solomon, 2012).

Additionally, our purpose here is not to provide an encyclopedic guide to every new law that has affected hedge funds. Indeed, there are entire books dedicated to many of the particular laws we will be referencing in this chapter. Furthermore, many law firms of late have built considerable dedicated practices toward helping hedge funds navigate the implementation of developing hedge fund regulations. Instead, it would be perhaps useful to read this chapter with the understanding that the focus is on how governance impacts laws on hedge funds. Should you find it helpful to gather more information on a particular law, and of course such further research is always useful to furthering your understanding of the topic, you can always leverage on these other texts and attorneys to navigate the specifics of each of the regulations we will address.

WHY SO MANY JURISDICTIONS?

Depending on your perspective, it may sometimes seem that the bulk of hedge fund investing is only centered around certain popular clusters such as midtown Manhattan, The City in London, or within walking distance of Hong Kong's Central Station.

As such, you may be wondering why we need to worry about so many different jurisdictions. If, for example, your US hedge fund makes investments in only US companies, then why do the hedge funds, and their investors, bother with these other far-flung locations? Similarly, if you are a hedge fund investor reading this book in London or Hong Kong and you only typically deal with the hedge funds in a handful of different countries, then is that all you need to worry about? Is there any benefit to understanding how the regulations in other jurisdictions, such as the United States, may impact governance structures closer to home? In short, yes.

Even if your hedge fund manager never leaves their office, they typically are affected one way or another by global hedge fund regulations. Indeed, even hedge funds that are unregulated, which is becoming increasingly more difficult these days, are impacted by regulation. This is because they often take measures to protect this unregulated status.

WHY THE INCREASED FOCUS ON THE IMPORTANCE OF OFFSHORE REGULATIONS?

In Chapter 2, we provided some general perspective on the growth in popularity among hedge funds and investors in utilizing offshore centers. As we outlined in the previous chapters, the primary reason for such continued growth is simple—taxes. People don't like to pay taxes. To qualify that statement, most people don't like to legally pay more taxes than they have to and hedge funds and their investors are no exception.

Until relatively recently in the United States, and indeed in most other jurisdictions, hedge funds did not have to be registered with financial regulators such as the US Securities and Exchange Commission (SEC). Related to this unregistered status were investor cap considerations that were prevalent in the 1990s. These caps limited most domestic and offshore hedge fund structures to 100 investors under Section 3(c)(1) of a law known as the Investment Company Act of 1940. For reference, this act is sometimes referred to as the 40 Act. Dealing with and seeking to get around this limit while still maintaining unregistered status and the tax benefits of offshore vehicles was a big deal (Adler). In 1996 these hard numerical limits were abolished with the passage of a law known as the National Securities Markets Improvement Act of 1996, but tax considerations were still prevalent in structuring funds throughout the hedge fund industry.

We have addressed in other chapters how this focus on taxes has facilitated the interest in different types of structures, such as master–feeder complexes, but for the purposes of our discussion on regulations it is worth highlighting another consideration related to taxes—their impact on hedge fund investment activities.

It's no secret that in the United States at least, and likely globally, the wealthier you are, the more money you can spend on hiring tax lawyers and accountants who specialize in legally minimizing tax obligations. Proving this point perhaps, Warren Buffett famously claimed on several occasions that he paid a lower tax rate than his secretary (Isidore, 2013). Not to single out offshore jurisdictions, there have been numerous articles written about how non-US citizens evade taxes in their home countries through US-based investments in assets such as New York City real estate (Hudson et al., 2014). Or if you would like to see a historical perspective on some of the more exotic tax planning techniques available, you could always read books such as *The Rich Die Richer and You Can Too*, which had received praise from the likes of famous hedge fund billionaire George Soros (Zabel, 1996). The tax rate people should pay is a contentious political and societal issue that we will not address here; however, taxes are a key consideration in hedge fund investing.

To clarify what were are talking about here is not the experience most of us have with taxes, such as in the United States making quarterly estimated payments if you run a business, or filing your annual tax returns by April 15. Making sure all the t's are crossed and i's dotted are certainly important considerations for hedge funds when filing out their tax returns; however, here what we are talking about relates to structuring. Consider, for example, a US hedge fund that wants to buy debt from a Portuguese company. Unlike a regular person a hedge fund doesn't just go negotiate a price and buy the debt. Instead, at least if they are smart, they consult the appropriate advisers and in-house tax personnel we referenced above to determine the best way to facilitate the purchase from a tax perspective. To be clear by best way, we mean the method that will result in the lowest tax obligation. Maybe the hedge fund didn't even themselves directly buy it at all, but have an intermediary entity buy it that they either create themselves or use as a facilitator to purchase it for them. This of course costs the hedge fund a bit of money, but the sometimes large sums of money that have resulted in savings as a result greatly offset the cost. By the way, we're not talking about anything being done illegally here. It's all perfectly legal, and I'm not commenting on the ethics of such practices; instead the point is to highlight how important tax considerations can be in hedge fund investing.

The important motivation of tax reduction and legal avoidance, not evasion, has also resulted in increasing boom in the use of offshore hedge fund jurisdictions for structuring purposes. This has led to the subsequent popularity of hedge funds from many different jurisdictions, the United States, Europe, and Asia, establishing hedge fund vehicles in popular offshore jurisdictions. The increasing popularity of these jurisdictions has directly correlated with the growth of the offshore directorship industry. As more hedge funds have utilized offshore jurisdictions the need for more directors has increased as well.

Therefore, to really understand the global implications of hedge fund governance we need to not only be conscious that tax minimization is an overriding motivating factor for the whole offshore director construct but understand the laws in these multiple jurisdictions as well. Not with the goal of being tax or legal experts. Instead, from the perspective of most investors, and even hedge funds operating in these jurisdictions, we need to have a general lay of the land. When specific questions come up, and believe me they do, you can of course leverage off the jurisdictional and functional expertise of different experts.

LEADING HEDGE FUND REGULATORS

Typically when most people think of the hedge fund regulatory environment, they logically think of the financial regulators themselves. With the understanding that the hedge fund regulations influencing governance are global in nature, it makes sense to provide some perspective on who actually produces these regulations. To provide some background in this area, it is perhaps helpful to summarize some of the key regulatory bodies that promulgate hedge fund regulations. We have included a summary of these key institutions in Exhibit 3.1.

PERSPECTIVES ON GLOBAL HEDGE FUND REGULATORY DEVELOPMENT

With an understanding of global regulators we can next proceed to a discussion of various key regulations themselves and how they impact fund governance. Before beginning this discussion it is perhaps helpful to understand some of the recent historical developments in hedge fund regulations. In Chapter 1, we focused our discussion around the development of corporate governance standards in the United States. As we have outlined above, however, the regulations influencing hedge fund governance are increasingly global in nature. As such, to provide more of a continental perspective in this manner we will focus here on certain key historical regulatory developments as they relate to hedge fund governance principles from a British perspective.

It is also worth noting another reason for our UK focus here. As we have outlined above, over the last decade in particular there has been an increased focus in the use of offshore jurisdictions by hedge funds. Many of these jurisdictions, particularly in the Caribbean, are heavily influenced not only by the courts of the United Kingdom but by the legislators and financial regulators in those jurisdictions as well. Therefore, understanding the growth of such regulations from a British perspective may add value as well.

Outside of the United States, the interest and acceptance in governance was slower to take hold, but by the 1990s there was more of a global push toward corporate governance reforms. In the United Kingdom one major corporate governance reform at the time was the development of Cadbury Code in 1992. This code was developed to address a number of recommended best practices in areas of corporate governance relating to areas including the independence of the corporate board of directors, evaluating executive compensation, properly structuring service provider contracts, and sufficient oversight of financial

EXHIBIT 3.1 Summary of Key Hedge Fund Regulatory Agencies

Country	Leading hedge fund regulatory agencies	Website
The Americas and Caribbean—the United States	United States Securities and Exchange Commission ("US SEC")	www.sec.gov
	US Commodity Futures Trading Commission ("CFTC")	www.cftc.gov
	National Futures Association ("NFA")	www.nfa.futures.org
	Financial Industry Regulatory Authority, Inc. ("FINRA"); nongovernmental agency	www.fingra.org
Cayman Islands	Cayman Islands Monetary Authority ("CIMA")	http://www.cimoney.com.ky
Europe		
Ireland	Central Bank of Ireland	http://www.centralbank.ie
Jersey	Jersey Financial Services Commission	http://www.jerseyfsc.org
Malta	Malta Financial Services Authority	http://www.mfsa.com.mt
Switzerland	Swiss Financial Market Supervisory Authority ("FINMA")	http://www.finma.ch
The United Kingdom	Financial Conduct Authority ("FCA"); formerly known as the Financial Services Authority	http://www.fca.org.uk
Asia		
Hong Kong	Securities and Futures Commission ("SFC")	http://www.sfc.hk
Singapore	Monetary Authority of Singapore ("MAS")	http://www.mas.gov.sg
Japan	Financial Services Agency	http://www.fsa.go.jp

reporting and internal controls. Additionally, the code espoused three central principles of openness, accountability, and integrity, which ran through its recommendations toward promoting better governance practices.

After the Cadbury Code was published a number of subsequent UK reports continued to focus on corporate governance reforms in the United Kingdom.

Examples of these reports throughout the 1990s and into the early 2000s included the:

- Greenbuy Report (1995)—focused on corporate directors' compensation.
- Hampel Report (1998)—focused on best practices in corporate governance within the corporation itself, as opposed to governance from outside regulators.
- Turnbull Report (1999)—made the controversial recommendation that public companies, on an annual basis, report to shareholders their risk assessment and decision-making process.
- Myners Report (2000)—made a number of recommendations to reforming the mismanagement of pension funds including increased training, enhanced intervention by institutional investors when investments underperform, and an increased use of independent custodians (Bob, 2003).
- Higgins Review (2003)—reviewed the role of nonexecutive directors with a focus on increased oversight of director independence and compensation. This ultimately led to the so-called Combined Code of the United Kingdom. Ultimately a separate Stewardship Code was issued in 2010 by the Financial Reporting Council that focused on guidelines of the relationship between institutional investors and companies they invest in (Mallin, 2009).

Turning away from England, other countries, in which many of the hedge funds do business today, also made similar efforts to increase the attention paid to corporate governance. These include:

- South Africa—the first King Report to establish a code of corporate governance in 1994 followed by an updated report in 2002.
- Cyprus—the country published its first code of corporate governance in 1992 followed by updates in 2006.
- Singapore—the country published its first code of corporate governance in 2001 followed by updates in 2005.
- Switzerland—the first policy documents relating to the corporate governance were published in 2002 with the updated formal Swiss Code of Best Practice for Corporate Governance codified in 2008.

Returning to the United States there were also a number of regulatory changes that pushed corporate governance reforms including Sarbanes–Oxley Act in 2002 and more recently the passage of Dodd–Frank Wall Street Reform and the Consumer Protection Act in 2010.

You'll notice that we conspicuously stopped our regulatory governance history in 2010. The reason for this is that 2011 was a big year for fund governance and we want to be sure to give it the attention it deserved. In 2011, the 2008 financial crisis was still fresh in many people's minds. A number of new reforms were passed and most people were having their confidence slowly restored in the financial system. This led to capital flowing back into hedge funds and, therefore, a continued growth in the use of offshore centers and fund directors.

Then the atomic bomb that was the Weavering case went was dropped as a wake up call to the directorship industry. The Weavering decision is covered in more detail in Chapter 8, but as you work through this chapter, it is worth noting that cases such as Weavering had an influence on governance regulations generally and the directorship industry in particular.

HOW DO REGULATIONS RELATE TO GOVERNANCE?

As you have been reading this background on hedge fund regulations in general you may have been questioning how this relates to governance. Good question! Let's answer it, but before we do we should address one important point about the relationship between the concept of compliance and governance.

The Relationship Between Compliance and Regulatory Governance

So far we have been talking the concept of governance as it relates to hedge fund regulations. In particular we've started to introduce an overview of the influence of regulations on oversight of hedge funds. As a preview, as this discussion progresses we'll address how regulations influence fund boards, fund structures, and overall governance structures. "Wait a minute," you may be saying suspiciously. "Are these compliance matters and not governance concerns?" This is a good question.

Let's say you have a hedge fund that is being sued. Most people would probably say that this is a litigation issue. Furthermore, most people would likely agree that if the fund has a dedicated General Counsel, then the oversight of resolving this matter would most likely be addressed by this individual. We didn't specify who was bringing the litigation. Let's say in the first part of our example, when the case was being handled by the General Counsel, it was a lawsuit brought by a nongovernmental entity such as a disgruntled investor. As you could likely predict from our description, now let's say that the lawsuit or proceeding is instead brought by a financial regulator such as the US SEC. Let's say the fund employs a dedicated Chief Compliance Officer in addition to the General Counsel. Does this change your opinion of who should be coordinating the fund's efforts in this regard? Some readers may take the position that the US SEC is a regulatory body and, therefore, such a proceeding lies more squarely in the compliance arena as opposed to the legal arena. Maybe both of them are involved? The point here is to show that the classification of issues in this area is sometimes not just a black and white issue.

The same can be said when comparing notions of the impact of regulations on compliance versus governance. The two areas overlap in many ways. This is not to say that they can be equated to one another, but that they are related. For example, a common area of investor inquiry when reviewing compliance during the due diligence process relates to whether or not hedge funds utilize third-party expert networks.

As background, these networks effectively connect hedge funds with so-called experts in different industries for research purposes. In certain cases, these experts were former executives and insiders at publicly traded companies who passed on illegal tips to funds. Although the expert networks and funds have ramped up their oversight and protections in these areas, certain investors frown on the use of such networks in part due to the enhanced potential for passage of insider information. As part of an industry-wide sweep of such practices a number of hedge fund managers found themselves in hot water. One of the more notable examples was the sentencing of Level Global LP cofounder Anthony Chiasson to six and a half years in prison (Hurtado, 2013).

With this perspective, is the hedge fund's use of such expert networks representative of poor governance? What about if, from a compliance perspective, they have a stringent oversight and a buttoned-up process? Does this mean that they could actually have better governance than a firm that bans expert networks but is weaker in other areas of analyst research oversight? The answers to such questions are largely dependent on the specific circumstances in place at each hedge fund under review. The point here is to highlight the related nature of the areas of compliance and governance. As you read through this material, it is important to keep in mind this relationship with the understanding that while the focus is on governance certainly due to the regulatory nature of compliance, there are also compliance underpinnings to this area.

Regulation and Fund Boards

One of the key players in discussions surrounding hedge fund governance has been the boards of offshore funds. The regulation, or lack thereof, in different offshore jurisdictions has had direct impact on several aspects of fund boards. These have included all the requirements for boards, the way these boards are structured, and the duties and obligations of board members. In Chapter 2 we provided an overview of varying perspectives on the practical effects of such regulations as they relate to the boards. Here we are taking a step backwards as it were, to provide some perspective on what these regulations actually are that influence this director activity.

Regulation's Influence on Other Aspects of Hedge Fund Governance

We have highlighted throughout this book that while fund boards are certainly critical elements of governance, they are not the whole story. In Chapter 4 we will outline how the role of service providers and those surrounding board members can influence governance. Additionally, the hedge fund itself has a number of influences on the way governance is implemented. These are discussed in Chapter 5. As can be expected, regulations not only address the role of the board themselves but can also influence the way the fund operates and is structured. These non–director-focused regulations are another important aspect to consider when evaluating the regulatory influence on fund governance.

KEY FUND REGULATIONS AND THEIR EFFECTS ON GOVERNANCE

By understanding how these regulations' influence on governance relates directly to the governance practices not only of the directors but also of the hedge funds themselves, we can now proceed to a discussion of the actual regulations. To accomplish this we will focus on summarizing key regulations in several different popular hedge fund jurisdictions. As we outlined earlier in this chapter, the goal of this analysis is not to provide a comprehensive overview of the regulatory guidance that a hedge fund manager seeking to establish a fund in a particular jurisdiction may need. Instead, we will highlight the direct effects certain keystone regulations have on governance for both directors and hedge funds as appropriate.

Cayman Islands

As we have noted above, there has been a growing interest in the use of offshore jurisdictions among hedge funds. Perhaps the focus of this offshore interest has been felt most prevalently in the Cayman Islands.

To take a step back for a moment we should clarify that under Cayman regulations the term hedge fund isn't utilized. Instead hedge funds fall under the broad definitions of mutual funds. The primary law that governs mutual funds, and therefore hedge funds as well, is the Mutual Funds Law. This law has been revised several times with the most recent revision at the time of this publication being the 2013 revision. For reference this most recent version of the law defines a mutual fund as follows:

> *Mutual fund means a company, unit trust or partnership that issues equity interests, the purpose or effect of which is the pooling of investor funds with the aim of spreading investment risks and enabling investors in the mutual fund to receive profits or gains from the acquisition, holding, management or disposal of investments but does not include a person licensed under the Banks and Trust Companies Law (2013 Revision) or the Insurance Law, 2010, or a person registered under the Building Societies Law (2010 Revision) or the Friendly Societies Law (1998 Revision).*

For reference a so-called Friendly Society, as mentioned in the law, is a membership association that can provide a wide range of services to members including health insurance and pensions. It is supported by members' dues and used to be prevalent throughout Europe and the United States in lieu of enhanced government benefits at the time.

Moving on, the Cayman Islands have also become one of the most important places, if not the center, of the debate surrounding hedge fund governance

EXHIBIT 3.2 Cayman Islands Mutual Funds Statistics: 2006–2013

	Registered	Master	Administered	Licensed	Total
2006	7,481	—	548	105	8,134
2007	8,751	—	543	119	9,413
2008	9,231	—	510	129	9,870
2009	8,944	—	448	131	9,523
2010	8,870	—	435	133	9,438
2011	8,714	—	424	120	9,258
2012	8,421	1,891	408	121	10,841
2013	8,235	2,635	398	111	11,379

Source: Cayman Finance, "Investment Funds in the Cayman Islands."

as it relates to fund directors. To put it in perspective the number of registered funds from the number of administered and registered funds has significantly increased from over 8000 in 2006 to over 11,000 at the end of 2013 as summarized in Exhibit 3.2.

As we noted above, the primary financial regulator in the Cayman Islands is the Cayman Islands Monetary Authority ("CIMA"). Recognizing that the role of directors continues to be a critical point of governance interest, in 2013 CIMA commissioned a survey of corporate governance trends with a focus on fund directors. This was a landmark survey and the first of its kind by CIMA.

In total, the survey had 179 respondents from all over the world and contained responses from the following groups of individuals:

Hedge fund managers: 57
Service providers (i.e., administrators, lawyers, accountants): 62
Investors: 28
Directors: 32

The reason I have included the figures above is that they are quite telling. The smallest group represented was investors. This may be because investors aren't simply interested in participating in surveys; however, this should be kept in mind when reviewing our discussion of the results in more detail below. To be fair, the survey does detail the breakout of how each of these different groups responded to different questions. The problem, however, is that certain groups have tried to point to the data as being representative of the entire hedge fund industry when investors were clearly underweighted as compared with the other groups. These generalizations, and it happens with all surveys so it's certainly not CIMA's fault, have been attempted to be utilized in particular to bolster arguments one way or the other regarding director capacity. We will not address capacity issues in this chapter. Instead a discussion of director capacity, including perspective on the CIMA survey results, can be found in Chapter 4.

As it relates to the concepts of governance and regulation some of the more interesting findings included:

- Only 7% of investors felt that "ensuring business practices adhere to legal and regulatory requirements" was on the three most important elements when assessing the corporate governance practice of the board and directors of Cayman funds. This was compared with 19% of directors, 28% of hedge fund managers, and 31% of service providers.
- Investors and directors were in agreement on several points including:
    - (i) No investors or directors felt that sufficient documentation of board discussion was one of the three most important elements.
    - (ii) Similarly no investors or directors felt that fewer governance standards should be implemented, as compared with 2% of hedge fund managers and 3% of service providers who were in favor of fewer governance standards.
- At least 20% or more of those surveyed wanted more corporate governance laws.
- Similarly, 90% of investors, 73% of directors, and 67% of hedge funds wanted a CIMA rule on corporate governance. This was compared with 37% of service providers.

The survey results highlighted that further regulatory guidance on governance and the role of directors was needed. Supporting this effort was the 2014 implementation of the Statement of Guidance ("SOG") for Regulated Mutual Funds. The SOG outlines a series of corporate governance principles for what is known as the so-called operating body of the fund that includes the fund directors. The SOG contains what are in effect best practice guidelines for fund governance for the operating body of the fund. It should also be noted that the SOG is on a so-called comply or explain basis. Effectively, once the SOG was adopted by a board, it was recommended that they either comply fully or describe the reasons they did not apply specific provisions of the SOG. More detail on the SOG is outlined in the interviews contained in Chapter 10.

One of the more recent changes in regards to Cayman fund directors was the passage of The Directors Registration and Licensing Law, 2014. This law will generally require directors, sometimes referred to in Cayman legal speak as professional directors, who act as directors for 20 or more entities (so-called covered entities), to obtain a license. Not to make the conversation overly technical from a legal perspective, it should be clear that these covered entities are certain entities regulated under the above-referenced mutual funds law as well as another Cayman law called the Securities Investment Business Law (2011 revision). Of course, as with most laws, the specifics are subject to a number of caveats and potential exclusions in certain cases. It should also be noted that the licensing law contemplates enhanced regulatory requirements for directors who hold more than 20 directorships.

The requirement of director licensing is part of a larger effort to facilitate oversight by CIMA of the directorship industry. As of the time of the writing of this book, the exact specifics of the practical implementation and oversight of this licensing requirement are yet to be seen. It is unlikely that this will have much of an effect, if any, on established directorship firms except that their directors will now need to obtain licenses. The practical ways in which CIMA will implement any ongoing monitoring of directors once licensed are also yet to be seen.

Finally, perhaps one of the more contentious points is that the licensing requirements do not seem to address the role of so-called associate directors that we outlined in Chapter 2. For reference the associate directors are not the so-called formal director named in the fund's offering documents, and they are the only ones who will be required to be licensed with CIMA under the new law. Instead, associate directors typically act as support staff handling the more mundane tasks required of directors. As we discussed in Chapter 2, the extensive use of these associate directors in some cases has raised concerns among certain investors regarding the level of engagement of the named directors. With a potential loophole for the continued work of these now unlicensed associate directors, concerns could be raised that the licensing requirements themselves still fall short of implementing best practice governance. Regardless, the mere fact of any licensing requirement is viewed by most to be a step in the right direction in continuing to promote governance in the Caymans. Furthermore, to draw a parallel to discussion in the next section regarding US SEC hedge fund registration, it may be the threat of ongoing oversight and examinations of directors by CIMA, as opposed to any actual reviews themselves, that could potentially have the biggest effect in chilling questionable governance practices going forward.

United States

If you attempted to print out all of the US regulations affecting hedge funds, you would likely break your printer. This would be especially true when you consider the recent explosion in compliance rules and regulations in the wake of the 2008 financial crisis. As noted above, we will not be going through the sometimes excruciating details of each regulation here. You're welcome. On the other hand, we will be focusing on the more critical regulations that relate to governance. In the United States one of the more interesting regulatory questions has been the ongoing debate regarding the regulatory requirement of hedge funds registration. It is this issue that we will focus on here.

Are Hedge Fund Registration Requirements Good for Governance?

If a hedge fund is registered with a regulator, does it imply or even promote better governance? This was an ongoing question in the United States. For many years hedge funds were required to be SEC registered. Then in 2006 a closed-end fund activist manager named Phillip Goldstein (Bulldog Investors) sued the SEC challenging it on policy and legal grounds (Scharfman, 2012). He won and the registration requirement was removed. To clarify it didn't mean that they couldn't be SEC registered but that many no longer had to be.

After the ruling many funds that were previously registered deregistered. Some didn't, however, because they thought it sent the wrong message to investors. This brings up an interesting question: "Does the mere fact that a hedge fund was US SEC registered imply to investors better governance oversight?" Many investors at the time would have likely told you yes. The fact that their hedge fund was SEC registered gave them a sense of comfort. It made them believe that someone was keeping an eye on them. This doesn't mean that investors would have been correct in blindly relying on the SEC and not performing their own due diligence, but many managers knew that many investors, particularly institutional ones, preferred to know that a hedge fund was US SEC registered. This trust may have been misplaced as demonstrated by colossal regulatory oversight failures in cases such as the Madoff scandal, which showed that the SEC wasn't exactly awake at the wheel with steadfast oversight at the time.

To take a step back in time though, the question should be asked as to whether or not hedge fund investors after the Goldstein decision were now privy to better governance under this new free-from-registration regime? Let's discuss the situation a bit further.

Consider the situation of a hedge fund that was previously required to be US SEC registered but after the Goldstein ruling deregistered. If you went to visit a hedge fund as a prospective investor in 2007, after the Goldstein ruling, and inquired about their governance practices with regards to say the area of compliance, you would likely get one of two responses. The first response from the now unregistered hedge fund would be something to the effect of "Well we're not registered anymore because we don't want the ongoing cost or hassle of registration but operate as if we are still registered." The second response could be along the lines of "It's not required anymore and we don't feel it's necessary."

Let's analyze the governance implication of each response under the post-Goldstein deregistration scenario. Starting with the second reply, at least this manager was being honest. This response also is based on the reasoning that we alluded to in the beginning of the chapter along the lines of "'if it's not illegal, then it doesn't represent bad governance." Well, we could offer up all kinds of arguments in favor or against this line of thinking but ultimately when registration is not required, as it wasn't during this time period, it was up to investors to make a determination individually as to whether good governance was in place by voting with their allocations so to speak. Said another way, even if a hedge fund was not required to be US SEC registered, investors were not forced to invest with them if they felt that the lack of registration, for example, translated to poor governance in the area of compliance.

We can now consider the remaining first reply from the hedge fund manager. As a prospective investor the question could logically be asked, "'If a fund was planning to operate as if it were still registered, then why not stay registered?" In reality many hedge funds that made such claims were in fact not being 100%

accurate in these statements. Many may have had the spirit of good governance in place in areas such as compliance oversight, but they were not in technical compliance with US SEC regulations. Some managers may have simply thought that many such regulations were frankly asinine.

Perhaps a story will help provide some perspective on this. There is an old hedge fund industry joke about the way the US SEC used to conduct its exams. There is this SEC examiner who is conducting a review of a smaller hedge fund. The hedge fund manager doesn't have any fancy compliance consultants, but is fastidious about keeping documentation and paperwork in order. During the exam the manager is completely forthcoming with the examiner, and the examiner is pleased with what he has seen.

There are no real deficiencies to report. Of course, there is room for improvement in certain areas, but certainly the examiner believes that the hedge fund is complying with the letter of the law. The examiner however has a problem. He can't end the exam without having something to put in a deficiency letter for the manager. After all, he has to show his bosses something to justify the time the examiner has spent on site. There can't be nothing wrong, can there?

Aha, he's got it. He asks the manager where his complaint folder is. The manager proudly tells the examiner that he places emphasis on instituting the highest level of integrity with his clients and has never had a single complaint. The examiner tells the manager that he is proud of him but again asks, "Where is the complaint folder?" The manager is puzzled and reiterates that he has never had a complaint. The SEC examiner then says, "Yes, I understand but the rules still require you to have an empty folder labeled complaints!"

Ok so maybe the joke wasn't that funny, but it still makes an important point. Do requirements such as the fact that a hedge fund manager must maintain an empty folder labeled complaints when he actually has none help promote better fund governance? As noted above, if we say no, we can point to the fact that certain US SEC–registered funds, which turned out to be total frauds such as Madoff, putting minor deficiencies aside, were registered entities in compliance with SEC rules. A fat lot of good these rules did to protect investors in those funds.

Is Registration Even the Key Governance Issue?

So where does this leave us? Is required hedge fund registration a good or bad thing for governance? Well, it could be argued that registration is not really the critical issue at all when it comes to discussing governance. A focus on registration could be viewed as miscategorizing the issue entirely.

Whether or not you think hedge fund registration regulations are good or bad, instead some focus on the product of what comes with registration. Namely, the potential for ongoing examination by the regulators. In addition to any governance benefits that may accrue as a result of registration, many believe that it is really the ongoing threat of an exam by the US SEC that has the real governance impact. To put it plainly it keeps hedge funds on their toes.

Consider if you ran a hedge fund. Wouldn't you be more relaxed if you knew that there was little to no threat of a regulator showing up at your door virtually unannounced and poking around? Compare this with the alternative. The regulator could show up any time, request all kinds of detailed information, and ask all kinds of questions. This would just be the start. They could stay as long as they wanted to and make you research and explain all kinds of historical activity. Oh and when you thought it was all over with, they could come back or require all kinds of follow-up. If they didn't like what they found, they could shut you down or fine you.

You could see how this latter scenario would likely put increased pressure on you to keep your ducks in a row. It is exactly this paranoia that helps to promote governance at funds. To be clear, this same threat is still equally valid not just for nefarious fraudster managers but also for those following the law. The threat of an ongoing exam is still the same. Of course, the fraudster has to work harder to cover up their crimes, but still both types of managers need to be prepared for the potential of an exam or inquiry. This fear while arguably a burden on hedge funds is generally thought of as being good for promoting governance.

Is This All Moot?

Today with mandatory registration in place for the bulk of hedge funds such questions may seem moot now but as we noted above, several years ago, when the requirements of such registration were narrower, this was a legitimate consideration for many investors.

After the financial crisis of 2008, under Title IV of the Dodd–Frank Wall Street Reform and Consumer Protection Act, most hedge funds were required to register with the SEC. But does this render the considerations we outlined above relating to a potential governance gap when there is a lack of registration a moot point? Particularly in light of enhanced oversight in places outside of the United States such as Europe's Alternative Investment Fund Managers Directive (AIFMD) effort (discussed in more detail below).

I would humbly suggest that the answer to this question is a resounding no. The reason for this is that despite increased oversight in the United States and in Europe, hedge fund investing is still global. Despite the movement toward increased oversight in certain places, including offshore centers, hedge funds are generally not required to register. Even if there is a technical registration requirement, it's not necessarily a strict one that is subject to exam requirements. Additionally although registration requirements may be in place for the onshore jurisdictions, there is still the potential for a governance gap between the onshore and offshore operations. Furthermore, while an exam requirement may be present, it is not necessary frequent or stringent.

On a related note, as scary as we might have made the threat of an exam seem, in the United States, for example, it was not uncommon as recently as a few years ago for a hedge fund manager to have not been visited by the SEC for several years or unbelievably never at all. Acknowledging that this was a problem, the SEC started something called a Presence Exam Initiative in 2012 to at least show their face with a portion, approximately 25%, of the deluge of newly registered managers after the new registration requirements were in place. This was not even a full exam but instead focused on five key areas: marketing, portfolio management, conflicts of interest, safety of client assets, and valuation. Big surprise, it was reported that they found a number of governance-related problems (US SEC, 2014) including:

- Poor conflicts of interest management
- Lack of appropriate disclosures
- Reporting misleading performance
- Wide-ranging problems relating to the handling of fund expenses including using fund capital to inappropriately pay so-called operating partners and the inappropriate shifting of expenses to limited partners
- A host of valuation issues ranging from deficient valuation policies and procedures to a lack of asset and sector-specific valuation methodology implementation

These were just some of the problems noted. Other violations included problems in distributing audited financials and custody rule violations. The argument could be made that these funds were new registrants and, therefore, more problems could be expected as compared with seasoned registrants. On the other hand, when looking at this list of violations, it could also be argued that the reason there were so many problems is because these funds were not required to be registered and there was no one making them implement what many would likely consider best practices and oversight that would promote enhanced governance. Particularly if you were an investor in a fund that cost you money as a result of these deficiencies, you would likely land on the side of the argument that regulations that require registration can be a factor in promoting better governance.

Europe

Europe has long been a leader in promoting hedge fund governance efforts. While we will address some of the country-specific development efforts in this area, it is also useful to comment on the growth of the European Union ("EU") fund governance framework.

One example of the EU efforts in this regards was the publication of the EU Corporate Governance Framework, sometimes referred to as the so-called Green Paper, in 2011. One of the key goals of this paper was to promote the increased qualifications of nonexecutive directors with appropriate training and skills, diverse backgrounds, and sufficient time to do their job (PwC, 2013). Other key focuses of this framework were to encourage executives to raise challenges and promote risk management oversight.

More recent European regulations that have directly influenced hedge fund governance have included the various Undertaking for Collective Investment in Transferable Securities (UCITS) regimes, the AIFMD, and Markets in Financial Instruments Directive (MiFID). To cover the technicalities of each of these regulations in detail would not be practical here. Nor is every aspect of each regulation relevant to our discussion of fund governance. As such, while we will not cover the intricacies of each regulation here, in summary some of the key areas of governance addressed include guidelines for a continued focus on risk management oversight by boards, appropriate conflicts of interest management, clean remuneration policies, distinct segregation of duties, board oversight of valuation transparency, and appropriateness.

Ireland

Ireland is important to the hedge fund industry. In fact, very important; based on estimates at least 40% of the world's hedge funds are administered out of Ireland and over 50% of the top 10 European hedge funds have set up Irish funds (PwC, 2014). According to the Irish Funds Industry Association ("IFIA"), 7% of those funds domiciled in Ireland are hedge funds as compared with 32% for bond funds and 25% for equity funds (Irish Funds Industry Association, 2014).

Administration in particular is a huge business. This was driven in part by the early movement by Ireland to create the International Financial Services Centre in Dublin as a portal to encourage financial services in Ireland. In large financial centers such as Dublin many of the larger administrator firms have neighboring offices. During the mid-2000s so great was the demand for fund administration personnel in large Irish financial centers such as Dublin that the job market was extremely competitive. So competitive in fact that the joke was that fund accountants could get a raise just by crossing the street. While Dublin still serves as a primary hub of administration and fund accounting activities, in recent years many firms have also spread out to other parts of the country, setting up facilities in more rural areas such as County Cork and Swords.

From a regulatory perspective, historically Ireland was a more popular destination for more traditional investment funds as opposed to alternatives. That is not to say that there were no alternatives there, but you were more likely to come across a mutual fund than a hedge fund. Increasingly Ireland began to become more popular with certain hedge funds. This was in part because they began listing their shares on the Irish Stock Exchange. The reasons for this were primarily marketing related as well as to facilitate investment from institutions that had restrictions on investing in unlisted shares.

Similar to the Cayman Islands, Ireland also has a fairly progressive regulatory environment that seeks to encourage continued hedge fund growth. As we noted earlier in this chapter, the oversight of hedge funds in Ireland is primarily coordinated by the Central Bank of Ireland ("Central Bank").

Over time the Central Bank began to focus on governance in the funds it supervised, including hedge funds. In Irish legal speak hedge funds are typically grouped under the definition of so-called authorized collective investment schemes. In 2011 on urging of the Central Bank the IFIA published a voluntary code of corporate governance (*HedgeWeek*, 2011). This code is commonly referred to as the IFIA code. The IFIA code focused in particular on the importance of independent nonexecutive directors, sometimes called by the acronym NEDs, in implementing fund governance. Some of the key recommendations of the code included:

- Guidelines for board member meeting attendance and training
- Specification of the time commitments expected from directors
- Recommendations to conduct a review of board performance and of individual directors at least once every three years
- An outline of criteria that focus on clarifying whether or not a director can be classified as independent
- Recommendation that the board should develop a conflict of interest policy and better document conflicts

It should be noted that the IFIA code also has to comply or explain provision similar to the Cayman SOG outlined earlier in this chapter.

The IFIA code was overwhelmingly adopted by the funds industry. Recent survey data have also shown that in line with IFIA code guidelines the majority of fund board members exceed the recommended minimum of three members to an average of five directors per board (PwC, 2013). The popularity of these five member boards is interesting when contrasted to the typical three-member board in jurisdictions such as the Cayman Islands.

The focus on corporate governance has continued to persist in Ireland. It has been reported that there have been continued efforts by the Central Bank to monitor fund board and manager compliance with the IFIA code (Cunningham, 2014). Additionally in 2014 the Central Bank announced that one of its priorities as part of its so-called themed reviews and inspections would be to assess corporate governance at funds.

Although less of a popular hedge fund offshore jurisdiction for structuring purposes as compared with some other jurisdictions, Ireland's progressive regulatory environment continues to be a leader in promoting governance oversight, director accountability, and transparency. These practices have and will likely continue to flow through to improve governance practices in other jurisdictions as well.

Switzerland

Similar to Ireland, or perhaps even more so, Switzerland has a long and storied reputation as being a popular hedge fund destination. From the shores of Lucerne to the slopes of Gstaad, in Switzerland's case the country is particularly famous as a capital raising and distribution haven for many funds seeking access to capital from regions including Europe and the Middle East.

Similar to the Cayman Islands a key motivation for Switzerland's hedge fund popularity in this regards has likely been two primary factors. First, it may not be a surprise to those familiar with the hedge fund industry that wealthy individuals generally prefer their privacy. Historically all one had to do is visit Zurich and count the private banking firms in Switzerland to know that the famous anonymity offered by Swiss bank accounts was alive and well, albeit hiding in plain sight. Fast forward to more recent times and due to a number of scandals related to money laundering and tax evasion recent reports have indicated that a number of long-standing private banks such as HSBC (Letzig and Walker, 2014) and Standard Chartered have exited the Swiss private banking business (Spanier, 2014). Second, as we suggested above, accompanying these notions of privacy in Switzerland is the country's favorable tax regime. It is still an open question whether such secrecy and lack of transparency in many cases promotes governance at the country oversight level, and is certainly a contentious issue with multiple sides to the argument. Regardless of your opinions on the matter, if you want to work with hedge funds globally, you have to accept the current state of affairs in Switzerland.

Switzerland however had been losing the hedge fund offshore popularity contest in recent years to other jurisdictions. Part of this can likely be attributed to the promulgation of regulations elsewhere in Europe, such as the above-referenced AIFMD, that put the role of Switzerland in question. To clarify although Switzerland is in Europe, the country is not a member of the EU. Therefore, it is not directly subject to AIFMD.

The Swiss eventually realized that the gap between AIFMD and Swiss regulations was bad for business. As a result the Swiss Financial Markets regulator, the Swiss Financial Market Supervisory Authority ("FINMA"), made changes to the primary law governing the distribution of hedge funds, the Swiss Act of Collective Investment Schemes ("CISA"). These changes sought to address the oversight and distribution of so-called foreign collective investment schemes ("FCIS"), which includes most alternative vehicles such as hedge funds. The old CISA framework used to feature a safe harbor exemption that effectively exempted most hedge funds from registration with FINMA as long as they only raised capital from so-called qualified investors.

In order to better harmonize the old regulations with AIFMD, CISA adopted revisions in March 2013. This together with a revision to the regulatory guidance known as Ordinance on Collective Investment Schemes ("CISO") detailed the new Swiss framework governing the distribution of FCIS. With an emphasis on enhanced regulatory oversight, these new rules made several material changes to the old CISA framework. These new changes have reportedly been an overall beneficial factor in promoting the growth of the Swiss fund industry (Sa'Pinto, 2013). While we will not address all the changes in detail here, from a regulatory governance perspective there is one change that is worth discussing in more detail.

To clarify we will use the term distribution here to effectively mean raising capital from hedge fund investors. To use the terminology itself, it can perhaps most easily be thought of as distributing shares in the hedge fund to investors. This is of course not a legal or technical definition of the term, but for our purposes this understanding of the term should be sufficient.

Returning to the revised CISA guidelines, as per the way they were written when they were adopted, it would not be considered a distribution for so-called regulated financial intermediaries to disseminate a variety of data relating to fund managers. This type of data would include tax data and current net asset values ("NAV"). The catch is that the intermediary cannot provide specific contact details for the manager. This construct seems a bit naive on the part of FINMA. Does giving investors raw performance data concerning a fund, but simply omitting contact details, due much by not providing investor protections or best practice governance?

We can illustrate this perhaps by way of an example. Let us consider a situation where a financial intermediary distributes the NAV of a fund. As part of this communication the financial intermediary, in compliance with the revised CISA framework, omits the manager's contact details.

Now let's say that the investor reviews the information and is impressed to notice that the fund's NAV has gone up over 70% over the last month. Of course, this investor most likely wants more information. Uh oh, we have a problem. Remember, according to the new rules this investor was not provided with the contact information for the fund. End of story? Probably not. The investors would have one of two options. They could reach back out to the financial intermediary to ask for more information. This intermediary would then most likely proceed accordingly.

The other option, however, is that the investor could take a do-it-yourself approach. They could simply locate the contact information for the fund, which most likely wouldn't be overly difficult, and contact them directly. It would be up to the fund then to cry foul if they learn that the investor learned about the fund through the Swiss-regulated financial intermediary, but what if this never comes up?

These types of regulations pose governance risks not only to investors but also to the funds themselves seeking to distribute through Switzerland. If the fund does deal directly with the investor under our scenario without looping in the financial intermediary, then they may be in violation of the regulations. Certainly this wouldn't be good for the fund's existing investors.

The potential performance distribution scenario outlined above demonstrates an example of the regulatory governance concerns that can come into play when dealing with emerging regulations. As we have outlined throughout this chapter, while it is admirable for regulations such as Switzerland to promote enhanced governance and investor protections through regulations such as the revised CISA framework, this does not mean that the job is done. Investors and funds need to analyze the ways in which exemptions and potential loopholes such as the one highlighted above may impact not only the practical details of compliance with new regulations but also the implementation of best practice governance standards for all involved.

Asia

Hong Kong

As is still unfortunately a problem throughout the hedge fund space globally and Asia in particular, Hong Kong has recently sought to promote the idea of governance in the area of insider trading. In particular the HK SFC, perhaps taking a cue from US insider trading prosecutions in cases such as Galleon as well as hearing increasing investor complaints about this issue, has taken a series of recent enforcement actions in this regard.

However, in other areas it is clear that their bark may be louder than the regulatory bite. Consider, for example, the May 14, 2014 ruling by the Hong Kong Easter Magistrates' Court against a futures trader, Ernest Fan Kwong Hung, for manipulating prices of index futures. After being found guilty on all six counts of false trading in the Mini-Hang Seng Index he was fined and sentenced to 200 hours of community service. Such similar community service–style sentences were proposed in sentencing of convicted insider trading conspirator Rajat Gupta. Mr. Gupta was found guilty of tipping off Raj Rajaratnam in an insider trading scheme.

Instead, Mr. Gupta was sentenced to a two-year prison term by Judge Jed Rakoff of the United States District Court in Manhattan. Granted the two offenses here are completely different, however, the threat of prison is generally taken more seriously as compared with light-touch approaches. Jurisdictions such as Hong Kong are slowly transitioning toward such harsher US-style approaches, but it is often at an excruciatingly slow regulatory cadence. Sentences such as community service time will likely have no material chilling effect on promoting better governance throughout the region.

HEDGE FUND REGULATORY GOVERNANCE IN OTHER JURISDICTIONS

As we highlighted above, the governance-related effects of these regulations also have shared commonalities with the effects of regulation on hedge fund governance in other jurisdictions as well. Rather than repeat effectively the same analysis over for each jurisdiction, it will be most efficient to then provide a regulatory summary of certain other jurisdictions in which hedge funds have traditionally operated. While reading this summary, it is important to keep in mind that we are not dismissing the importance of the governance implications of regulations in these jurisdictions or seeking to overgeneralize them. On the contrary, the unique aspects of different jurisdictions' regulations are important to understand. Here, however, our focus is on highlighting the shared impact of these regulations on governance, and as such a summary is appropriate. For reference, where available, we will also include links to provide further information to the source text of these regulations.

British Virgin Islands

In previous years, the British Virgin Islands ("BVI") was a somewhat popular offshore hedge fund destination. BVI's popularity declined in recent times as it lost market share to other Caribbean jurisdictions such as the Cayman Islands. Indeed recent statistical data from the financial regulator, the British Virgin Islands Financial Services Commission ("BVI FSC"), have shown year-over-year quarterly declines in active BVI mutual funds (BVI FSC, 2013). To clarify, similar to the Cayman Islands, hedge funds fall under the definition of mutual funds under regulations including the BVI's Securities Investment Business Act ("SIBA").

Recognizing that BVI was perhaps losing steam, in 2013 BVI revised its laws. The new Investment Business (Approved Managers) (Amendment) Regulations from 2013 came into force on January 2, 2014. One of the primary changes from this regulatory revision was the provision under the new framework of so-called approved managers (i.e., those registered and approved in BVI) of non-BVI funds that are located in certain other jurisdictions. These other jurisdictions have to be recognized as being effectively similar to BVI. There are also of course exemptions to this for certain funds that relate certain asset cap levels.

What the new BVI regulations allow for is that a fund from other jurisdictions, such as a Cayman exempt fund, could still retain their Cayman fund while becoming licensed under the BVI FSC (Williams, 2014). The reasons for doing this would include further distribution options for funds. It has also been highlighted that this new BVI regime removes many of the more stringent old licensing requirements under the SIBA manager licensing regime prior to the revisions (Doyle, 2014).

While the new regulations have been popular with hedge funds, whether the removal of certain SIBA ongoing monitoring requirements is good for governance of BVI funds is still an ongoing question. Investors who deal with BVI-based funds, or those who distribute through BVI to take advantage of these new structures, would do well to inquire how hedge funds have adopted to this new regime. Have they taken it as an opportunity to strengthen governance oversight or lessen it due to enhanced regulatory flexibility?

China

While hedge funds have been investing in mainland China for a long time, it is only recently that they have been formally recognized. One of the primary laws governing the registration of hedge funds in China is called the Securities

Investment Funds Law. In June 2013, this law was amended to expand regulatory oversight to include hedge funds (Dickinson, 2013). In general, those funds that manage over 100 million Yuan or that have more than 50 investors are required to register with a self-regulatory agency known as the Asset Management Association of China (http://www.amac.org.cn/), which is sponsored by the government regulator, the China Securities Regulatory Commission (http://www.csrc.gov.cn).

This approach to regulating funds is reminiscent of the argument promoted by many hedge fund industry groups. Namely that the hedge fund industry is best left to its own devices and self-regulation as opposed to formal government regulation. It could be argued that such thinking, particularly in the larger hedge fund financial centers of the world, was one of the contributing factors to the financial crisis of 2008. Without formal regulatory oversight, do hedge funds really have any accountability to these industry self-regulators? This is particularly true when there is little to no information sharing within these self-regulatory organizations ("SROs"). In particular, many members of SROs or industry lobbies are at the end of the day market competitors. You can see perhaps how they would be less than comfortable sharing information with either the SRO or their competitors. Furthermore, in many cases the only tool many SROs have is public pressure. That is to say if one hedge fund is acting in a manner that they deem inappropriate, then they will make them feel bad about it. It's not as if they have any legal authority to shut down a fund or levy fines to an unwilling hedge fund.

Other SROs have effectively morphed into hedge fund industry lobby organizations rather than actually oversee. In an attempt to legitimize themselves they often put out codes of conduct that some firms subscribe to. There are several problems with these codes. First, there is little to no ongoing oversight; it's primarily a self-certification effort. Sure a firm can hire an auditor to check if they have complied, but complied with what exactly? In many cases the codes are so vague as to be useless. They typically follow a comply or explain mentality. As we have highlighted above, such protocols can have a great deal of flexibility in the nature and quality of explanations.

That is not to say that SROs are all bad; some governance oversight is better than nothing; the point here is that letting the funds industry self-regulate could be equated to giving the fox the keys to the hen house in some regards. In Asia such SROs and light-touch oversight of hedge funds have unfortunately led to insider trading both in the region and for hedge funds that trade in stocks in the region. One example of this was the case of Sun Sung Kook "Bill" Hwang, the founder and portfolio manager of Tiger Asia Management, Tiger Asia Partners, and Tiger Asia Partners LLC (US SEC, 2012). In 2012 Mr. Hwang pled guilty to using material nonpublic information to illegally profit for his funds by short selling shares of Bank of China Ltd. and China Construction Bank Corp. (Taub, 2012). Eventually the firm forfeited $16.3 million and paid a US SEC settlement of $44 million (Voreacos, 2012).

The desire here is by no means to criticize the Chinese effort to regulate the hedge fund industry. Efforts to promote oversight, particularly at relatively low AUM levels, is an admirable step in the right direction. Rather it is to suggest that due to all the potential governance failings present in SROs, it is perhaps advisable to speed up the pace at which more formal regulation is implemented, and more importantly enforced by government authorities with real ability to act.

Singapore

Singapore has waxed and waned in popularity in the hedge fund space. Thanks in part to ostensibly stricter regulatory changes, Singapore has regained some of its popularity. But in Singapore's example, is what's good for business necessarily good for governance? Not necessarily.

Background on Singapore Regulatory Environment

In 2012 Singapore announced a major change in its approach to hedge fund regulation—and the hedge fund community celebrated. Prior to that time Singapore-based hedge funds were not required to be licensed as long as they were classified as exempt fund managers (EFM). As long as they only marketed themselves to so-called qualified investors and met some other basic criteria, there wasn't much oversight or regulation of their activities. All hedge fund managers had to do was provide notification to the Monetary Authority of Singapore ("MAS") of their choice as to whether to be licensed or not—and most chose the latter. This fast and loose approach to hedge fund regulation was originally utilized as a marketing tool to lure fund managers to Singapore, and "put the city back on the map" as an Asian hedge fund destination (Ismail, 2010).

In an attempt to revise their hedge fund regulatory structure and improve governance, the MAS studied ways to increase regulation of hedge funds. After two years of study, and seemingly taking cues from the US Dodd–Frank legislation and recent SEC registration requirements, the MAS decided to effectively require all hedge fund managers above S\$250 million to register. Specifically, under the Securities and Futures (Licensing and Conduct of Business) (Amendment No. 2) Regulations (2012), hedge funds were classified into two different categories: Fund Management Companies ("FMC") and Registered Fund Management Companies ("RFMC"). RFMC replaces the old "EFM" classification. RFMCs can serve up to 30 qualified investors and manage up to $250 million in Singapore dollars (commonly written as S\$). RFMCs do not need a license but FMCs will need a license.

According to the MSA at the time these regulations were enacted, FMCs would be subject to "enhanced business conduct and capital requirements." These included rules requiring independent custody and valuation of investor assets, as well as requirements for FMCs to undergo independent annual audits by external auditors and have an adequate risk management framework commensurate with the type and size of investments managed by the FMCs. All of this sounded pretty good, and as if it would work to better promote governance. Let's dig deeper into some of the guidelines as they were written at the time of implementation.

Requirements for Independent Custody

Does anyone remember Bernard Madoff? The potential for manipulation in self-custody relationships is too great and does not promote best practice governance. While it is commendable that the Singapore financial regulators now require independent custody for FCMs, investors should avoid self-custodied managers, as such relationships are generally not worth the potential risk to investors.

Additionally, it could be asked, why did the MSA only require independent custody for its larger managers? Perhaps a custody-related fraud below S$250 million does not outweigh the burden and costs of hiring a third-party custodian placed on smaller fund managers in the mind of the MSA; however, such considerations would likely hold little recompense for the investors who could lose capital in such a situation.

Requirements for Independent Valuation of Investor Assets

"Independent" is a vague term at best. Does this mean that a hedge fund that trades highly liquid positions such as equities, and is able to price such positions from a third-party source such as Bloomberg, has satisfied this requirement? Or instead is the work of a third-party firm engaged by the hedge fund manager, such as a fund administrator, required? Does this mean that it is now a violation of the Singapore regulations for FCMs to self-administer?

What about situations where positions are thinly traded or initially manager marked? Would the hedge fund manager hiring a third-party administrator, who may not have the competency to independently price such thinly traded positions, still satisfy this requirement?

An overarching concern relating to the use of such third-party administrators is that administrators themselves are hired by the fund managers. While they work for the fund, there are legitimate questions about the true independence of such relationships.

Requirement for FCMs to Undergo Independent Annual Audit by External Advisors

Would this requirement be satisfied by a hedge fund manager's regular annual financial statement audit? Does this "new" requirement mean that it was previously fine for a manager not to be audited?

Once again, it seems the MSA is finally catching up to what is common sense to investors. While investors should in no way outsource their operational due diligence responsibilities to a third-party auditor, the work of an auditor and the subsequent financial statements are extremely valuable to investors during due diligence. If a hedge fund manager is not audited, investors should move on.

If on the other hand the "independent annual audit" language does not imply that a financial statement audit will not encompass the "independent annual audit" language of the MSA, will FCM hedge funds now be required to have a separate audit performed in addition to the financial statement audit?

Requirement to Have an Adequate Risk Management Framework Commensurate With the Type and Size of Investments Managed by the FMCs

Once again, this is perhaps so vague as to be useless. Many logical well-intentioned hedge funds may take different approaches, some less conservative than others, in regards to the definition of the word "adequate." Certainly, it would be considered adequate to have an independent dedicated risk manager, but other fund managers may feel that nondedicated oversight is sufficient. How will the MSA regulate this?

Form Over Substance Governance?

On the surface investors' initial reactions to such enhanced regulatory reforms may be that more regulation is better for investors and results in better governance. However, it is important that investors take measures to understand not only the technical requirements of new regulatory requirements but also whether these additional requirements will be effective. Singapore has grown as an Asian hedge fund center in the past few years and is increasingly nipping at the heels of Hong Kong for hedge fund business. Additionally, despite recent efforts to create a more hospitable environment for hedge funds in other Asian countries, scandals such as the AIJ fraud in Japan and continued concerns related to fraud in mainland China, continue to push Singapore to the forefront ahead of other Asian jurisdictions.

In the case of Singapore's measures to further regulate the domestic Singapore hedge fund industry, the MSA, at the time of the writing of the law at least, has unfortunately stopped short in its attempts to implement real oversight and reform in order to enhance governance.

By setting artificially low limits for hedge fund transparency and independence, the MSA has demonstrated that it is still partially a captured regulator in the shadow of the hedge fund industry it seeks to regulate. Of note, one of the more concerning themes of the recent MSA reforms is the shifting of the onus toward hedge funds themselves. It is up to hedge funds to ensure adequate risk management procedures are in place and that assets are independently valued. Yet, the MSA stops short of saying how it will police these items.

Effectively, the MSA is hoping the largest hedge funds play by the rules. The 2014 reports have shown that the new regulations have also been a boom to many Singapore-based industries that support hedge funds' compliance

(Wille, 2014). This includes lawyers, auditors, and compliance consultants. In many cases, these increased expenses as part of the cost to comply are being passed along as fund expenses. That is fine as such expenses are indeed likely legitimate fund expenses, but does it represent good governance if investors are effectively paying for funds to comply with light-touch regulation?

While it may be the general perception that more hedge fund regulations equal better governance, this is certainly not always the case. We highlight the case of Singapore here to outline that in some cases ill-constructed regulations can arguably do more to hurt governance than to help it. To clarify the goal of this discussion is not to pick on Singapore. Rather, it is to show that in many cases more carefully crafted legislation without so many loopholes, lack of clear regulatory guidance, and unanswered questions would likely be more beneficial to promoting overall governance as opposed to leaving key governance issues open-ended or for the courts to decide. Of course, some may argue that some regulations are better than no regulations and certainly these arguments have their merits as well.

CONCLUSION

This chapter provided an overview of the influence of financial regulations on hedge fund governance. In summary, these regulations have resulted in changes in the way hedge funds approach governance. Certainly, as with most regulations, they make it more expensive and complicated to conduct business. These expenses don't just come from the army of lawyer, compliance, accounting, and support personnel required to navigate the requirements of these new laws and regulations. That is just the tip of the iceberg. There's also the cost on productivity and then there is the ongoing cost of monitoring any changes to laws that monitor governance and implementing ongoing compliance. As noted above, in many cases these expenses are passed on to hedge fund investors.

Of course, it can be argued that these regulations have increased corporate governance and accountability. As we have outlined above, there is not necessary a single answer or perspective that can determine whether the cost, and burden, of such an enhanced regulatory environments is a good thing for governance. Certainly, as we discussed in this chapter, the threat of ongoing oversight from regulators due to hedge fund registrations regimes has made strides in promoting better oversight practices, but it is yet to be determined whether such registration regimes will make wholesale improvements to governance globally.

REFERENCES

Adler, J.A. Onshore Investors in Offshore Funds. Available at: http://www.hedgefundnews.com/news_n_info/article_detail.php?id=44.

Bob, B., 2003. Thin to Top: Why Corporate Governance Matters & How to Measure, Manage, and Improve Board Performance. Nicholas Brealey Publishing, March 25.

BVI FSC, 2014. Statistical Bulletin. Vol. 34, BVI Financial Services Commission, March.

Cunningham, B., 2014. Ireland: the Central Bank's themes reviews, inspections and enforcement priorities for 2014. *Mondaq*, March 14.

Dickinson, C., 2013. China introduces registration for hedge funds. *Hedge Funds Review*, March 11.

Doyle, M., 2014. Extension of BVI approved manager regime. *HedgeWeek*, May 2.

HedgeWeek, 2011. IFIA issues voluntary corporate governance code for collective investment schemes and management companies. *HedgeWeek*, December 12.

Hudson, M., Stănescu, I., Adler-Bell, S., 2014. How New York real estate became a dumping ground for the world's dirty money. *The Nation*, July 3. Available at: http://www.thenation.com/article/180516/how-new-york-real-estate-became-dumping-ground-worlds-dirty-money#.

Hurtado, P., 2013. Level Global co-founder gets 6 1/2-year prison sentence. *Bloomberg*, May 13.

Irish Funds Industry Association, 2014. Irish Funds Industry April 2014 Monthly Statistics Factsheet.

Isidore, C., 2013. Buffett says he's still paying lower tax rate than his secretary. *CNNMoney*, March 4. Available at: http://money.cnn.com/2013/03/04/news/economy/buffett-secretary-taxes/.

Ismail, N., 2010. Singapore's new hedge-fund regulation puts city 'back on map'. *Bloomberg*, July 28.

Letzig, J., Walker, I., 2014. HSBC sells Swiss private banking portfolio. *The Wall Street Journal*, June 24.

Mallin, C., 2013. Corporate Governance, third ed. Oxford University Press, February 7.

PwC, 2013. Understanding the finder details: Irish Funds Corporate Governance Survey, July.

PwC, 2014. Hedge Funds. Available at: http://www.pwc.ie/asset-management/am-hedge-funds.jhtml.

Sa'Pinto, M., 2013. Hedge funds find new Swiss rules good for business. *Reuters*, April 22.

Scharfman, J., 2012. Private Equity Operational Due Diligence: Tools to Evaluate Liquidity, Valuation and Documentation. Wiley Finance, April 10.

Solomon, S., 2012. With lax regulation, a risk industry flourishes offshore. *DealB%k*, September 4.

Spanier, G., 2014. Standard Chartered to sell Swiss private banking arm. *The Independent*, February 13.

Taub, S., 2012. The downward spiral of Bill Hwang and Tiger Asia. *Institutional Investor's Alpha*, December 14.

US SEC, 2012. Hedge Fund Manager to Pay $44 Million for Illegal Trading in Chinese Bank Stocks, December 12. Available at: http://www.sec.gov/News/PressRelease/Detail/PressRelease/1365171486854#.U73TurEzT2Q.

US SEC, 2014. Compliance Outreach Program National Seminar 2014, January 30.

Voreacos, D., 2012. Tiger Asia admits guilt in $60 million court settlement. *Bloomberg*, December 13.

Wille, K., 2014. Hedge-fund startups adapt to new Singapore rules: Southeast Asia. *Bloomberg*, April 30.

Williams, J., 2014. Extension opens door to managers with non-BVI funds. *HedgeWeek*, February.

Zabel, W., 1996. The Rich Die Richer and You Can Too. *Wiley*, March 16.

Chapter 4

The Role of Fund Service Providers in Implementing Governance

Chapter Outline Head

INTRODUCTION TO HEDGE FUND SERVICE PROVIDER GOVERNANCE

Service providers serve critical functions in the overall governance structures of hedge funds. This chapter will provide an overview of key hedge fund service providers and discuss the ways they influence hedge fund governance.

The work of service providers can both support the internal governance efforts of the hedge funds and provide third-party oversight of hedge fund governance practices. With the increasing outsourcing of certain functions to service providers by hedge funds, they may also directly manage certain elements with governance implications at funds.

Hedge Fund Governance
97

To pause for a moment, perhaps we should ask, what exactly is a hedge fund service provider? It may seem like an overly simple question whose answer is obvious to any investor or other individual who works as part of a professional hedge fund allocation organization, such as an operational due diligence analyst, but let's get it out of the way so we are all on the same page with regards to terminology. It's a pretty straightforward question, isn't it? Let's propose as a general definition that a service provider is any kind of third-party company that does work for a hedge fund. Is this definition practical from a governance perspective?

ARE SOME SERVICE PROVIDERS MORE IMPORTANT TO GOVERNANCE?

If we accept that service providers do play an important role in fund governance, as we have outlined above, does this mean that we should be concerned with all service providers when evaluating governance? Your gut reaction may be, yes. When you think about the answer in a little more detail, however, you might see that there may be some differences in responses among the groups you ask this question to.

If you asked a hedge fund manager, for example, for a list of service providers, they would likely present the usual suspects including the auditor, administrator, prime brokers, and law firm. An operational due diligence analysts may, however, seek to expand this list using the above-referenced broader definition and include service providers such as trading counterparties, fund banks, compliance consultants, and information technology providers. After all, aren't these third-party companies that do work with the funds?

Let's take it a step further. What if we asked a hedge fund controller who was responsible for overseeing payment to third parties for their services for a list of all third-party firms the hedge fund pays? Well, under this perhaps broadest definition service providers may include catering firms and office cleaning services. You may be thinking something to the effect of, "who cares who cleans the office?" To be clear this last example is not the type of service providers we will be focusing on in our discussion here. The question could be raised, however, beyond a core set of generally agreed-upon key service providers, could there likely be reasoned disagreement around how an investor and hedge fund should think about so-called "important" service providers?

ISN'T CASTING A BROADER NET BETTER?

If an investor wanted to be truly inclusive in evaluating a hedge fund's service providers, as a function of a larger evaluation of the overall hedge fund governance framework, then wouldn't it be simply better to include a larger sample of all service providers? This would include not only what most investors would agree on to be the core base of critical providers but also simply all providers ranging from the most critical to the least critical. This data set of all service providers could be collected using the broad definition of service providers outlined above of any third party that does work for a hedge fund.

In the interests of completeness of review, such an approach would certainly be valid. That being said, there are certain practicalities of evaluating a hedge fund governance framework that likely preclude this. These include:

- Transparency limits
- Declining fund responsiveness beyond what it deems to be reasonable due diligence norms versus the amount of capital being invested
- Service provider disclosure limitations
- Investor's inability to proceed beyond transparency limits due to concerns raised by the signing of liability releases with service providers

As such, to focus on more of the practical and less of the theoretical, our discussion here will primarily focus on those service providers that are commonly reviewed during most investor due diligence processes with consideration of the above-referenced, albeit sometimes frustrating, practical restrictions.

ARE "ANCILLARY" SERVICE PROVIDERS IMPORTANT IN EVALUATING GOVERNANCE?

Putting the limitations above aside, many investors would be hard-pressed to make a legitimate argument that there is a need, from either a due diligence perspective or a governance evaluation perspective, to evaluate what we will deem to be ancillary service providers, such as office cleaning services. We are not arguing here for less due diligence, particularly when it comes to evaluating governance relationships. Just the opposite, to truly evaluate a hedge fund's complete governance landscape, more due diligence is preferred to less.

This is not to say, however, that there is no value in a high-level review of the controls surrounding such relationships, as well as the relationships themselves.

Let's continue our cleaning service example to highlight this point. If a hedge fund manager happens to hire a very high-priced cleaning service that is owned by the brother-in-law of the portfolio manager, this would raise legitimate conflict of interest questions. If a hedge fund manager would take liberties in areas such as this, who's to say they are not taking similar liberties in the hiring of other service providers? Certainly if the firm has no infrastructure in place to monitor, or correct, such actions, this would be representative of poor governance.

Furthermore, how is an investor supposed to even know about this relationship if it's not even on their list to inquire about it? In particular, if there are any legitimate conflicts of interest in place, the hedge fund portfolio manager is not going to necessarily volunteer this information. This represents the chicken or egg dilemma of due diligence information collection. When evaluating governance, as with most due diligence processes, investment, operational, or otherwise, an investor cannot evaluate information they have not inquired about and collected. As such, we are not advocating that investors simply put blinders on and not inquire at all about what certain groups may deem to be ancillary service provider relationships. Rather due to the constraints referenced above an investor may only get so many bites at the apple in evaluating the governance roles of hedge fund service providers; the lion's share of attention should practically be focused on a core group of service providers you would want to make sure you certainly evaluate.

It is also worth noting that with increasingly limited due diligence resources to evaluate a whole host of areas, including governance, picking which service providers to focus on beyond a core set can present a bit of a Sophie's Choice. As the number of hedge fund service providers has continued to expand in recent years, investors run the risk of being overwhelmed. By developing a due diligence plan of action in this regard, investors can be better prepared to ensure that they cover the low-hanging service provider fruit so to speak, and do not lose the forest for the trees. To start this planning process off you need to first understand the roles of common hedge fund service providers and their impact on governance.

COMMON HEDGE FUND SERVICE PROVIDERS

The primary service providers that modern hedge funds employ include the auditor, prime brokers, custodians, administrator, legal counsel, compliance consultant governance, and information technology providers (Scharfman, 2008). Directors, whether they may want to admit it or not, are also service providers that can be grouped alongside the rest. From a governance perspective, they are certainly currently the group of service providers that receive the greatest attention, but this doesn't mean the other service providers aren't equally, if not more, important to governance.

Directors seem to garner special attention when it comes to governance due, in part, to their oversight role with managers. Most other service providers perhaps have the general perception of being less involved with managers as compared with the directors. This is certainly not always the case and as we highlighted in Chapter 2, some directors are certainly too hands-off for certain investors' tastes. We will provide some more perspective on the capacity aspects of director governance later in this chapter; for now let us begin our discussion here by outlining the role of other key service providers.

ISN'T SERVICE PROVIDER GOVERNANCE SIMPLY FUND OPERATIONS?

Before we begin to analyze the governance roles of service providers it is worth pausing for a moment to clarify what we mean by the term governance in this case. You may remember from Chapter 1 that we developed a general working definition of governance as "an interconnected systems of controls and procedures which seek to promote independence, transparency, and oversight through the hedge fund ecosystem." Service providers can play a key role in enforcing controls and promoting independence, oversight, and transparency through their work with funds. These activities are what we are talking about when we discuss service provider governance.

You may be questioning how these service provider governance activities are different from the actual nuts and bolts of operational practices. Does it change anything if we call it governance? To put it in perspective, this is similar to the question raised in Chapter 3 when we discussed the relationship between compliance and regulatory governance. The answer here is effectively the same. Service provider governance and fund operations are related concepts that influence each other. Governance is a concept that overlays the area in question, fund operations in this case, to gauge the effectiveness of notions of control, oversight, independence, and transparency. An example may help to further clarify the related nature of service provider governance and operations.

As we outlined above, it might be counterintuitive to think that certain service providers have really much to do with governance at all. Consider a hedge fund that has a particular information technology need. It calls up an information technology provider and bam problem solved. Is there really anything more to say about the relationship? Beyond that, what really does this have to do with governance? First, governance does not have to be a binary concept. That is to say that a hedge fund doesn't necessarily have to either have governance or not. Furthermore, isn't it a bit of a generalization to say that a hedge fund has either good governance or bad governance? Similar to many concepts in the hedge fund space governance is really an umbrella term encompassing many related subtopics that are addressed throughout this book.

Continuing our information technology example we can say that under the broad term of hedge fund governance, there is also information technology governance. Now you might be thinking to yourself, "Wait a minute. This is ridiculous. Besides the fact that there really isn't much governance related to IT service providers themselves, couldn't it simply be argued then that every little aspect of a hedge fund, and by association its service providers, can be categorized according to this governance subtype architecture?"

Let us address each of these points individually. First, the information technology function and the associated service providers do involve aspects of governance. Consider the structure by which the hedge fund provides and controls access by information technology personnel to its systems. Does the hedge fund simply allow IT personnel to access its system willy-nilly, or instead does the firm have policies and protocols in place that govern such arrangements? A common example of an arrangement that highlights the types of issues we are discussing here relates to the use of contract consultants for IT projects. It is not uncommon for a hedge fund, for example, to hire a firm or freelance consultant to assist with a specific project that requires unique technology expertise that the firm may not have in house. In those cases, the consultant may work for the firm for a few months and then the engagement would end. So focusing on the way the hedge fund may govern these relationships, with a particular focus on IT security, what does the firm do when the consultant's tenure ends? Some hedge funds have robust policies in this regard that outline that the consultant's access to systems is limited to only relevant areas on the network, and even physically within the firm while they are employed there for the engagement. For example, if an IT consultant is working on software issues, then they don't need access to the firm's server room to do their job. In such a case it would overwhelmingly be thought to be best practice for the firm to implement such access restrictions.

Furthermore, once the employee leaves the firm, some hedge funds will have policies that outline that the contractor's passwords and network access will expire on that day. You could see potentially how a firm without a rigorous policy in this regard may either completely forget to block this access when the consultant leaves the firm or implement it with a lag. Once again it would be considered best practice to implement such protections in order, for example, to prevent a nefarious consultant from continuing to access the firm's systems after they leave the firm to do who knows what. By the way, it might go without saying, but a policy such as the one we are discussing is only as good as its enforcement. That is to say the real gauge of best practice is how well the fund implements the policy. If a fund chooses not to implement it, then it's not worth the paper it's written on.

Returning to the potential objections to our argument that may be raised, we can now visit the second part of the proposed objection. Namely, whether or not you can reasonably call the different aspects of a hedge fund functionality, which for the purposes of simplifying our argument we can classify broadly into investment and operational duties, as being subtypes or subcategories of governance. It would be perhaps easy for us to just take the stance that it doesn't matter what you call it. After all, at the end of the day we're all talking about the same issues here, aren't we? As we outlined above, it is a nuanced but important difference between fund operations and the governance oversight of them. In this case, the hedge fund had poor information security controls over the IT consultant. The nature of such controls can be thought of as a fact. It is what it is. The governance elements of it can be thought of assessing the quality of the controls and these are the types of differences that a governance focus attempts to highlight.

With this distinction clarified we can now turn to discussing some key governance aspects of different core hedge fund service providers. In the interest of space we will focus on administrators, prime brokers, and directors here, but certainly as we have noted, other service providers such as auditors, law firms, and information technology consultants can play critical governance roles. For reference we will discuss techniques for investors to evaluate the governance aspects of such providers in more detail in Chapter 6.

When reading through this overview, please keep in mind that our goal is not to cover the full gamut of services provided by these service providers. Other texts do that in detail. Instead, here we will be focusing on select aspects of the role and duties of these service providers as they relate to fund governance.

THE ADMINISTRATOR'S GOVERNANCE ROLE

Introduction to Administration Governance

At first glance most investors view the primary, or perhaps the most important, function of administrators as being related to the valuation function. For the most part they would be correct, providing oversight or support for the hedge fund's internal valuation work being certainly a critical administrator function. Now whether the administrator's work in this area can be classified as truly independent is certainly a contentious point. We will table this discussion of the administrator's role and arguable independence in regards to valuations in Chapter 9, which focuses in more detail on the subject of governance in valuations.

For the purposes of our discussion here we will focus on the governance-related functions of the other services performed by the administrator. To take a step back we should cover some initial background on what it is administrators actually do, and how they interact with both hedge fund managers and other service providers. Once we are on the same page with this background information, we can focus on the governance roles administrators play. For those already familiar with this background information, I invite you to skip ahead to the next section, which will begin our governance discussion in this regard.

So let's get this discussion out of the way. First off, what do administrators actually do besides valuation? The other key duties of administrators have traditionally included:

(1) Processing capital contributions, sometimes called subscriptions, to the fund from investors
(2) Processing capital withdrawals, sometimes called redemptions, from the funds to investors
(3) Distributing statements to investors throughout the life of their investment in the fund on typically a monthly, quarterly, or annual basis

In addition to valuation oversight by the administrator, which ultimately feeds into the production of the above-referenced investor statements, these have been the core traditional administration functions. As I noted above, this list of administrator duties is not meant to be comprehensive, but to serve as a framework for our discussion.

Is That All Administrators Do?

In more recent years administrators have begun offering more services to hedge funds including a host of valuation support services. Outside of the valuation arena other services offered by administrators have included asset verification services, where the administrator will verify the holdings and asset balances (i.e., cash) with the fund's prime broker, custodian, and fund banks as applicable. With the increased investor focus on fund directors, some administrators have sought to capitalize on the director boom through the offering of services that support both the hedge fund's work with the board and the boards themselves. These services are sometimes sold under the heading *secretarial services*. Some of these services include assisting hedge fund in preparing reports for the board and acting as a general coordinator of board meetings. Sometimes these secretarial services step on the toes of traditional director activities. To this end, some administrators have broadened these secretarial services to include items such as facilitating local offshore regulatory filings and preparing meeting minutes.

This is worth noting because it can theoretically put directors' and administrators' business interest at odds. This can present a bit of a governance paradox, as we will discuss in more detail below, because these same groups often rely on each other through the cross-delegation of certain duties. Such an arrangement is by no means unique to administrators and directors, as increasingly service providers have begun to offer services that were traditionally offered by others. Another recent example as it relates to administrators was the completion of Form PF filings in the United States. Many hedge funds were required to first file Form PF after the US registration requirements were implemented that we discussed in Chapter 2. Traditionally, such filings may have been the realm of legal counsel. For Form PF a number of other service providers including compliance consultants and administrators came out of the woodwork seeking to offer services for such filings. While there is nothing wrong with such competition, it is another situation where the business interests of different service providers may be at odds with their reliance on each other.

Directors in Sheep's Clothing? Administrator Similarities to Directors

Before the more recent focus on the governance-related aspects of hedge fund directors, investors traditionally focused the spotlight on fund administrators. One of the biggest criticisms of fund administration relationships related to many of the same issues raised when criticizing fund directors. Namely, conflicts of interest, or should we say the perceived conflicts that are in place between the hedge fund, administrators, and investors. Sound familiar to the conflict questions raised surrounding hedge funds, directors, and investors? The arguments are very similar.

Administrators, just like directors, service funds. As such, it has been a much debated issue as to whether or not administrators ultimately represent the interests of investors over those of hedge fund managers. Fueling this fire, it is traditionally the fund managers, not investors, who actually make the hiring decision regarding which fund administrator to hire. While of course investors have input into this process, it's ultimately the fund manager's decision, not theirs. Once again this process is similar to directors. Although to be fair this issue is not limited to just administrators and directors; this is the way all service providers are hired and fired. That is of course with the exception of situations such as separately managed accounts where investors may direct the selection of service providers such as custodians.

Another similarity between administrators and directors is the delegation of responsibilities. In Chapter 2 we addressed the common practice of director delegation that outlined that the directors were not responsible for day-to-day management and administration of the fund. Instead, they rely on not only the fund manager but also other service providers to pick up the slack as it were and provide day-to-day oversight. One of the main entities they rely on is fund administrators.

To pause for a moment it is interesting to highlight that often times director's delegation clauses as it were will outline that the day-to-day outsourcing of responsibilities is left to the fund and other service providers. The reason this is of note is because administrators themselves may not be engaged with funds on a daily basis or even weekly basis. On a historical basis, if a hedge fund even had an administrator, it was not uncommon for them not to talk to the administrator on a daily or even weekly basis. The administrator might have been receiving information with such frequency from the fund (i.e., daily trade files) or from other service providers such as prime brokerage feeds, but the administrator themselves may not have been actively involved with the manager on a daily basis. Particularly when the administrator was cutting a net asset value (NAV) for funds on a monthly basis, there could have been periods of weeks where the administrator and the manager didn't really communicate.

Some managers may have even preferred this. For starters, they weren't being bothered. More likely, this somewhat reduced level of service likely cost them less. Over time, as investors and the hedge fund market in general have grown to adopt the perception that third-party administration is a good thing, such infrequent communication is increasingly uncommon, although it still does happen particularly in smaller hedge funds. Indeed, today it is not only is it far more common for a managers speak to and interact with their administrators on a daily basis, but they also increasingly shadow the work of administrators internally.

Returning to our discussion regarding the director delegation of duty, it is worth noting that administrators themselves delegate certain responsibilities to other parties as well. Or at least they rely on the work of other service providers such as auditors. Similar to the same questions we raised when we discussed directors, the same question can be asked here—does the delegation of duties in this manner promote good governance?

Can't I Just Resign? The Lancer Example

The answer to this question is directly related to the notions of administrator conflicts of interests as outlined above. Often administrators attempt to use these concepts to draw the line at the extent of their duties. When things go wrong and investors end up losing money and sue, administrators often use these delegations as a technique to limit liability. One example of this was the case of the Lancer Management Group LLC and in particular two of its British Virgin Islands–based funds, Lancer Offshore Inc. and Omni Fund Ltd. Investors with Lancer included Britney Spears and former jailed Sotheby's chairman Alfred Taubman (Lashmar, 2003). To summarize the case investors who lost money through investments in the Lancer funds sued a number of parties including the hedge fund administration firm Citco Fund Services ("Citco") and affiliated subsidiaries. Ultimately, the Lancer Group's founder Michael Lauer was acquitted of stock fraud (Feeley and Lucoff, 2011).

One of the key issues in debate was whether the investor capital statements that were produced by Citco contained appropriate valuations for the positions held by the funds. An April 2011 *Forbes* article discussing the case outlined that a Citco employee, Declan Quilligan, sent an internal e-mail questioning valuations in one of Lancer's funds. "It appears to me," he wrote, "that they have put absurd valuations on illiquid stocks since the start of the year in particular in order to compensate for serious losses" (Touryalai, 2011).

This same article goes on to describe how the administrator reportedly followed up on these concerns. Specifically the article outlined that Citco's lawyer, Lewis Brown, stated to *Forbes* that the firm appropriately raised its concerns with Lancer's auditor, Pricewaterhouse Coopers, and confronted Lauer, the portfolio manager, but was not required to do more (Touryalai, 2011). Citco eventually resigned as administrator.

As part of the initial legal wrangling in the case in 2009, Citco had argued in US District Court that it should have been dismissed from the case in part because it had resigned as administrator. The judge in that case, Judge Shira Scheindlin of the US District Court for the Southern District of New York, didn't buy that argument.

Interestingly as part of the argument, Citco outlined that it attempted to rely on the work of others to support the fund NAVs that were being reported on statements to investors. Who did Citco reportedly outline that they relied on in particular? Well, the fund directors of course. Judge Scheindlin didn't buy that argument either reportedly stating, "Citco Group makes much of its efforts to 'obtain certifications from the board of directors of the Lancer Funds attesting to the propriety of the valuations,' its 'full disclosure … regarding its concerns over the valuations,' and its seeking and following of 'legal advice of the law firm of Shearman and Sterling in New York with respect to its resignation'" (Caulfield, 2009). She reportedly continued, "Although these actions demonstrate Citco Group's questioning of the numbers, they could also be interpreted as Citco Group's efforts to shield its own involvement in the process" (Caulfield, 2009). Interestingly, the investor claims against the administrator who took over, International Fund Services (Ireland) Ltd., were dismissed via summary judgment. Ultimately the claims against PricewaterhouseCoopers and Citco were settled with investors (Uhlman, 2011).

While we have outlined some of the details regarding the Lancer case here, a review of historical records could likely find a whole history of similar claims against other administrators. The aim here is not to single out Citco in particular.

Rather the facts of cases such as this demonstrate a number of relevant governance considerations. As our discussion of the Lancer case has highlighted hedge funds and their service providers interact through a series of relationships that can often be rife with complicated delegations of duty and competing interests. Putting aside whether you think this is a good or bad thing, this is the framework under which hedge fund investing occurs. That said, the specific obligations and duties of these parties are not always black and white situations. If they were, they wouldn't need to be so extensively litigated when problems arise. Furthermore, assuming such relationships are indeed technically clearly defined from a legal perspective, there is always the issue that they are overwhelmingly opaque to most investors. Ignorance is no defense of the law, and certainly investors have an obligation to dig deep into such relationships during due diligence.

Yet, I wonder if prior to the losses in the Lancer situation, if you asked any of the investors, who had perhaps taken comfort in the hedge fund's use of a brand name administrator such as Citco, whether or not they felt that it was the duty of the administrator to protect them, as compared with an obligation to raise concerns over issues such as this, what the response would be? As a follow-up to that, perhaps not just to even simply raise such issues with the fund and other service providers, but to stop it from happening as soon as they may have suspected something was wrong. Wouldn't this have arguably been best practice governance? Furthermore, shouldn't the other service providers have raised a flag?

This brings us to a discussion of the interaction between the directors and administrators. Even if we do not consider the Lancer situation, it's a bit like a game of hot potato, where one group passes the buck to the other. For example, the administrators notice a problem in fund valuations and raise concerns. They then seek certification from the board of the fund regarding the valuations. The board hasn't been involved on a day-to-day basis; remember they delegated this responsibility to the administrator. Now the administrator comes back to the directors and says something to the effect of, "Hey you know that work you asked us to do. Well we've been doing it, but we've noticed some potential issues. We know you haven't been involved but can you certify that these valuations are accurate?" Even if the directors certify the valuations when a problem may arise, then they could of course go back to the administrator with the argument to the effect of, "Yeah ok we certified the valuations but that certification was based in part at least on the information that you the administrator gave us. We delegated our duty to oversee the valuations to you. So we certified something that was your obligation. If we're wrong then we'll point the finger back at you." You see how this is starting to become a somewhat blurry infinite game of tag.

These types of examples highlight the problem for investors. If service providers can't agree who's really responsible, then how are investors supposed to figure it out? Furthermore, if investors can't figure out who is actually in charge, then how are they supposed to assess the governance of the situation?

Today, frankly investors are en masse more sophisticated regarding general awareness of such issues. Even though they're not Hetty if they do look green. Rather, the problem is what are they supposed to do about it? If you want to deal with hedge funds, such relationships and potential conflicts are inherent. However, these are not cookie cutter arrangements. Without due diligence investors may not even learn of the specifics of the ways such relationships among service providers may present conflicts. Then, they would have no one to blame but themselves.

CUSTODIAN AND PRIME BROKER GOVERNANCE

Prime brokers provide a wide range of service to hedge funds. These services can typically range from trade execution and leverage financing to custodial services and securities lending (Scharfman, 2008).

From a due diligence perspective, investors traditionally focused on the counterparty and default risks of prime brokers. Such risks were highlighted by the failure of Lehman Brothers in 2008. Immediately after the Lehman Brothers failure investors increasingly turned their attention to the hot button issue of the day, which was analyzing prime brokers during due diligence. This type of shift to the flavor of the week has become known as a *Madoff effect* where investors, influenced by recent failures and frauds, refocused their due diligence efforts on risk areas where leading operational red flags were present (Corgentum Consulting, 2010).

Increasingly this focus on prime brokers led to an increased acceptance in the marketplace that prime brokers played an important role in overseeing hedge fund governance. For example, during the 2008 crisis many hedge funds violated what are known as NAV triggers in ISDAs. For reference an ISDA is an agreement that governs derivatives transactions, such as swaps. These are agreements that are typically in place between the hedge fund and the prime broker and often contain a number of specific terms and provisions. One such provision relates to declines of a hedge fund's NAV. If the NAV declines by more than a predefined amount over a certain period, then the counterparty to the ISDA agreements (i.e., the prime broker) has the right to terminate the agreement early. This can put the hedge fund on the other side of the agreement in a tough spot, because not only are they facing a declining portfolio but they now also have to come up with capital to meet the obligations of the now terminated contract.

During the 2008 financial crisis many hedge funds violated these NAV triggers as the market crashed. Prime brokers, however, don't stay in business by terminating these agreements and in effect firing their clients. So they told hedge funds not to worry about it and just keep trading. It was their right after all. It didn't work out so well for investors in some of those funds that just continued to lose more money. Whether the prime brokers should have taken a tougher stance with hedge funds is up for debate, but what is not an open question is that simply the ability to implement decisions such as this demonstrates the key governance role played by prime brokers.

ADDITIONAL COMMENTS ON FUND DIRECTORS AND GOVERNANCE

Director Resignations—You Can't Fire Me; I Quit!

In our example above regarding hedge fund administration we discussed the Lancer case. In that case, Citco eventually resigned as administrator. Situations such as this highlight a related interesting question with regards to director governance that hasn't been addressed yet. Can a director just quit if they have governance concerns?

Consider the following scenario. It's 2007; you are a fund director and you have a booming business sitting on tons of hedge fund boards. Getting even better, as the hedge fund industry is going gangbusters and fund launches are happening at breakneck speed you're joining more boards all the time. Then 2008 comes and the bottom drops out of the market. All the funds that you were going through the motions with on autopilot now have significant losses. As a result all kinds of shenanigans ensue. Funds start throwing up gates, side pocketing investments and even liquidating. Some investors are so upset that they start to sue everyone including the directors. You don't want to be involved with all of this. So what can you do? Who needs the headache? How about you simply walk away from these sticky situations before things get any hotter, and stick with the stable funds that don't have any problems? It's not like you're necessarily going to get paid much more as a director to walk a fund through the liquidation process. Any extra fees are not likely worth the headaches. But no one would do this, would they? What about all those fiduciary duties and stalwart oversight obligations directors talk about?

Unfortunately, the answer is yes. During the 2008 crisis and beyond certain directors simply left fund managers and investors holding the bag and walked away. The fact that they gave up doesn't necessarily mean that they were off the hook from a liability situation, but most investors would agree that a director resigning in the middle of tough time does little to help the situation. Should directors even have the right to resign during such situations? Would it be considered better governance to oblige them to finish the job they started? The goal of course would not be to tie directors to sinking ships, but instead not to make the lives of investors any more difficult during turmoil by losing a key governance resource. Perhaps one solution may be to obligate directors to serve for certain fixed terms or require them to be unable to resign until they finish certain duties. Perhaps a requirement could be implemented that requires directors to seek permission from investors before resigning outside of a predetermined service period.

A good analogy to this may be when an attorney needs to request permission from the court in certain instances before resigning from a case. In this instance the court weighs the disadvantage to the clients from the attorney resigning against the potential detriment to the attorney for sticking with a bad case. Is this situation really so different here? Wouldn't it be considered better governance for investors and funds to at least have some mechanism by which to sound off on such proposed resignations? There are of course two, if not more, sides to such issues. Some of the arguments from directors in this area would likely include that they are free citizens and should be able to resign whenever they want, particularly if they have concerns over the prudence or legitimacy of actions of funds. Investors would likely agree, however, that the crux of such arguments resides not with a director's right to resign or not. Instead, here we are talking about the timing of the resignation and in particular when funds are in crisis. Often in such tenuous situations, investors are left in a better position with a director support system in place.

Capacity Consideration in Evaluating Governance

Earlier in Chapter 2 we covered in detail perspectives on the governance role of fund directors. In that discussion we alluded to issues relating to director capacity but didn't really dig too deeply into the subject. Rather we opted to table the discussion to this chapter as capacity considerations are a key issue in assessing the overall service provider effectiveness of directors in implementing governance.

Introduction to Hedge Fund Director Capacity

What exactly do we mean by director capacity? Well, it depends on who you ask. If you went up to an average person on the street who has no idea what a hedge fund was, and you asked them what was thought by director capacity, they would likely refer to how many positions the director could hold. They would of course be correct. The solution, however, is in pinning down what is meant by the term "positions" in our example. Perhaps it's easiest to illustrate the confusion through an example.

A Director Capacity Example

Let's say we have an individual, Mr. Moran, who recently retired from his job working at a fund administrator in Dublin and migrated from Ireland to the Cayman Islands, and he opens up a new directorship firm, Moran Directors Inc. He is currently the only employee of this firm. Pursuing his entrepreneurial dream of building a directorship business Mr. Moran sets off to market his services.

By luck one of his former colleagues, Mr. Moriarty, launches a new hedge fund. The hedge fund management company is called Moriarty Asset Management, LLC ("MAM"). Calling in a favor, Mr. Moran is subsequently hired to serve as the director of an offshore Cayman-based hedge fund investment vehicle run by MAM known as Fund A. The other directors of Fund A by the way are Mr. Moriarty and Ms. Mycroft, who is Mr. Moriarty co–portfolio manager. At this point how many directorships does Mr. Moran have? Pretty stupid question, right? Well, at this stage everyone would of course agree it's one. That's fine; pardon my stupidity, you would be correct. Let's proceed.

Let's next say that Mr. Moran does such a good job as a director at Fund A that word starts to spread. Before you know it Mr. Moran is then called upon by another hedge fund manager Mr. Lestrade. He runs a hedge fund management company called Lestrade Asset Management, LLC ("LAM"). Mr. Moran is hired to sit on the board of his offshore Cayman fund; let's call this Fund B. To simplify things, let's say somewhat unusually Fund B has only two directors, one affiliated (Mr. Lestrade) and one independent (Mr. Moran). To take stock, at this point how many directorships would you say Mr. Moran has? Two of course. Fine, we're all on the same page.

Continuing along let's say that Mr. Moran's friend who gave him his first directorship position, Mr. Moriarty, is a great hedge fund manager. He consistently outperforms both the markets in general and his specific hedge fund peers and has decided to grow his firm by launching more funds. This, of course, means he needs more directors. Well, he knows the field-tested Mr. Moran has done a good job on Fund A so he calls upon him for his new fund; let's call it Fund C. Mr. Moriarty, however, still has a problem. You see because it has been awhile since Mr. Moran was first engaged as a director, over time investor focus and perception of the importance of the directorship role have changed. Directors are now more important than ever before. With the passage of time, it is no longer en vogue for the majority of the board of a hedge fund, such as the offshore vehicle in this case, to consist of a majority of affiliated personnel.

To clarify, for those who are reading this book out of order and have not read our previous discussion in Chapter 2 of the term, "affiliated" can be read for the purposes of this example as being those employed by the hedge fund. In this case, this would, namely, be Mr. Moriarty and Ms. Mycroft.

Returning to our example, Mr. Moriarty is still left with a problem. Yes, of course, he can select the more than capable Mr. Moran to serve on the board of his new fund, Fund C, but where is he going to get another independent director from? Well, it must be Mr. Moriarty's lucky day. You see while his hedge fund business has been going gangbusters, Moran Directors Inc., the directorship firm started by Mr. Moran, has been growing as well. In light of anticipated new demands Mr. Moran has hired a new director Mr. Wiggins to work alongside him. The hire was just made and Mr. Wiggins has not undertaken any directorships as yet. As his first post, Mr. Wiggins is hired to be the second director of

Fund C alongside his colleague, and boss, Mr. Moran. The third director for Fund C will be Mr. Moriarty. In order to keep the board of the new offshore, Fund C, majority independent Ms. Mycroft has been dropped from the board. So the current board construction is two independent members (i.e., Mr. Moran and Mr. Wiggins) and one affiliated member (i.e., Mr. Moriarty). By the way, Ms. Mycroft doesn't mind being dropped from the board of directors of Fund C; she is busy enough working as co–portfolio manager of the growing hedge fund firm anyways. Over time Mr. Wiggins is also elected to the board of Fund B at LAM to support further board diversity.

To take stock yet again, how many directorships would you say Mr. Moran has now? For reference Exhibit 4.1 summarizes the current state of affairs.

Let's see one at Fund A, one at Fund B, and now one at Fund C. So three, right? What about the other independent director Mr. Wiggins? Wouldn't it be correct to say he has two directorships? Easy enough, isn't it? By this point you might find my straightforward questions annoying. Why do I keep asking them? Well, because not everyone would necessarily answer these questions in such a straightforward way. To show you what I mean you have to understand the distinction between so-called *director relationships* as compared with directorships.

The term director relationship, or equivalent, is used to portray a concept that a director does not just have a relationship with a particular fund, but with

EXHIBIT 4.1 Board Membership Summary

	Fund A (run by MAM)	Fund B (run by LAM)	Fund C (run by MAM)
Mr. Moriarty (co-PM at MAM)	Yes	No	Yes
Ms. Mycroft (co-PM at MAM)	Yes	No	No
Mr. Moran (independent director from Moran Directors Inc.)	Yes	Yes	Yes
Mr. Wiggins (independent director from Moran Directors Inc.)	No	Yes	Yes
Mr. Lestrade (PM at LAM)	No	Yes	No
Total number of independent directors	1	2	2
Total number of affiliated directors	2	1	1
Total number of directors (i.e., independent plus affiliated)	3	3	3

the entire management company organization that a particular hedge fund is affiliated with. So how would the concept of director relationships play into our example?

Let's see. Mr. Moran sits on the board of two funds run by MAM and one fund run by LAM. So rather than classifying Mr. Moran as sitting on the board of three funds we could also say he has two hedge fund relationships. Not rocket science, and a pretty intuitive concept. Why then should we care about this?

What about the other independent director from Moran Directors Inc., Mr. Wiggins? Well, he sits on two boards (Fund B and Fund C) and similarly has two relationships. So both Mr. Wiggins and Mr. Moran maintain two relationships, but different number of boards. This is summarized in Exhibit 4.2. Ok, you need to pay attention, but not overly confusing as yet.

Well, let's increase the complexity of our example a bit. Let's say instead of two funds that require directorships, MAM runs seven funds that require directors. Let's also say that LAM launches five new funds that require directors. Let's further say that there are five new hedge fund management companies (i.e., HF1–HF5) that also launch additional funds that require directors. For the purposes of our example, let us also assume that Moran Directors Inc. also now employs multiple directors in addition to Mr. Moran and Mr. Wiggins. Several of these individuals, in addition to Mr. Moran and Mr. Wiggins, now sit on the boards of funds. Oh and as one final wrinkle in certain cases, funds no longer have a maximum of three people but some have up to five directors. In certain cases, not all the independent directors are staffed with directors from Moran Directors Inc. but with other individuals. Also the majority of these fund boards are still majority independent. This revised example is summarized in Exhibit 4.3.

Let's look at some key points in Exhibit 4.3. Let us consider Mr. Moran for starters. He sits on a total of 26 different individual funds. These 26 funds are run across a total of 7 different hedge fund managers. This represents 19 more boards versus management companies. We can next compare this with

EXHIBIT 4.2 Board Membership Summary—Relationships Versus Fund-Level Directorships

	No. of fund-level directorships	No. of management company relationships
Mr. Moran (independent director from Moran Directors Inc.)	3	2
Mr. Wiggins (independent director from Moran Directors Inc.)	2	2

EXHIBIT 4.3 Summary of Different Board Member Relationships

	Independent director from Moran Directors Inc.					
	Mr. Moran	Mr. Wiggins	Mr. Anderson	Mr. Magnussen	Ms. Donovan	Mr. Frankland
Fund A (run by MAM)	Yes	No	No	No	No	No
Fund B (run by LAM)	Yes	Yes	No	No	No	No
Fund C (run by MAM)	Yes	Yes	No	No	No	No
Fund D (run by MAM)	Yes	No	No	No	No	No
Fund E (run by MAM)	Yes	No	No	No	No	No
Fund F (run by MAM)	Yes	No	No	Yes	No	No
Fund G (run by MAM)	Yes	No	Yes	Yes	Yes	Yes
Fund H (run by MAM)	Yes	Yes	No	No	No	Yes
Fund I (run by LAM)	Yes	No	No	No	No	No
Fund J (run by LAM)	Yes	Yes	No	No	No	No
Fund K (run by LAM)	Yes	No	Yes	Yes	Yes	No
Fund L (run by LAM)	Yes	No	No	No	No	No
Fund M (run by LAM)	Yes	Yes	No	No	No	Yes
Fund N (run by LAM)	Yes	No	Yes	Yes	No	No
Fund O (run by HF1)	Yes	Yes	No	No	No	No
Fund P (run by HF1)	Yes	Yes	Yes	No	Yes	Yes
Fund Q (run by HF2)	Yes	No	No	No	No	Yes
Fund R (run by HF2)	Yes	No	No	No	No	No

Fund S (run by HF2)	Yes	No	No	No	No	Yes
Fund T (run by HF3)	Yes	No	No	No	Yes	Yes
Fund U (run by HF3)	Yes	Yes	Yes	Yes	No	No
Fund V (run by HF4)	Yes	No	No	No	No	Yes
Fund W (run by HF4)	Yes	No	Yes	Yes	Yes	Yes
Fund X (run by HF5)	Yes	No	No	No	No	No
Fund Y (run by HF5)	Yes	No	No	No	No	No
Fund Z (run by HF5)	Yes	No	Yes	No	No	No
No. of fund-level directorships	26	8	7	6	5	9
No. of management company relationships	7	4	6	4	5	6
	19					
	0.730769231					

Mr. Anderson. He sits on seven different boards across six different management companies. Finally, let's look at Ms. Donovan. She sits on five different fund boards, each of which is managed by five different management companies. An equal number for each category.

What's the point of all this analysis? Well, for starters we can see that when directors are classified by number of relationships as compared with number of fund-level directorships, the results can vary. In the case of Ms. Donovan, for example, it doesn't matter whether she states her directorships as fund director-ships or relationships; it's the same number since the two are equal. For Mr. Anderson and Mr. Moran it's a different situation. Stating the number of direc-torships as the number of relationships can paint a different and more cloudy picture. Why would a director prefer to frame the discussion in terms of the number of relationships as opposed to the actual number of boards that he or she sits on? The answer relates to the notion of director capacity we had previously been discussing.

Questioning Director Capacity Classifications

You must consider who is often asking the directors how many boards they sit on. Traditionally, such questions come about in one of two venues. The first being when hedge funds themselves pose the questions to directors. This may come about, for example, when a hedge fund is considering hiring a director and is performing some pre-employment due diligence screening as it were to determine the director's current commitments. This would likely give the hedge fund manager certain insights into director capacity levels, but we will table these considerations for the moment.

The second type of situation in which this type of director questioning of-ten occurs is from investors. Typically, this investor questioning comes about after a hedge fund has already hired a director and the investor is interview-ing the director as part of their overall due diligence process. In this type of situation the investor is still effectively making a hiring decision based on the director's response (i.e., should they hire the hedge fund or not). One of the distinctions of course is that the investor's opinion of a director's current commitments is not the sole factor in the overall investor hedge fund alloca-tion decision. Additionally, the investor of course is not deciding whether to hire the director themselves as it were, but to invest with (i.e., hire) the hedge fund manager.

To pause for a moment, it is also worth highlighting that capacity is not the only consideration. A director may have plenty of capacity but have a bad reputation, have a poor infrastructure at their directorship firm, and charge ex-orbitant fees. Most investors would not likely want this type of director to sit on the boards of any hedge funds they invest in. So as you can see, capacity, while important, should certainly not be the sole determining factor in evaluating director quality or effectiveness.

When investors are evaluating directors, it is important to clarify how they approach the issue of capacity. Some questions you may want to ask include:

- As a firm do you institute any strict capacity limits?
- If not:
  (a) Why not?
  (b) Who determines when a director is running thin on additional capacity? For example, is this decision left up to the individual directors themselves? Or instead, are other people at the firm monitoring this?
  (c) How do fund-specific considerations you consider impact director capacity limits for more challenging hedge fund engagement (i.e., one that has many illiquids vs. one that is completely liquid—and therefore there may be less time required to valuation oversight issues)?

This doesn't mean that valuation considerations are not important for liquid managers but if a director, for example, is presented with multiple reports from the administrator and manager showing that a hedge fund manager's portfolio, sometimes called their book, was 100% priced via readily available market quotes and the manager didn't effectively exercise any discretion in this matter (i.e., there is no manager valuation memorandum for the director to review), then they are likely spending less time with the hedge fund manager discussing such issues. In aggregate, there could be several issues like this and in total the director can reasonably spend more or less time with different managers.

Therefore, the argument could be advanced that if a manager spends less time with some managers and more time with others, then on average this may also influence the capacity discussion to bode more favorably one way or the other. Let us consider the following example to clarify this point.

Related Director Resource Allocation Capacity Considerations

Let's revisit our old friend Mr. Moran. As you may remember Mr. Moran is the founder of a directorship service company and he himself works as an independent director for hedge funds. Mr. Moran's firm is full of other high-quality directors. These include a newly hired director, Mr. Doyle. Let's say that for the purposes of this example, Mr. Moran and Mr. Doyle sit on three different hedge fund boards among them. In one of these three instances let's say both of them sit on the same board. Let us further assume for the purposes of this example that they have been sitting on these fund boards for a while and can on average estimate how much time in total they spend working on each particular fund. The detail of their board memberships is outlined in Exhibit 4.4.

We can now analyze the implications of this scenario with regards to director capacity. For starters based on the amount of time each individual director allocates, we can see that they rank the following in order of time taken: Fund 3 (2 days), Fund 2 (0.5 day), and then Fund 1 (1.5 days). This can imply a few things. As noted above maybe there are certain things relative to Fund 3's strategy,

EXHIBIT 4.4 Summary of Average Board Member Time Allocations

	Mr. Moran	Mr. Doyle
Fund 1 (run by HF manager X)	Yes; 1.5 days per year	No
Fund 2 (run by HF manager Y)	Yes; 0.5 day per year	Yes; 0.5 day per year
Fund 3 (run by HF manager Z)	No	Yes; 2 days per year

such as a relatively greater presence of illiquid holdings as compared with Fund 2 and Fund 1. Or perhaps in the past Fund 3 was embroiled in a number of issues such as litigation, structural changes, key personnel turnover, etc., that require more attention from directors. Alternatively, it could be that hedge fund manager Z simply is more actively engaged with their directors than the other funds.

As an aside does this mean hedge fund manager Z is a better hedge fund manager? Not necessarily; it just plainly means that they devote more time to talking to their directors. Maybe it's because they genuinely value the directors' input. Or maybe it's because they are unsure how to handle many basic issues and they need the director to guide them. Perhaps it's because they don't want to be accountable for very much and are looking for a scapegoat (i.e., the director) on which to blame problems regarding certain decisions if they don't work out. Who knows, maybe it's all of these reasons and some other ones. The point is that the director spends more time with this fund than with others.

Compiling Director Capacity Figures

When discussing director capacity so far, we have presented different scenarios that nicely summarize all of the different positions held by different directors. Even when such information is presented in a succinct and organized format, as we have discussed, there are still many potential open-ended questions and gray areas that may come about when determining whether or not a director is over or under acceptable capacity levels. Another problem, however, facing investors and hedge funds in the market is that of course the real world isn't as simple as we make it seem.

Wouldn't it be nice if directors were required to provide a detailed list of all the funds they currently sit on and historically sat on? Wouldn't it also be nice if regulators collected, reviewed, scrubbed, and made these data publicly available to investors? Of course it would, but they typically don't, not under the current regimes anyways. The Cayman Islands has discussed a proposal for such a database, but the time frame and final nature of any eventual database is yet to be determined. For reference, perspectives on database proposals are contained in the interviews in Chapter 10.

Depending on whom you ask it's not even that the information is necessarily a secret; it's just not easy to find. So let's discuss some ways that you could collect this information on your own. First, you could approach the directors themselves. You could go directly to them and ask for a list of all the funds they sit on and compile it yourself. Good luck with that.

Since that didn't work, you could then approach the problem from other side. namely, with the hedge fund themselves. You could go around to hedge funds and ask them who sits on their boards. Once again likely a dead end. There is another option that is to search the regulatory filings related to the hedge funds on which these directors serve, which can provide details concerning who serves on the boards of funds. This approach has been taken by journalists who report on this subject to research hedge fund US Security and Exchange Commission filings such as Form D. Of course such searches will not provide a complete picture of how many boards directors serve on, but it may point you in the right direction. Ultimately, conducting massive searches of the full universe of hedge fund regulatory filings is not very practical either. As such, the best approach is still just to do direct due diligence with the directors themselves. Talking to others in the industry may also help provide some perspective on the matter, but once again pinning down specifics unless the directors disclose it themselves can be nearly impossible.

Evaluating Director Capacity—How Many Directorships Are Too Many?

Ultimately, from the perspective of hedge funds, investors, and indeed directors themselves the question becomes, how many directorships are too many?

I would propose that this is a bad question that seeks to oversimplify the issue. Certainly there are extremes (i.e., over 300 directorships) but when you get more within the realm of reality, what is more commonly acceptable these days? Is 15 appropriate? What about 20? A better question would be perhaps as a reader, whatever your situation in the hedge fund food chain, how many do you think are too many?

The lazy way out is just to pick a number and use it as your benchmark. However, does this really accomplish anything? This isn't to say that you shouldn't have guidelines; it is rather to emphasize the need to make informed decisions about director capacity as opposed to simply being overly inclusive or exclusive. As we have highlighted in this discussion when analyzing directorships sometimes the numbers can be misleading. You know, it's a bit reminiscent of how many traditional investment consultants work to screen funds for different searches. Let's briefly summarize this process and you'll see how setting overly rigid benchmarks can lead to bad decision making.

Let's say that you are a university endowment and you work with an investment consultant to assist in determining what sectors and how much they should investment in order to fund their obligations. Sometimes all kinds of fairly complicated actuarial assumptions and analysis can go into determining what the appropriate returns on investment actually are, but we're putting those aside for the purposes of our example. Continuing along, let's further assume that the investment consultant suggests that the endowment should invest $30 million in global macro hedge funds as part of their overall allocation strategy. Assuming they agree, the consultant would then begin the search process of locating the appropriate hedge fund manager(s) by typically issuing a request for proposal, which is typically abbreviated by the initials RFP. As part of the RFP process, the managers who wish to throw their name in the hat would be required to answer a series of questions about their firms and their funds. Think of it like a due diligence questionnaire they are asked to complete. As part of this process, the consultant may request that certain pieces of information be completed in predefined charts that generally can't be changed. They could, for example, request this information either in an Excel file or via a form on the consultant's website.

As anyone who has ever completed an RFP may know, each hedge fund manager is different and each hedge fund manager's information might not fit neatly into the consultant's predefined categories. Problems for hedge fund managers in completing these forms typically arise more often in the quantitative categories of information such as assets under management, fund performance, or personnel figures. Of course, in many instances the manager may have the ability to submit accompanying disclosures and notes surrounding the data they fill in the form. The problem is that by the time anyone on the consultant's side gets around to reading any of these disclosures, if they read them at all, it may be too late. This is not to disparage the work of consultants at all. On the contrary, it is to highlight that that they are not typically given enough credit based on the resources available for the task at hand. You see, for many of these searches the consultants are deluded with responses. In order to facilitate the sorting process many of them set firm requirements as to what is acceptable and what is not.

This allows them to winnow down the field and devote more resources to vetting those managers that, in their opinion, are more qualified for the search. Additionally, many consultants already have the details of many managers on file and they have to sort through them as well, which further broadens the initial search field.

Returning to our example, in this case the consultant may say that they only want to invest with managers that have over $200 million in commingled global macro funds. Well, let's consider a fund that has $180 million in a master–feeder complex of pooled vehicles and $60 million in a separately managed account. Let's further assume that in the consultants' predetermined forms there was only one space to put in historical assets under management of pooled vehicles and not separate accounts; there was a different table for that. Seeking to fill out the consultants forms correctly let's say that the manager split up the two amounts and included the appropriate statements elsewhere in the RFP clarifying how they are over the $200 million required limit. Ok, they have now just been disqualified by the consultants' screening process. Typically, the consultant may not dig any deeper into the manager to find out more details.

Not fair, you say? Well, it's really a no win situation for the manager. If they would have included the pooled vehicle assets as being the total of the pooled vehicles ($180 million) and the separately managed account ($60 million), then that would not exactly have been accurate, would it? After all, the question asked for total in commingled funds, not separate accounts.

You might think this example is splitting hairs a bit, and that it shouldn't matter. Why should the consultant care, as long as the manager has a chance to explain themselves later? Well, first off the manager often has to attest at the end of the RFP that all the information is true, but besides that it doesn't really reflect too well on the manager if they are seen as being less than accurate in providing certain details. We also should mention that many hedge fund managers are conscious of the intricacies of this process. Indeed some larger asset management firms employ ex-consultants who are familiar with expertise in how to successfully navigate the consulting process including how to best fill out these types of forms so that managers are included in searches and reflect well in overall rankings.

Lest we digress too much into the equitableness of investment consultant searches, let us return to our discussion of how this relates to capacity limits. As we have highlighted earlier in this discussion, there are difficulties in determining how many boards certain directors serve on. Some investors have taken the approach to flat out ask directors to put the answer in writing as part of a director due diligence questionnaire they are asked to complete.

So, for example, let's say for whatever reason an investor determined that a director should not sit on more than 30 individual fund boards. They set this as a hard rule and if a director sits on more than 30 boards, then it doesn't necessarily imply that the investor won't ultimately allocate to a hedge fund, but rather that this will be noted as a deficiency when assessing the overall risk of the hedge fund.

Now let's say in the director DDQ the investor asks the following question, "How many individual fund boards do you sit on?" Let's say the director responds as follows, "I have 25 board relationships with hedge fund managers." Similar to the issues presented with our consultant search example above, it doesn't exactly answer the precise question being asked, does it? If we take it a step further and say that the director was only asked for a number, perhaps in a chart, and had to put the details clarifying the response of 25 somewhere else. Do you see how a similar scenario to our consultant search example may also arise?

Let's assume that the investor interprets this answer to mean that 25 board relationships equals 25 directorships. Who knows, maybe it does. We can't say for sure based on the limited information we have. In either case, the investor would likely deem this to be below the limit of 30 and move on.

What if an investor is unsure how to interpret this figure? Ideally they would go back to the director for clarification. Unfortunately, for a number of reasons not all investors take the time to do this. Some may even foolishly take the perspective that it's not their job to verify this information. After all, directors wouldn't lie, would they? Others may go back and follow up with the director.

Now let's change the scenario a bit and clarify that the director's "25 board relationships" actually means that this director works with 25 hedge fund management firms but sits on 65 different fund boards across these relationships. In our example, let's say the director wants to pursue full disclosure, and answers the question asked. They respond with an answer of 65. As absurd as it may seem, some investors, just like the consultants in our previous example, may not follow up on this matter and simply view 65 as being greater than 30 and note this as a deficiency.

What about the scenario where a director may respond with both figures? That is to say both 25 board relationships and 65 individual different fund boards. It's anyone's guess how an investor may interpret this.

So once again why all the smoke and mirrors and careful language surrounding this topic? Well, when asked with this question, perhaps fearful of negative connotations of director's spreading themselves too thin, some directors may similarly respond with a number that reflects the lower number of relationships as opposed to the larger number of total board positions. Not to repeat myself, but once again this is not to imply in any way that directors are dishonest or seeking to mislead anyone. To be gracious, perhaps this is how they have become used to answering the question. Or perhaps indeed, they prefer to show a smaller number in response to this question to assuage any capacity concerns. Similarly, the previous example is not to suggest that investors cannot ask follow-up questions or are incapable of deciphering director speak. Instead, the point is to demonstrate that there can be reasonable confusion regarding this point and it is worth asking some additional questions to clarify exactly what figures we are talking about.

Director Capacity Survey Data

Earlier in this book, in Chapter 3, we referenced recent survey data from the 2013 Cayman Islands Monetary Authority ("CIMA") survey. For reference, this survey collected 179 respondents from hedge fund managers, service providers (i.e., administrators, lawyers, accountants), directors, and investors all over the world. This survey covered a wide variety of topics relating to many different aspects of governance and the role of fund directors. As it relates to our discussion here, to provide some practical perspective on this matter we can examine some of the survey results regarding director capacity:

- 53% of the entire survey group felt that it was a weakness that directors didn't have enough capacity. The survey frames this as "ensuring directors have sufficient time to fully apply themselves to every board." Only 49% of hedge fund managers and 47% of service providers surveyed viewed this as a weakness. Not surprisingly, a greater percentage of investors, 64%, viewed this as a weakness. Somewhat surprising, however, is that the survey data showed that 63% of directors agreed with investors that this was a weakness.

- When asked "What information was needed to assess the robustness of the corporate governance standards in Cayman Islands domiciled fund?" overwhelmingly investors at 89% felt that knowledge of the number of directorships held by each director was needed to make a corporate governance assessment. As with the previous item we discussed, investors and directors were once again surprisingly more closely aligned in this area with 65% feeling the information was needed. Similarly, hedge funds and service providers were more closely aligned, albeit further apart, in this area. Specifically 42% of service providers felt that disclosing the number of directorships was required as compared with 72% of those hedge funds surveyed.

- 46% of investors surveyed indicated that they had requested but not received information regarding the number of directorships held.

- With regards to capacity one of the more interesting questions asked was, "When considering the independence of a director, is it important to implement regulatory standards requiring a director to hold positions for more than one manager, or that no more than 50% of their revenue relate to one manager (25% when the services are provided by a company) or to implement an 'independence' standard similar to this?" Directors were effectively split in their responses with 50% in favor versus 44% against, with 6% uncertain. Investors were once again aligned with directors with 50% in favor and 32% against, with 14% unsure. A slim majority of hedge funds, 51% were against limits on the number of positions held. Service providers were similarly divided over the issue with 45% in favor of such limits while 48% were against them.

- 61% of those surveyed felt that limits on directorships should be based on the number of manager relationships as compared with 39% who were in favor of limits on an absolute number of directorships.

- 91% of those surveyed felt that director limits would contribute to improved corporate governance practices.

The survey also inquired about the controversial question on what limits on the number of these directorships should actually be. Interestingly these results show that 11% of investors supported more than 50 manager relationships for directors as compared with no support for this among investors. Similarly, directors showed no support for limits fewer than 10, between 41 and 50, and between 31 and 40. Investor support was also mixed among the different categories, showing a continued lack of consensus in this area. However, as we outlined in Chapter 3 these results should perhaps be taken with a grain of salt as investors were the smallest group represented. In general, hedge funds' and directors' opinions were aligned with over 30% of both groups expressing support at limit levels between 11 and 20.

It is also interesting to note that out of the group of those who did support limits on manager relationships, no group supported more than 100 relationships. Hedge funds at 72% overwhelmingly supported limits between 26 and 50 relationships. Although investors in general favored lower limits of fewer than 10 and between 11 and 25, the majority of the other groups (i.e., investors, directors, and service providers) were largely split over the issue.

The CIMA survey data provide a number of interesting insights into opinions regarding director capacity. As we outlined in Chapter 3, CIMA should be commended for taking proactive approach to gauging market opinions in this area. The Caymans has since passed regulations outlining enhanced oversight of directors that was likely informed by these survey data. For reference a further discussion of these laws and trends in this area is outlined in the interviews in Chapter 10.

Final Comments on Director Capacity

By now you may feel we have covered the issue of director capacity ad nauseam. You might also be thinking that it's a bit ridiculous that such a seemingly straightforward issue should merit such industry attention. You would be correct on both accounts; however, this doesn't make the issue any less contentious or important. Understanding current director commitments is a key piece of information that should be considered by both hedge funds and investors when evaluating fund governance. As we have highlighted throughout this book, however, capacity itself should not be the sole or determining factor in evaluating directors, but rather a contributing factor to an assessment of a director's overall effectiveness in implementing governance.

GAUGING INDIVIDUAL SERVICE PROVIDER QUALITY AND WEIGHT IN EXTERNAL GOVERNANCE

If a service provider charges a hedge fund more, compared with other service providers that perform different functions, should an investor give that service provider more weight in evaluating their importance in the overall external governance of the fund? Most investors would likely say no. But what if that service provider performs what an investor deems to be more critical services for a fund? This question perhaps gets a bit of a different response from investors. But what services are "critical" to one investor may not be to another. What about the importance to investors of service providers that are investor facing versus internal to the fund's daily investing activities?

These questions illustrate some of the issues investors may have in assigning importance levels or weights to the governance roles of different external service providers. Investors will likely find that this is more art than science. Similar to the field of due diligence, investors are often better served in many areas by attempting to gauge more broad assessments of service provider quality as opposed to creating what may seem to be overly precise external governance measurement scales. So, for example, does it really mean anything if an investor scores one administrator on a scale of 1–10 as a 2 and another as 3? Certainly you could have predefined criteria that cause different administrators to earn different scores; however, this approach suffers from two major problems. The first is that general scoring categories do not take into account the unique differences of each administrator. Second, if the criteria for each category are not designed correctly, there can be too much subjection within each of the criteria. So, for example, let us say that one of the categories by which an investor attempted to score an administrator was "quality of fund accounting team." "Quality" is a subjective term. Some may view the fact that a fund accounting professional was a certified public accountant, commonly referred to as CPA, as an indication of quality. Others may view the fact that an individual is knowledgeable of a particular hedge fund's account and has been with the team for a number of years to be a better indication of quality. It is not necessarily a black and white decision for all investors. As such, in evaluating the quality of a particular service provider, which relates directly to their ability to provide efficient governance oversight, an investor would perhaps be initially better served by establishing core criteria that are easily determinable.

So continuing our fund administration example, it would be much easier for an investor to evaluate if a fund administrator has undergone a SSAE 16 (formerly known as SAS 70) type 1 or 2 review. The administrator either has or hasn't undergone this review. Investors can then definitively determine if an administrator has met a definable minimum set of criteria. The weight assigned to the importance of such definable criteria, as indicated above, can then be subjective to investors. However, from a best practice perspective, the majority of investors would agree that it gives them an additional level of comfort if an administrator has undergone such a review. Such reviews also give many investors an enhanced sense of confidence that a third party other than the administrator is checking certain internal controls mandated by the SSAE 16 review process. This then further suggests to many investors that the administrator has better controls, and a lower operational control failure risk profile as compared with other administrators. This confidence gives many investors, therefore, enhanced confidence that the administrator is less likely to deviate from certain processes, and therefore have more consistency in their implementation of governance at the fund level. Of course, this line of thinking only analyzes one area of the overall administrator external governance evaluation process and should not be taken in isolation to summarize the entire administrator governance evaluation process.

CONCLUSION

In this chapter we have discussed the relationship between hedge fund service providers and governance. As part of this discussion we highlighted the practicalities of investors, focusing on certain so-called traditional key service providers, as opposed to ancillary providers. Our discussion also provided some perspective on the distinction between hedge fund service provider operations and governance oversight. We then provided examples of the ways in which service providers such as administrators and prime brokers can implement governance at the hedge fund level. Finally, we provided an overview of discussions of director capacity.

In seeking to evaluate hedge fund governance, it is important to focus on not only the hedge fund itself but also service providers. While fund directors are clearly a key component to evaluating service providers, they are not the entire story. As we have highlighted in this chapter, other service providers such as auditors, administrators, and prime brokers can also play critical roles in the overall hedge fund governance framework.

REFERENCES

Caulfield, C., 2009. Citco still on hook in $550M hedge fund fraud suit. Law360, January 6.

Corgentum Consulting, 2010. The Madoff Effect—An Analysis of Operational Due Diligence Trends. Available at: http://www.corgentum.com/research/the-madoff-effect-an-analysis-of-operational-due-diligence-trends.html.

Feeley, J., Lucoff, M., 2011. Lancer Group founder Michael Lauer acquitted of stock fraud in hedge funds. Bloomberg, April 27.

Lashmar, P., 2003. Oops, I lost cash again. The Independent, May 11.

Scharfman, J., 2008. Hedge fund operational due diligence: understanding the risks. Wiley Finance, Hoboken, NJ.

Touryalai, H., 2011. Protection racket. Forbes, April 6.

Uhlman, L., 2011. Lancer Group receiver, Citco Group reach $5M settlement. Law360, August 31.

Chapter 5

Hedge Fund Internal Governance Mechanisms

Chapter Outline Head

INTRODUCTION TO HEDGE FUND GOVERNANCE MECHANISMS

Throughout this chapter we will be discussing governance as it functions from within the hedge fund. If you're reading the chapters of this book sequentially, you may be asking why we didn't start with analyzing governance at the hedge fund itself. Well, for starters, this is traditionally, in large part, not where discussions of governance have been focused. As we outlined earlier in this book, such governance concepts traditionally focus on fund boards. Governance is much more than just the board of directors and there is a continuing acceptance of this expanding definition.

Governance is an interrelated concept. It's analysis in a hedge fund context and it should not be limited to a single segment of the hedge fund investing relationship. Nor should control and implementation of governance be thought of as residing within a single particular silo of authority such as the board of directors. Rather governance is a multifaceted concept over which several different parties have influence.

WHY ARE HEDGE FUNDS NOW TALKING ABOUT GOVERNANCE?

Increasingly investors may have noticed the word governance cropping up in hedge fund market presentations. The question could be asked as to why hedge funds have recently taken such a renewed interest in the subject. Has anything materially changed in the way that they operate their funds that has massive governance implications, which now requires significant new explanation?

Perhaps one of the factors contributing to the rise of governance in these presentations, which are appropriately commonly referred to as pitchbooks, is the increased marketing flexibility afforded in the United States at least by regulatory changes such as the Jumpstart Our Business Startups Act, which is more commonly known as the JOBS Act. Are such changes good for governance?

IS THE JOBS ACT GOOD FOR HEDGE FUND GOVERNANCE?

In July 2013, the SEC adopted a rule that overturned an 80-year advertising ban. Under the lifting of these restrictions hedge funds now gained the ability to advertise publicly, well kind of, for the first time. The rule, which passed by a 4-1 vote, came about because of initiatives from the JOBS Act to be completed by the SEC (Primack, 2013). When the removal of such bans happened, there was much media fanfare made that this would open the flood gates for fund-raising from the masses. Some in the media had even suggested that we might start to hear hedge fund ads on the radio or see hedge fund billboards (Goodman, 2012).

Many in the hedge fund community, at least those looking to raise capital or start new funds, likely welcomed the rule change due to the increase in the flexibility in marketing it provides them. Their zeal may only be matched by the deluge of marketing and advertising professionals who are now seeing a new channel of potential business open up. Perhaps as an example of how exciting they were at the potential advertising revenue, I even started receiving calls from radio stations explaining how they were dedicating resources to this area and were expecting to be running hedge fund radio advertisements. Was all this excitement much ado about nothing? Well, I've never heard a hedge fund radio advertisement or seen a billboard posted along the side of the road during my commute to the office, but hedge funds have begun to advertise more. Some have not taken to producing outright advertisements as such, but have instead begun adding more information to their websites, including video interviews with key personnel, and making more frequent media appearances. Others have taken a more direct approach, and have even taken to make video commercials complete with floating formulas and peppy Starbucks-style background music (Stevenson, 2014). Makes you want to invest, right? Joking aside, we should consider the impact, if any, such marketing freedom, called "general solicitations" in legalese, has on governance. Is such increased marketing flexibility even a legitimate concern for investors who allocate to established hedge funds?

DOES ENHANCED FLEXIBILITY PROMOTE BETTER GOVERNANCE?

For starters, many established large hedge funds have simply not wanted to proactively put themselves in the spotlight (FINalternatives, 2014). Additionally, many hedge funds build their businesses around institutional capital. This can be from endowments and foundations, pension funds and sovereign funds, and the like. While these types of institutional clients typically read the papers and may be subjected to advertising, they generally are first introduced to managers in a number of different ways and don't necessarily interact with the traditional type of advertising that the JOBS Act rule changes influence. One such method is via industry conferences. At the time of its implementation, the new JOBS Act rules didn't really impact this sector at all. Another method that used to be more popular but has perhaps waned slightly is the traditional capital introduction services. Once again the rule changes really had no ramifications on this. With such wide-ranging areas of the hedge fund asset raising lifecycle uncovered, the question should be raised whether simply technical compliance with the law is enough to promote good governance.

Yet another common method used to locate hedge funds by these institutions is through the use of traditional investment consultants. Another group that the JOBS Act rules don't directly address. These investment consulting firms typically assist institutions in crafting searches and locating managers who are attractive from an investment perspective. As we outlined earlier in this book, hedge funds typically get on the consultants' radar by reporting into industry performance databases, applying directly to be listed in consultant databases, and through many of the traditional institutional industry channels such as industry conferences and events.

In the past, certain traditional investment consultants may have recommended hedge funds to large institutional investors making broad marketing claims related to the fund managers they recommend or the due diligence that the consultant themselves had performed on the fund manager. Sometimes these claims come up for debate as was the case where investors alleged that a consultant, Hennessee Group LLC, didn't perform adequate due diligence before recommending the fraudulent Bayou fund. In Hennessee's case one suit brought by investors was South Cherry Street, LLC v. Hennessee Group LLC [573 F.3d

98 (2d Cit. 2009)]. Ultimately, Hennessee Group and Charles J. Gradante, the firm's cofounder and principal, settled with the SEC in this matter for $814,000 (Halonen, 2009).

As part of a settlement, Hennessee Group and Mr. Gradante were "required to adopt policies to ensure adequate disclosures in the future" (Halonen, 2009). A few years after cases such as this, however, the SEC missed an opportunity by not including these types of fund-raising relationships when redesigning the marketing rules via the JOBS Act. Once again we can raise the question, does technical adherence to such incomplete rules therefore represent good governance?

This is not to fault the investment consulting industry, which provides a valuable service to many institutional clients. Rather it is to highlight that regulators such as the SEC may have missed the boat with regards to taking the opportunity to establish effective due diligence and governance standards around both hedge funds directly and, more appropriate to this discussion, those that promote and recommend hedge funds such as traditional investment consultants. Such regulations would likely be more impactful in influencing the largest hedge fund investor groups (i.e., institutions) rather than the smaller retail marketplace. The goal is not to single out the SEC; instead, it is to highlight that investors should consider that a hedge fund's technical compliance with rules may not be enough to implement good governance.

IS TECHNICAL COMPLIANCE ENOUGH FOR GOOD GOVERNANCE?

First, while the specifics of the rule change do provide more flexibility with regards to hedge fund advertising they do not completely remove them. Funds must still make efforts to verify that a person is an accredited investor. This is a bit of a paradox, because certain reports suggest that this will increase hedge fund marketing toward the retail market, but many in the retail market would not necessarily meet the accredited investor hurdle. Perhaps the theory is that those hedge funds with lower minimums seeking wealthy individuals will be able to have success in raising capital via broader more traditional marketing efforts.

Such technicalities can present legitimate compliance-related governance concerns. For example, a hedge fund may claim that it is in full compliance with the law before accepting new subscriptions. This can include review of the investor's suitability and anti-money laundering checks. In reality, however, many hedge funds simply ask investors to attest that they are suitable. That is to say they don't typically ask to see investor bank statements and asset holdings to verify suitability for hedge fund investing. Second, many related investor presubscription checks, such as anti-money laundering reviews, are delegated to service providers such as administrators. Uh oh, not the magic "d" word again! Yes, and with this delegation as we have outlined earlier, you can see how it can start to become a bit messy to determine who's really in charge.

Returning to the compliance-related governance concerns, it is worth noting that much of the JOBS Act governance concerns come not from the actual subscription process itself but the marketing that goes on prior to such subscriptions. There are reams of technical rules regarding what hedge funds can and cannot say during the marketing process. This includes ensuring that pitchbook presentations, and other materials, have the appropriate disclosures. Furthermore, in actual in-person meetings and conference speeches, for example, hedge funds can't use magic legal words such as "guarantee"; otherwise they can find themselves in violation of the law. As an aside, this isn't simply a US problem. In certain jurisdictions, for example, hedge fund personnel must be accompanied by registered local representatives as well; otherwise the whole process could be deemed illegal.

From a governance perspective the question becomes: not only does a hedge fund understand the technicalities of such rules but are they implementing them? To take it a step further, if the hedge fund is indeed implementing such changes, the real governance assessment question is how well they are doing it. A common hedge fund reply when posed with such questions may be something to the effect of "We have that covered. Everything goes through legal before we send it out." With such an answer are we now convinced that this fund has instituted best practice governance oversight in this area? Well, certainly the hedge fund's in-house general counsel would likely know if something is illegal or not, but what about beyond that? For example, wouldn't it be possible, despite the new freedoms of the JOBS Act, for a hedge fund marketing person to take a perfectly buttoned-up presentation replete with appropriate disclosures, and make claims or promises about performance that violate the law? I can hear the objections at the trial of the investor who then loses money with the hedge fund and sues now. "Ah but the hedge fund marketing person protected herself. She said the magic words that 'past performance is not indicative of future results' so she's now protected." Or, "Any comments made by my client were simply marketing puffery, the investor should have read the documents more carefully." These arguments may be accurate, but the point we are highlighting here is that just because a hedge fund is in technical compliance with the JOBS Act rules, for example, this doesn't mean that they necessarily are implementing best practice governance oversight.

So what else is to be done? Well, for example, does the hedge fund institute new hire training for marketing personnel with regards to what they can and can't say to investors? Furthermore, as the laws change, is such training updated on an ongoing basis? You can see how perhaps a legal review of all materials plus ongoing compliance training for marketing personnel can lead to a better governance oversight situation of such issues as opposed to simply technical compliance.

This example highlights two important points about hedge fund governance. First, it shows how in many cases, mere technical compliance does not represent best practice governance. Indeed, there is often room for improvement in the governance area beyond simple technical compliance.

Second, it demonstrates the interconnected nature of governance. In our example, we discussed what many would initially consider to primarily be a business development and fund-raising issue, the JOBS Act, and expanded the issue to areas of hedge fund legal and compliance. This is the interconnected nature of governance and demonstrates how governance issues often are influenced by not only a variety of external factors, such as the regulatory impact of the JOBS Act, but multiple in-house hedge fund elements as well.

I SAID GOVERNANCE, DIDN'T I?

Returning to our initial discussion of why there has been an increased focus on governance by hedge funds, another more likely contributing factor is that investors are increasingly enamored and concerned with governance. They are asking more questions about the subject and hedge funds want to show that they are paying attention. The problem, however, as we have pointed out, is that governance is sometimes difficult to define. Outside of the board of directors, what else would go in the governance sections? Well, as we have discussed, this perhaps would be a good opportunity for funds to highlight the way in which they implement appropriate controls and oversight. As this issue has become more controversial, some funds seemingly do not even want to draw investors' attention to offshore fund boards when discussing governance as they may not even be mentioned in pitchbooks at all. Indeed, many of these governance sections may not even mention the board of directors. Other funds seem to be framing governance as being equated to compliance oversight. Yet others attempt to demonstrate strong governance through organizational charts that demonstrate dedicated personnel for certain functions. While we are not saying that all of this is not well and good, do the choices of what to include or omit in these presentations do much to promote a better understanding of governance? Well, this type of information certainly doesn't hurt, but as we have outlined governance is a much broader subject than any one area. To further clarify this, let's continue our discussion of governance classification in the next section.

GOVERNANCE MECHANISM CLASSIFICATION CHALLENGES

Before we proceed to discuss internal hedge fund governance mechanisms, it is worth pausing for a moment to highlight some disagreements that may arise with regards to the classification of these mechanisms. Depending on a number of factors including your role in hedge fund industry, different readers of this book might take different perspectives on classifying certain governance mechanisms and responsibilities. So, for example, later in this chapter we will discuss the issue of hedge fund compensation arrangements and its relationship to hedge fund governance.

Some may argue that this area is not a governance issue at all. Even if it is, it's not something that investors should focus on when discussing governance.

How much people get paid should be the exclusive purview of hedge funds, shouldn't it?

After all, couldn't it be argued that hedge fund management companies, not investors or the funds they invest in, are the ones actually writing the checks to their employees? As such, why should investors care or even have a right or interest in looking into the way hedge funds structure their compensation arrangements? Is a practice correctly being classified under the category of governance if it doesn't have the potential to hurt investors? Or taken a step further, if a hedge fund manager tells you something to the effect of "this is a management company, not a fund level expense so don't worry about it," does this mean that an investor should not, or even doesn't have a right to, classify the issue under governance?

On the other hand, the perspective could be taken that hedge fund manager compensation involves simply more than cutting checks to employees. It could further be argued that these compensation arrangements have implications in numerous aspects of the continued operation of the fund, including retaining employees, the attracting of new employees, and risk taking within the funds, to name a few. Furthermore, if you look at the world of traditional corporate governance, compensation has historically been a key issue (Bebchuk and Fried, 2006). Which side of this argument is correct?

If you work at a hedge fund, and are happy with your compensation arrangement, you may fall on the side of the manager. If you are an investor who wants more transparency, oversight, and influence in this area, you likely are in the more conservative camp. The point is that from a governance perspective it ultimately doesn't matter whether you as a reader decided that this is an issue that falls squarely within the responsibility of the hedge fund or whether the investors should have more influence in this respect. This is the wrong way to think about governance.

Instead, a better approach is to think about the issue itself. At the end of the day, what is the best approach to promote good governance at the hedge fund? Period, end of story. Developing a solution that works to promote this governance is what matters. Both fund managers and investors are partners in establishing, policing, and monitoring the implementation of these good governance solutions in each of these respective areas and the obligation cannot be outsourced or ignored. Continuing our compensation example, regardless of whether you file the issue of undergovernance or not, an investor would be foolish to assume that the hedge fund manager should maintain sole discretion in this area and they don't have to worry about it. This puts too much power in the hands of the manager.

Similarly, a hedge fund that kowtows to every investor demand about how compensation should be structured isn't doing their job to promote good governance either. In summary, the bottom line is that while classification of governance mechanisms and responsibilities can help to think about a framework for good governance, reasonable minds may disagree over the classifications.

Whether you agree or disagree with the classifications outlined in this book, the core governance concepts are what are important. By focusing on the core governance concepts, different classification systems may be perfectly acceptable as long as the issues are still being addressed. You should keep this in mind as you read this chapter and Chapter 6, which provides an overview of techniques for investor analysis of governance. If you wanted to, you could swap certain items we cover in this chapter into the next one and vice versa. Once again, the implementation and analysis of the governance practice is the key issue.

HEDGE FUND INTERNAL GOVERNANCE BY COMMITTEE?

Now that we have provided an overview on some of the governance classification challenges as well as highlighted the interrelated nature of governance to multiple parts of the hedge fund, we can now begin to discuss some common internal hedge fund governance mechanisms. To start off, we can highlight the role of one of most common internal governance mechanisms, namely, committees.

Corporations, especially publicly traded ones, have all sorts of committees. Examples of these can include audit committees, corporate governance committees, regulatory committees, and compensation committees. Typically the members of these committees include a mix of senior management and external third-party independent board members. In the United States the focus on corporate committees was increasingly galvanized in recent years due to the passage of laws such as Sarbanes–Oxley legislation, which focused on committees including the external oversight of audit committees.

Hedge funds, just like corporations, have committees. One of the key differences between hedge fund committees and the committees of public corporations is that the board of directors of the offshore funds hardly ever sit on the hedge fund committees. This is not to say that they might not be privy to the details of committee meetings, but the fact that, as we highlighted earlier in this book, independent offshore fund directors are not involved on a day-to-day basis or even monthly basis with fund operations and this would make their participation on committees difficult. This would be particularly true for hedge fund committees that meet more frequently. Generally, the involvement and oversight afforded by the board of directors is considered to be a positive for the overall governance structure of the firm. Why then do hedge fund investors accept an impliedly lesser standard of governance as compared with public companies?

Taking a page from the world of more traditional corporate governance, certain hedge funds have taken to forming internal policy committees that have often been seen in the public corporation world. We will proceed with our discussion by focusing on several common internal committees maintained by hedge funds and discuss the role they play in implementing governance oversight. This list is by no means comprehensive. Furthermore, some hedge funds may maintain committees that perform certain duties here, but do not have these exact names. That is fine. The goal here is not to provide a due diligence committee checklist. Instead we are trying to highlight the governance role played by these committees in overseeing hedge fund practices and resolving conflicts.

Investment Committee

As the name suggests, many hedge funds maintain investment committees to facilitate portfolio management and the overall investing process. In larger hedge funds in particular, investment committees can also assist in facilitating the sharing of information throughout the firm. The members of management committees typically include the fund's analysts and portfolio managers.

As with all of the committees we will discuss here, the installation of an investment committee is voluntary. That is to say it is completely a discretionary decision for the hedge fund whether to implement an investment committee or not. Similarly, once such a committee is in place, there are no laws or rules that outline who is on the committee, what information they review, who has decision-making authority, what the decision-making mechanism is (i.e., simple majority, 3/4 majority, etc.), or how frequently the committee meets. With all of this ambiguity you may be asking yourself, what benefit to governance, if any, such committees have.

Well, there are two points to note about this. First, based on common market practice, there is a general perception among investors of what constitutes a common set of committee practices. That is not to say that you won't find hedge funds that manage large sums of money with committee practices that constitute less than best practice governance. You definitely come across them. Why do investors tolerate this? Well, this relates to the second point we want to make in this regard. That is that a hedge fund generally doesn't attempt to conceal the rules of committees. At times if you ask, they may have a policy that addresses some of the key considerations we outlined above (i.e., committee membership, decision-making mechanism, etc.).

The fund is generally obligated to stick to these rules once they communicate them to investors. Of course, the hedge fund can change the rules once they are in place. An example of this would be switching from a simple majority decision-making mechanism to a 3/4 majority requirement; however, generally this information is available for investor review. That said, if investors don't inquire about such information, then they can't make any sort of informed assessment about the committee. Furthermore, this highlights the fact that simply having certain committees does not represent that the hedge fund will have continued good governance.

Consider two hedge funds that have investment committees. One meets weekly and one meets quarterly. Does one necessarily have better governance than the other? Well, generally more frequent meetings imply better oversight. There are also considerations, as noted above, as to what actually happens at such meetings. Investment committees are a good example of this because they may meet frequently, but if a single decision maker, such as the portfolio manager, controls the entire process as a dictator, then there is little independent oversight provided by this committee no matter how frequently they meet.

Management Committee

Management committees are typically responsible for all noninvestment functions of the firm. The items these committees address can include legal questions, personnel issues, oversight of information technology functions, business development, office administration, and marketing support. The members of management committees typically include the fund's senior management.

Valuation Committee

Valuation committees are generally responsible for overseeing the implementation of the fund's valuation policies and procedures. These committees are often multidisciplinary in nature and include representatives from multiple departments throughout the fund, including investments, operations, and compliance. Often times at these meetings the valuation committee will review not only any internal pricing work done by the fund but that of the fund's administrator or other third-party valuation consultants as well. Valuation committees are increasingly important from a governance perspective for hedge funds that value portions of their own holdings. This importance rose in the post-2008 financial crisis as many funds were left holding increasingly large percentages of illiquid positions. For reference the subject of valuation as it relates to governance is discussed in more detail in Chapter 9.

Business Continuity and Disaster Recovery Committee

After the events of widespread disaster events in hedge fund centers such as the Hong Kong SARS outbreak or Superstorm Sandy's impact on the East Coast of the United States business continuity planning and disaster recovery planning ("BCP/DR") has received increased attention from hedge funds and investors. To clarify BCP/DR can encompass a number of issues ranging from backup power generation and data replication to maintaining designated backup facilities from which employees can continue operations.

This attention has resulted in more hedge funds developing BCP/DR committees. The members of BCP/DR committees typically include representatives from senior management, facilities, and information technology. In practice, such committees primarily focus on plan updating and management while day-to-day oversight and implementation of BCP/DR typically falls to employees who are more in the weeds, so to speak, such as information technology personnel.

One of the key considerations that has been bumped up in the priority list of many BCP/DR committees has been oversight of plan testing to ensure functionality in the event of a business disruption or disaster event. Does a BCP/DR committee that implements any sort of testing at all comply with best practice governance standards? As you probably guessed by now, the answer is no. There are a wide range of testing options hedge fund's BCP/DR committees can implement that lie on different aspects of the governance spectrum.

Evaluating a fund manager's BCP/DR is a critical part of the overall BCP/DR committee governance assessment process. As noted above, as funds have continued to place increased focus on BCP/DR, plans have become increasingly detailed. This detail, however, is useless if the functionality of the plans is never tested. This is an important point to note from a governance perspective that relates not only to BCP/DR planning but also to other areas of fund governance. If, for example, a hedge fund has detailed compliance policies and procedures, but never checks to make sure they are being implemented, then what good are they?

Returning to BCP/DR as noted above, the detail in BCP/DR plans can often run the gamut from data backup and alternative backup power generation plans to phone notification trees and alternative gathering locations.

The best laid plans, however, can be useless if they are not properly implemented during a business disruption or disaster event. This is where the role of plan testing oversight by BCP/DR committees comes into play. Funds that test their BCP/DR plans more frequently are better prepared to deal with disaster events. More frequent testing via enhanced BCP/DR committee oversight represents better governance oversight of the function in this regard.

There is not one single prescribed method of testing that represents best practice. BCP/DR committees can design and oversee testing plans that can come in many different forms. There are technology-based tests that solely focus on restoring the fund's systems and hardware after a business disruption or disaster event. Other types of tests can be more focused on the role played by the fund's personnel in the event of a disaster event. If a fund's BCP/DR testing plan calls for the ability of the fund's employees to access the fund's systems remotely should the fund's primary office become inaccessible, then one type of test could have employees attempt to connect to the fund's network from outside of the office. Other types of tests can include more realistic simulations where employees stay home for the day and try to continue operations or instead continue working from a remote location.

To promote oversight in this area, the BCP/DR committee should take measure to not test one singular aspect of the fund's plans, but test how the different components work together. Furthermore, it is considered best practice from a governance perspective for a BCP/DR committee to work with the hedge fund's different departments, such as information technology, to evaluate test results. If deficiencies are noted, then the BCP/DR committee should monitor the implementation and subsequent testing of the appropriate fixes for such deficiencies.

Some key questions funds should consider when either implementing such committees or seeking to evaluate the governance oversight effectiveness of such committees include:

- Have we ever tested our BCP/DR?
- If so, when was the most recent test?
- What kind of test was it?
- How was the test carried out?
- Who at the firm was responsible for evaluating whether the test was a success?
- How has the firm's BCP/DR changed as a result of test feedback?
- How frequently does the firm plan to perform such tests going forward?

Another key consideration related to BCP/DR testing is whether or not employees have the necessary information and tools to remain in contact after a business disruption or disaster event. If a fund's BCP/DR does not contain this information, then it is up to the committee to ensure that such information is transparently available throughout the fund. But is information sharing enough to constitute best practice from a governance perspective?

As with BCP/DR in general, there is a wide range of options ranging from minimal levels (i.e., just sharing the information) to making it readily available throughout the fund. As an example, some funds provide employees with remote mobile devices. As part of BCP/DR and testing, a fund may load each employee's contact details onto these devices so employees can utilize this information to contact others in an emergency. If employees' details change or new employees join the firm, the revised information is automatically pushed out to employees' phones. Do BCP/DR committees that take advantage of more advanced technology in this regard represent better governance? Many would say yes.

Utilizing the BCP/DR committee as an example, we have highlighted here some of the range of options committees have in not only performing basic committee functions but also taking a step further to promote more active governance oversight within the hedge fund itself.

Risk Committee

Similar to the fact that investment committees are responsible for overseeing a fund's investments, risk committees are responsible for, you guessed it, overseeing risk. Specifically, these committees are traditionally responsible for monitoring market and credit risks as well as for risk reporting. As part of this process, the risk committee may be responsible for running a number of risk statistics for the funds including scenario analyses. The general goal of such risk committees is to provide oversight to ensure that the fund is not taking inappropriate levels of risk such as overweighting certain sectors or holdings. In regards to committee membership, the members traditionally include representatives of portfolio management and trading. Some hedge funds maintain dedicated chief risk officers or risk departments that consist of multiple individuals. In these cases, those individuals typically participate in this committee as well.

In some cases, risk committees may also be tasked with oversight of trading counterparties. In other cases, as we will discuss in the next section, this role is delegated to a separate counterparty committee.

Counterparty Committee

The counterparty committee is traditionally responsible for the review, approval, and monitoring of all counterparties and credit exposure undertaken by the firm's funds. These committees are typically involved in the initial vetting of counterparties. This vetting process can include background checks, credit reviews, and financial statement reviews. Once approved, these committees typically work with either in-house legal or third-party counsel to finalize counterparty agreements. Typically these agreements are negotiated around predefined fund terms such as requirements for limiting excess margin held by counterparties via bilateral arrangements with low threshold amounts.

These committees can also assist with ongoing oversight of counterparties. This oversight can include monitoring overall counterparty aggregate exposure across the firm's funds, credit spreads, counterparty stock prices, and news that may mention counterparties.

In certain cases, the actual nuts and bolts work of these counterparty reviews and oversight may be handled by individuals from different departments whose representatives sit on the counterparty committee. The members of the counterparty committee typically include members of portfolio management, legal, operations, and trading. If the firm maintains dedicated risk management or credit oversight personnel, they are generally members of this committee as well.

In some cases the counterparty committees may also provide broader oversight of all the firm's vendors including third-party consulting firms for functions such as compliance and information technology.

Compliance Committee

With the increased focus on compliance, increasingly hedge funds are maintaining dedicated compliance committees. These committees are typically in place to supervise the work of the firm's compliance function and facilitate discussion of compliance issues throughout the firm. Common issues discussed by these committees include:

- The ways in which new regulations may impact the firm
- The implementation of any new compliance policies and procedures

- Review of any compliance policy violations or near misses by the firm, funds, or employees
- Updates on the work of the compliance groups with regards to testing and training programs

Additionally, it is not uncommon these days for hedge funds to make use of third-party compliance consultants. In these cases, the compliance committee will typically discuss the work of these consultants including the results of any third-party mock audits or topic-specific training sessions. Members of the compliance committee typically include representatives from throughout the firm, including individuals from compliance, portfolio management, investor relations, and fund operations. It should also be noted that from a governance perspective, the presence and activities of compliance committees are particularly important for those hedge funds that are typically smaller in nature and that do not maintain dedicated compliance personnel. Without the presence of dedicated compliance personnel, such compliance committees can often provide enhanced oversight of the compliance function, which likely improves information sharing, oversight, and overall governance throughout the fund.

Best Execution Committee

Best execution is an umbrella term that relates primarily to the costs for executing trades. The exact categorization of these costs, however, is not always purely an issue of how much money is spent on commissions from trades, as often times execution quality can also depend on the amount of effort exerted in pursuing trade execution (Harris, 2002). When hedge funds discuss best execution, it can also include a number of other related concepts such as the speed of execution and information flow obtained from brokers.

For example, consider a hedge fund that trades in energy markets. Let's say this fund has a number of large brokerage firms who are willing to trade certain energy stocks on its behalf. Some offer commissions ranging from 1¢ to 3¢ per share. Another smaller broker charges 5¢ a share. This broker is located in the heart of an energy trading hub such as Houston, Texas. They often share valuable information with the fund regarding the energy sector. To clarify this is not illegal information, simply high-quality information they are able to put together based on their focus on the energy sector and on-the-ground knowledge. Is the hedge fund not following best practice governance if they trade with this higher-commission broker?

These are the types of issues the best execution committees would typically evaluate. On the one hand, it's more expensive compared with the lowest execution costs the fund could obtain with a larger broker. On the other hand, the information obtained from the Houston-based broker has legitimate value for the fund. There is not necessarily a clear-cut best practice answer to this question. That is why the quality of oversight of best execution committees can be crucially important in governance in general and in assisting to resolve conflicts of interest in particular.

In recent years, a growing trend among best execution committees has been to ask the firm's employees who are involved with brokerage, including traders, to rank brokers based on the quality of services provided. This can include any additional research brokers provide. This ranking process can often help guide the best execution committee's oversight of this matter.

Best execution committees will also typically have oversight in:

- Vetting new proposed brokers
- Performing ongoing monitoring of brokers
- Managing the sharing of brokerage commissions among multiple parties to prevent overconcentration to any one broker
- Reviewing actual commission rates paid to ensure both that the fund is utilizing its negotiating power and that the rates paid are competitive with the market
- Analyzing the decision to terminate counterparties

Best execution committees may also typically be involved in conducting ongoing monitoring of counterparties. In some cases, this oversight may also be carried out by other parts of the firm or other committees including the above-referenced counterparty committee.

As we have noted above, some hedge funds may not even have best execution committees. Certainly, from a governance perspective, having such a committee would be preferable to not having one. However, as we have also highlighted, vetting the specific duties and responsibilities of the committee is also crucially important to understanding the governance structure in place at the fund. Returning to our original example regarding energy trade commission rates, the question could be asked how the best execution committee may have become comfortable with paying higher commission rates based on additional beneficial broker information flow concerning the energy sector. This will help to evaluate whether there is actually any governance oversight in place, or if they are simply a rubber stamp committee.

Steering and Legislative Committees

In addition to the committees outlined above, hedge funds can also maintain a number of other committees. These committees may include:

- New products and accounts committees
- Steering committees
- Strategic planning committees
- Legislative policy committee
- Compensation committees
- Trade error committees

It is also worth noting that simply because a fund doesn't call a meeting of people a committee doesn't mean that the fund has no governance oversight over certain issues. Here we are talking about the distinction between a so-called formal committee and an informal committee. Formal committees, which are typically referred to by with the word "committee" in their title, are generally formal in the sense that they regularly schedule meetings with agenda, reports are prepared for them, and committee meeting minutes are taken. There can of course be other elements to formal committees but this is just a general outline.

Informal committees are typically just meetings of people to discuss certain issues. They can have agendas, reports prepared, and follow-up items too, but they are typically not formal in the sense that detailed minutes are recorded. That is not to say that an informal committee cannot have meeting minutes. However, the distinction we are drawing here is to show that some funds have more formal committees and some more informal ones. In some cases, an informal committee at one hedge fund may be more "formal" than a so-called formal committee at another hedge fund. It can be a case of semantics. On the whole, however, formal committees are generally considered to be more rigorous in their oversight as compared with informal committees. In analyzing governance it is often useful to inquire about the entire universe of hedge fund committees, both internal and external. The presence of informal committees can often serve to fill in the gaps of funds with weaker formal committee structures. Once again, the key issue here is to determine not only whether an internal hedge fund committee is formal or not but also how effective they are in implementing governance.

As we have outlined above, not every hedge fund will maintain these committees. This doesn't mean that these are necessarily bad hedge funds with poor governance. Just the opposite, in certain instances the presence of such committees could signal red flags from a due diligence perspective. Consider the example of a start-up or midsize fund with a large committee structure. Such a structure may be too detailed for the fund to be realistic or useful.

Often times in their zeal to prove to investors that they have institutional quality and robust governance procedures hedge funds may sometimes utilize boilerplate materials that may not be applicable to the funds. Feeding the funds these materials in many cases are those that assist them in formation and starting up such as law, accounting, and finance firms and compliance consultants. There is nothing wrong with such boilerplates as a starting point, but when a fund begins creating committees solely for the sake of making investors feel that more oversight is in place, it is a problem. As we have noted above, while it is easy to have the initial reaction that more committees imply better governance the key point is what these committees actually do. A handful of active committees may do more to promote internal governance oversight as compared with many nonactive committees.

HEDGE FUND CAPACITY AS A GOVERNANCE INDICATOR

In Chapter 4 we discussed the issue of fund director capacity. The notion of director capacity is similar to that of capacity for a hedge fund itself. To clarify, when applied to the context of a fund itself, as opposed to a director, the term capacity is often meant to provide an upper limit or range on the assets under management ("AUM") a particular fund or strategy could manage. This limit is typically contemplated so that it would not cause a detrimental impact on the strategy.

Looking at hedge fund AUM capacity, traditionally, capacity limits have been thought of as primarily artificial marketing limits. As such, the issue of hedge fund capacity has been largely ignored. Can notions of hedge fund capacity provide any governance insights?

Ambitious Capacity Limits Versus Reality

One way to attempt to answer this question is through an example. Let's say that a current hedge fund strategy manages $400 million across a master–feeder complex. This fund may tell investors that the strategy has an estimated capacity ranging from two to two-and-a-half billion.

Continuing our example, at this point it is worth clarifying what this capacity level quoted by the manager actually means. When a hedge fund manager quotes an investor a strategy capacity limit, this doesn't necessarily mean that the hedge fund strategy would be unable to allocate capital above this range, but rather that it believes it would be less effective.

Typically capacity guidelines are generally ambitious in nature and aren't overly technical in their calculations. To clarify you may be thinking well if a hedge fund has a down year, then couldn't one of the contributing factors be that they had to put too much capital to work and couldn't stick to their knitting as it were to focus on more profitable opportunities? As such maybe seeking to raise assets above more realistic capacity limits demonstrates poor internal governance of this matter?

Of course, you might be correct in this line of thinking and it certainly would be a valid question for the hedge fund manager exhibiting poor performance; however, that is not the focus of our discussion, but still a point worth noting nonetheless. Continuing our hedge fund AUM capacity example, in addition to being ambitious we should also note another key related capacity point, with regards to who decides when capacity limits may be revised.

Revisionist History—Are Manager Capacity Limit Changes Overly Discretionary to Promote Good Governance?

Hedge fund managers' capacity limits may change over time. This change may come based on a number of factors including changing market conditions that may legitimately have expanded the opportunity set of the manager over time.

There is nothing wrong with this and a hedge fund manager may have a number of well-reasoned and legitimate reasons to raise previously determined capacity limits.

The problem, however, is that in many cases increasing capacity limits is driven more in part by the opportunities presented by new potential investor capital inflows into a strategy, as opposed to market opportunities. In addition to strong performance, a component of running a successful hedge fund is also related to continuing to raise, and keep, capital. Would it be possible that such asset grabs may become overly ambitious and that a hedge fund could raise too much capital too quickly? Yes, this not only is possible, but also, traditionally, when hedge fund inflows into certain well-performing sectors outpaced outflows, this is a frequent problem for certain funds. It is worth considering what kind of governance oversight is in place, if any, internally at the fund to monitor manager capacity versus internal capacity to not only maintain consistent investment performance, but also appropriately manage the internal operational and personnel requirements of managing additional capital. Such considerations are especially important when you consider that the manager generally maintains sole discretion over this decision. Wouldn't it perhaps be better from a governance perspective if above certain predefined limits, the decision to increase capacity was subject to input by more parties such as investors and fund directors? Or instead would such input actually hamper the fund's ability to perform, thereby serving as more of a detriment to the fund than a governance benefit?

Capacity Can Be an Umbrella Term

It is also worth considering here when we use the term capacity whether we are discussing the capacity of a particular strategy (i.e., series of funds) or the capacity of an individual fund. Typically hedge fund managers talk about strategy capacity rather than individual fund-level capacity. Does this distinction seem somewhat similar to the discussion of board member relationships versus fund-level relationships? Does it matter from a governance perspective if a fund considers only total strategy capacity?

Couldn't it be argued that adding additional capacity to an entire strategy, but concentrating the bulk of those additional inflows into a single vehicle such as an offshore fund in a master–feeder complex, could in fact damage or help the investors in one vehicle (i.e., the onshore) versus another one? From a governance analysis perspective, if not from a purely equitable perspective, it is worth considering whether a fund manager has not only considered fund-level capacity limits, but also how they would be implemented. Furthermore, what oversight, if any, would be in place to ensure that any such implementation was handled appropriately? Without such oversight, questions relating to the continuing governance in place at the fund may arise.

Are "Closed" Funds Good for Governance?

Another point worth noting with regards to hedge fund capacity is the notion of fund closures and the associated governance implications. Sometime a hedge fund will tell an investor that it is no longer open to accepting new capital at the present time. This is referred to as a so-called "closed" fund. Of course, as with most hedge fund jargon, there are multiple variations on this term. A fund may be "soft closed." This can mean several things, including that it may be open to accepting capital only from existing investors (and not new ones).

The term "soft closed" could also mean that the fund won't accept new capital from any investors (either existing or new) for some period of time, which by the way it may not overtly define. To clarify a fund may be soft closed but still opt to accept capital from certain investors (either new or existing) depending on whatever internal guidelines it sets for itself. Generally it's completely in the manager's discretion. The funds will sometimes explain the reasons for this soft close period as wanting to be able to put existing capital to work effectively before accepting more capital.

Of course, as a nice benefit the hedge fund slowly builds up a pipeline of capital waiting to join its fund creating a sort of pent-up demand. Sometimes investors may feel unjustifiably jerked around for lack of a better term by funds that play these games. While it may ultimately be beneficial to the fund from a business perspective, does such asset raising gamesmanship promote best practice governance? Or instead is it perhaps representative of the type of arrogance that caused the fall of C.E.M. Joad in the train ticket scandal of 1948? As remote as such considerations may seem there are more recent reports, for example, of an unnamed UK hedge fund manager being fined £43,000 after manipulating the UK's Oyster train system when traveling from Stonegate, East Sussex to the city (Bains, 2014).

Returning to our discussion, under a soft close it is contemplated that the funds will open up to accepting new capital again at some point in the future. This is to be contrasted with the term "hard closed." A hard closed fund is typically interpreted to mean that the fund will no longer accept any capital from anyone at any point in the future. As can be expected a hard closed fund may magically open up to new capital again in the future at the manager's discretion showing that the initial close may not have been so "hard" after all.

In addition to building up demand, as outlined above, when funds close, they also sometimes use it as a mechanism to encourage investors to allocate capital before a particular deadline. So, for example, a hedge fund may tell a prospective investor who they have been talking to that the fund will likely implement a soft close (or hard close) in two months' time. After that point the investor, ostensibly, won't be able to contribute more capital so this forces them to make an allocation decision. In some cases, funds simply utilize such threats of closes to push inflows. For existing investors in the fund does this do much to promote good governance or instead, as we have outlined above, potentially damage the nature of governance practices in place? Furthermore, how do such potentially high-pressure tactics relate to the governance in dealing with prospective investors?

The aim here is not to criticize hedge funds that implement capacity limits. Just the opposite, instituting capacity rather than letting the fund get ahead of itself can allow a fund to focus on not only implementing strong internal governance oversight but actually improving existing governance programs as well. Funds and investors should be conscious of the way hedge fund AUM capacity levels are set and monitored by not only individuals such as portfolio managers but also internal committees and operational personnel to ensure that funds can appropriately manage new inflows without sacrificing governance oversight capabilities.

THIRD-PARTY OPERATIONAL CONTROL AUDITS AS GOVERNANCE PROXIES?

In certain cases a hedge fund may look to external parties to opine on how well its internal control mechanisms are being implemented. These reviews often include by implication the quality of governance oversight within the hedge fund.

Historically, such reviews used to have only been performed by certain hedge fund service providers such as administrators or prime brokers. Today, a hedge fund will typically engage an audit firm to conduct these reviews according to the methodology of certain industry certifications. Due to the increased focus on operations and control frameworks in place at hedge funds themselves, many larger hedge funds have taken to having such audits performed. The primary reason these types of reviews have been undertaken by primarily larger hedge funds is due to the expense and time commitment involved in having such a review performed.

Traditionally, one of the more popular such reviews has been the Service Organizational Control ("SOC") review. As a disclaimer SOC1^{SM} is a service mark of the American Institute of Certified Public Accountants, commonly known as the AICPA, which reserves all rights. The SOC1^{SM} reports were previously based on an AICPA audit standard known as the Statement on Auditing Standards No. 70 ("SAS 70"). In June 2011, the SAS 70 standard was replaced by a new standard known as Statement of Standards for Attestation Engagements No. 16 ("SSAE 16").

SOC1^{SM} reports typically come in two forms. A SOC1^{SM} Type I report focuses on the auditor's opinion as to the fairness of the presentation of an organization's description of controls as well as the suitability of the design of such controls. A SOC1^{SM} Type II report includes all the Type I information as well as the auditor's opinion regarding whether the controls operated effectively during the review period.

The type of controls reviewed range from information technology and trading controls to compliance oversight and processing of client-related documentation. Auditors, in these reports, will increasingly use the term governance in describing a hedge fund control environment. As an example, they may describe a summary of the firm's "organizational and governance structure" or the "governance bodies" or "governance committees."

Many feel a key benefit from a governance perspective is the testing of controls by the auditors. Typically during these tests when deficiencies, sometimes called exceptions, are noted, the hedge fund will respond to them in the report. Often these responses will include remedies to rectify the problems that caused the exceptions. Exhibit 5.1 outlines an example of how such a test and fund manager response may appear.

If we put two hedge funds of similar size next to each other and one has undergone a SOC1^{SM} review or similar type of audit, and another has not, then can we automatically say that the one that has undergone the review has better governance? Not necessarily. After all, such a review could have been rife with deficiencies noted by the auditor. It is worth noting, however, that the mere fact that a hedge fund has undergone such a review implies that they take the issue of oversight and controls seriously. This can result in a dangerous signaling effect however, that certain investors may automatically take to imply that good

EXHIBIT 5.1 Example Test Results and Management Response in Hedge Fund Control Audit Report

Control specified by hedge fund	Testing performed by auditor	Results of tests
The hedge fund's reconciliation personnel utilize an automated reconciliation process. This process encompasses the reconciliation of both cash and positions between the custodian and the firm's portfolio management system on a daily basis. Any exception reports are produced and reviewed by senior reconciliation personnel. All cash and position breaks are monitored until such time as they are cleared. Comments on any breaks are maintained with the aforementioned reports containing detail of breaks as needed	For a random selection of dates, auditor inspected the automated reconciliation and associated reporting	For 3 of 15 reconciliation reports reviewed comments on breaks were not accurately documented by reconciliation personnel **Hedge fund response:** The hedge fund acknowledges the importance of this procedure. The reconciliation team will implement a series of review procedures around comments to ensure that initial logging and ongoing monitoring of comments are appropriately included in reports

governance is in place. Investors should take advantage of the opportunity that a fund has had such a report by digging deeper into the reporting process and what changes, if any, the manager has implemented as a result of the review. Similarly, for managers who have not undergone such review investors should inquire why the managers feel that such reviews are unnecessary. While the fact that a hedge fund has undergone a review of this type won't on its surface correct poor governance, as we noted above, regardless of whether such a report has been undertaken, it is the way a fund approaches correcting any internal governance deficiencies that is key and not necessarily whether they recognized it themselves or an auditor pointed it out to them. Of course, such third-party reporting doesn't hurt either.

CONCLUSION

This chapter provided an overview of hedge fund internal governance mechanisms. We began by outlining some of the motivations as to why hedge funds have increasingly focused on governance. As part of this discussion we included motivations for this increased attention to both increased regulatory flexibility, under regulatory reforms such as the JOBS Act, and increased investor focus on this topic. Next, we addressed the challenges presented in classifying governance. We then proceeded to cover the role of a key component of internal hedge fund governance, committees. Our discussion outlined how committees can play a crucial role in implementing internal hedge fund control and oversight as well as resolving conflicts of interest. Finally, our discussion covered the governance considerations of AUM capacity and the implications of third-party operational control audits. As can be expected hedge funds play crucial internal roles in managing and implementing governance at the fund level. When seeking to analyze the internal governance mechanisms, attention should be paid not just to the formal structures in place such as the number of committees but also to the actual ongoing implementation and oversight of these structures.

REFERENCES

Bains, I., 2014. High-flying fund manager spends five years dodging rail fares … then coughs up £43,000 after being caught. *Daily Mail*, April 13.

Bebchuk, L., Fried, J., 2006. Pay Without Performance: The Unfulfilled Promise of Executive Compensation. Harvard University Press, United States of America.

FINalternatives, 2014. No billboards, but experts say JOBS Act is lifting veil on hedge fund industry. FINalternatives, April 3.

Goodman, B., 2012. Hedge funds arrive on Madison Avenue. *Barron's*, April 28.

Halonen, D., 2009. Hennessee, Gradante settle SEC charges over Bayou. *Pensions & Investments*, April 22.

Harris, L., 2002. Trading and Exchanges: Market Microstructure for Practitioners. Oxford University Press, New York.

Primack, D., 2013. Hedge funds can now advertise. What it really means. *Fortune*, July 10.

Stevenson, A., 2014. With bank on ads removed, hedge funds test waters. DealB%k, February 20.

Chapter 6

Developing a Framework for Investor Analysis of Hedge Fund Governance

Chapter Outline Head

INTRODUCTION TO DEVELOPING GOVERNANCE ANALYSIS FRAMEWORKS

Investor interest in analyzing hedge fund governance has gained steam in recent years. In large part, this is due to an increased focus on due diligence factors not purely related to a fund's investments. This type of analysis is commonly referred to as operational due diligence (ODD). We have introduced the concept of ODD earlier in this book. For reference, ODD typically refers to a review of the noninvestment-related risks inherent in hedge fund investing. This book, however, is not about ODD, so why are we talking about the subject to begin with? Well, as we have also mentioned in previous chapters, analyzing hedge fund governance typically falls within the purview of ODD reviews.

This does not mean, by the way, that if you are an ultra-high-net-worth investor, family office, or even midsized hedge fund allocator without a dedicated ODD department, you should stop reading. Instead, rather than having a dedicated person or group review governance, you probably should incorporate a review of governance-related factors into your existing review process that covers these non–purely investment-related items. In fact, by incorporating a review of those governance factors more closely aligned to your overall due diligence process, you are actually more likely to be better positioned than some larger, well-heeled allocators with more resources. This is because governance, while generally thought to be primarily focused on operational issues, also involves the investment-related aspects of a fund's portfolio. We will highlight some of these issues in this chapter.

This is not to say that by having ODD groups coordinate governance reviews, we are missing something. Rather it is to imply that, because governance is an area that cuts across both the investment and operational aspects of a firm, ODD groups should be engaged with investment personnel in analyzing governance. By taking a review approach that classifies different pieces of information into silos, a less than complete assessment of governance can often result. As an aside, this is also true when reviewing the operational risks in place at a hedge fund. Even though certain issues are primarily operational in nature, engaging in discussions with investment due diligence personnel, or considering both issues side-by-side in smaller allocators that do not have dedicated ODD groups, often leads to a more informed assessment of risks.

So where should investors begin in seeking to analyze fund governance? As we have noted earlier in this text, as investors have sought to analyze fund governance, many have fallen into the mindset that analyzing governance simply requires focusing squarely on fund boards and their directors. There has been growing acceptance, however, that hedge fund governance constitutes more than just the fund directors. If you've been reading the chapters of this book in order, hopefully we have convinced you of this by now and shown that governance includes every different aspect of the hedge fund life cycle including regulators, service providers, and, of course, the hedge funds themselves. This doesn't mean investors should ignore the directors when seeking to evaluate governance, but, clearly, they need to consider other factors as well.

DO STRONG OPERATIONS IMPLY GOOD GOVERNANCE?

At this point you might be thinking to yourself, "If governance is so similar to ODD, then can't I just conduct an ODD review and call it a day?" That's certainly a fair question. What if we were to rephrase it a bit? Said another way, does a fund with strong internal operational controls (i.e., low operational risk in certain areas) automatically have strong governance (i.e., low governance risk)? The crux of both questions is the same: does low operational risk equal good governance? Certainly, as we've outlined earlier in the book, the two areas are not identically equivalent, but aren't they similar enough, and with sufficient overlap in both areas? After all, based on the sometimes difficult to pin down definition of governance in practice, isn't it impractical to attempt to tease governance out of ODD reviews? Such a question, however, may frame the issue incorrectly. Governance is perhaps best thought of as an overlay to operational risk rather than being contained within it. As the focus of this chapter is on practical application of governance analysis at hedge funds, let's return to the original question of whether an ODD review is sufficient to cover governance.

Let's attempt to answer this by way of example. Consider three hedge funds. One that self-administers, and two that use a third-party administrator. Of the two that utilize third-party administrators, one fund completely outsources the function to the administrator. The other one conducts a full internal shadow review of the administrator's work. Which one has better governance?

To start off, it certainly couldn't be the self-administered one. That's not best practice, right? Ok, let's go with that assumption for now. Moving on, let's look at the other two. The one that utilizes a third-party administrator is following what today is considered standard operating procedure. That is, it is in line with the majority of the practices in the market. We're simply not looking for average here; we want the best practice governance. Well then, it must be the one with the most oversight. That is the fund that not only uses a third-party administrator in line with normal market practice but also goes beyond this by shadowing the work of the administrator internally. More oversight and more controls imply better governance. All done? Not quite. First, one issue we didn't address was the operational strength of each hedge fund in our example.

The fund that self-administers could have an army of highly qualified and experienced operations and accounting personnel dedicated to the job. On the other hand, the two that use third-party administrators could have had multiple historical net asset value ("NAV") restatements, extensive delays in producing investor statements, and junior personnel on the account with high team turnover. Or alternatively, the situation could be reversed and the self-administered fund may have much weaker operations as compared with the third-party–administered fund. We are by no means attempting to espouse the benefits of self-administration. On the contrary, as we have outlined above, self-administration rationally implies poor governance. Here instead, we are focusing on an assessment of the operational practices in place.

Returning to our example, you see then how a fund with seemingly strong operational procedures could have a poor governance structure in place and vice versa. Yes, there are traditionally correlations between strong operational practices and good governance. Such relationships, however, are backward looking in nature. They also present a dangerous precedent that may lead many investors down the wrong path. While some comfort may be taken that strong operations imply good governance, such implications are by no means iron clad. As we have suggested throughout this book, it is the responsibility of investors, or those who manage capital on their behalf, to conduct detailed due diligence assessments of managers. All hedge funds are not created equal. The unique particularities of each fund's operations and governance frameworks must be analyzed before an assessment may be made. Without such detailed reviews there is a real danger of thoroughly investigating one aspect of the relationship, such as fund operations, and failing to analyze the remaining aspects under consideration (i.e., fund governance).

IS GOVERNANCE A MOVING TARGET?

It is also worth noting that our example above is time dependent. By this we mean that certain operational practices that were considered common at one time are no longer, in large part, considered acceptable. The classic example of this is hedge fund administration. In the early days of the hedge fund industry, it was not uncommon for a hedge fund to conduct their own administration (i.e., self-administer). In fact, there were only a handful of funds that utilized third-party administrators. Fast forward to today, and the situation is completely reversed with the majority of hedge funds using third-party administrators. In certain cases, hedge funds have taken to using double administration models, where effectively one administrator checks the work of another. One widely reported use of such a model was the case of a large hedge fund named Bridgewater Associates, LP who hired one administrator, Northern Trust, to independently replicate and back up certain middle- and back-office services provided by existing administrator BNY Mellon (Clancy, 2013).

Such double administration relationships are not the norm today in the hedge fund industry, but who knows; as investor scrutiny on fund operations increases, perhaps they will become more popular. Couldn't the question be posed, however, that such double administration relationships, now that they are being used, may rightly be considered the new best practice? As compared with other hedge funds, do those without double administration models have less oversight and therefore, by implication, worse governance? After all, not speaking specifically about any manager, would not such increased double administrator oversight suggest enhanced oversight that implies better governance?

As you may have guessed by now, the answer depends, of course, on the implementation of such oversight and control throughout the firm. Just as we have outlined in Chapter 5, as well as through our discussion above, the fact that a mere committee is in place or that a third-party administration is in place does not, in and of itself, guarantee that good governance is in place. Only by learning the facts of each relationship and governance practice can you make any sort of informed assessment of the situation. The point of this single versus double administrator example is to show that, like the definition of best practice operations, the definition of governance is a moving target that evolves over time. In Chapter 12 we will outline some industry trends and comment on future progressions in this area. In the meantime, let's turn our focus back on the discussion of how investors can go about assessing governance. Before outlining some key considerations in this area, it may be useful to analyze some existing investor governance assessment models.

INSTITUTIONAL INVESTOR GOVERNANCE: THE CalPERS MODEL

As it relates to investments in general, large, influential institutional investors have led the charge in increasing the focus on and broadening the definition of governance best practices. From a traditional corporate governance perspective, many of these large institutions have, over the last decade, increased their focus on corporate governance practices at the companies in which they invest. One of the leaders in this area has been the California Public Employees' Retirement System ("CalPERS"). Examples of proposals in their work have included the publication of Global Principles of Accountable Corporate Governance (CalPERS, 2011) and the 3D plan for a so-called Diverse Director Database to better empower shareholder's use of proxy rules, under proxy access plans, to better control the membership of corporate boards (Chon, 2010).

This focus on traditional corporate governance has also flowed through to investments made by groups such as CalPERS into their investments with fund managers, including hedge funds. In 2009, for example, the group that coordinated the hedge fund investing activities at CalPERS issued a memorandum on this subject. Specifically, in the memorandum CalPERS outlined three primary governance areas that it felt were in need of improvement in the hedge fund industry: alignment of interests, control of investments, and transparency of information and risks (Silberstein and Dandurand, 2009).

Although over five years old, this type of effort is a good example of the linkage between traditional corporate governance notions and hedge funds, as well as of a broadening of the definition of governance beyond that of simply the directors. Interestingly, perhaps showing how investor attitudes have changed in this area, the guidance itself doesn't even mention hedge fund directors. The key areas of the memo with their associated subareas of governance concern and CalPERS guidance are outlined in Exhibit 6.1.

EXHIBIT 6.1 Summary of 2009 CalPERS Hedge Fund Governance Recommendations

Primary area of governance concern	Subarea of governance concern	Related issues	CalPERS governance recommendations/ requirements
Alignment of interest	Fee structure	(1) Misalignment of interest in fees (2) Incentives for managerial risk taking including lack of clawbacks	(1) Both management and performance fees should be based on factors including fund's strategy, allocation size, and fund and firm size (2) Managers without hurdle rates should explain why they maintain a fee structure under which they earn a performance fee even when funds post positive returns but less than cash
	Crystallization of performance fees	(1) Fee crystallization annually, or, more frequently, skew manager to focus on short-term gains over long-term performance	Fee crystallization timing should better align investors and fund manager incentives

EXHIBIT 6.1 Summary of 2009 CalPERS Hedge Fund Governance Recommendations *(cont.)*

Primary area of governance concern	Subarea of governance concern	Related issues	CalPERS governance recommendations/ requirements
	Business management	(1) Talent retention during down performance periods (2) Lack of sound business practices	Enhanced explanation and demonstration of how managers plan to retain talent and run their businesses
Control of investments	Misalignment of interests in commingled funds	Fund documents that are too broad or too narrow	Enhanced investor control, typically via separately managed account structures
Transparency of information and risks	Lack of security-level transparency	Transparency regarding risk data	(1) Full security-level transparency via managed account and separate account structures (2) Complete transparency through so-called aggregators such as administrators or via other methods such as prime broker fees

If Separate Accounts Are So Good for Governance, Why Can't We All Have Them?

Are proposals such as this too pedantic to be meaningful? In practice, some may consider some of these recommendations to be rote didactic lecturing and may not be fully practical for every investor or fund. On the other hand, such assessments can often contain useful guidance for investors both big and small, with different parts of the recommendations being applicable in different ways.

For example, let us consider the issue of separately managed accounts. It is generally thought that separately managed accounts offer increased transparency and investor control as compared with pooled funds. Therefore, some may consider them to be more beneficial from a governance perspective and certainly preferred to pooled vehicles. From the perspective of a hedge fund, it is more operationally intensive, and therefore expensive, for hedge funds to offer separately managed accounts. That is why most hedge funds require large minimum subscription levels for such accounts at levels that are typically drastically above the subscription minimums required for investments into pooled vehicles that are already up and running.

The reasons for increased expense are, as noted above, the same reasons that many investors would ideally prefer such accounts from a governance perspective. That is, their segregation, and often enhanced investor oversight and involvement, comes at the price of having to run what is sometimes referred to as a fund of one. In some cases, this includes dealing with investor-designated service providers such as custodians, which may be different than those that the hedge fund manager deals with for their other vehicles. There are of course the expenses associated with other standard operational procedures to account for, the separate account trades such as execution, settlement, and reconciliation. The fund also has to produce separate investor reports and statements for the fund.

If you are a large institutional investor such as CalPERS, you are writing large enough checks to hedge funds that they are generally willing to bend over backwards, and would likely pay some or all of the extra expense of creating these separate accounts, because the fees earned on the large allocation greatly offsets the associated expenses. For the smaller hedge fund investors, however, separate accounts are not necessarily an option, and, therefore, if they want to invest in the fund, they have to go invest in a shared pool of capital and sit alongside other investors. This doesn't mean, of course, that they cannot perform a governance evaluation. As we have outlined throughout this book, they are certainly capable of doing this.

To digress for a brief moment, this is a good time to highlight the point that certain hedge fund investors, particularly smaller ones, when discussing governance analysis may take a perfectly logical perspective along these lines:

> Look, this is great, and I'm all for better fund governance, but I'm not writing $100 million allocation tickets like some of these large institutional investors. I could do the best governance analysis in the world and come up with great recommendations that would benefit not only myself but all the funds investors, and the hedge fund itself. The problem is, they wouldn't listen to me, or even if they do listen they won't make any changes because they don't have to. If they are a functioning hedge fund, why would they rock the boat with new governance initiatives their larger investors aren't demanding? Also, implementing those changes will likely take time and money, wouldn't it? Finally, can't I just solve my whole governance problem by investing in large established hedge funds? By default, they must be operating at best practice in multiple areas including governance. If they weren't, why would they have so much in assets under management?

These are certainly valid arguments and are common questions and perceptions among many smaller investors and allocation groups. Let's consider some responses to these objections. First, whether you are writing a large or small check, you have the right, if not the obligation, to ask certain questions, including those about governance, and get answers. Second, as an investor, you also have the right to have the hedge fund listen to your feedback and expect reasonable process changes to be made along a reasonable timeline. We will address this in more detail below. Third, it is naive to think that institutional investors are necessary conducting adequate due diligence in all areas. While not usual, it is certainly not unheard of for mistakes to be found in the audited financial statements of funds that larger investors, and the funds themselves, didn't notice. Also, since you likely have little to no insight into what level of due diligence these larger allocators are performing, isn't it a bit unreasonable to blindly rely on them?

Finally, simply because a hedge fund has been in business for a while or has a large number of assets under management doesn't mean that it's operating in line with best practices. Sometimes some of the largest funds are the ones that are the last bastions of inertia, clinging to antiquated practices and technology. A good example of this is a speech from the 1991 movie, which was based on a play, called *Other People's Money*. A character in that movie, Larry the Liquidator, is a corporate raider seeking to convince the shareholders of a company, New England Cable and Wireless, about the dangers of holding on too tightly to old practices. The character cites the following example: "You know, at one time there must've been dozens of companies making buggy whips. And I'll bet the last company around was the one that made the best goddamn buggy whip you ever saw. Now how would you have liked to have been a stockholder in that company?" And it makes a good point. The world changes and sometimes hedge funds have to overcome their stubbornness and adapt. Some of the last holdouts with the self-administration issues discussed above were some of the biggest hedge funds. Were these shrewd businessmen not jumping on the bandwagon of the latest operational trend, or were they not promoting best practice governance for investors through their reluctance to change?

Returning to our separate account example, it is not meant to imply that these smaller investors should strive for any less transparency than might be found in a separate account. On the contrary, these are admirable goals. The problem, of course, is that they have less leverage to force such changes because, to state it plainly, they're simply not big enough and many hedge funds feel that their bark is louder than the pain of their bite if they were to redeem. Of course, it doesn't mean such investors should simply throw their hands up in frustration either.

Bad Blood Driving Good Governance?

It should also be noted that toward the end of the above-referenced memo, CalPERS outlines the caveat that there is no "one-size-fits-all" approach to implementing these changes. This perhaps demonstrates clearly that the implementation of governance improvements at hedge funds is less prescriptive than it is flexible in its implementation. That is, as long as it complies with the spirit and economics of their goals. Indeed, not everyone took the proverbial governance bait, and some of the high-flying hedge fund managers at the time were not interested in kowtowing to the CalPERS governance concession program as it were (Williamson, 2009).

Institutional investors such as CalPERS have increasingly taken these governance standards more seriously. While on the surface the motivation may ostensibly be to promote better governance in hedge funds, large hedge fund losses during the 2008 financial crisis were definitely motivating factors for these investors to make some changes in the way they did business. It may also have been the case that institutional investors didn't like the fact that they, during and after the 2008 crisis, couldn't redeem their capital timely because many hedge funds instituted what are known as gates. For reference, gates are effectively limitations on how much capital investors can withdraw from funds. In general, the effect of gates is to slow the flow of redemptions out of a fund and space them out over time, in some cases a year or more.

Other sore points of contention that may have led to some bad blood between hedge funds and these large investors around 2008 was that certain funds side-pocketed certain investments that also effectively locked up the capital. Hedge funds were perfectly within their rights to take such measures, but many large institutional investors, particularly because of the size of their allocations and length of relationship with certain managers, didn't think it would ever happen. Some groups, such as CalPERS, reacted to measures such as gates and side pockets by eventually redeeming from hedge funds once they could (Tunick, 2009). Whether it was because of a true desire to improve hedge fund governance, or instead use governance as a shield to hide the bit of egg on their face for selecting losing hedge fund managers, is up to you to decide.

Not to single out CalPERS, but often times, as we outlined in Chapter 2 when discussing criticisms of directors, it is easiest for those who live in glass houses to throw stones. While such recommendations by institutional investors such as CalPERS, one of the former largest hedge fund investors in the world, have likely done much to advance the cause of better governance for all, CalPERS itself has had some governance failures over the years. These include reports that Kurt Silberstein, one of the authors of the above-referenced governance memo, was forced to forfeit 10% of his salary for six months and was placed on brief administrative leave as a result of alleged revelations that CalPERS had been using two outside advisors, UBS and Paamco, without a contract for several years (Harper and Lifsher, 2009). Perhaps more famous were allegations of improprieties related to the use of placement agents. In particular were allegations that CalPERS CEO, Federico R. Buenrostro, and his friend, a former Los Angeles Deputy Mayor and CalPERS board member, were involved in a conspiracy that resulted in millions of dollars in placement that were inappropriately earned and not appropriately disclosed (U.S. Securities and Exchange Commission, 2012). I'm sure that pensioners who have been victims of such poor governance practices would likely have some governance prescriptions for investors such as CalPERS as well. This is not to single out CalPERS by any means, but rather to demonstrate that sometimes it is important for investors to practice what they preach and institute governance best practices not just at the funds in which they invest but also at their own organizations. Often this may result in a renewed focus and enhanced due diligence on governance at the fund level as well. By the way, in an attempt to bring the story to an end, it was reported in late 2014 that Mr. Buenrostro himself had entered into a plea deal to cooperate with the investigation (Lifsher, 2014). Additionally, seeming not to get over the bad taste left in their mouth by hedge funds, in September of 2014 CalPERS announced that they planned to eliminate all $4 billion of their hedge fund investments over the following year.

CLASSIFYING GOVERNANCE ANALYSIS INTO TWO CAMPS: INVESTMENT AND OPERATIONAL

Despite the pros and cons of any proposals by large institutional investors, we can all likely agree that such discussions do increase the focus and debate surrounding hedge fund governance. This has, as we noted above, increased investor's focus on analyzing the issue. Before we begin developing a governance evaluation plan for investors, it is first useful to frame our discussion with a backdrop of a typical hedge fund's general operations.

Putting any discussions of governance aside for a moment, we can broadly classify the activities that take place in a hedge fund as falling into one of two camps. The first group of hedge fund actions involves the core functions of what a hedge fund is supposed to do—make money. These investment-related activities can include things such as the research process, the firm's investment process, and buy and sell disciplines.

The other category of hedge fund activities is to actually make the business function. Hedge funds are more than just prop trading desks. Instead they are businesses. Just like any other business, be it a hedge fund or a McDonalds, they have employees, offices, lawyers, accountants, insurance, and a long list of other things you would associate with a business. Where hedge fund business operations differ from say, a McDonalds, is that in order to perform their investment operations they also need specific operational support. This can include items such as the hiring and managing of prime brokers and trading counterparties to actually execute trades, custodians to hold the securities, and fund accountants to, among other things, keep track of the securities traded and specialized technology to support the trading process.

As we have previously outlined, a governance evaluation should incorporate not only reviews of investment activities of funds but their operational activities as well. As part of this governance analysis, investors should be careful not to silo such areas but rather analyze the way the shared governance aspects of these funds interact. For example, if a hedge fund, as part of its investment trading strategy, works with multiple investment counterparties, is the operational side of the house providing adequate oversight of these counterparties? Through these types of shared examples, investors will produce more complete governance evaluations as opposed to simply investment or operational governance reviews.

DEVELOPING A GOVERNANCE PROGRAM

So far in this chapter we have provided an overview of the relationship between operational risk and governance. We have also provided some perspective on historical institutional investor attitudes toward investor governance evaluations as well as some considerations for smaller allocators when seeking to evaluate governance. In this section we will outline where the rubber hits the road so to speak, actually conducting a governance review of a fund. One of the first questions to consider, however, is what standards should we apply?

UNDERSTANDING GOVERNANCE
EVALUATION STANDARDS

What exactly do we mean by governance evaluation standards? To clarify what we are talking about here, we are referring to the evaluation standard or benchmark against which we are comparing the hedge fund under review. For example, should a multibillion dollar hedge fund be compared with the same governance standards as a $100 million fund? What about comparing a fund in Hong Kong with one in New York or London; should the same governance standards be applied? Should factors such as asset size or regional considerations matter?

There are two schools of thought on the subject. One takes a hard-line approach and says that all hedge funds should be judged on the same best practice standard. Frankly, the thinking goes, it's not the investor's problem that a hedge fund can't implement best practice.

The second school of thought argues that "best practice" is actually a bit more of a flexible term. This thinking considers that, while there is certainly an absolute or universal standard of best practice, there are also subclasses of best practice that are appropriate in different situations. Examples of these different situations would be for funds of different asset sizes or in different regions. The point of this line of thinking is not to give these funds a free pass, but rather to acknowledge the practicalities of the situations. In many cases, it is not economical for funds to implement certain governance protocols. In other cases, the governance oversight changes that may be considered applicable from a universal best practice approach aren't expensive to implement but they are simply not appropriate for a firm of smaller sizes. For reference we will provide an analysis of such a case in our example of a business continuity plan discussed later in this chapter.

When reviewing the following information in this chapter regarding governance evaluation, it is worth nothing that, depending on which school of thought you subscribe to, the actual assessment of how well a hedge fund stacks up from a governance perspective could be up for debate in certain instances.

BEGINNING GOVERNANCE ASSESSMENTS

So where to begin in analyzing governance? The chances are that you've already begun. By this we mean that, as we highlighted earlier in this chapter, often the raw data that facilitate a governance assessment come from the operational and investment due diligence review processes. Once again, the goal of our discussion here is not to provide details on how to conduct ODD or investment due diligence reviews; rather it is to highlight how to evaluate governance. Due to the interrelated nature of governance, the best way to proceed with beginning a governance assessment is to focus on examples of investment and operational procedures and data. In our discussion of these items, we will highlight how governance can be assessed as an overlay in each area.

"Wait a minute!" you may be thinking. "What a cop out, isn't this a bit of a circular reference argument?" Isn't that like saying we will evaluate governance "holistically" by evaluating the components that make up governance? You may feel that this does you little good in the real world. While I empathize with your frustration, this is, for better or worse, the way governance should be evaluated. It's not likely, for example, that hedge funds employ Chief Governance Officers whom you can just interview. Instead governance is simply one of those interdisciplinary areas that touches on many parts of the firm. Therefore, to thoroughly review governance you have to review these other areas by association and then analyze the quality of the governance oversight and control environment overlaid upon them.

Ok, I know you're unhappy with my answer. Let me try and make it up to you. Would it be better if I told you that I reviewed the entire universe of hedge funds and developed a cheat sheet of governance best practices? Would you like me to tell you I've boiled this down into a governance due diligence questionnaire you could just ask every hedge fund you review to fill out? That way, if they do poorly on the questionnaire, then you know they have bad governance.

Since I feel so badly about my conduct earlier, what if I take it a step further for you? Remember I said I evaluated every hedge fund ever. Ok, now assume that when I did these reviews, I used my proprietary black box governance scoring system and assigned a governance risk assessment to every fund. They have either "good governance" or "bad governance"—et voilà, Bob's your uncle. See, you wouldn't have to do any work at all! Is this too simple? Ok, let's say I get technical about it and on a scale from 0 to 10, I rate the governance in place at each fund. This seems more precise. Let's say I even have a predetermined set of categories such as "control environment" or "director capacity constraints" and I further assign more detailed ratings across each category. Sure, I could bundle it all together under a governance assessment system. You trust that I'm doing detailed due diligence, and I'm assigning what seem to be somewhat intricate ratings. Do you feel better now?

We're not trying to be facetious. Seeking to apply such ratings and detail in governance assessments is not necessary a bad thing. In many cases, however, such approaches can oversimplify the issue. While making everyone feel better, this type of analysis often does not get to the heart of the issue. That said, let's discuss some practical ways that you can begin to conduct your own assessment. Once again, this list is by no means comprehensive. Rather our discussion will highlight the interrelated nature of governance to investment and operational factors through examples. You can certainly select a whole host of other factors that we have not addressed and analyze the governance frameworks in place in those areas as well.

ANALYZING DIRECTOR GOVERNANCE

If you've been reading this book in order, by now you're likely sick of directors. Love them or hate them, we've talked about them a lot. With good reason, of course, as they are not only a critical cog in the overall governance gearbox but also an area of increased investor governance focus. As such, we would be remiss in this chapter not to discuss some of the additional considerations investors should consider when evaluating governance.

Are You Underestimating the Benefits of Director Engagement?

There is an old joke about a patient who goes to visit a doctor. The story goes something like this. There is a man waiting in the doctor's office. The doctor comes in and before the man can even speak the doctor starts to examine him. The doctor continues his examination without asking any questions or asking what the matter is. Several times the man attempts to interrupt the doctor but the doctor asks the man to be quiet. Finally the man stands up, the doctor and states that he isn't even the patient; it's his wife who is parking the car that is sick.

This story is a good analogy for analyzing the role of the board of directors. Sometimes investors are so quick to dismiss directors that they may not even review who they are, much less actually engage with them. Many investors would be surprised to find out what they might learn from directors if they actually asked. Still others, just like the doctor in our story, are so sure of themselves and of what questions they need to ask directors that they forget to take a step back and actually listen to what directors may have to say.

Of course, the same is true of many other elements of analyzing fund governance. Many investors simply do not think that certain factors are important or risky and simply minimize them. Others may not realize the full extent of the information they could obtain from hedge funds and their service providers during the due diligence and governance analysis processes if only they would ask.

Analyzing Director Turnover

Directors are not immovable. Hedge funds may indeed fire and hire directors. In certain cases, the change is often made because the surviving directors view the new director to be an upgrade over the previous one. In more recent times, this has been the case when investors have increasingly focused on legacy directors and raised questions concerning a number of factors that we previously discussed in this book ranging from capacity considerations to general qualifications and level of support staff. Obviously, directors may, in certain instances, resign from a fund. In previous chapters we outlined the prevalence of such situations surrounding the aftermath of the 2008 financial crisis.

Investors, when seeking to analyze directors, tend to focus on the here and now. That is to say, their focus is on the current board of the fund that they are investing with today. Sometimes, however, it may be useful to look backwards with regards to the historical makeup of the board. In certain instances, such as when the opportunity is taken to upgrade, board turnover can be a good thing. In other cases, the reason a director was fired may be for other reasons. For example, let's say a director decided to ask a number of questions and demand a great deal of information from the fund. Such inquiries may have indeed been merited based on practices or decisions made at the fund. As we outlined in other chapters, some funds may not have been overly interested in what directors have to say. Instead they just want them to collect a check and sit quiet. As such, hedge funds may have decided to terminate these noisy directors in favor of others who know how to fall in line. Most investors would likely be quite interested to know about situations such as these. The problem is that the hedge fund will not likely volunteer such information. So what's to be done?

Well, to start off, an investor can inquire directly about fund director turnover. If indeed there has been any historical turnover, then the next question should be: why? Furthermore, when directors get let go under contentious circumstances such as those described above, it can often present an opportunity for investors to gain further insight as to the governance practices at play. In certain instances these former directors may be willing to have off-the-record conversations with you. They are, of course, precluded from discussing the specifics of any particular fund relationships, but they could discuss generalities that may give you a sense of what kind of directors they are.

For example, how many funds have they been associated with besides the one in question that terminated them? What other kinds of hedge fund boards do they serve on? If they had never been fired from anywhere else and they serve on the boards of large funds, perhaps this suggests that it might have had more to do with the fund itself than the hedge fund may have let on. To play devil's advocate, could it be that this person is a bad director, and is simply popular because they don't rock the boat and the hedge fund did the right thing by terminating them? As an investor seeking to evaluate the governance implications, you really can't get a sense of such issues unless you put in the time to ask the questions from a due diligence perspective.

Director Background Investigations

Investor-performed background investigations on key fund personnel have become increasingly popular in recent years. The reasons for this are obvious.

With the deluge of hedge fund frauds, nobody wants to invest with a criminal. Beyond that, of course, there are numerous stories of multiple issues arising including overexaggeration of credentials, claims of degrees never earned, unreported arrests, and undisclosed lawsuits. It should also be noted that, in order to cast a broader net in this area, many investors increasingly perform investigations not only on key individuals but on fund management companies as well.

Depending on a number of factors including the number of jurisdictions, the individual under investigation has lived in, and the scope of the investigation, background investigations can appear to be quite expensive. Often times, investors are increasingly penny wise and pound foolish in this area. If you're making a multimillion dollar investment, is a few thousand dollars too much to spend to cover your bases in this area? Some may argue yes, while others say no. Additionally, there are considerations as to which individuals to investigate. There are a number of models in this area such as those individuals who have equity ownership in the firm, those with the ability to move cash, or those with the ability to execute trades (Scharfman, 2008).

Due to the increasing focus on governance and the board of directors, it has slowly become popular among investors to run background checks on fund directors. The question could be asked as to why directors get this special attention. After all, as we have highlighted earlier in this book, aren't administrators equally important from a governance perspective? One of the reasons directors may be singled out is because of the ostensibly more personal nature of directorships. When a hedge fund hires an administrator, they are hiring a firm. On the other hand, when a hedge fund hires a director, it often is based more on the personal relationship with a particular director.

As we know by now, however, this is not necessarily the case as the director is often supported by associate directors and may not even be the one attending the fund's meetings. Nonetheless, the fiction is that a single director fills the role and, as such, they frequently are the ones who receive additional scrutiny from a background investigation perspective. This is not to say that investors should just pass on performing background investigations on directors because of this arrangement. Nor should they necessarily seek to perform checks on all the associate directors. Rather, here we are just highlighting why directors receive more background investigation attention from investors as opposed to other service providers. Additionally, as a practical matter, due to the expenses involved as noted above, most investors simply do not have the budgets to run detailed background checks on everyone.

Let's assume that you decide to run a background investigation on a director. How would you undertake such an investigation? Due to the nature of these searches and the types of information required, investors often find it more economical to work with third-party firms to conduct these reviews. That being said, investors can still often perform basic searches on their own such as high-level media reviews and regulator searches via publicly available regulator databases. These databases, of course, may not be as complete as those that require subscriptions, which many third-party firms have access to and are experienced in using efficiently. As such, rather than obtain their own subscriptions, third-party firms can be a cost-effective solution.

What are some of the key areas that you could investigate? For reference, the areas of investigation typically covered by my employer, Corgentum Consulting, are generally grouped into five main categories. Corgentum typically performs these investigations on behalf of investors investigating both fund managers and directors. While we have outlined them below, please note that this list is not necessarily inclusive of all areas of search and is provided for example purposes only:

Criminal checks:
- Arrest records
- Parole and probation records
- Sex offender searches
- Driver's license search/traffic citations

Litigation searches:
- Docket searches across all federal and state courts
- Bankruptcy, foreclosures, and tax case searches
- Judgments and liens

Regulatory:
- Regulatory records searches
- OFAC and global sanctions searches
- Judgments and liens

Factual information:
- Employment and education verifications
- Asset searches including property and vehicles
- Social security verification
- Fictitious names/doing business as searches

Media:
- Web content searches
- Broad media searches
- Industry-specific periodicals and scholarly articles
- Social media screens

A few words about the list above. First, these types of searches are not necessarily applicable in all jurisdictions. Second, privacy laws vary among different jurisdictions and performing such searches may require liability releases. Additionally, you may need to obtain releases from directors themselves in order to verify items such as previous employment and educational history.

It is also worth noting that the list above could also apply to investigations conducted on hedge fund managers themselves. As we noted above, investors have increasingly focused on conducting investigations on key hedge fund personnel to mitigate what is commonly known as reputational risk. The oversight by the hedge fund itself of such reputational risks through mechanisms such as preemployment screening of potential candidates to monitor for criminal activity can be another item that investors evaluate as part of a review of not only the reputational risks of the hedge fund itself but also the governance oversight of reputation management in general. This can apply not only to new hires via preemployment screening but also to ongoing reputation oversight. In certain cases, to facilitate such efforts, select hedge funds have taken to conducting reviews of key personnel, such as annual criminal checks, to ensure that no new reputational risks have arisen that, among other things, would likely signal poor governance oversight to investors in this area.

It is also worth noting that investors are increasingly integrating such background investigations with ODD reviews. Corgentum Consulting is a leader in this field and one of the first firms to assist investors in implementing this hybrid background investigation and ODD model. The benefits of this model to investors include the fact that, during the ODD review process, third-party ODD consultants such as Corgentum already engage with, in this case, directors as part of the broader ODD review. For administrative process issues, such as, the signing of releases, the integration of the processes streamlines and reduces the overall time and cost of services for investors and directors. Additionally, should any issues come up during the background investigation, most investors feel more comfortable with having the group assigned with ODD discuss the issue as opposed to another third-party investigator. Finally, during the ODD process, the group responsible for ODD will likely become familiar with the directorship firm as well as the hedge fund and associated entities.

When reviewing any historical litigation in particular, a party who has not been involved in the rest of the ODD review process, such as a third-party investigator, may be less effective. This could include not conducting searches on appropriate directorship-related entities as well as thinking certain litigation represents a negative issue, when, in fact, it came up during the standard course of business as part of the directors' relationships with the funds. As such, investors are increasingly combining the ODD and background investigation process with industry's leading ODD groups such as Corgentum that offer integrated background investigations as well.

Director On-Site Visits

Another key component to most due diligence reviews, be they investment or operational in nature, is the on-site visit. In the case of directors who reside in offshore jurisdictions, such visits may be either cost prohibitive or not practically feasible for investors to conduct prior to subscribing to the fund.

Consider, for example, a United States–based pension fund that is allocating to the offshore vehicle of a fund. This pension fund may have already conducted the on-site visit with the fund manager, wherever in the United States their offices may have been located. Now the investor would have to make a separate trip internationally, let's say to the Cayman Islands, to visit with the offshore directors.

Just because it's more complicated and expensive to go on-site with directors, does this mean they shouldn't do it? As you can imagine, there are two sides to this argument. On the one hand, it should matter. Hedge fund investing may be a long-term commitment, and particularly if the investor is managing money on behalf of others, they should have duty to visit directors. On the other hand, the world is becoming increasingly virtual. Yes, there are benefits to an on-site visit, but if it is not practically feasible, then can't due diligence via emails and conference calls be sufficient?

Obviously, an on-site visit is preferred, but the level and detail of review in place depends on the circumstances of each arrangement. Therefore, an inflexible set of rules would not be prudent in this regard. As an aside, why should directorship firms get special attention? After all, does a prime broker deserve less scrutiny than a fund's directors? What about an administrator or law firm? The notion of how important a service provider is can inform this decision, but ultimately, the investor has to analyze the specifics of each situation. To put it in perspective, in many cases, investors do take measures to conduct on-site visits with administrators and prime brokers.

Additional Director Governance Analysis Considerations

In Chapter 5 we outlined some critical hedge fund internal governance mechanisms. As part of that discussion we discussed a number of internal hedge fund operational procedures such as business continuity and disaster recovery ("BCP/DR") planning and internal oversight committees. Many of these types of considerations are also applicable to investor analysis of fund directorship firms. That is to say, in the same way that a hedge fund may maintain a BCP/DR plan, so too can a directorship firm.

Of course, there are differences. For example, a directorship firm does not execute trades as a hedge fund does. As such, there are no director counterparties such as prime brokers to review. This, however, does not mean that an investor cannot evaluate the process by which a directorship firm vets new service providers that they may use before they hire them. Directorship firms may also share common core operational governance considerations with hedge funds across multiple other areas. Another example would be the directorship protocol for information security management. In the same way that it would be considered best practice from a governance perspective for a hedge fund to not only maintain such committees and protocols but also provide appropriate implementation of oversight and controls in such areas, so too are these concepts applicable to directorship firms.

Consider an example where an investor is considering two operationally identical hedge funds with two different directors. The director of one fund is associated with a directorship firm with detailed BCP/DR planning and testing, and the other is not. Which one has a better overall governance infrastructure? As we noted above, it of course depends on the specific implementation involved, but in general it is considered to be an indicator of better governance to have such planning in place.

It should also be noted that it is increasingly accepted among investors that such considerations of best practice governance requirements at the hedge fund level should be reviewed for service providers other than directors as well. This would include, continuing our example, the information security, BCP/DR planning, and committee structures in place at service providers such as fund administrators and prime brokers.

GOVERNANCE ANALYSIS OF SERVICE PROVIDERS CONTINUED

Hedge Fund and Administrator Interaction as a Governance Indicator

As we highlighted in our discussion of service provider governance in Chapter 3, administrators continue to be a focal point of investor's service provider reviews during the due diligence process. In light of the importance of the administrator's role in implementing governance oversight, the focus on fund administration relationships has continued to increase.

Further increasing their importance is the fact that administrators are expanding their relationships with funds and providing more services beyond the traditional shareholder services and fund accounting. Service providers such as administrators can provide investors with a key source of information about fund governance. Such information may be particularly useful because it is coming from a source other than the fund manager themselves.

As the frequency and scope of investor ODD has increased, administrators have become increasingly willing to interact with investors. Investors should not pass up the opportunity to communicate with administrators as part of the overall governance assessment process. Similar to our discussion of director engagement above, investors may gain useful insights by seeking to evaluate the level of administrator engagement with the hedge fund.

In seeking to provide a resource for investors in analyzing the governance role played by service provider such as administrators, some key questions investors should consider asking in order to start off the fund review process should include:

(1) How often do you speak to the fund? Do you ever visit the fund's offices? Does the fund ever visit you?
(2) Has the fund accounting team that services the fund account experienced personnel turnover? If so, how does this turnover compare with industry standards? How did the firm deal with that turnover?
(3) What systems and technology are utilized by the fund's administrator? How does this compare with the software, such as fund accounting systems, utilized by the fund itself?

(4) Has the administrator undergone an SSAE 16 or equivalent review? If so, will they share a copy of the report with investors?

(5) How does the administrator deal with fair valued positions? Are they actually making any attempt to independently value these positions themselves? Or instead, is the administrator simply collecting documentation and taking the manager's word for it?

(6) Can the administrator, independent of the fund, provide a list of brokers utilized by the fund? If so, how does this compare with any broker information provided by the fund? Furthermore, how is the administrator notified of new brokerage accounts?

(7) What is the administrator's role in overseeing cash movements? For example, how often does the administrator reconcile cash (i.e., daily or monthly)? Is the administrator involved in reviewing invoices to process fund expenses?

(8) What pricing sources are utilized by the administrator? How does this compare with valuation sources utilized by the funds?

(9) How does the administrator resolve pricing variances or disputes between itself and the fund manager?

(10) What is the month-end NAV distribution timeline? Has this timeline changed (i.e., become longer or shorter) over time? How does this compare with the timeline presented by the manager?

In addition to asking questions such as those outlined above, investors may be surprised to learn that an administrator may share a wealth of documentation with investors if they simply ask for it. For example, many administrators will share with investors basic marketing materials about their firm, BCP/DR plans, and copies of engagement letters (or the actual reports) of their SOC1 or similar reviews.

By engaging in dialogues with fund service providers such as administrators, investors may gain not only useful insight into the working of the fund's administrators but also the broader picture by which fund managers interact with their service providers. This type of information often provides meaningful insights into the hedge fund's overall attitude toward implementing governance. Investors should seize this opportunity to not only evaluate administrators but also understand the work they perform in order to conduct a more complete ODD review.

Evaluating Prime Broker Governance

In Chapter 4 we provided an introduction to the role prime brokers have in influencing fund governance. As an example of the risks to investors of dismissing this primer broker governance oversight, we highlighted the example of the failure of Lehman Brothers. As we highlighted in this discussion in that chapter, after Lehman failed investors increased their due diligence focus on prime brokers. That was a positive step toward more thorough diagnosis of overall fund governance. Unfortunately, investors have short-term memories when it comes to frauds and financial crises.

A 2012 Corgentum Consulting study demonstrated that, in the post-Lehman environment, investors have increasingly and somewhat dangerously downgraded the roles of prime brokers (Hedge Fund Law Report, 2012). The majority of those surveyed ranked fund administrators and auditors as being more important than prime brokers. Specifically, only 17% of those investors surveyed indicated that they felt that prime brokers were the most important hedge fund service providers (McCann, 2012).

When investors perform due diligence on hedge fund managers, evaluating the fund and firm service providers is a critical element of the process. Included in this list of service providers should be a fund's prime brokerage relationships. These survey data suggest a trend whereby investors are increasingly minimizing the roles of prime brokers. As a result of this minimized importance, resource-limited investors run the very real risk of focusing their due diligence efforts away from prime brokers, and instead on other service providers that they view as being more important. As the failure of Lehman Brothers has demonstrated, investors cannot solely rely on the fact that a prime broker is a big name bank or a leader in the industry.

Additionally, different fund managers may be receiving different levels of services from prime brokers. Without delving into the specifics of such relationships, during the due diligence process, investors may not have the information they need to make an effective determination as to the service provider risks to the hedge funds.

Investor due diligence on prime brokers also provides investors with a useful avenue for independent fund manager asset verification. Investors who do not even attempt to contact prime brokers, or who are only confirming a fund manager's relationships with a prime broker and doing nothing more, are missing this valuable opportunity.

For those investors who wisely perform evaluations of fund manager prime brokerage relationships during the due diligence process, a word of caution is necessary. Perhaps taking a cue from the audit industry and on the advice of their legal departments, prime brokers have become increasingly difficult to deal with.

So, for example, if an investor reaches out to a prime broker to ask certain questions regarding the nature of their relationship with a fund manager, many times prime brokers will send back generic responses that do not address the investor's questions in detail. Furthermore, such responses are often rife with legal disclaimer language, making them difficult to evaluate in certain circumstances. The onus is then put back on investor to follow up with the prime broker to attempt to have their specific questions answered. In many cases, prime brokers may be unresponsive or slow to respond that can elongate the due diligence process and make it more difficult. However, just because it may be difficult does not mean that investors are not up to the challenge.

By acknowledging the importance played by prime brokers in implementing fund governance and constructing a detailed service provider review program that encompasses the specifics of prime brokerage relationships, investors will develop more comprehensive ODD solutions, and perhaps avoid indirect exposure to the next Lehman.

Analyzing Legal Counsel Governance—Does Service Provider Clustering Improperly Minimize Governance Weights?

When evaluating service providers during the due diligence process, many investors may tend to focus their initial efforts around certain specific service provider functions. The short list of the common cast of characters includes fund administrators, auditors, fund directors, and counterparties such as prime brokers. This is known as *service provider clustering* because investors cluster their efforts around certain select groups of service providers that they feel are important. By association, as a result of this increased attention, these service providers often receive more weight in the overall governance evaluation process.

Other service providers may, unfortunately, receive less attention that, as noted above, can set a dangerous precedent, not only from a total due diligence perspective but also with a specific focus on governance evaluations. After all, several years ago many investors would not have necessarily added fund directors to the list of so-called important fund service providers, yet attitudes in this area have progressed over time.

In regard to governance analysis, certain service providers may have traditionally received less attention because of the perceived importance, of the roles they play. For example, investors may feel, and rightly so, that valuation is a key issue for hedge funds. Therefore, understanding the role played by the service providers related to valuation oversight such as the fund administrator may receive more attention at the expense of the analysis of other service providers.

Another motivation for many investors in clustering their service provider evaluations around a limited subset of all the hedge fund's service providers is the notion of a risk-based approach. Continuing our valuation example above, many investors view valuation as not only a highly important issue for hedge funds but also one that is fraught with potential risk. That is to say, there would be direct negative implications for investors if a hedge fund began playing games with valuations.

Such a risk may be compared, for example, with the risks associated with a hedge fund, or even a director or other service provider, utilizing a slightly less than cutting-edge piece of hardware for data storage. While we will address the example of information technology (IT) hardware as a tool for governance analysis in more detail later in this discussion, for now let us consider the implications of IT hardware as simply representative of a type of risk factor here. When framed against valuation concerns, investors may feel that the valuation risks outweigh the technology concerns. For some investors, this trade-off unfortunately results in a lesser degree of analysis of third-party IT service providers that may have participated in assisting the hedge fund in overseeing its hardware management.

Often this service provider clustering effect also influences the ways in which certain investors overlook the role played by service providers such as a hedge fund's legal counsel. During the governance assessment due diligence process, some investors may simply check to see if a hedge fund is working with a large, well-known law firm. Other investors may go further and attempt to confirm the relationship with the legal counselors, but may be unsure what other items they should evaluate.

The role played by a law firm working for a hedge fund is not cookie cutter in nature. As could be said with all service providers, they are not created equal. This is particularly true when it comes to fund legal counsel. A number of differences may exist with regards to not only the quality of work they perform for the hedge fund but also the type of areas they cover. The specific nature of such relationships can not only provide indications of the quality of governance in place between the hedge fund and its lawyers but also have a signaling effect with regards to governance practices in place at the fund itself. As with all hedge fund service providers, investors would be well served to capitalize on the opportunity to vet the role played by a hedge fund's legal counsel during the initial governance assessment process.

For starters, investors should endeavor to cover what could be considered the nuts and bolts of the relationship with a law firm by attempting to understand answers to questions including:

- What is the hourly billing rate charged to the hedge fund?
- Are any hourly billing rate or fee caps in place?
- Is a blended rate charged or instead does the rate vary by the experience of the law firm employee (including non-attorneys) performing the work?
- Is the hedge fund notified if fee caps are being approached?
- Are flat fees charged for any projects?
- Does the law firm have any particular expertise that may be applicable to the hedge fund (i.e., jurisdictional expertise, or experience in performing legal work related to certain investment products)?

This above list is, of course, not comprehensive, but is intended as a guide with which an investor could start a conversation with a law firm in order to gauge certain basic issues regarding its relationship with the hedge fund. You could, of course, take issue with any of the items of the list above. For example, what does it matter from a governance perspective how much a hedge fund pays its attorneys? As we outlined previously throughout this book both in our conversations related to fund employee compensation and more germane to our conversations related to the rates of service providers, questions such as this can have direct governance implications. For example, if a hedge fund is blatantly overpaying for legal services, couldn't it be argued that this suggests that the firm has poor governance with regards to oversight of the reasonability of fees paid to service providers?

Beyond the basics, an investor could inquire further into a number of different topics in an attempt to understand the extent of the law firm's work with the hedge fund. Examples of some items an investor could cover may include:

- Does the law firm provide any compliance-related services to the hedge fund?
- If the hedge fund works with a separate compliance consultant, does the law firm interact with them?
- Has there been any personnel turnover among the key individuals servicing the hedge fund's account?
- Can the law firm provide an example of a recent matter on which it has worked for the funds?
- If the funds or hedge fund management company was (or currently is) involved in any litigation, can the law firm walk the investor through the litigation (and any outcomes)?
- Does the law firm interact with any other law firms used by the hedge fund?
- Can the law firm provide a summary of the routine legal tasks performed for the firm?

Additionally, other more broad questions could be asked of the law firm to gain an understanding of how much they interact with and understand the hedge fund's business. Examples of these questions may include:

- Does the law firm generally understand the hedge fund's investment strategy?
- If there have been any recent material developments that have occurred at the hedge fund, is the law firm aware of them?
- Who at the hedge fund does the law firm primarily deal with?
- Has the scope of the work the hedge fund has given the law firm increased or decreased over the past two years? If so, why?

A law firm can play an important role in supporting the successful overall management of a hedge fund. In particular, in light of the increasingly complex regulatory and legal environment, investors should be cautious not to minimize the due diligence they perform on third-party service providers such as law firms. This can be stated in regards to both the functional operations between the hedge fund and the law firm and the overall governance in place in such relationships. Similar to other service providers, including fund directors, by delving into the details of such third-party relationships investors will likely be surprised at the useful governance insights they may learn.

Reviewing Information Technology Consultant Governance

It is increasingly common for many hedge fund managers, especially smaller ones, to leverage the efforts of external IT consultants. As we outlined in

Chapter 4 with the information security example regarding the use of IT consultants, the actual work performed by these consultants within the hedge fund itself, similar to other service providers, can have direct governance implications as well.

These consultants can support the work of internal IT personnel as well as be fully outsourced consultants. Specifically, IT consultants come in many different forms and can provide a wide array of services for fund managers. In general, common services provided by IT consultants can include:

- Help desk support
- Software development and support
- Hardware maintenance
- New software or hardware vendor and package selection
- Implementation of new systems or hardware
- BCP/DR program design, testing, and maintenance

During the due diligence process, investors may sometimes find it difficult to obtain a straight answer from their hedge fund managers with regards to the nature of the work of these IT consultants. Perhaps it is because certain fund managers want to emphasize the arguably more important role played by dedicated in-house IT personnel, be they dedicated or shared, while minimizing the external resources. Such evasiveness may provide a signal with regard to the governance oversight and extent of use of such providers. Said another way, certain investors may think that if a manager is coy in their response to such questions, what are they trying to hide? Invariably, such evasiveness can cause certain investors, particularly those focused on the governance controls in place surrounding such consultants, to ask more questions, in an attempt to kick the tires harder as it were.

Additionally, many hedge funds may utilize certain consultants on an ad hoc or as-needed basis and, therefore, perhaps don't feel that highlighting such relationships matters much to investors.

Investors should not be discouraged, however, and should take measures to evaluate the role of IT consultants. A good starting point is speaking directly with the hedge fund managers about the use of such consultants.

Learning What Consultants Do

From a governance standpoint, there are direct diagnostic benefits to gaining a hedge fund's perspective regarding the use of such consultants. Similar to the ways in which we described the benefits of letting directors explain in their own words what they do, so too can it be useful to hear from the hedge fund what exactly it is a service provider does. By comparing the two sides of the story, investors can often gain valuable governance insights with regard to any potential operational as well as oversight and control discrepancies that may arise.

By inquiring about these third-party firms, investors will likely learn about the duties performed by different IT consultants. Investors can also learn where a hedge fund may be weaker internally from a technology perspective and feels the need to augment these deficiencies with external resources. Examples of the types of questions that can provide valuable insights in this area include:

- Has there been turnover among IT consultants in a particular function? If so, why?
- If the hedge fund utilizes a consulting firm, as opposed to an individual free-lancer, what personnel from the IT consultant are actually doing the work?
- How often are the IT consultants in the offices of the hedge fund manager? If not frequently, do they access the firm's systems remotely?

Does the Hedge Fund Control Information Access?

In addressing the governance oversight of IT consultants, we should follow up in more detail regarding the example we provided in Chapter 4 relating to information access and control protocols. Specifically, after an investor has obtained a detailed understanding of what a third-party IT consultant may actually do for a hedge fund, investors should next inquire as to how the hedge fund controls the third-party's access to, and use of, fund data. Some questions investors may want to consider asking in this regard may include:

- Has the hedge fund taken policy-based measures to ensure IT consultants keep information confidential (i.e., signing a confidentiality agreement)?
- Are technological measures in place to limit the IT consultants' access to certain information? Or does the hedge fund trust the IT consultants blindly?
- How does the hedge fund oversee the implementation of any data security measures either agreed to with the IT consultants or in place from a technology perspective (i.e., is there any testing of such controls)?

The Importance of Governance Assessments on Information Technology Consultants

Hedge funds are information-based organizations. Technology supports the way in which a fund organizes, utilizes, and trades upon this information. When a hedge fund effectively opens up its doors to a third-party firm to assist in managing or improving upon this technology, investors should take notice. By incorporating an analysis of the role of third-party IT consultants into the larger governance assessment process, investors may learn new pieces of information, which can provide valuable insights into their overall assessment of a hedge fund's IT function.

GOVERNANCE ANALYSIS CONTINUED—AUDITED FINANCIAL STATEMENTS EXAMPLES

From a due diligence perspective, investors have long focused on analyzing the hedge fund audit process. As an offshoot of this process, investors also typically collect and review a hedge fund's audited financial statements. The focus on the analysis of such statements has become increasingly popular in recent years in conjunction with the overall increased focus on hedge fund operational risk analysis.

The analysis of audited financial statements can also highlight a number of related governance issues. In this section, we will analyze three such issues: the source by which investors collect such statements, related-party transactions, and expense disclosures.

Does the Source of Financial Statements Matter to Governance Analysis?

As we noted above, audited financial statements have increasingly become a critical part of the investor's due diligence process. Today, it certainly would be considered prudent for prospective investors in a particular hedge fund (i.e., those who have not already allocated to the fund) to request historical audits as part of the due diligence process. While many investors tend to justifiably focus on the content of the statements, the source of the statements however, tends to often be overlooked, particularly from a governance perspective.

Authenticity and Accuracy — Considering Audited Financial Statement Source Independence in Governance Assessments

To clarify, the source in this case refers not to the auditor; they of course produce the audited financials. Rather here we are referring to what organization the prospective investor is receiving the financial statements from. Many times the hedge fund itself will maintain an internal library of audited financials and simply forward them along, directly to the requester. When receiving documentation such as audited financials that were supposed to be prepared by a third party directly from the fund, however, there are legitimate governance concerns that may be raised relating to both the authenticity and accuracy of the documentation.

Taking authenticity first, an investor may be concerned about whether or not the auditor themselves actually produced the audits that the investor received. A hedge fund manager, for example, could simply steal the letterhead of an existing auditor or make up their own digital facsimile. Indeed, by reviewing the audits of other hedge funds produced by any big four accounting firms, it would not be overly difficult for a hedge fund manager to go online, download a logo, and make what may look like auditor letterhead. Similarly, taking a skeptical perspective, we could consider, for example, a fund that, for whatever reason, did indeed have accurate information in the financials (i.e., the liabilities figure on the balance sheet was indeed the correct liabilities amount for the fund); however, perhaps they prepared these figures themselves and used fake documentation to imply they were audited. If you don't believe that someone would go to such lengths to manufacture false documents to hide impropriety, consider the case of fraudster Marc Dreier, which included the use of such fraudulent statements (Wesier, 2009). Next, consider the question of accuracy of documentation. Of course, creating fraudulent numbers, which appear to make sense, that go into the actual audits may be slightly more difficult; however, this is certainly not outside the realm of possibility.

As we noted above, to those unfamiliar with such practices, it may be thought that it would be highly unlikely that any hedge fund would ever take such measures. Indeed, for the most part, the skeptics would be right. However, there certainly have been historical cases of hedge fund managers claiming relationships with auditors they did not have, such as the case of Andrey Hicks and Locust Offshore Management (Corgentum Consulting, 2013). There have also been other cases of hedge funds altering existing financial statements such as the Pinn fund case in 2002 (Murphy, 2002). Taking matters further, some hedge fund managers have even created fake audit firms to produce their own fraudulent audits. This scheme most famously took place in the Bayou fraud, but has also unbelievably been repeated as recently as March 2012 in the James Michael Murray case, where a hedge fund manager not only created a fake audit firm but went so far as to make a website for it as well (Egelko, 2012).

Can Administrators Serve as an Independent Statement Sources to Enhance Governance Oversight?

Recognizing the potential risks outlined above, some investors may feel it is better to obtain historical audited financials from a source other than the hedge fund manager. Of course, the most logical source would be to go straight to the horse's mouth, so to speak, and obtain the financial data directly from the auditor.

As any investor who has tried to conduct a review on an audit firm in the past will know, it is a bit of thorny issue. Indeed, many audit firms will barely confirm their relationship with a hedge fund. Seeking to obtain historical audited financials from them is virtually unheard of. As an aside, do such difficulties in dealing with auditors promote governance of the overall hedge fund investing relationship? After all, isn't the emphasis supposed to be on transparency? If investors aren't privy to the details of such audit relationships, how can they be expected to make any sort of assessment on the nature of the auditor's oversight and controls?

While hedge funds and investors may be unhappy about it, perhaps as a proposed compromise toward independence, the next party looked to is the fund administrator. The way it typically works is that the administrator, in the course of their business, interacts with the fund auditor and obtains the financial statements. The administrator can then forward the audited financials from the auditor directly to the prospective investor performing the review.

It seemingly would give investors some level of comfort to know that the audits are not coming directly from the manager, but instead from a third-party source. But are such notions of independent oversight misplaced?

When an administrator sends an investor audited financial statements, they are merely acting as a messenger. By transmitting these statements directly to investors, the administrator is not in any way attesting to the authenticity or accuracy of the statements. Of course, it would be nice to believe that the administrator at some point is not simply receiving the statements and filing them away, but actually reviewing them. In practice, in recent years auditors and administrators have increased the level of interaction between them. Although there is delegation of duty considerations among service providers that we discussed earlier in this text, such enhanced collaboration is, in general, believed by most to be beneficial for the overall governance relationship.

This increased collaboration is, in part, likely a result of the need for more transparency and information to perform each group's respective role, as well as a desire to better insulate themselves from allowing a manager to overly manipulate one relationship (i.e., an administration relationship) without the other firm (i.e., the auditor) knowing about it.

That being said, the theory behind receiving audits from a source other than the manager does rest on some solid governance ground. Principally, the more third parties that are involved, the more difficult it is to coordinate some sort of fraudulent deception. So when the administrator is placed in the financial statement distribution loop, assuming of course that they are not involved in the scheme, the manager would then need to trick the administrator into somehow believing that they received the audits from the auditor. Once again, not impossible, but a bit more complicated.

Additional Comments on the Governance Implications of Financial Statement Source Considerations

At the end of the day, the information contained in the audited financial statements should not be viewed in isolation during the due diligence process. This includes not only the actual financial data but the source of the financial statements as well. Certainly, just because a financial statement comes from an ostensibly more "independent" source such as the fund administrator as compared with the manager, this in no way means that an investor should not take measures to independently confirm the audit relationship outside of the manager.

Furthermore, investors should not let hedge fund managers attempt to dodge further inquiry regarding the auditor or the financials, simply because they were forwarded to the investor from the administrator. It is ultimately up to each investor if they take any additional comfort from receiving the audited financials from the administrator as opposed to the manager; however, for the reasons outlined above, the addition of a third-party–audited financial statement source to your governance assessment toolkit certainly couldn't hurt.

Governance Considerations Related to Interpreting Financial Statement–Related Party Transactions

Continuing our examples and discussion of governance-related considerations that may arise throughout the analysis of audited financial statements, we can now turn our attention to related-party transactions. When reviewing audited financial statements during the due diligence and governance assessment process, investors should consider not only the actual numbers contained in the different sections of the financial statements but the financial statement notes as well. One key part of the notes is the so-called "related-party transactions" section. For reference, related-party transactions typically refer to transactions among the firm's funds, or between the fund and the management company. These entities typically share common ownership and are therefore related. One reason related-party transactions are particularly important from a governance perspective is because of the enhanced potential for conflicts of interests among the firm's entities that engage in related-party transactions. It may be easy for investors simply to look at this section and dismiss it as a boilerplate language; however, often times meaningful details may be buried within this section.

Analyzing Related Party Fees

The financial statement disclosures pertaining to related-party transactions often start off with a general summary of the fees the investment manager receives and how often they receive them. This section then typically proceeds to include general disclaimer language, which, unfortunately for investors, effectively gives the fund manager a great degree of fee flexibility. This language generally mimics similar language in the fund's offering memorandum, and reads something to the effect of "The Investment Manager, in its sole discretion, may reduce or waive the management fee with regards to certain limited partners."

The fee section then typically concludes with the actual amount (i.e., not a percentage) of what the fee actually was. This last piece of information, the actual amount of the fee, can be used by investors to further analyze the various sections of the financial statements contained earlier in the audits. For example, the actual amount of the management fee provided in the related-party transaction section can be compared with the management fee figures in other parts of the financial statements such as in the Statement of Income. Similar comparisons can be made for other related-party fees such as the incentive allocation. Additionally, it may also be useful to compare the fee information disclosed in this section with fee details that may have been disclosed in previous year's audit.

Considering Related Limited Partner Capital Balances

Returning to the related-party transaction disclosures in the financial statement notes; generally this section also includes details of related limited partner capital balances. This figure can then be compared with "skin in the game"–type asset information provided by the fund manager outside of the audited financials. The amount of capital invested by managers is often considered to be a powerful governance mechanism to better coordinate the interests of fund personnel with investors. The thinking is, the more personal capital a hedge fund manager has invested in the firm's funds, the less likely they are to try and lose it.

Similarly, these figures may provide clarity with regard to the balances of actual funds that are invested in other funds. This information can then be used to facilitate a comparison to provide insights into any discrepancies on a vehicle-level basis between the fund's reported figures and those contained in the financial statements.

Fee Waiver Considerations

In addition to the information listed above, related-party transaction disclosures may also contain other pieces of information including any specific fee waivers among related parties and transactions made among the firm's different funds. Items such as fee waiver disclosures should be considered by investors, not only in the context of a review of the audited financial statements themselves but in the broader governance assessment as well.

For example, during an on-site interview, a fund's representative may have made a statement to the effect that "all employees invest with the same terms as everyone else." If a fee waiver is then disclosed in the audits, does this mean that the fund employee was lying? Not necessarily, the argument could perhaps be made that the fund employee was referring to liquidity terms and not necessarily fee waivers. As this example highlights, certain disclosures made by the funds in this instance may be open to interpretation. As such, it is better to not blindly take the fund's word for it and instead perform your own double checking with regard to related-party transaction terms that may benefit the fund such as fee waivers. Such analysis can serve as a useful tool during the governance assessment process to assist in determining not only the accuracy of manager statements but also the seriousness by which the fund manager takes items such as the equitableness of fee arrangements between fund personnel and investors.

Interfund Transactions

Transactions among the firm's funds is another area that investors should inquire about during the broader due diligence process, particularly when focusing on a governance assessment.

One reason for this is that, in a master–feeder complex, investors may run the risk of having one vehicle (e.g., the offshore fund) take advantage of another vehicle (e.g., the onshore fund). As an example of the potential risks related to an interfund complex transaction, one could look at the SEC allegations in the Martin Currie China fund case (US SEC, 2012).

Once again, general information learned during the ODD process regarding the potential for funds to participate in transactions with each other can be revealed and supported by disclosures in the audited financial "related-party transaction" section. In certain cases, specific details related to the transactions may be disclosed in the audits. Often times such disclosures can give investors another perspective on the magnitude, nature, and frequency of such transactions.

Additional Comments on the Governance Implications of Financial Statement Source Considerations

From a governance perspective, there is nothing inherently wrong with related-party transactions. In some cases they come up during the normal course of business of a fund complex. When analyzing fund governance, the aim should be for investors to understand the nature of such transactions, controls in place surrounding any such transactions, and their economics to both the fund and investors. By reviewing related-party transaction disclosures in the audited financial statements, maintaining a focus on potential conflicts, and the associated overseeing of such transactions during the governance due diligence process, investors may gain useful insights into the risks surrounding such arrangements.

Incorporating Fund Expense Disclosure Analysis Into Governance Reviews

When considering a hedge fund's audited financial statements, another common consideration relates to the nature of fund expenses. The typical concern in this area is whether such expenses are reasonable. The next logical consideration is: how do we define what reasonable means? There are also a number of governance considerations with regard to the oversight and control of fund expenses. When considering fund expenses from a governance perspective, investors should also be conscious of the aforementioned related-party transaction considerations that may be related to the allocation of such expenses as well.

Within the audits themselves, investors are generally provided with some guidance through a series of expense-related disclosures. But do these disclosures add any real value to investors in analyzing fund expenses? Additionally, what should investors' governance goals be in analyzing fund expenses?

Governance Implications of Legitimate Versus Illegitimate Expenses

For risk assessment purposes within the context of a due diligence review, many investors would most likely agree that, in general, fund expenses can be grouped into two categories. The first category could be so-called legitimate expenses. That is to say, those expenses that occur as part of the course of a hedge fund's normal business and trading activities. These expenses could include both investment and trading-related costs such as interest and dividend expense and stock loan fees. Other expenses that many investors would likely place in the "legitimate" bucket would include performance and management fees. Fees for items for operational or noninvestment-related purposes such as fees paid to members of the board of directors, audit, and legal expenses could also be placed in the legitimate bucket with little investor argument.

The second category of expenses investors tend to look for could be called illegitimate expenses. These are effectively the polar opposite of legitimate expenses, and, as the name implies, would not be items investors expect to be charged to the fund during the normal course of business. These could be items such as lavish expenses for fund-raising, paying for the fund manager to travel to a sales meeting in a private plane, or the unreasonable salary of any individual employee being charged directly to a fund. During the due diligence process, from a governance perspective, investors who come across any of these illegitimate expenses should certainly raise a red flag and inquire further as to why such expenses are being charged to the fund.

Beyond this fairly basic legitimate versus illegitimate framework, investors face more complex additional governance assessment challenges in reviewing fund-level expenses.

Evaluating Gray Area Expenses

As noted above, it may be easy for investors to classify expenses at either end of the spectrum as being legitimate or illegitimate. The classification of expenses may become less clear, however, when investors start to dive into the details of actual fund expenses. It is with regard to these gray area expenses that difficult governance questions may arise and, as is the case with many similar gray area issues, more than a cursory expense analysis is often required before a comprehensive assessment may be made.

For example, consider a hedge fund manager that invests in the distressed debt of companies. As part of their research process, the fund manager sends analysts to visit with the management of the target companies in which it is considering purchasing debt. Most investors would likely agree that such research trips are not lavish or excessive, but rather part of the hedge fund manager's standard operating procedure. Where investors may differ in their opinions is whether the expense of such research trips should be charged directly to the funds themselves, or rather if the expense for such trips should be posted at the management company level. From a best practice governance perspective, do you believe such trips should be covered by the fund or the management company? Perhaps the answer may depend on other information such as what other types of expenses are charged to the fund? This type of example highlights the necessity to conduct a comprehensive review of multiple factors before making a rash, uninformed governance assessment.

There are many other examples of areas where investors and fund managers may disagree as to the appropriateness of allocating all or a portion of an expense to the funds versus the management company. Additional examples of these types of expenses may include the allocation of a hedge fund's office rent expense and expenses related to acquiring and maintaining the IT function including hardware that may be used to execute the fund's trading strategies.

Regardless of which side of the argument a particular investor lands on, from a governance perspective, it is important that investors have transparency with regard to such expenses. Additionally, investors should seek to evaluate the consistency of a hedge fund manager's approach in allocating gray area expenses. Said another way, from a governance perspective, it is up to the investor to understand what a particular hedge fund's rules of the expense allocation game are before they can evaluate if a manager is following them.

Figuring Out the Expense Allocation Rules

At this point, you may be asking yourself, how is an investor supposed to figure out what the hedge fund's policy is with regard to allocating such expenses in order to facilitate a governance review? A hedge fund's offering memorandum might be a good start. The offering memorandum often contains valuable information about not only what expenses are anticipated to be charged to the fund (i.e., legitimate vs. illegitimate) but also the way in which they will be allocated.

It is worth noting here the importance of incorporating documents other than the offering memorandum and audited financial statements into the overall governance expense analysis process. Clearly, investors should not be hesitant to seek out information from other sources to guide their analysis. This produces a more comprehensive, well-rounded review, which runs less of a risk of ignoring key risk areas simply because they may be interdisciplinary in nature.

Returning to our discussion of expense allocation rules, it is instructive to discuss the information that can be gleaned from the audited financial statements themselves. Often times the statement of operations, also known as the income statement, will provide valuable information about the detail of total fund-level expenses. The problem, however, is that the figures presented in these statements are often in summary format. For example, the statements may indicate that interest and dividend expense was $100. It would arguably be more useful for investors to know more detail. For example, something to the effect of interest expense was $30 and the dividend expense was $70.

Another problem investors often encounter when attempting to make a detailed governance inquiry of fund expenses relates to so-called rollup categories of expenses. These are groups of expenses that are bundled together into a single line item. An example of such an expense category would be "Professional Fees and other." Under US GAAP, there is no universal rule as to what exactly should be lumped into such a category. Furthermore, there is not even a general agreement among hedge funds or investors as to what exactly may go into this line item. Typically, an expense category such as this would contain items such as board of director's fees and legal fees; however, investors should not make any such assumptions. A hedge fund manager could just as likely use such a broad category to bundle gray area expenses that, if brought to the attention of some investors, may raise questions. Some investors may feel that the fund manager should be more transparent with such fund expense details, particularly when they have the information available. Furthermore, it could be argued that providing investors with such transparency would promote enhanced governance oversight of such issues by investors.

Additional Comments on Expense Analysis During Governance Due Diligence

Are investors left with any options when faced with such rollup categories? One resource investors should consider when faced with such issues is the notes accompanying the financial statements. These notes can sometimes provide additional clarification as to what is included in rollup expense categories. Although there are some general guidelines under US GAAP with regard to minimum mandatory disclosures, once again there is no universal requirement to provide such detail in all cases.

Furthermore, as we have outlined earlier in this discussion, a typical hedge fund auditor is not generally incentivized from either a financial or liability perspective to write detailed, clear disclosures. In this case, investors should then not be afraid to approach the fund manager directly and inquire as to what actually goes into each category. If a manager is willing to engage in such discussion, it may be a signal, subject to further inquiry of course, that the manager supports enhanced governance transparency in other parts of the firm as well. As noted above, manager's expense allocation disclosures may provide investors with more data to judge whether allocation rules are being followed. Additionally, investors engaging in such discussions with managers may be surprised to learn about how much discretion a fund manager may have in making determinations as to how expenses are allocated.

One of the goals during expense analysis therefore should be not only to diagnose the way in which a hedge fund allocates expenses but also to oversee that discretionary choices by the manager are equitable to all investors and in the best interest of the particular fund vehicle in question. By engaging with fund managers to conduct such reviews, investors may find their review of the fund expenses and disclosures may bear fruit, with regard to transparency as well as other parts of the overall governance due diligence process.

GOVERNANCE ANALYSIS CONTINUED—BUSINESS CONTINUITY EXAMPLES

Business Continuity Pandemic Planning—Example of a Governance Indicator?

As noted earlier, during the due diligence process, one of the key areas frequently reviewed is BCP/DR. As we discussed in Chapter 5, the assessment of BCP/DR plan implementation and testing, as overseen by internal BCP/DR committees, is an example of an in-house hedge fund governance mechanism that investors can assess to gauge the competence and risk associated with a given fund's governance.

Part of the investor review process of BCP/DR plans typically includes requesting that a hedge fund provide investors with actual copies of their BCP/DR plans. The response to this request may, in and of itself, contain revealing governance data. For example, some funds may not have a separate BCP/DR plan and instead may incorporate this into other documentation such as a compliance manual. Other firms may have a document entitled "BCP/DR Plan," but instead the plan may be heavily focused in one specific area such as technology planning. Assuming that a fund does provide a BCP/DR plan that covers more than just technology, however, investors may find several pieces of interesting governance information that may not be immediately available on reviewing a short summary of the BCP/DR plan in another document, such as a DDQ.

One point of information that may surprise investors is that certain BCP/DR plans may address how the firm would respond to a wide range of exogenous events including terrorism and even epidemics of infectious diseases known as pandemics. At first glance, investors may think such planning is surely overkill. Of course, employees can become sick, or during the winter season there may be a spread of diseases such as the flu, but generally they do not rise to the point of a widespread pandemic. Are such concerns completely unfounded and representative of the use of boilerplate documentation and, therefore, representative of poor governance as evidence by prefabricated recycled documentation? On the other hand, is planning for such unlikely, outlier events representative of well-thought-out governance planning? After all, isn't that the point of BCP/DR planning to make plans so that the fund can continue operations should an unexpected or unlikely event occur?

Pandemic Scares Do Happen: SARS and Swine Flu

A real-world example of a pandemic event that directly affected the hedge fund industry was the 2002 severe acute respiratory syndrome ("SARS") outbreak in Asia. At the time, many Asian hedge funds, including those in the hedge fund centers of Singapore and Hong Kong, were suddenly faced with the problem of attempting to continue their operations in the face of regional travel advisories and compulsory quarantines. After the outbreak had subsided, many Asia-Pacific hedge funds put SARS plans in place (AsiaHedge, 2003). Another more recent example was the 2009 global swine flu outbreak. In such situations, a fund with a detailed and tested pandemic plan would have likely fared much better than those who had never considered it.

Pandemic Boilerplate; Fear Mongering or Best Practice Governance?

If a fund does have a BCP/DR plan in place, the next question facing investors is whether the plan is appropriate for the firm. A good place to start when analyzing pandemic plans is with the language in the plan document. First, investors should consider if the language in the plan is appropriate for the size of the firm. Investors may realize that in some cases, perhaps in their eagerness to provide what they deem to be complete BCP/DR plans, funds may include wide-ranging boilerplate descriptions of pandemic planning that may be more in line with episodes of *The Walking Dead* zombie-type apocalyptic breakouts, and may not be appropriate for a firm of their size. Disconnects between the realities of the scale of practical planning based on the firm's size and broad, widespread plans more appropriate for large publicly traded corporations suggest not only that was there poor governance oversight in the creation of such plans but also that there is little ongoing oversight or control regarding actually implementing such plans. This is certainly not representative of good governance practices.

Consider, for example, a BCP/DR plan for a hedge fund with less than 10 employees that has a detailed pandemic plan with 9 levels of different escalations depending on the nature of the outbreak. On first glance, does this seem appropriate for a fund of this size? As we outlined above, this isn't to say that a small hedge fund shouldn't plan for a pandemic event. An excessive level of detail, however, suggests that the plan may not have been designed with the firm in mind, and may not be practically implementable for the firm. It would be likely considered better from a governance perspective, once again depending on the specific facts at hand, that a relatively small firm such as this may benefit from a smaller-scale BCP/DR pandemic plan that is more appropriate for a firm of their size. This, by association, suggests that poor governance oversight regarding the development of such plans may be in place.

Regardless of the firm's size, investors should also consider whether they feel the language contained in the fund's BCP/DR plan is something the firm will actually follow or is just boilerplate in nature. Consider, for example, the following sample language from a BCP/DR plan related to pandemic planning: "In the event of the first human outbreak case in North America, the fund will minimize face to face contact by conducting transactions with vendors, investors/investees via email, telephone, and electronically wherever possible. Face to face interactions will only occur when every other option has been used." Do you think that such planning would be appropriate for a smaller firm? Is such unrealistic planning likely inappropriate for the firm and representative of poor governance?

When assessing governance, investors should not simply take language from the BCP/DR plan at face value and instead inquire further with the firm. An investor could perhaps start such questioning by asking a fund to generally describe its BCP/DR plans. If they omit the subject of pandemic planning altogether, perhaps they don't take this subject too seriously from a governance perspective. Furthermore, if they have a BCP/DR that does address pandemics, but they do not address it when describing the plan, then how can investors be reasonably expected to believe some of the detailed descriptions contained in such plans?

Consider the following sample language from a BCP/DR plan related to pandemic planning structured in a Q&A format:

Question: In the event of an outbreak in the United States, describe how you will provide for new employee onboarding to familiarize replacement resources with their duties as quickly as possible?

Response: The fund's business function processes have been documented in our policies and procedure manuals. The fund's teams consist of multiple investment professionals. Weekly meetings are held for all investment professionals for status updates of active investments as well as potential investments. New employees would be familiarized with the documented procedures and policies and included within the weekly meetings.

Putting aside the fact that the response doesn't really answer the question, does such boilerplate language make an investor feel as if the fund really has a detailed plan in place to onboard new employees in the event of a pandemic? Furthermore, do investors really believe that the fund will go on a hiring spree in the event of a pandemic? This is an example of where there may be a disconnect between practicality and overplanning to feign good governance.

Additional Comments on BCP/DR Pandemic Planning and Governance

Analyzing the language of a BCP/DR plan and having frank discussions with fund managers regarding the fund's planning can not only provide insights into how seriously the fund takes BCP/DR but also alert the reviewer of other potential yellow flag governance issues that may be in place at the fund. Focusing on areas such as pandemic planning may seem to be outside of the scope of governance assessment, but as recent examples demonstrate, there are situations where such planning can insulate funds from risk should a disaster strike.

Business Continuity Backup Planning—Another Governance Indication Example

Reviews of a fund's BCP/DR infrastructures, however, are a bit counterintuitive from a governance perspective. The goal of evaluating a fund's BCP/DR plans seems simple enough on its face—can a fund continue operations in the event of a disaster? As we have outlined above, however, from this simple enough question comes a myriad of quite complex technology, process, and planning considerations. One such area that we will focus on in this chapter relates to backup power generation. Similar to pandemic planning examples above, the way a hedge fund approaches the concept of backup power generation in regards to BCP/DR planning can also serve as a valuable governance indicator.

At this point, you may be asking why we are seemingly focusing on such minutia of details such as pandemics and backup power. The reason is that these are exactly the types of issues that run the risk of slipping through the cracks. The level of transparency, oversight, and controls in areas such as these are often the best indicators of how genuinely a fund approaches governance. It may be easier to address so-called big-ticket governance items, such as the board of directors, but an additional level of effort is typically required to institute good governance in these seemingly ancillary areas.

Can Keeping the Lights On Be Representative of Good Governance?

The concept behind a fund manager's backup power generation capabilities may seem to boil down to a singular goal—can a fund manager keep the lights on, literally and figuratively, if the power goes out? From a due diligence perspective, the question of how a fund manager approaches this issue can actually be further distilled into two distinct questions.

First, does a fund manager have backup power capabilities to allow for an orderly shutdown or protection of the firm's hardware? Second, can the firm continue operations, and perhaps most importantly, investing activities, in the event of a prolonged power outage? Let us consider each of these questions individually.

When considering backup power that provides an orderly system shutdown, we first have to understand exactly what hardware is being turned off. On its most basic level, fund managers generally have two primary types of hardware: desktop computers and servers. When the power is suddenly cut to either of these types of equipment, bad things could happen if they were to immediately just shut down. First, important data that was not saved properly before the shutdown could be lost. Besides the loss of data, a sudden power loss could potentially cause actual physical damage to the hardware itself.

To combat these problems, a fund manager can typically install a piece of hardware known as an uninterruptible power supply, which is commonly referred to as a UPS. On their most basic level, a UPS provides protection from a power loss. It does this by automatically switching on when the power is cut. Once switched on, a UPS will minimally provide sufficient battery power to the computer or server so that it may be properly shut down without data loss or hardware damage.

The length of battery power provided by a UPS can be relatively short (i.e., 15 minutes) or may even extend up to a number of hours. A UPS may not only serve as a backup to power loss. These devices can also protect equipment against power surges, spikes, and high-frequency power oscillation from other equipment. All UPSs are not created equally, and there are many different types including offline/standby UPS, line-interactive UPS, double-conversion online UPS, double-conversion on demand, ferroresonant UPS, and diesel rotary UPS.

While UPSs range in price and capabilities, it is generally considered best practice for a fund manager to have dedicated UPSs for both their desktop computers and servers. Additionally, it is important for fund managers to perform ongoing testing of UPSs to ensure that they are appropriately holding battery power.

We can now turn to the second primary concern most investors have to backup power generation: the ability of a fund manager to continue operations in the event of a prolonged power loss. This area is most likely the more common of the two major investor concerns related to backup power generation. To clarify, a prolonged power loss generally refers to a loss of power that extends for more than a few minutes.

Depending on the fund manager's geographic location, inclement weather such as snow storms or hurricanes may potentially cause power outages that can extend for a number of days. The problem, of course, is that the entire world does not lose power all at once, and the markets remain open.

A fund manager who cannot continue trading operations for an extended period of time is likely to be at a severe disadvantage and may potentially pile up serious losses. As an aside, it should be noted that a fund manager's approach to continuing operations may encompass a number of concepts not directly related to backup power generation including securing alternative work locations and maintaining backup phone lines and Internet connections. Returning to the issue at hand though, what approaches is an investor likely to encounter during the governance assessment process?

The most common solution that fund managers take to address this issue is a backup generator. Backup generators are different from UPSs in that they actually have the ability to generate power for an extended period of time. Emergency backup generators come in multiple types including natural gas, gasoline, and diesel powered. Generators must be sized to meet anticipated demands and must be capable of starting automatically when needed unless on-site personnel are capable of operating the units. Regardless of the type and size of generator employed, a preventive maintenance program needs to be implemented to ensure the unit will function properly when needed. Additionally, standby generators need to be run under load several times throughout the year to ensure that the equipment will function reliably when needed. It is important to ensure that the generator has an appropriate supply of relatively fresh and contaminant-free fuel in its tank and provisions to refill the tank as needed during a long-duration power outage need to be in place before the event. Depending on their location, a fund manager may have a dedicated generator or one that is shared with multiple tenants in the same office building. Large generators, which may need to generate power for periods of multiple days, certainly require a significant investment of capital and ongoing maintenance expense from a fund manager. Depending on the nature of the fund manager's strategy, some investors may consider the importance of such extended generator capabilities to be more or less important.

For example, some investors might be of the opinion that a high-frequency trading hedge fund would likely suffer greater losses by having an extended power outage than a low-frequency event-driven manager. Regardless of the particular specifics associated with a given manager's funds, it is generally considered best practice for a fund manager to have both UPSs and a dedicated emergency backup power generator.

Investors who take the initiative to evaluate the way in which a fund manager approaches loss of power issues lessen the risk of being left out in the dark when the power goes out. As noted above, in addition to providing a sense of comfort with regard to the actual backup power practices employed, this can also be a strong indicator that the hedge fund is focused on governance. Of course, investors should reserve judgment until a more detailed review of the unique circumstances of each fund is conducted, but certainly, detailed planning in this area is representative of overall management attention to detail and can't hurt the situation.

INFORMATION TECHNOLOGY GOVERNANCE REVIEWS

Although elements of BCP/DR planning often incorporate many aspects of IT, reviewing additional IT-related factors can also provide valuable indications of overall fund governance. In this section, we will discuss several typical hedge fund IT issues. Like our BCP/DR examples highlighted above, we will utilize the opportunity to focus on these specific IT issues as illustrative of the type of governance analysis that can be employed across the wide variety of operational and investment-related factors reviewed during the investor due diligence process. Specifically we will analyze the use of the cloud including its use in BCP/DR planning, information security risk frameworks, and approaches to technology hardware management.

If a Hedge Fund Uses Cutting-Edge Cloud Technology, Does That Imply Good Governance?

Cloud computing–based IT and cloud-based BCP/DR solutions have becoming increasingly popular in recent years among the hedge funds. Indeed, many investors performing due diligence on fund managers may have come across more and more funds utilizing the cloud. The question could be asked, however, whether the increased use of this technology, or really any new technology for that matter, is representative of best practice governance. On the other hand, does this show that the hedge fund is merely an aggressive early adapter of new technologies that it may not have fully vetted but are simply the flavor of the day?

While considering such questions, it is perhaps useful to provide some background before seeking to answer them. It is important for investors to understand exactly what the cloud is and both the challenges and opportunities it presents to fund managers, particularly in relation to BCP/DR.

What Exactly Is the Cloud?

In the context of evaluating fund BCP/DR infrastructures, the cloud can effectively be thought of by investors as an Internet-based off-site IT solution. There are three types of cloud computing, all of which are typically classified with the ending "as a service." They include:

- Platform as a service ("PaaS")—Under this model service providers provide a computing platform solution to funds such as an operating system or web server.
- Software as a service ("SaaS")—This model allows funds to run and access applications on cloud-based servers.
- Infrastructure as a service ("IaaS")—Under this model, service providers offer funds access to virtual computing equipment, storage space, and data centers via the Internet.

Depending on the way these different PaaS, SaaS, and IaaS services may be applied, hedge funds may be exposed to more or less governance risks. For example, under an IaaS, virtual equipment is utilized. Has the hedge fund appropriately taken measures to institute robust controls regarding the information sharing through the use of these virtual machines? Similarly, what oversight mechanisms have the fund put in place to ensure any controls are being appropriately implemented? This is an example of the ways in which governance consideration can play into issues such as the use of the cloud.

How Do Fund Managers Utilize the Cloud for BCP/DR Planning?

Hedge funds are increasingly incorporating cloud-based components into their BCP/DR plans in several ways:

- Data storage—Increasingly it is cost-effective for firms to archive data off-site on cloud-based servers. This reduces expenditures on new servers and frees up office space for other equipment and personnel and may reduce in-house IT personnel requirements.
- Data backup—Cloud-based data storage centers typically serve a high volume of customers and are therefore designed to handle large-scale data transfers. These facilities are also typically designed with BCP/DR planning in mind, and may be more robust in both equipment and design than an individual fund manager's system.
- Application backup—Fund managers may utilize cloud-based solutions to serve as a backup location from which applications could continue to be run in the event of a business disruption or disaster-type event. The continued operation of applications during such an event may be particularly critical for quantitative or high-frequency trading strategies.

Similar to the questions we have previously raised, when conducting a governance assessment, investors should consider how a hedge fund has balanced the benefits of cloud utilization with the appropriate governance countermeasures. For example, a common concern relating to off-site data backup relates to questions regarding the security of such information in off-site facilities. Has the hedge fund coordinated the efforts of any internal IT personnel and third-party providers involved in this process to ensure appropriate oversight over data integrity? Similarly, are sufficient controls and oversight in place to ensure the integrity of the process does not break down?

Inquiring About Hedge Fund Cloud Governance

As noted above, the cloud can present a number of attractive benefits to fund managers. As part of an evaluation of a hedge fund's BCP/DR planning, investors should take the time to understand how their fund managers may make use of such technologies. Some key issues investors may want to consider addressing when conducting a governance assessment include:

- What measures has the hedge fund taken to evaluate the BCP/DR planning procedures of the cloud provider?
- How does the hedge fund monitor the testing and oversight of the BCP/DR plan at this provider?
- What measures has a hedge fund taken to address security concerns related to storing data and running applications at third parties?
- Does the fund manager incorporate testing of access to cloud-based data and applications as part of its own BCP/DR tests?
- Has the fund performed a cost–benefit analysis of the use of cloud-based technologies versus bringing such technologies in house? At what point would any cloud benefits be outweighed by internal cost considerations?

While the increased use of the cloud may be a hot trend among hedge funds for functions including BCP/DR data storage and application development, investors should take care to understand if a hedge fund has carefully evaluated their use of this new technology, or if they are simply jumping on the bandwagon. Additionally, by taking measures to ensure not just the technical implementation of the cloud but also the overall governance oversight environment including controls on data integrity, investors will likely be able to make more informed governance assessments in this area.

Are Strong Information Security Controls Representative of Good Governance?

Hedge fund managers are often undertaking a number of different technology projects at once. These can range from mundane software updates to full-scale hardware upgrades. Additionally, with the increased acceptance of virtual work environments and increased cloud usage noted above, many fund management organizations are eschewing further investment in more traditional technologies and ramping up the resources allocated to these emerging technologies. As we have discussed, some investors question whether the aggressive adoption of such technologies represents good governance.

With all of these changes taking place, investors may be tempted to focus the efforts they make during their due diligence review on these more cutting-edge advances, in lieu of spending appropriate time and effort reviewing technology basics. These basics can typically include an evaluation of the appropriateness and quality of software systems utilized across a number of operational functions including order management, settlement and reconciliation, and fund accounting. Other traditional IT-related items that may be covered during due diligence reviews include hardware-related items such as understanding the types and number of servers utilized and the type of network connections in place. A common item that may become lost in the due diligence shuffle between an increased focus on a fund manager's use of new technologies and more traditional technology concerns is information security.

The focus on information security and cyber attacks on hedge funds has rapidly increased in recent years. Indeed, there have been continued reports that hedge funds have undergone attacks from hackers who have stolen data and disrupted high-frequency trading operations (Strohm, 2014). As another sign of the increased risks in this area, in April 2014, the US SEC Office of Compliance Inspections and Examinations announced that its 2014 examination priorities would include a focus on hedge fund cyber security preparedness (US SEC, 2014). With the increased focus on risks in this area, it is relevant to consider the governance implications of the way in which funds address such risks.

A fund manager is not like a traditional factory—they do not manufacture anything an end user can touch. Rather, a fund manager is in the investing business—and this is a field that is centered on information. Funds deal with all types of information, not limited solely to investment data. For example, they typically maintain data related to daily operational procedures (i.e., books and records, data from accounting systems, trade confirmations, etc.) as well as information about their employees (i.e., employee addresses, payroll figures, etc.), and data about who their clients are. During the due diligence process, a key question to consider is, "how does a fund manager go about protecting this data?" Are appropriate governance controls and protocols in place to adequately ensure initial and ongoing data security? Perhaps the more appropriate question from a governance perspective should be, "who is this fund manager protecting this data from?"

The most common consideration that first comes to the minds of most investors is that a fund manager's approach toward protecting data is often focused almost exclusively on external threats. For example, it would obviously be a serious threat if a hacker were able to log onto the fund manager's internal network and steal data. During the governance assessment process, investors can take a number of steps to evaluate the quality of a hedge fund's information security defenses from external threats including:

- Has the firm performed any penetration testing?
- If yes:
    - **(i)** Has the firm employed a third-party firm to conduct an evaluation or did they perform the testing themselves?
    - **(ii)** What were the results of the penetration testing?
- If not, does the firm have any plans to perform such testing in the future?
- What are the firm's standard information security procedures to prevent external attacks?
- What types of firewalls are in place?

Another often overlooked area of information security due diligence relates to segregating and protecting data within the fund management firm itself. Often, particularly in a larger fund management organization, different employees will have access to certain pieces of information.

This can be both to protect the confidentiality of certain employees (i.e., the administrative assistant does not have access to everyone's personnel files in the same way a human resources professional would) and to implement checks and balances throughout the firm. In this regard, a fund manager who takes measures to protect or limit access to certain pieces of information would do so among the firm's employees itself. Some key considerations investors may want to consider when evaluating the governance framework in which a fund manager attempts to protect data internally may include:

- Are IT consultants utilized? If so, how does the firm monitor consultant access to and use of proprietary data?
- Can employees utilize remote storage devices such as zip drives?
- If employees can access the firm's systems remotely, are equivalent data protection procedures in place to system access from within the office?

A fund manager that does not take measures to appropriately protect data from threats, both internal and external, can have critical information literally walk out the door. From a governance perspective, putting aside any loss of competitive advantage from loss of investment-related data, a fund manager that does not protect data may be exposing their client's information to others and run the risk of future fraudulent activity or even identity theft. Clearly, neglecting to protect data using best practices does not represent good governance. By asking the right questions, an investor can effectively diagnose whether a fund manager approaches this subject seriously or instead is in denial that such attacks won't happen to them. Even if a fund manager does have some controls in place, conducting a thorough governance assessment can make headway in determining what ongoing oversight is in place to prevent ongoing cyber threats. Without such ongoing oversight, it is likely only a matter of time until a fund manager is hacked.

Governance Implications of Hardware Management—Dusty Servers or Organized Efficiency?

When performing due diligence on IT-related matters, investors have a tendency to focus intently on software applications and less on the actual infrastructure in place. Software is, of course, crucial to a fund manager's operations and certainly evaluating the ways in which software interacts with other functions can provide critical insight into the operational infrastructure of a fund. But what about hardware? Isn't all hardware created equal? Often times analyzing the way in which a fund approaches hardware management can provide a better understanding of governance approaches in place. To take a step back for a moment we should clarify what type of hardware we are addressing here.

What Kind of Hardware Are We Talking About?

First of all, in evaluating a fund manager's hardware it is important to clarify what exactly we are talking about. Fund managers effectively interact with hardware in one of two ways. The first is that they purchase or lease hardware that is under their control. We can classify this type of hardware as *internal hardware*.

The second type of hardware is not owned by the hedge fund but by a third party, and is where a fund manager's data is stored or passes through in the case of trading platforms. We can classify this type of hardware as *external hardware*. One of the more recent examples of the ways in which fund managers interact with external hardware is the increased use among fund managers of colocation solutions, such as cloud computing and cloud-based storage solutions. In these cases, managers are often utilizing large, third-party servers on which they have space allocated to them. It is important for investors to understand the distinction between internal hardware and external hardware in order to effectively evaluate a fund manager's hardware infrastructure.

As we noted above, with the increased use of third-party off-site services, there are increased concerns of maintaining the control and integrity of such data. Similar to the concerns outlined earlier in this discussion, from a governance perspective, investors should inquire how a fund has achieved comfort with colocation solutions. Additionally, what oversight protocols have the fund put in place to appropriately monitor colocation oversight?

Often times the equipment utilized in both internal hardware and external hardware situations is similar. Common types of IT hardware and peripherals include desktop computers, routers, and servers. In addition to this standard equipment, many fund managers may also have additional hardware that provides backup power generation capabilities such as generators or UPS devices.

It is worth noting that each of these types of equipment is a broad umbrella term, which encompasses a wide variety of meanings. So, for example, a fund manager could have several different types of servers (i.e., email/Exchange Server, SQL Server, BlackBerry Server, etc.). It is important for investors to understand the different types of equipment in each category so that they can effectively evaluate the overall IT function.

Investors should take stock of a manager's hardware inventory when reviewing the IT function during the ODD process. With this inventory in place, investors will have a road map by which they can navigate and evaluate the hardware review process.

Is the Use of Brand Name Hardware a Sign of Better Governance?

After an investor has developed an understanding of the types of hardware utilized by a fund manager, it is also important for investors to learn of the brand names of the manufacturers of such hardware. Brand names do not necessarily imply better operations, or that better governance was employed in the purchasing of such hardware. That being said, certain types of hardware are considered to be of higher quality than others. Some manufacturers may be better positioned to support the equipment they sell after the purchase. Additionally, different types of hardware from different manufacturers may have different capabilities. By inquiring not only as to the types of hardware in place but also as to the brand names of the manufacturers of such hardware (in conjunction with evaluating hardware capabilities), investors may be able to make more fully informed decisions when evaluating the overall governance oversight of the IT function.

Can Too Much Hardware Indicate Poor Governance?

During the due diligence process, investors will often take a tour of a fund manager's IT closet. This room is often loud, due to the buzzing of cooling fans, and cold so that the equipment does not overheat. When many investors walk into these rooms, they often see large columns of equipment in racks with numerous flashing lights and wires running between them.

Many investors may not be able to distinguish between different types of hardware, because they may not be aware of what these different pieces of hardware actually look like. Putting this aside, investors seeking to evaluate the strength and scalability of a fund manager's IT function may also be unable to answer a more basic question: how much hardware is enough? Can too much hardware signal poor oversight and control of hardware management?

This question is perhaps most easily thought of in terms of data storage space. Consider the following two fund managers: Fund Manager A is a small fund manager who has five employees and has been in business for three years. Fund Manager B is a larger firm with 35 employees and has been in business for eight years. Which Fund Manager is likely to need more data storage space? The answer is obvious when such a stark comparison among organizations is in place. Although it is clear that Fund Manager B would require more data storage space, the next logical question is: how much is enough?

Consider a prospective investor who is considering making an allocation to Fund Manager A. During the due diligence process, they take the tour of the aforementioned standard clean, cold, and loud server closet. To most investors, unfortunately, if everything looks and sounds good, they stop their hardware due diligence. Evaluating a fund's hardware infrastructure can provide valuable insights beyond just the specifics of the hardware. By asking more detailed questions during the ODD process, investors can glean information as to how the firm approaches other operational issues, such as business planning and scalability as well. This in turn can lead to insights with regards to governance approaches.

Returning to our question of how much storage space is enough, there is no definitive answer. Each fund manager's situation will be different. However, to gain perspective in this area investors should consider asking the fund manager questions such as:

- How do you evaluate how much storage space you need?
- How much space do you currently have?
- Have you taken measures to plan ahead so that the firm's storage architecture is scalable?

By digging deeper into the hardware evaluation process during due diligence on IT, investors will not only have a much more detailed picture of a fund manager's overall IT framework but be also able to gain perspective on how to gauge the manager's approach to the governance of not only purchasing hardware but also maintaining it. Such an analysis can also be augmented by combining the information garnered during a hardware review with reviews of related governance mechanisms such as a hedge fund's IT planning committee.

CONCLUSION

In this chapter we have introduced topics related to developing a framework for analysis of hedge fund governance. We covered a wide variety of topics ranging from approaches taken by institutional investors in this area to conducting analysis of fund directors. We also provided a number of examples of governance considerations when analyzing specific hedge fund issues such as fund expense analysis, BCP/DR planning, and IT analysis. As we noted above, the items covered in this chapter were by no means meant to be a comprehensive list of all the governance-related factors investor can analyze during due diligence. On the contrary, we only scratched the surface in this chapter. As we outlined earlier in this chapter, for the purposes of facilitating an investor's analysis of governance-related factors, we framed our analysis of governance as an overlay on top of the analysis of operational and investment risk factors. This type of analysis framework represents the interconnected nature of governance. By leveraging off the operational and investment-related due diligence reviews, investors can conduct more comprehensive governance reviews of funds with a focus on transparency, oversight, and controls. This focus on governance will typically not only enhance the other aspects of an investor's due diligence process but produce an overall more detailed picture of the risk landscape of funds under review.

REFERENCES

AsiaHedge, 2003. Managers Put SARS Plans in Place, April 1.

CalPERS, 2011. Global Principles of Accountable Corporate Governance, November 1. Available at: http://www.calpers-governance.org/docs-sof/principles/2011-11-14-global-principles-of-accountable-corp-gov.pdf.

Chon, G., 2010. Calpers aims director list at increasing board sway. *The Wall Street Journal*, June 18.

Clancy, L., 2013. Northern Trust to shadow BNY Mellon at Bridgewater. *Risk Magazine*, January 15.

Corgentum Consulting, LLC, 2013. The preposterous fraud of Andrey C. Hicks and Locust Offshore Management. Corgentum Consulting Blog, January 11. Available at: http://corgentum.com/blog/due-diligence-news/preposterous-fraud-andrey-hicks-locust-offshore-management/.

Egelko, B., 2012. SEC accuses James Michael Murray of investor fraud. *SFGate*, March 16.

Harper, E., Lifsher, M., 2009. CalPERS proves oversight of two outside hedge fund advisors. *Los Angeles Times*, November 25. Available at: http://articles.latimes.com/2009/nov/25/business/la-fi-calpers25-2009nov25.

Hedge Fund Law Report, 2012. Corgentum Survey Illustrates the View of Hedge Fund Investors on the Roles, Duties and Performance of Service Providers, July 26.

Lifsher, M., 2014. Ex-CalPERS chief to plead guilty. *Los Angeles Times*, June 30. Available at: http://www.latimes.com/business/la-fi-calpers-scandal-20140701-story.html.

McCann, B., 2012. Investors downgrade prime brokers, new survey shows. *Opalesque*, July 17.

Murphy, V., 2002. Too good to be true. *Forbes*, February 18.

Scharfman, J., 2008. Hedge fund operational due diligence: understanding the risks. Wiley Finance, Hoboken, NJ.

Silberstein, K., Dandurand, C., 2009. Improving the Relationship Between CalPERS and Its Hedge Fund Partners, March 27. Available at: https://www.calpers.ca.gov/eip-docs/investments/bus-opportunities/rmars/rmars-memo.pdf.

Strohm, C., 2014. Hedge-fund hack is part of bigger siege, cyber-experts warn. *Bloomberg*, June 23.

Tunick, B., 2009. The Calpers challenge. *Institutional Investor*, August 25.

US SEC, 2012. SEC Charges Scotland-Based Firm for Improperly Boosting Hedge Fund Client at Expense of U.S. Fund Investors, May 10.

U.S. Securities and Exchange Commission, 2012. SEC Charges Former CalPERS CEO and Friend With Falsifying Letters in $20 Million Placement Agent Fee Scheme, April 23. Available at: http://www.sec.gov/News/PressRelease/Detail/PressRelease/1365171488576#.U7mKhvldWWE.

US SEC, 2014. OCIE Cybersecurity Initiative, vol. IV, issue 2, April 15.

Wesier, B., 2009. Lawyer get 20 years in $700 million fraud. *The New York Times*, July 13.

Williamson, C., 2009. CalPERS tightening its control over hedge funds. *Pensions & Investments*, April 20.

Chapter 7

Investor Activist–Driven Governance and Ongoing Monitoring

Chapter Outline Head

INTRODUCTION TO ONGOING MONITORING AND ACTIVIST-DRIVEN GOVERNANCE

In the previous chapter we provided some perspective and techniques for investors seeking to implement a governance evaluation of a hedge fund. In that chapter we demonstrated the interrelated multidisciplinary nature of governance as being directly related to the data collected during both the investment and operational due diligence processes. What happens after all these data have been processed from a governance perspective and the decision as to whether to allocate to a hedge fund has been made? Are investors done with governance considerations? This chapter seeks to address these questions. To start our discussion off we will consider the question of ongoing governance evaluations.

DO ONGOING GOVERNANCE EVALUATIONS ADD VALUE?

So what happens after an initial governance assessment has been performed if for whatever reason, be they governance considerations or other concerns, you decided not to invest with a hedge fund manager? Well, then that is effectively the end of the discussion for our purposes here. You could conduct a new governance assessment, or update your initial assessment, should you decide to reconsider the manager, but effectively there are no governance considerations to consider with regards to the manager who was not hired. Simply move onto reviewing the next one.

Now let's consider that an investor did decide to allocate to a hedge fund that had gone through an initial due diligence review, which included a governance assessment. What happens next? Well, investors have two basic options from a governance evaluation perspective. The first option is to do nothing and reply solely on your initial governance assessment work. Simply throw any governance memos or reporting in a file and never look at it again. You may even sleep better at night with the security of knowing that you conducted an initial review. However, such thinking would be foolish as this is a bad idea.

Governance, just as with all aspects of hedge fund investment and operations is mutable. For example, hedge funds implement new computer systems, hire and fire people, and launch new strategies. As we noted above, service providers change as well. For example, a hedge fund administrator may lose 10 large accounts, have to lay people off, and they may not be appropriately able to service the remaining accounts. Prime brokers and other trading counterparties may experience problems resulting in credit rating downgrades. Some event may occur that influence both service providers and hedge funds themselves, such as widespread business continuity and disaster recovery events, for example, terrorism or storms. Another example of such widespread change that may influence multiple parties in the hedge fund space would be industry wide regulatory changes.

Let us return to our initial governance report where our example investor had thrown the findings in the circular file as it were. This old analysis would not incorporate any of these new changes. You can see how this presents a problem for investors who are still invested in the hedge fund. The overall risk profile has changed, which may have included changes to governance risks. How has the hedge fund adapted to these changes? Is the same strong oversight and control environment that was in place initially, that convinced you to invest in the fund to begin with, holding strong under the new stresses of these changes? If not, has the hedge fund made appropriate adaptations in governance oversight and controls to react and mitigate these governance risks?

ONGOING GOVERNANCE MONITORING INFORMATION DECAY CONSIDERATIONS

As you can imagine, the review that was conducted when an investor first subscribed to a hedge fund is stuck as of a point in time. A good analogy is that it is like a snapshot of the fund. It describes how it is today. At the time you allocate the review is current to the fund for the investor. Over time, however, similar to any due diligence information collected, the value of the report decreases. For the purposes of this discussion we will refer to this as *information decay.*

This information decay influences the value of all due diligence data collected. Certain information may decay slower than others. Why is this? Well, the rate of information decay is typically correlated with the rate of change of the underlying data. Historically certain information has changed at a faster rate than others. As an example, hedge funds that actively trade are likely to have the details of their portfolio holdings change quite frequently on a daily, if not minute by minute, basis. Other information, such as a list of the key fund accounting and operational systems used, has historically changed at a much slower rate. That is to say, hedge funds don't frequently switch fund accounting systems, and if they do, such changes are infrequent.

The rate of information decay may also be contingent on the particular circumstances of a fund under review. For example, if a fund suddenly realizes significant reductions in assets under management over time, then it may have to lay off personnel. A fund with historically low personnel turnover may all of a sudden experience significant turnover associated with asset declines. This is an example of how the rate of change or historically low rate of change factors can change more rapidly depending on the particular circumstances of the hedge fund under review. As such, while general guidelines may be helpful in guiding an assessment of which areas experience the greatest information decay, any such guidance should not be blindly followed.

What does this have to do with governance? Glad you asked. Due to the fact that information decays over time, which includes investor-collected governance information and the historical assessments of that information, there is a need to update the information after the initial assessment is performed. This is the second option available to investors, to conduct ongoing governance monitoring. From a best practice perspective for investors, this clearly represents a much better option than doing nothing on an ongoing basis.

Additionally, it's also a good investment. If you have already expended the resources, and associated costs, in conducting such a review, then the cost to update this review is significantly less. Furthermore, from an overall due diligence cost budgeting perspective it is best to think of such historical due diligence, and associated governance assessment costs, as sunk costs. For our purposes here, sunk costs can be thought of as money already spent. It's gone, get over it. Focusing on the here and now, the money and resources you spent previously on conducting a due diligence review shouldn't necessarily influence your decision to conduct an ongoing review. Such thinking is penny wise and pound foolish. Besides if an investor has already produced a detailed understanding of a fund's internal governance framework, then the cost to update and monitor reports on an ongoing basis in general should be significantly less, as less time and resources are often required to conduct such ongoing monitoring on the whole.

DEVELOPING AN ONGOING GOVERNANCE MONITORING PROGRAM—A META-ANALYSIS PROGRAM?

Now that we've convinced you of the benefits of conducting ongoing governance monitoring, we can next address the ways that investors can think about beginning to develop an ongoing monitoring program. Ok, I know what you're thinking. How are we supposed to do this? After all, if you've been reading the other chapters, you'll know that we demonstrated that analyzing governance requires conducting what is effectively a meta-analysis on operational and investment-related due diligence data. To clarify what we mean here is the concept of metadata referring to data about data. One way to think of it is similar to descriptive statistics. The meta-analysis describes or draws conclusions about the underlying data. With this understanding, you might rightly raise the question similar to one that was raised in Chapter 6 when we discussed developing an initial governance assessment program. Namely, what is the difference between ongoing governance monitoring and ongoing investment and operational due diligence monitoring? Said another way, if I am going to conduct ongoing investment and operational monitoring, then how is governance monitoring any different?

To answer this question, let's first remember, as we noted above, that assuming you are conducting thorough investment and operational due diligence assessments, you have collected the bulk of the raw data needed to conduct a governance assessment. This is not to say that further questions, framed in a governance context, could not be asked, which would require further data collection and follow-up at either the fund or service provider level. Such inquiries are often merited. Rather what we are outlining here is that due to the interrelated nature of governance, an ongoing governance evaluation should be incorporated into the ongoing investment and operational due diligence reviews. This is particularly true because the items that you are applying a governance assessment to are the investment and operational factors at the hedge fund that you have already reviewed and are conducting an ongoing risk assessment of.

It is also worth clarifying, as we noted above, that just because an investor seeks to update their initial operational due diligence review work, that they are necessarily conducting an updated governance evaluation. Just the opposite, as we highlighted earlier in this book, fund operations and governance are not concepts that can be necessarily interchangeably equated with one another. Instead, as we have shown, the concepts are related to one another.

Returning to the question at hand then, how is an ongoing governance assessment different from ongoing investment and operational due diligence? The answer, as we have intimated above, is that these assessments are not distinctly separate from each other, but rather related. As we highlighted above, data collected during the review processes are used to evaluate governance. In the same way that governance is interrelated to these concepts, it is also distinct in other aspects in the fact that, for example, it may dive deeper into the nature of control and oversight of operational and investment factors. We have provided many examples of this throughout this text including the way that the pure raw facts of the allocation of expenses represent an operational process. While the assessment of the equitableness, controls, and oversight of such expenses, and subsequent allocations among the funds, is representative of governance. Notice how the items are interrelated, but more inquiry of these issues with a governance focus can also add value.

BEGINNING ONGOING GOVERNANCE ASSESSMENTS

We just highlighted the interrelated nature of governance, and its similarities and distinctions with ongoing operational and investment due diligence monitoring. Due to these interrelated relationships it is perhaps easiest to demonstrate the ways that an ongoing governance assessment can be performed by outlining examples of governance considerations that arise when conducting this other ongoing due diligence. To start off we will outline the governance considerations relevant to the area of information technology. As we noted earlier in this book, information technology can be a key area that can have strong governance signaling effects. From an ongoing governance monitoring perspective, focusing on information technology is particularly relevant because it is an area under frequent change. Therefore, any governance assessments made during the initial investor governance assessment process may decay at a faster rate (i.e., become stale faster) as compared with other more seemingly stable data.

ONGOING GOVERNANCE MONITORING—INFORMATION TECHNOLOGY EXAMPLES

Analyzing Software Upgrade Cycles as an Ongoing Governance Assessment Indicator

Consider the following scenario. A hedge fund utilizes a multifunction third-party software application. This system, with all its bells and whistles, is used in the front and back office and to assist with risk analysis to perform several other key functions including preparing nightly portfolio reports. The fund has used the system for over two years, and has been happy with the system and the level of ongoing support provided by the third-party vendor that makes the software.

One morning fund personnel come into the office and find that the system isn't functioning properly. After having their internal IT department investigate and run a series of tests they determine that there is no problem with their network or systems. They contact the software provider who informs them that overnight they rolled out a new software update and that might be the culprit. The fund had been using this software application for quite some time and had not experienced any problems with upgrades in the past. Why was this one different?

Well, it could be a myriad of reasons. Unfortunately for our hypothetical fund, they must now work with the software provided to not only remedy the immediate problem but also ensure that this problem does not occur again. In the real world these types of fixes often take time. The fund might be able to implement a temporary solution such as reverting to a previous instance of the software application, but there is still a delay that could ultimately affect profitability. This scenario highlights some of the risks related to software version updates that might impact a fund.

Ongoing Governance Implications—Exclusion by Preclusion?

Software version controls and oversight may be overlooked by investors during the initial due diligence assessment process. Similarly, the specific implementation and governance oversight of controls may also not get covered during the initial governance assessment process. Such a lack of coverage runs the risk of being extended into the ongoing monitoring process as well. After all, if an investor didn't think it was important to focus on the controls in this area to begin with, why would they suddenly have an epiphany and begin focusing on this area?

This is perhaps a good opportunity to highlight another important consideration relating to ongoing governance monitoring. If an investor did not analyze a certain issue during the initial governance review process, does this mean they are precluded from ever addressing the issue? Of course not, the sins of the past as it were should not condemn present desires to further expand the governance assessment process. The difference of course is that an investor may have to put more work in now to first build an initial understanding of the issue under review, than they would have if they had already covered the issue, and were simply working during the ongoing assessment process to update the review.

An OMS Example—Ongoing Governance Assessment Information Compromises

To illustrate the ongoing assessment governance implications of software versioning and upgrades let us consider the example of a specific software application utilized by many funds. Most funds typically employ some sort of order management system, commonly referred to as an OMS, which facilitates the entry, processing, and general organization of fund trades. An OMS is a piece of software and, therefore, falls within the realm of a fund's larger information technology architecture.

When a fund manager purchases and initially installs an OMS, they typically receive the most recent release version of the application. As we have outlined above, in order to keep applications such as OMS fresh and add different system upgrades, third-party vendors often go through series of ongoing software upgrades. These upgrades are typically not automatically pushed out to users of the systems (i.e., fund managers), but instead the fund manager has to actively install such an upgrade. This makes sense because if it is a major upgrade, the third-party vendor does not want to force a disruption on a fund manager.

As noted above, the version of OMS used by fund managers is an area that runs the risk of being overlooked during the initial due diligence process. Furthermore, assessing the initial controls and oversight surrounding the potential for upgrades in the future often becomes overlooked during the initial governance assessment process. For example, does the firm maintain a written policy in this regard? Does the information technology committee, if the firm has one, oversee the process for determining if a fund should implement a new OMS at the current version? What if the vendor informs the hedge fund that a new version of the OMS is due to come out within the month of the planned installation of the current system? Which individual or group at the firm makes the decision as to whether the firm should proceed with the current installation or wait a week? By default do these decisions go to a Chief Financial Officer (CFO) or other senior manager with limited information technology experience? Does this necessarily represent best practice governance oversight in this regard?

This analysis process becomes even more complex because fund managers typically do not utilize just one OMS, but instead utilize multiple software applications within their organizations. No, rather fund managers may use dozens of different third-party software applications. Investors may feel inquiring about software versioning across all of these multiple applications is too cumbersome or they may feel unsure what to do with this information. By collecting such information during the initial assessment processes investors then have a benchmark by which to compare the information obtained during ongoing assessments. We will provide an example of how this works in practice below.

Further complicating matters, if you are a current hedge fund investor, why don't you do a quick exercise? Poll all of your hedge fund managers and ask them the following:

- What version of their OMS they are on?
- What is the most recent available version?
- If they are not using the most recent OMS version, why not? Who made the decision to hold off?

The results of such inquiries may surprise you and provide some interesting governance insights. Some fund managers may either not have this software version information readily available or simply not want to share this information with investors.

In these cases, there are a number of strategies and techniques that can be employed during the initial assessment process by which an investor can come to a compromise with a fund manager, in terms of information required and burden on the manager. A key caveat to the previous statement is that just because a fund manager eventually may object to a certain request and an investor then accepts less information than they originally asked for, it does not mean that an investor should draw this conclusion on their own.

That is to say, an investor should ask for software versioning information from a manager, and if the manager objects, that is where the negotiation and compromise may begin. Such considerations may be applicable not only to the collection of initial raw operational data such as what version of an OMS is utilized but also to more governance-related assessments regarding the controls over such OMS upgrades. That being said, in some instances, an investor may also choose to draw a line in the sand and state that this is a "deal breaker" issue, and that if the manager does not provide this information, the investor will walk away.

But returning to the issues of fund manager OMS software versions, beyond the actual data itself (i.e., what version of a particular software application a fund manager is utilizing), an investor can often garner valuable metadata about the nature and quality of a fund manager's operations by inquiring as to software versions employed. Perhaps it is best to illustrate this point by example as we outlined above.

Let us consider two hedge fund managers: A and B. Fund manager A began using an OMS, which we will call System1, in June 2012. When fund manager A purchased the system, the most recent version available was version 2.0, and this was the version of the OMS the fund manager had installed. Fund manager B also utilizes System1 and began utilizing the system in September 2013. At that time, System1 was on version 2.5. Similar to fund manager A, fund manager B had the latest version of the system installed.

Fast forward to today. The most recent version of System1 is version 4.0. This version contains many upgrades that were not available in the older versions.

Today, after subsequent upgrades since the initial installation, fund manager A utilizes version 3.5 of the system. Fund manager B has similarly undergone several upgrades since the initial installation and is now on version 4.0. A logical conclusion may be that fund manager A is behind the times. Perhaps fund manager B has a better governance infrastructure ensuring that it is on top of latest operational developments and therefore has the most recent system. Is such a formulaic quick assessment based on version number correct? Such shorthand conclusions, while expeditious, may not necessarily be accurate.

For example, perhaps version 4.0, the most recent version, was recently released and fund manager A just completed an expensive upgrade to version 3.5 last year. Fund manager A may be waiting for version 4.1 to come out before completing the next upgrade. Does such a reluctance to upgrade software represent poor governance? This type of question is an example of the types of questions that investors may be faced with from an ongoing monitoring perspective, and the answers are not always cut and dry. Returning to fund manager A, perhaps it is rather prudent for them to wait for an upgrade. The juice of upgrading now may not be worth the squeeze. If the benefits of an upgrade are not worth the costs, then fund manager A may actually be representing better governance through restraint rather than action. Conducting an upgrade can be an expensive proposition. This expense may come from not just the actual cost of the upgrade but also business disruptions from switching from one version to another, as well as the use of employees' or consultants' time in implementing these upgrades.

Similarly, turning to fund manager B despite the fact that they are utilizing the most recent version, this might be masking crumbling governance inefficiencies behind the new facade. For example, perhaps fund manager B never conducted any other previous upgrades in between version 2.5 and the current version 4.0. An argument could perhaps be made that fund manager B had poor governance oversight during this period as compared with fund manager A because some of the interim system upgrades (i.e., between versions 2.5 and 4.0) during this period may have helped fund manager B. Of course, in either of the cases of fund managers A and B, an investor wouldn't be able to make any further assessment of the strength or weakness of the governance programs in place without further inquiry. This example highlights not only the benefits of conducting initial deep-dive governance assessments but the importance of digging deep into ongoing governance assessments as part of the overall due diligence process as well.

Representations of Continued Internal and External Governance Risks

Continuing our general discussion of software version control example, when issues occur related to software updates, particularly for critical systems, they can cause a number of problems ranging from prolonged business disruptions to data loss and trade errors. The good news for investors is that these types of problems are avoidable for funds, and an ongoing governance assessment of these areas can provide insights into how well a fund acknowledges these risks not only initially but also on an ongoing basis. This is particularly an important consideration for areas such as software versioning. Not only may the hedge fund itself adopt new software, but also as new software is released often new risks can arise.

In Chapter 6 we highlighted the growing cyber security threats facing hedge funds. The issue of software upgrades is directly related to this. As new software versions and patches are released often to correct prior information security holes that have been exposed by hackers additional potential problems can arise. If a hedge fund is slow to adopt such updates, they may be overexposed to these types of information security risks as compared with other hedge funds. This implies that funds that are slow to adopt such changes have worse governance oversight in this area. Consequently, this demonstrates how issues such as software updates can represent governance challenges from an in-house hedge fund perspective as well as related challenges that come from outside the firm.

Many software updates involve software vendors pushing updates automatically to users of the software. Under this push update model the fund may not even know that the software has been updated until the next time they log in. In many cases, updates are pushed out by vendors to repair or enhance existing behind-the-scene functionality, which is not immediately apparent to system users. Other types of push updates may be more visible to end users and may add new system features or functionality.

Another type of software update may require the fund to proactively install the updates. One example of these so-called pull updates would be when a new version of a fund accounting system is released. Often times the decision to upgrade to a newer version can be expensive and require a support team from the application vendor to work with the fund to assist in the upgrade. This is why some funds opt to sit on the sidelines through several new software releases before installing major version upgrades. Waiting for these upgrade cycles to pass before taking the leap to switch to a new version allows the fund to both save on costs and see how other users react to the upgrades. Regardless of whether the updates are push or pull type, funds can take a number of proactive steps to avoid disruptions. Such proactivity in this area often is a signaling effect of better governance oversight in this area. From an ongoing monitoring perspective, inquiring about how a fund approaches such updates may be a good governance indicator. Furthermore, with regards to ongoing governance monitoring, an investor could ask a fund to demonstrate how recent software version upgrades were implemented.

Each hedge fund's information technology infrastructure is different. These different infrastructures and software environments interact differently with third-party technologies. For example, one fund may be using primarily a Windows 7 environment while another uses Windows XP or UNIX. In designing their new software update, the vendor may not have taken into account that the upgrade may negatively affect users who run an older version of an operating system. Or perhaps the vendor did perform checks in this regard, but a fund has a number of proprietary software applications that interact with the third-party application and they will not function properly with the new upgrade. Additionally, the software vendor may not have the visibility into the client's systems to accurately predict that the upgrade may cause problems. Similarly, under a pull upgrade format, the client may not believe that the software upgrade would cause a problem, and therefore they would proceed with the upgrade only to identify problems after the fact.

During the initial governance assessment process, investors should inquire if their funds are appropriately acknowledging and addressing these software upgrade risks as well as establishing an appropriate oversight and control environment for such upgrades. When implementing an ongoing evaluation process, investors should consider how frameworks are implemented and tested. If a fund did a good job in demonstrating how controls were in place at the time of an investor's initial investment into a fund, can they demonstrate that they have maintained this oversight going forward? This is one of the goals of ongoing governance assessment.

In order to determine if their funds are appropriately managing the risks surrounding software upgrades, on an ongoing basis from a governance perspective, some questions investors may want to ask could include:

- What is the firm's general approach to providing oversight of the software upgrade process?
- Who controls the upgrade process (i.e., is it vendor driven, internally at the fund, or both)? Has the fund proactively made the decision to coordinate upgrades in this manner or is this by default?
- Does the fund work with third-party vendors to remain informed of upgrades before they happen?
- Has the fund had any issues related to bugs or similar system disruptions with regards to upgrades?
- Does the fund have the ability to easily restore a previous instance of an application if an upgrade caused a disruption?
- Before an upgrade is rolled out to a fund's users, does the fund's information technology function review upgrades in a test environment?
- Does the information technology function review any security or data integrity changes that may be caused by upgrades?

Additional Comments on the Ongoing Assessment and Governance Implications of Software Versioning

When an investor begins to delve into the issues and circumstances concerning system versions and upgrades, often times they can begin to get a sense of the larger operational planning going on within the organization. Additionally, as outlined above, an investor can often develop a dialogue with a manager about why certain upgrades may or may not have been conducted at certain time periods. During the governance assessment and due diligence processes, such discussions can often provide useful perspective in evaluating software versions rather than simply conducting an exclusively quantitative comparison among managers of software versions.

When evaluating the versions of software employed by a fund manager, some considerations include:

- How many versions behind the most recent version are they?
- Is this version delay limited to only one software application or multiple applications?
- Why has the fund not decided to upgrade to the most recent version?
- Will the fund be able to complete the upgrades themselves or will they need to work with a third-party consultant?
- If the upgrade will involve more than clicking a few buttons or downloading a new upgraded version of the software, how has the fund planned to handle any software disruptions?
- Has the fund taken appropriate steps to ensure data loss will not occur during any system migrations?
- If any changes were required to be made to users or access points for the new upgraded system, has the fund checked to ensure any unauthorized security holes have been properly closed?

Investors who inquire about such seemingly minor issues as what versions of software are being used by a fund manager may be surprised about how this information can yield valuable insight into the larger governance framework in place at a fund manager.

By taking measures to inquire whether or not a fund has proactively addressed the issue of overseeing and controlling software upgrades investors will be making more informed governance assessments. Without such oversight, investors may find themselves invested with a fund that may find itself left behind when an upgrade occurs. By actively engaging in the upgrade process funds can be better prepared to control such risks, and investors will likely have more comfort with the ongoing information technology control environment, at least from a software perspective.

BONUS BOARD GOVERNANCE OVERSIGHT BONANZA? DON'T WORRY, WE'VE HIRED SOMEONE FOR THAT

A key focus of late for investor's governance inquiries relates to a hedge fund's board. As we have highlighted throughout this book, analyzing the exact duties of boards can sometimes present a bit of a challenge when we consider the common practice of board members, in addition to other service providers, delegating their more frequent oversight of certain areas to the fund manager and other service providers. This delegation analysis problem is also prevalent for ongoing governance analysis. Somewhat further potentially complicating this problem has been the rise of so-called fund advisory boards. These boards consist of individuals who are hired by the fund manager not to serve necessarily on the board of any particular fund, but rather to be general advisors to the hedge fund in general. In some cases these advisory boards, which are sometimes referred to as qualified boards, can also provide oversight at specific fund levels such as the master fund level in a master–feeder complex. These boards can perhaps be thought of as being similar to private equity–style advisory boards in some regard, although in practice private equity advisory structures may be quite different. These boards are discussed in more detail in the interviews contained in Chapter 10.

For the purposes of our discussion here the question could be asked if these additional bonus boards, referred to as such because they are in addition to the existing fund boards already in place, should give investors any comfort with regards to ongoing monitoring of governance considerations at funds.

To answer this question perhaps we should look at the potential motivation for a fund manager to hire an advisory board. For starters, as you may have figured out by now from reading this book, investors are increasingly focused on governance. This includes an ongoing focus on the board. As we noted in Chapter 2, and elsewhere, some investors are very critical of fund boards including related capacity issues. Effectively by installing an advisory board a fund manager is seeking to take the heat off the board of the offshore fund in some respects. Perhaps one way to think of it is as wearing a second parachute. If the first board completely fails, shouldn't it give investors additional comfort, and by association allay any ongoing oversight governance concerns, that there is a second advisory board rip cord to pull?

Another motivation for the hiring of such boards may be because hedge fund managers are seeking specific board qualifications or experience that is more germane to their day-to-day management that an offshore board member may not be able to offer. For example, as we have highlighted above, information technology can play a crucial part in the operational functioning of the firm. The oversight and control of many aspects of information technology can have a number of governance implications. While there may be some board members out there with experience in this area, this is not the direction of the experience slant of the vast majority of offshore directors. As such, a hedge fund may be looking for an advisory board member with more experience in a particular functional area or investment space (i.e., a CLO expert if the fund trades heavily in CLOs) that the offshore board may not have.

Finally, a third motivating factor for funds utilizing such boards may be the issues we highlighted above of delegation. Funds may be looking for boards that are more involved on a day-to-day basis as compared with offshore board members.

For all these reasons and more, hedge funds may view advisory boards as adding value. Of course, hedge funds also know that the mere fact of having such a board sends a strong governance signal to investors. Think about it. If as an investor you had one fund with an advisory board, and one without it, at first glance which one would you say had a strong ongoing governance oversight infrastructure in place? Of course, as we hopefully have convinced you by now, such a broad generalization without further digging to back it up is ill-advised. That being said, most investors would likely prefer an advisory board versus not having one from a governance perspective.

Ok, so now we've convinced you that by having an advisory board in place a fund has not checked the box with regards to ongoing governance monitoring. Instead, investors should not simply rely on the fact that an advisory board is policing ongoing governance monitoring. Instead, during the initial governance assessment process investors should inquire what the advisory board actually does. There is no one cookie cutter approach to the way these boards are constructed or what they do. Furthermore, investors should attempt to determine the nature of the interaction between the advisory board and the offshore fund directors. With this initial understanding in place investors can then consider the role of the advisory board with regards to ongoing governance monitoring. Some questions investors should consider asking include:

- How often does the advisory board meet?
- Is attendance at such meetings mandatory?
- Will the fund share the minutes of advisory board meetings? If not, why?
- If no meeting minutes are taken, are any reports or documentation prepared?
- What are examples of recent issues discussed by the advisory board?
- Are there situations where the advisory board has disagreed with the fund manager or offshore directors? How were the situations resolved?
- Does the advisory board perform any internal testing oversight work or do they simply provide advice?
- Does the advisory board review the work of the offshore board? How do they interact with them on an ongoing basis?

Having an advisory board in place can be useful tool to promote the implementation and management of ongoing fund governance structures. Investors should not simply rely on the work of advisory boards to be their eyes and ears with regards to monitoring ongoing governance oversight. Rather they should take active roles in engaging with the advisory board to support investors' own ongoing governance monitoring assessments.

ONGOING BACKGROUND INVESTIGATION AND NEWS MONITORING FOR FUNDS, PERSONNEL, AND DIRECTORS?

In Chapter 6 we discussed performing background investigations on hedge funds and directors. As you can imagine after an initial investigation is performed, there are questions regarding whether ongoing investigations should be performed. Investors take all kinds of different approaches in this area. Similar to the points we raised about the expense of such investigations involved, many investors are penny wise and pound foolish with regards to conducting ongoing investigations in the same way they were with initial investigations.

While some investors wisely conduct initial background checks, some investors do not do any sort of ongoing monitoring. This is a bad idea. As you can imagine as part of daily life people get sued, arrested, purchase new assets, newspaper articles are written, people get married and divorced, and the list goes on and on.

All of these types of issues can have an impact on your initial background investigation assessment. Simply putting your head in the sand as an investor because at some point historically you reviewed the information is frankly not good enough to constitute sufficient oversight. Similar to the points raised in our California Public Employees' Retirement System (CalPERS) example, consider if you were considering allocating to two different funds of hedge funds. One did ongoing background investigations on fund managers and directors and one did not. What is your initial reaction about which fund of funds implements better governance oversight of underlying reputational risks in this area?

The other fund of funds understands the risks involved and decides to perform ongoing monitoring, but establishes seemingly arbitrary rules such as every three years, or if there is a problem. Can you guess what our opinion is of such approaches? In general, they are too haphazard to be effective.

Other investors take this area more seriously and perform ongoing monitoring. Once again some investors take a miserly approach and feel setting up Google alerts for managers and directors is sufficient. While certainly not a bad idea, this is not necessarily a comprehensive background search on an ongoing basis. Others establish what are effectively ongoing monitoring alerts, typically with firms that assist in providing such searches, to monitor for new litigation, arrests, criminal convictions, etc. Some investors fall in between these groups and do not have alerts, but instead run certain more limited searches with predetermined frequency such as annually.

As we noted above, some hedge funds perform ongoing searches on their employees as well. The goal here is not to create a big brother state, but rather to ensure that investors are aware from a governance implication of both the nature of any potentially concerning background information and the governance oversight in place to monitor for such information. For example, consider a fund that does not provide ongoing background searches on employees and board members. If a third-party board member of a fund is sued, do you think they are going to proactively raise the issue with the fund? If not, and the fund is not doing any sort of ongoing monitoring, couldn't it be argued that from the perspective of an investor you add value to the fund's governance by monitoring for such information yourself? While this would certainly add value to the fund, it would also serve to potentially benefit you as an investor by having earlier insight into such information.

Ongoing background investigation and news monitoring concerning funds, fund employee and directors can add valuable governance insights to the investor ongoing governance assessment process and should be considered by all investors as part of their ongoing governance management programs.

THE GOOD GUY PROBLEM: DO "HOUSE VIEWS" RESULT IN WEAKENED ONGOING GOVERNANCE OVERSIGHT?

Let's say that you've taken the advice in this book to heart and conducted a deep-dive institutional quality governance assessment of a hedge fund as part of your larger due diligence process. You've further been convinced of the benefits of conducting ongoing governance assessments. Great, we're on the right track. There is a common problem, however, that can influence both initial and ongoing governance assessments that may set a dangerous precedence for your reviews that is worth mentioning.

The issue in questions relates to what, for the purposes of this discussion, we will affectionately refer to as the *good guy* problem. With the increasingly number of female hedge fund managers perhaps this is more appropriately called the *good person* problem. As an aside, many of these types of non-gender-neutral terms are still prevalent in the hedge fund industry. A common example is so-called key man risk. This refers to the risks associated with the hedge fund overly relying on any single individual or groups of individuals. As we noted earlier in this text, typically key man clauses refer to a hedge fund's lead portfolio manager or in the case of shared responsibilities co–portfolio managers. From a risk management perspective investors understandably prefer a situation where they have certain protections in place to mitigate the risks associated with these key individuals. Interestingly, key person clauses rarely, if ever, refer to noninvestment personnel. The question could be reasonably asked as to why investors do not demand similar protections for key operational personnel. Wouldn't it have a material impact on the firm if the CFO, Chief Operating Officer (COO), or Chief Compliance Officer (CCO) suddenly departed, died, or was no longer capable to work at the firm? Certainly from the perspective of an investor having such key man clauses across both types of functions, namely, investment and operational, would promote better governance controls. The focus of our discussion here is not to cover the ins and outs of key man clauses, but rather to highlight the use of the term "man." Many people in the hedge fund industry still refer to these protections as key man clauses. To a lesser extent the gender-neutral term "key person clause" is also utilized. These perhaps dated terms are largely a function of the primarily male-oriented history of the hedge fund industry. As such to comport with convention we will use the term good guy here, but certainly the same problem can of course apply regardless of the declination in gender of the term we use, or of the investors that suffer from this problem.

But we digress; let us return to the *good person* problem and how it relates to weakened due diligence of both initial and ongoing governance protocols. If you have ever conducted due diligence on a hedge fund before, regardless of whether you were focused on the fund's investments, operational risks, or both, you will likely have noticed that there is a lot of detailed information flying around the conversation. This can include detailed fund specifics of portfolio holdings, fund terms, risk management data, fund back office process charts, and the like.

During these meetings, merely the fact of making sure that an investor captures all the data can sometimes be challenged. Forget about the difficulties associated with actually processing, analyzing, and asking follow-up questions on any of it. To do this often requires several key skill sets. The first is familiarity with common hedge fund practices. The second is preparedness. By this we mean devoting time beforehand to collect and review documentation from the hedge fund. By doing this in advance, an investor can, for example, tell if what the hedge fund personnel are saying is consistent with the documentation. Next there is a wide breadth of certain topic-specific knowledge that is required.

So let's, for example, say that an investor is only conducting an operational due diligence review. Let us further assume that the investor or analyst conducting this review is a Chartered Public Accountant (CPA) or equivalent, is very familiar with hedge fund accounting practices, and even used to work as a hedge fund auditor. Let us further assume that during the course of the meeting with the hedge fund manager, the manager goes on and on about how great their compliance function is. They get into the details of kinds of interesting compliance controls and procedures. Unfortunately, the former auditor in our example knows only the basics of hedge fund compliance. This doesn't make them a bad person, or even worse a bad analyst; it's just that it is easy to see how they could quickly get out of their depth. When this type of information starts getting discussed, the intricacies of the conversation quickly get lost. Furthermore, key follow-up questions might not be asked because of this lack of familiarity.

Similar examples can also be pulled from the investment side of the business. Let's say an investor, perhaps from a Japan-based family office, is familiar with a certain hedge fund investment strategy such as long/short investing in Asia. This investor might be lost, for example, when the hedge fund investment personnel begin to discuss portfolio-level risk management, such as the assumptions built into the various risk management scenarios they run, or why certain hedging or leverage strategies may be reasonable. Once again the point here is not to overly criticize investor's backgrounds or one type of operational due diligence analyst over another. Rather what I am saying here is that a lack of experience and training in certain areas can result in information leakage as it flows from the hedge fund to the analyst or investor during due diligence process.

Additionally, this type of data loss can result not only from a lack of familiarity as indicated above but also from a lack of detailed note taking during the meeting itself. Some investors and analysts are frankly lazy and feel that they don't need to write, or type, a lot of information. Others may make excuses that they can memorize it all or that it is written down somewhere else in the managers' materials. This is a mistake. Information, some of which might be useful, will get lost. To be fair, it is hard work to have a conversation, take notes, review the notes, and ask follow-up questions, but if investors take shortcuts, this will lead to an incomplete due diligence process that will suffer from weak information.

As a result of these types of problems what typically happens under the good guy problem is that investors and those who may be performing due diligence on their behalf turn more away from the actual facts relating to certain hedge fund investment or operational practices, and instead develop what can be called for lack of a better term a gut feeling or general perception about a manager. To put it into words, these gut feelings can then result in an overall assessment of the manager being reduced to the something of the effect of "we did due diligence on them and they are good people." They might be nice, friendly people. They might like the same sports teams you do, have gone to the same college, be of the same religion, or even have shared mutual acquaintances. That's all well and good, but it does not replace the fact that you may not have conducted as detailed a due diligence review of the manager as you thought you did, or dare I say you should have. These generalized perceptions can be damaging to initial governance assessments as well as lulling many investors into a false sense of comfort regarding ongoing monitoring.

It should be noted that here we are not seeking to discount the importance of qualitative factors or intuition in the hedge fund investing process. Just the opposite, such insights can be extremely valuable. The point here is that investors should not blindly rely on this intuition. The inclusion of reference to blind reliance here does not mean, as our examples above have also suggested, that doing any due diligence at all simply serves as an escape hatch from this problem. Just the opposite, even if an investor is performing due diligence, the problem can still persist due in part to lax due diligence process as alluded to above.

An investor's evaluation of governance directly relates to this *good person* problem. Returning to our earlier example, that governance in a hedge fund involves multiple players including the hedge funds themselves, investors, and service providers. Now let us further assume that an investor is evaluating a hedge fund's service providers including the fund administrator. The evaluation of an administrator, as with directors and most governance issues, typically lives in the operational due diligence camp.

If an investors walks through the services of the fund administrator from a purely checklist perspective, certainly they would not be meeting what would be considered a best practice review from either an operational due diligence or governance perspective. But let's give our example investor the benefit of the doubt, and say that they are average at operational due diligence. They go beyond the checklist approach, but there is still room for improvement. The reasons for this gap could be perhaps because the investor is resource constrained and does not have the time or resources to more fully vet the administrator. It could be because, as we outlined earlier, the investor simply doesn't have the background to know what else to ask the fund administration personnel.

Regardless of the reason, the point is the investor leaves some information on the table, and some of the due diligence and governance landscape uncovered. Let's further assume that this is a brand name administrator who is popular in the hedge fund industry. Would it be unreasonable to assume that this big name may give the investor a certain level of comfort? That they would perhaps be more inclined to do less due diligence out of notions of brand name familiarity or lack of counterparty concern for well-capitalized firms with large market shares? It would be naive to assume that certain investors, even large allocators, don't think this way. Sometimes you will even hear administrators and consultants boast that they have a so-called *house view*, that so-and-so prime broker or administrator is a good firm. The bottom line is in the same way that an investor may have given a hedge fund manager a pass in certain areas because they were *good people*, so too in many cases is the same courtesy afforded to brand name service providers. As an aside, hedge funds often know this bias exists and that is why, in part, they are willing to pay higher prices to these larger household name firms. Of course, these larger firms also typically perform good work, but the historical investor bias in this area doesn't hurt either.

In summary, this *good person* problem can often result in a due diligence and governance research gap because of the perception that the managers have strong operational and governance procedures in place without necessarily the detail to back it up. Investors who fall victim to this trap are making decisions based on less complete information. These types of biases can negatively influence not only investor's initial governance assessments but ongoing governance evaluations as well.

FAST AND FURIOUS—INCREASING GOVERNANCE MONITORING FREQUENCY THROUGH SHALLOW DIVES

If you are reading this book, you may be seeking a quick resource to evaluate governance. It could be a questionnaire that you could give the appropriate people (i.e., hedge fund manager, directors, etc.) to fill out, or perhaps a reference checklist or scorecard you could use to make a quick assessment of a fund's overall governance. Of course, if ease or speed of evaluation of hedge fund governance is your concern, then really you may care less about the method of evaluation, but more about the results, that is to say does the fund have "good governance" or "bad governance?" As we noted earlier in the book, from an initial assessment perspective, this approach perhaps takes too simple an attitude to a complex problem.

By seeking to reduce a concept like hedge fund governance to a binary "yes" or "no," or a "good" or "bad" discussion, you may be shortchanging yourself of fully understanding the full governance framework in place at a fund. This is not meant of course to minimize the practical concerns of analyzing governance. Indeed as with many aspects of the hedge fund world, evaluations and due diligence capabilities must also be balanced with time and capacity considerations. Furthermore, this is not meant to say that investors should cut corners because they are understaffed or overwhelmed, but rather that above certain minimums resource questions may come into play.

Such quick governance assessments may be more practical, however, to facilitate ongoing governance monitoring. For example, let's say that as an investor you conduct detailed initial governance monitoring. Furthermore, let's assume that you decided to update your initial governance assessment in conjunction with updating your initial due diligence. For our purposes let's assume that you conduct an annual on-site revalidation of your initial due diligence, and have been for many years. This annual revalidation could be an extensive review that seeks to update your initial deep-dive work in many areas including fund governance. Is there any more you could be doing?

Some investors have taken the view that more frequent lighter-touch monitoring to compliment the sometimes long gaps in so-called formal due diligence visits and revalidations can be beneficial. Certainly, the more frequent the oversight, the less chance of something slipping through the cracks. There is nothing necessarily wrong with more shallow due diligence dives that incorporate governance analysis, if they are used to support the gap between more extensive governance assessment reviews. Of course, if you learn anything during these so-called shallow dive governance reviews that may merit further inquiry, then you of course have the right, if not the obligation, to dive deeper to more fully vet the situations.

One example of the implementation of such a so-called shallow dive would be for an investor to conduct quarterly shallow dive reviews of a fund manager. During these quarterly inquiries a number of governance questions could be asked as well. Obviously the nature of the inquiries would be dependent on each fund, but examples of the types of questions that could be asked include:

- Has there been any turnover among board members? Is any turnover contemplated?
- When was the most recent board meeting? What was discussed?
- If there was a board meeting, will the fund share a copy of the minutes, or a summary, with investors? If no, why not?
- Have there been any new committees added?
- In regards to the firm's existing committees, were there any meetings held? If so, what happened at those meeting? Will the firm share reporting of such meetings?
- What measures has the firm taken to react to any regulatory changes that may have occurred throughout the quarter?
- If the firm conducts ongoing background monitoring of employees, were there any issues noted?

- Have there been any changes in service provider practices that may influence governance controls?
- What measures has the firm taken to test the implementation of governance controls and oversight? Have any reviews such as internal audit or compliance testing been performed? If no, why not? What were the results of any governance testing?
- What has the firm done to strengthen governance oversight and controls throughout the quarter?

GOVERNANCE ACTIVISM

As we outlined in Chapter 1, governance from a hedge fund investing perspective has traditionally been associated with concepts of shareholder activism. Concepts of activism from a governance perspective can also have fund-level investment implications. As they are related to the concept of governance we will introduce some of these concepts here. The initial implementation and ongoing monitoring of the implementation of so-called fund-level activism, which we will outline below, may be restrictions on certain investment activity. This can be similar to the other areas discussed throughout this chapter, and provide insight into the effectiveness of ongoing governance implementation.

Activism in Promoting Good Governance-Linked Goals

In addition to promoting best practice governance in the hedge funds in which they invest, certain investors may also seek to promote other goals that they feel are aligned with this good governance.

These could be a wide variety of goals that we can classify into two primary categories. The first category of governance-linked goals comprises those who relate to the nature of the hedge fund's investments themselves. This goal can be further classified into *prohibitive* and *permissive* investment guidelines. The second category can be those governance-linked goals that relate to the hedge fund management company guidelines. We will address each of these categories separately.

Prohibitive Investment Guidelines

For a variety of reasons, certain investors do not want the hedge funds that they allocate capital to, to make investments in certain industries or companies. The reasons for this can include that they are not aligned with the mission statement or organizational goals of a particular investor, or that they present a conflict of interest. An example of such a scenario would be the pension fund of a charitable organization that works to prevent lung cancer, implementing a prohibition on any hedge fund in which they invest from investing in tobacco stocks. In a traditional investing context, these prohibitive guidelines can be thought of as the rules and preferences an investor sets out when hiring a financial advisor and filling out what is commonly known as an investment policy statement, which is commonly referred to as an IPS.

As we have outlined earlier in this book, structurally many hedge funds operate as pooled investment vehicles. This means that all investors allocate to a shared pool that follows the same investment guidelines. Of course, there are exceptions to the pooled vehicle structures through mechanisms such as side letters, which may offer preferential terms and transparency to certain individual investors in the pool. However, the popularity of such side letters has declined in recent years.

Instead, to implement specific custom mandates that provide investors with more control over a number of items, including instituting prohibitive investment guidelines, hedge funds often propose what is known as a separate account structure. Under this structure, which can be thought of as a fund of one for a single investor, the investor can still benefit from the fund manager's general strategy, but can often customize certain restrictions to their liking. As we discussed earlier in this book, the catch for many investors is that the minimum investments required for a manager to implement separately managed accounts are much higher than those for the pooled investment vehicles. To put some numbers around these concepts, it would not be uncommon for a hedge fund's minimum initial investment required to be US$1 million but the minimum investment requirement to establish a separate account may be US$20 million.

It should be clarified here that the prohibitive guidelines we are discussing here do not refer to prohibitions at the fund level as specified in its offering documents ("OM") or other marketing materials. An example of such a guideline in that context would be when a fund's OM outlines that it can't invest in either a certain type of security or geographic region. Another common example would be a cap on the maximum percentage on the weight of a single security or sector that a fund is allowed to invest in. Instead, these types of guidelines would be investment restrictions that all investors participate in. Indeed, as we have outlined throughout this book, one of the key goals of hedge fund governance is to ensure that a fund follows these prescribed guidelines. Here, however, we are focusing on the prohibitive investment guidelines mandated by specific investors on top of the general investment mandate of any particular fund.

Permissive Investment Guidelines

As the name would imply, permissive investment guidelines are those that investors seek to encourage. Unlike prohibitive investment guidelines, permissive ones are often closely aligned with the core strategy of the hedge fund's strategy.

ALTERNATIVE ACTIVISM IN ACTION ESG, SRI, AND FAITH-BASED INVESTING

The use of both permissive and prohibitive guidelines in promoting fund-level activism is perhaps best outlined through examples. This type of alternative activism works by directing fund managers' investments as opposed to direct investments, and can be introduced through an overview of three popular areas in this regards: environmental, social, and governance ("ESG") criteria, socially responsible investing ("SRI"), and faith-based investing.

Environmental, Social, and Governance Criteria

ESG criteria are examples of the ways that certain investors attempt to direct the investment strategies of their hedge funds through permissive investment guidelines. As noted above, these ESG principles are often linked directly to notions of investor activism and good governance in part because in addition to outlining these criteria, investors often seek to monitor the way in which hedge funds implement ESG policies on an ongoing basis. The investor ESG focus is typically geared toward encouraging investments in certain companies that investors feel comport with their ESG notions, and avoiding others that do not. As such, an ESG is an example of both permissive and prohibitive investor guidelines.

Putting any benefit to society or the environment aside, it is up for debate whether ESG principals are actually profitable from a purely dollars and cents perspective. Some have argued that the track record of ESG funds is too short to be able to draw any meaningful conclusions about their profitability (Staub-Bisang, 2012). Others have argued that to be profitable, hedge funds cannot follow ESG principals (Rice et al., 2012). Other studies have shown that hedge funds are largely ignorant of ESG principals (Röhrbein, 2012). Despite questions regarding investment benefits of ESG investing in general, large institutional investors such as the CalPERS use them. Additionally, funds that have promoted such efforts have realized inflows from institutional investors as well (Hua, 2011).

Socially Responsible Investing

One such common example would be what is known as "SRI." For the purposes of our discussion of fund governance, an investor seeking to adhere to SRI would make allocations only to managers who agree to follow certain guidelines. Indeed this is representative of broader public market efforts to promote social responsibility and good corporate citizenship (Lohr, 2011). Similar to ESG, some funds that follow SRI principles have realized significant institutional inflows as well. Some hedge fund groups have even taken to giving out awards to funds that promote SRI investment approaches (Lindsay, 2013).

As an example of the way a hedge fund would implement SRI guidelines in practice let's consider the following. We have an investor investing either directly into a hedge fund whose sole focus is SRI or via a separate SRI account. Let's say this investor, or the fund based on its predetermined SRI guidelines, is concerned with the environment. Under this type of green SRI initiative, for example, the fund or investor, as the case may be, may choose to not invest in oil companies because of any perceived pollution problems. Instead they may invest in companies that are thought to promote cleaner energy, which is sometimes referred to as clean tech. Examples of this would be solar power companies or electric car companies.

Faith-Based Investing

Other investors may seek to make investments in hedge funds that are more aligned not necessarily with broad social responsibility goals, but more in-line with particular religious beliefs. For example, a Middle East–based family office that makes investments in hedge funds may have a requirement that any such investments be made in a manner that is compatible with Sharia, sometimes spelled Shariah, law. To meet this demand several hedge funds have launched Sharia-compliant funds (Fieldhouse, 2008).

Hedge funds have increasingly sought to provide transparency, supporting investment structures and restrictions to facilitate investments from institutions concerned with SRI. Another example would be hedge funds that seek to better align with the corporate activism and religious beliefs of Catholic institutions (Dugan, 2005; Williamson, 2012).

Additional Comments on Activism Investing

In this section we have introduced three of the more popular fund-level activism trends. There are of course others, many of which are similar to the principles outlined above with slightly nuanced differences in some cases. These may include so-called economic, social, and environment ("ESE") principals and corporate social responsibility ("CSR") principals. Other investors may decide to leverage off the principles of others such as the UN Principles for Responsible Investment ("UNPRI").

At the end of the day whatever a particular investor chooses to call it, ultimately it is a hedge fund's adherence to the goals laid out by investors that is the critical point. While the focus of such initiatives is to generally promote what investors may deem to be good corporate governance principals at the underlying companies in which they invest, as noted above, these frameworks also have fund-level implications. When performing an initial or ongoing governance assessment of a hedge fund, the ways that the funds are structured to both initially comply with these guidelines and monitor them going forward can be important indicators of the level of governance controls in place at the fund level. After all, what's the difference between a particular hedge fund's risk limit guidelines that leverage cannot exceed 140%, or an ESG guideline that outlines that no more than 5% of a portfolio can be in tobacco companies? From a governance control perspective the two concepts aren't that different. As such, if investors pursue governance principals at funds, they should also use them as an opportunity to monitor the fund-level signaling effects and their implementation on an ongoing basis.

CONCLUSION

We began this chapter by introducing considerations or ongoing governance monitoring. To begin our discussion we highlighted the benefits of performing ongoing governance evaluations of hedge funds. In designing an ongoing governance monitoring program we outlined considerations including information decay, and a meta-analysis of raw operational and investment due diligence data. We then proceeded to outline examples of the types of considerations that may arise during ongoing governance analysis. As part of these discussions two examples we highlighted were the governance signaling effects of hedge fund software upgrade cycle implementation and the ongoing governance monitoring required of the role of advisory boards, should they be in place at a hedge fund.

As part of our discussion of ongoing governance monitoring we also highlighted the benefits of ongoing background investigation and news monitoring for funds, personnel, and directors. We also outlined the risks to ongoing governance assessment associated with developing house views via the *good person* problem. To sum up our discussion of ongoing monitoring we outlined the potential to increase governance monitoring frequency through shallow dives. To conclude the chapter we introduced fund-level activism, and discussed several governance investment trends including ESG, SRI, and faith-based investing. The development and monitoring of ongoing governance assessment programs can add substantial value to investors' overall governance monitoring efforts. As we highlighted earlier, monitoring a fund's adherence to investment governance considerations such as ESG can also provide useful insights with regards to the way funds approach governance in general and not just in their portfolios.

REFERENCES

Dugan, I., 2005. Hedge funds attract catholic institutions into the fold. *The Wall Street Journal*, May 24.

Fieldhouse, S., 2008. Islamic hedge funds come of age. *The Hedge Fund Journal*, October 6.

Hua, T., 2011. ESG gains wider acceptance. *Pensions & Investments*, January 24.

Lindsay, M., 2013. Hedge funds need ethical guidelines. *Hedge Funds Review*, February 13.

Lohr, S., 2011. First, make money. Also, do good. *The New York Times*, August 13.

Rice, M., DiMeo, R., Porter, M., 2012. Nonprofit asset management: effective investment strategies and oversight. Wiley, Hoboken, NJ.

Röhrbein, N., 2012. Hedge funds largely ignorant of ESG principles. *Investments & Pensions Europe*, July 23.

Staub-Bisang, M., 2012. Sustainable investing for institutional investors: risk, regulations and strategies. Wiley, Singapore.

Williamson, C., 2012. Hedge fund firms accepting screens to get faith-based business. *Pensions & Investments*, August 23.

Chapter 8

Case Studies and Example Scenarios in Hedge Fund Governance

Chapter Outline Head

INTRODUCTION

As we have outlined throughout this book, governance is a broad multidisciplinary subject touching on multiple areas of a hedge fund. Governance considerations should not be solely limited to the fund itself, but should include service providers as well. Due to the broad and interconnected nature of governance it can sometimes be challenging to evaluate in the real world. To make inroads in this area, in Chapter 6, we outlined techniques for investors seeking to conduct an initial governance assessment. Then in Chapter 7, we covered techniques for investors seeking to conduct an ongoing governance assessment.

The purpose of this chapter is to provide further perspective on how investors can go about considering real-world applications of governance. For starters, we will review several case studies of hedge fund failures with a specific focus on key governance issues. Then we will proceed to provide several hypothetical scenarios that highlight some of the governance evaluation challenges that investors may face when evaluating hedge funds. For reference, all situations and persons described in these scenarios are purely fictional and these situations and persons are described solely for demonstrative purposes.

CASE STUDIES

Hedge funds fail for all kinds of reasons. Many of these failures are nothing sensational. Funds realize losses, lose capital, and go out of business. It's obviously not a good situation for investors who lose capital, but some of these failures are a result of bad investment decisions. Other funds have voluntarily shut their doors and simply returned capital because of a combination of losses in a sector or a general lack of promising future prospects in particular markets (Stevenson, 2014; Kishan, 2014). In other cases, however, there are situations where poor operational practices result in, if not significantly contribute to, hedge fund failures. In those cases, it is not necessarily that fraud or even illegal activity was involved, but simply that poor operational planning and risk management were in play. Finally, there are the situations of outright illegal activity. It is this last situation, where illegality is involved, where there are often a number of governance failings that either contributed to the situation or helped perpetrate it. To illustrate the real-world implications of these governance breakdowns we will proceed with our discussion of several case studies.

Case Study 1: Governance Considerations of Madoff Ponzi Scheme

"Fraud is, of course, always a primary concern to us. I emphasize that I do not intend to imply that hedge funds or their managers generally engage in nefarious or illegal activities. I have no reason to believe that fraud is more prevalent in hedge funds than it is anywhere else" (investor protection: Donaldson, 2003). These comments were taken from the April 10, 2003 testimony of William H. Donaldson, the then chairman of the US Securities and Exchange Commission, to the Senate Committee on Banking Housing and Urban Affairs. When read with hindsight, particularly after the Madoff scandal occurred, these comments are telling of the pre-Madoff perspective at the time, at least from the perspective of certain regulators.

If you have ever been sued or sued anyone yourself, you'll likely know of the breakneck speed with which it takes litigation to run its course. Indeed, there are famous experiments on the speed at which pitch can take to drip that likely proceed at a more expeditious rate. Facetiousness aside, believe it or not, as this book is being written there is still ongoing litigation related to the Madoff case. To those with experience in this area this may not surprise anyone, but it certainly doesn't come as comfort to any investors still involved in such suits.

While numerous other books, articles, and research papers have been written about the Madoff scandal, here we will focus on the governance implications of a particular aspect of the Madoff scandal. In particular, we will highlight a recent decision in a Madoff-related case that came about in the United Kingdom. This case highlights the role of directors in Madoff's London operation, which was named Madoff Securities International Limited ("MSIL"). The decision was from the English High Court in the case of *Madoff Securities International*

Limited (In Liquidation) v. Raven and Ors [2013] EWHC 3147. For those unfamiliar with UK law, it is of particular interest because as we have outlined
earlier in this book, the decision in this case came out of the United Kingdom.
This is because the law of the Cayman Islands is greatly influenced by British
law. Additionally, many Cayman court decisions will be heavily influenced by
UK court decisions. As such, the decisions by UK courts such as this typically
are viewed as having direct implications in popular offshore directorship centers
such as the Caymans.

Turning to the case itself, as indicated by the parties named above, the focus of this case related to the activities of MSIL. In this case, the legitimacy
of the trading operations conducted by MSIL was debated. Some argued that
the operations were merely a so-called warehouse for stolen cash, while others
argued it was a legitimate operation (Croft, 2013). Related to our discussions of
governance and directors, MSIL maintained a board of directors, the composition of which varied over time. These directors reportedly included Leon Flax,
Christopher Dale, Philip Toop, and Malcolm Stevenson (Tobin, 2010). One of
the key governance issues in the case, and the one we will focus on here, relates
to the oversight role of these directors.

To provide some factual background in this matter, it was reported that
between 1992 and 2007, reportedly at Madoff's request, MSIL made a series of
regular payments, totaling over $27 million, to companies owned by an individ-
ual named Sonja Kohn (Partington, 2013). For reference Ms. Kohn, an Austrian
banker and the former Bank Medici AG chairwoman, worked with her firm to
serve as a major source of funds to Madoff, including a large number of assets
reportedly from Russian oligarchs (Sarna, 2010). The money was ostensibly
paid for research provided by Ms. Kohn's companies to Madoff. During the
case, Grant Thornton, the liquidator of Madoff's UK operation, alleged that this
"research" was useless and according to reports by the *Financial Times*, "com-
piled partly by a US literature student with no financial services experience and
'in large part copied wholesale from other sources' or 'cut and pasted from the
internet'" (Croft, 2013).

One of the key questions in this case was whether or not the directors
breached their duties by allowing these payments to be made. Without getting
into all of the legal technicalities in the decision, which was rendered by Judge
Andrew Popplewell, the court found that there was no breach by the directors
of their so-called duty to exercise independent judgment with regards to their
oversight of the payments to Ms. Kohn. One of the key tests in this case was if
the directors were satisfied that the payments were appropriate. As part of this
assessment the directors are not necessarily responsible for being experts at assessing, as it was in this case, whether the information was valuable or not, but
merely that they made an appropriate inquiry in this regard. According to the
decision, they are even allowed to rely on other directors in this regard. To pause
for a moment, does this sound familiar to the concepts of delegation of duties
we had addressed earlier in this book?

Returning to the case, one of the directors, Mr. Flax, reportedly appreciated that MSIL's trader believed that the research from Kohn's firm was of little value, but that he was ultimately satisfied by Bernard Madoff himself that the research was of value to the firm (Walton and Jackson, 2014). After making inquiry and being satisfied, then whether there was actual value received or indeed the research was worthless no longer mattered to the court. Ultimately, the inquiry was made and the director duty was satisfied. So, the director was now effectively off the hook. Oh, and the court also outlined that a director doesn't have an obligation to make a fund act the way that the director would necessarily act. Under this do as I say not as I do standard, do you think a director and a fund having divergent practices is a good thing for overall fund governance?

It is interesting to think how this would apply in a different hedge fund context. For example, let's say a hedge fund was paying exorbitant fees to execute trades with a particular broker. In return the broker was providing research service. The director gets wind of this and calls the fund's traders who say that the research provided by the broker is useless. The director then asks the head of the fund who tells them that there is value in it and not to worry about it. At this point the director could either accept this reasoning and move on or ask another director, who may say they heard the same story from the head of the firm and they were satisfied. In either case, the situation wouldn't change and the hedge fund would continue to pay high commission rates for what may have been effectively useless research. Shouldn't the director be liable here?

Not if we extend the court's reasoning in this case; then the director did their job and are therefore not liable. The point of this discussion is not to focus on the failings of any particular director and certainly not those in the MSIL case; however, the point is to highlight the difference between the beliefs that some investors may have and how the law works. As we have highlighted throughout this book, some investors may take the perspective that the board should protect them in such situations and make further inquiries, perhaps even going outside of the fund to determine whether the arrangement is reasonable. Cases such as this demonstrate that directors do not necessarily have a responsibility to do this.

Another director, Mr. Raven, reportedly did not believe that MSIL was receiving value for money in regards to the payments made to Kohn's companies and, after continuing to pester him, eventually persuaded Bernard Madoff, in July 2007, to stop making the payments (Walton and Jackson, 2014).

The case also highlighted and focused on the role of Madoff's sons Andrew and Mark. Since the Madoff fraud was revealed in 2008, Andrew was reportedly diagnosed with and undergoing treatment for a type of cancer called mantle cell lymphoma (Lattman, 2013). Andrew later passed away in September 2013. Madoff's other son, Mark, committed suicide in 2010. Madoff himself isn't fairing much better in prison as reports have surfaced that he suffered a heart attack and is suffering from stage four cancer (Gorman, 2014).

Allegations of the brothers' knowledge of the Ponzi scheme and associated guilt have continued. In 2014, Irving Picard, the Madoff bankruptcy trustee, filed an amended complaint seeking the return of more than $153 million that the suit alleges was taken improperly from the Madoff fund in the form of inflated bonuses and salaries, sham loans, and fabricated trading profits (Sterngold, 2014). Other reports have emerged that in a plea deal a former Madoff accountant, Paul Konigsberg, identified so-called Madoff coconspirators that renewed suspicions among some that Madoff's remaining living son, Andrew, may still be charged in the case (Ax, 2014).

This decision also has further wide-reaching implications for director defenses. In particular, under UK law, the so-called "statutory defense" traditionally invoked by directors under UK Section 1157 of Companies Act 2006 may find itself embraced by courts with more sympathy now than prior to the decision in this case (Gordon, 2013).

What do you think, does this represent best practice governance? Should directors be able to raise such defenses going forward or should the laws change to cut off such defenses? Outside of the United Kingdom, should the legislatures of offshore jurisdictions with directors change the laws to proactively stop such defenses or instead should it be up to investors to adjudicate such matters in the courts? It is likely that no immediate changes in the laws will be made. Instead, it will be up to investors to take matters in their own hands after unfortunate losses incur. Examples such as this show the need for investors to dive deep into the role of boards of directors and the decisions that they make.

Indeed, if many investors in Madoff's fund had been privy to the questions raised by directors with regards to the Kohn payments, perhaps they would have come to different conclusions than the directors. However, without asking such questions investors are relying on the directors, which as this case outlined may be insulated from liability beyond a certain point.

Case Study 2: Weavering Capital (UK) Ltd.—A Fund Governance Milestone

By hedge fund fraud standards, the allegations in the Weavering capital case probably are not that sensational when compared with the likes of Madoff. This is not to minimize the damage done to investors, but the total amount of capital lost, reportedly around $600 million, certainly does not compare with Madoff's billions.

As background, Weavering Capital (UK) Ltd. (WCUK) was a hedge fund that managed a global macro fund called the Weavering Fixed Income Fund. In the Weavering situation, the fund collapsed after the 2008 financial crisis following the bankruptcy of Lehman Brothers because it could not keep up with onslaught of redemption requests; however, there were also allegations of wrongdoing contributing to the collapse. For example, according to PricewaterhouseCoopers among the failed investments made by Weavering were investments in a music video production company and a failed stage musical production (Bowers, 2012). Not exactly what we would call traditional global macro bets.

After Weavering failed, investors understandably sued. In 2012, Mr. Peterson, his wife Amanda Peterson, who was a director at the firm, along with two other directors, Edward Platt and Charanpreet Dabhia, were found guilty of negligently permitting fraud to happen that resulted in an award of $450 million against them (Wilkes, 2012).

In 2014, the United Kingdom's Serious Fraud Office ("SFO") alleged that Weavering's founder, Magnus Michael Peterson, committed fraud by misrepresentation, false accounting, forgery, and obtaining the transfer of capital by deception (Binham, 2014). Interestingly, the SFO dropped its initial inquiry into Weavering only to reopen it later after a change in leadership at the agency (Scott, 2012). In response to the 2014 charges, Mr. Peterson pled not guilty to the charges and his trial is, at the writing of this book, scheduled for 2015.

For the purposes of our discussion here, we will focus on the role of the fund directors that was highlighted in litigation that followed in the 2011 Cayman Islands case of *Weavering Macro Fixed Income Fund Limited (the "Fund") v. Stefan Peterson and Hans Ekstrom Cause No. FSD of 2010 (AJJ)*. That case focused on the role of the directors of Weavering's offshore open-ended fund, Weavering Macro Fixed Income Fund Limited. As background, this fund was registered with the Cayman Islands Monetary Authority. This fund was also listed on the Irish stock exchange (Ridley, 2011).

As part of the Irish listing requirements the fund was required to have two directors. The first director was an individual named Stefan Peterson. Stefan, a Swedish resident, was Magnus's younger brother. The second director was also a Swedish resident named Hans Ekstrom. Mr. Ekstrom was Magnus's stepfather (Fletcher, 2011). Hopefully this is not a difficult question, but do you think having relatives of the portfolio manager serve as fund directors represents best practice governance? Of course, it doesn't. It may be of interest if we provide further details on these individuals.

Returning to the decision in this case, written by Honorable Mr. Justice Andrew J. Jones QC for the Grand Court of the Cayman Islands, it was outlined that, "on paper both Mr. Ekstrom and Mr. Stefan Peterson had appropriate professional credentials and met the ISE's [Irish Stock Exchange's] independence requirement." Despite all of the good governance steps taken by Ireland, many of which we outlined in Chapter 3, there was obviously a problem with close relatives serving as fund directors, so much so that I would argue that this should not have met the spirit, rather than the technical rules, of any ISE independence requirements. The decision in the case provided the several interesting facts about the fund's directors including:

- While serving as a director, Stefan Peterson was also a full-time employee of Storebrand Investments, a large insurance company. Specifically, he was working as the portfolio manager of the fund's credit hedge fund in Oslo. Does anyone else see a problem with a fund director managing his own hedge fund?

- Mr. Ekstrom was 79 years old at the time of his appointment. Thirteen years prior to his appointment he retired as head of the Trustee Department of Skandinaviska Enskilda Banken, commonly known as SEB, which is a large Swedish financial group. Not to criticize the benefits of experience, but do you think it represents best practice to have an almost 80-year-old hedge fund director who had retired from industry almost 15 years ago?

Putting the familial relationship aside, we can turn to the way the directors operated, or should we say didn't operate. To address this issue we must of course focus on one of our old friends, delegation of director duty. As background, acknowledging that a keystone of the directorship industry is the ability to delegate decision making, the decision by the Honorable Mr. Justice Andrew J. Jones reads, "The Cayman Islands investment fund industry works on the basis that investment management, administration and accounting functions will be delegated to professional service providers and a company's independent non-executive directors will exercise a high level supervisory role." The court then acknowledged that in this case the directors did properly delegate these duties to the fund's aforementioned investment manager WCUK and the fund's administrator PNC Global Investment Servicing (Europe) Limited (PNC). We will return to the role of these groups later in our discussion, but for now let us simply remember that the directors appropriately delegated certain duties appropriate to them.

The decision in this case also focused on the duty of directors under Cayman law to exercise independent judgment. In implementing this judgment, under Cayman law, the directors have a duty to exercise "reasonable care, skill and diligence." What exactly do those three magic words mean? Well, that's open to interpretation. The court in this case even clarified this point by stating that the directors' duty to act with reasonable care, skill, and diligence "... in the interests of the Macro Fund, which means what they—not the Court—bona fide considered to be in its best interests." Translated from the legalese, this implies that even if the directors are completely off base, as long as the directors themselves thought the decision to delegate decision making was in the fund's best interest and followed up on any issues with reasonable care, skill, and diligence, then they are safe from liability and the Court shouldn't really pursue the issue further.

This is a good example of how in governance and director analysis, there is a major difference between the way an average hedge fund investor is likely to think about an issue and how this issue is handled in a courtroom. This is by no means meant to disparage the average hedge fund investor, as they are often quite sophisticated, but rather to show how in many cases issues of obligations and duties, which may seem logical and straightforward to some, can become quite perverted in the courtroom.

While we are discussing the decision of a court here, which is a legal analysis of a case, it is important to understand the disconnect here. While what courts decide has very real-world implications, as did the decision of the court in this case, the way the law works does not always comport with investors' common notions of right and wrong. For example, would it be "reasonable care, skill and diligence" to take the word of a firm's head that potentially useless research was worth millions of dollars? Well, that was one of the director scenarios we outlined in the UK Madoff case, wasn't it? Now, if I stopped your average Joe on the street, they would likely think me crazy not only for saying it wasn't reasonable but also for not agreeing that the director should be thrown in jail. Courts applying the law? Well, you saw the result. As you read this you may be thinking, oh of course, it's obvious that the directors didn't perform their duty. However, please remember there is a difference, for better or worse, from an investor thinking this and a court actually applying it. That was one of the reasons this Weavering case was such a big deal, because the court took a stand on certain issues and clarified some of the key duties of directors in this regard.

Returning to the decision, the court rightly outlined that there are both objective and subjective elements to analyzing directors' duties. In regards to objectivity, on the one hand, the court acknowledged that the directors "rarely have the technical expertise and experience to be able to monitor sophisticated investment strategies and trading techniques in a direct hand[s]-on manner." On the other hand, the directors were "not expect[ed] to supervise WCUK's trading activities ..., but they were expected to satisfy themselves that it was complying with investment restrictions." Not to oversimplify the situation but how would you feel if I asked you to make sure I was doing something, but you couldn't be involved in watching me do it? Is this a fair governance proposition? Think about that as we proceed.

Moving on, the court addressed the issue of willful neglect or default. The court effectively did not even get into the details of applying the legal test as to whether there was willful negligence or default since, in the court's words, "'they did nothing' and carried on doing nothing for almost six years." From this the court surmised that if the directors knew that they had a duty to perform their duties and "utterly ignored their duty," then it must have been intentional. Didn't the directors do anything at all? In summary, here are some of the highlights that provide clarity on what they did and did not do:

- The court found the directors "went through the motions of appearing to hold regular quarterly board meetings but, in reality, did nothing."
- The court also stated, "[t]he directors should have made enquiry to ensure that they properly understood the nature and scope of the work which each of the professional service providers were proposing to do, perhaps more importantly, proposing not to do, and that it would result in proper division of responsibility." The directors did not do this. Additionally, the court went further to clarify the nature of the directors' review of service providers, including specifying that "a desktop review of the contract documents is inherently unlikely to be sufficient. ... especially if the promoter/investment manager is a start-up operation with which the other service providers have no prior business relationship and working experience."

- In commenting on the potentially different interests of service providers the court stated, "... it is important to understand that the lawyers' duty to their client is quite different from that of the directors' duty to the company. ... It is their [, the directors,] duty to stand back, review the various contracts and satisfy themselves that each one is appropriate and consistent with industry standards and that, taken together, they do create an overall structure which will ensure a proper division of responsibility among the service providers." This did not happen either in Weavering's case.
- The decision outlined that directors had passed a resolution to appoint Price-waterhouseCoopers as auditors. What's the problem with that? Well, the directors learned only after the event that Ernst & Young had been appointed instead. Doesn't necessarily suggest that they were too involved, does it?
- Another interesting point raised by the court related to the directors' analysis of the fund's audited financial statements themselves. The court found that if the directors sign the financial statements, as they did in this case, then "they are required to exercise the skill and care reasonably to be expected of investment fund's independent non-executive directors. They must also bring to bear the expertise they actually possess." How would this scenario play out if we compared two different types of directors? Let's say we have one with experience with financial statements and another with perhaps less experience and sophistication with financial statements. Is the one with less experience and sophistication held to a lesser standard as compared with the other one? Does such a floating standard seem fair from an investor's perspective? What about, as we outlined earlier in this text, investors who take the opinion that directors are useless and the fund managers do all the work, and therefore completely ignore fund directors? How can they claim that they have any understanding of a director's skill set and qualifications to assess to what standard a director would be held? Furthermore, would a more qualified director be necessarily better for investors in this regards? If a director is more qualified, then couldn't they make the argument that based on their extensive qualifications they had satisfied their own standard of applying reasonable care? On the other hand, a less qualified director perhaps could simply play dumb. In either case, are investors left with few good governance options here? Once again, how can they know if they don't dig into the role and backgrounds of the directors?
- A related question that the court contemplated, but did not directly address in this case, was whether a director could properly delegate all their functions with respect to the financial statements to the investment manager and administrator. What do you think about this? Couldn't the argument be made that the administrator in particular is more heavily involved with the fund as compared with the directors and it would perhaps make more sense to put the administrator in an oversight role in this regards? Additionally, this argument is further bolstered with the increased interaction of late between administrators and auditors. On the other hand, the directors can provide a

valuable level of independent oversight of the financial statements in this regards. As an investor do you feel you are asking the appropriate questions to determine if directors are adding real value to provide sufficient oversight of the financial statements? Do you have any evidence to support this?

- In regards to the actual offering document for the fund, the court outlined that the directors have a duty to "satisfy themselves" that the document complies with the Mutual Funds Law. On this point the court stated, "[t] hey could not discharge their duty by saying to themselves that the content of the offering document must be alright because the promoter/investment manager, its lawyers, the prospective administrator, auditor and other service providers are all reputable firms having experience in their respective fields. Every offering document should be subjected to a verification exercise." As you likely guessed, the court determined that the directors did not do this either. If you are currently a hedge fund investor, what response do you think you would get from the fund manager and the fund's directors if you inquired how they verified that the fund's offering documents were in compliance with Cayman law? Did the directors simply rely on the fund's legal counsel or did they do anything else to pursue this further verification standard? How would a hedge fund check to make sure the directors did this? Do they even have an obligation to?

- The decision by the court outlined that at the first board meeting the directors passed a resolution that "[a]t each meeting we will assess the performance of the Company and the work done by the investment manager. ... This will be closely looked upon at each board meeting and the Directors will have weekly discussions with the investment manager about the Company's position and fixed income markets in general." On cross-examination one of the directors, Stefan Peterson, explained that the purpose of this seemingly robust resolution was because "[w]e wanted to be ambitious here. ... we want this fund [to] operate well and to make an effort to make it to be a good company." Ok, well, step one would be to actually do something substantive here. As you can imagine by now, the court found this to be "a self-serving resolution" to which "they never made any attempt to comply with …."

- The court also highlighted that the directors never asked for any reports to be prepared for themselves or other service providers other than Mr. Peterson from WCUK. This was in spite of the fact that the administrator for the fund even asked the directors to "[p]lease confirm what information you would like reported on." The directors never even bothered to respond to the question. Furthermore, the directors didn't ask for representatives from the other service providers to attend board meetings. This is an interesting point to mention; from an investor governance perspective, and putting legal technical notions aside, do you think that if a director asks no follow-up questions, the administrator should raise an alarm or follow up with the fund directly? What about the other service providers? Should they have an obligation to raise the issue with investors? The court tangentially addressed this issue by accepting the directors' defense argument, which outlined that the evidence presented in the case suggested that the administrator, PNC, must have known that a related entity was a counterparty because of exposure level in place. However, the court further clarifies that this analysis misses the point because it wasn't the administrator's responsibility to "take any action on behalf of the Fund." Would you as an investor feel that this represents an appropriate level of transparency and collaboration among fund service providers to protect your interests?

The list of issues, and subsequent failures, of directors' duties in this case goes on and on. The issues discussed include those related to the signing of financial statements without comment or further review, allegation of signing sham contracts, and issues relating to the conflicts among investors with regards to the execution of side letters.

Weavering was an extreme example of what were effectively figurehead directors who did virtually nothing. All that being said, the fund still managed to raise approximately $600 million. Did those investors know about the role of these figurehead directors? Did they not even ask questions or instead did they just not care?

Now, of course, it's easy to make the directors scapegoats and place all the blame on them. While they were certainly very culpable in this area, there were multiple other parties involved in this fund. We are not implying that any of them were necessarily negligent for the purposes of this discussion, but rather to illustrate that the directors here, as in all funds, were part of a larger system. In this case, it appears that through the complex web of delegation of duties multiple parties may have dropped the ball. Of course, they may not be technically liable, but the question can be raised as to who was supervising these parties? Certainly the directors did not provide any meaningful supervision.

Another consideration that warrants discussion is how does the Weavering case stack up against traditional objections against directors. As we have highlighted throughout this book, a contentious point of debate for many investors is the issue of director capacity. We will once again revisit this issue in the Sark Lark case study in this chapter. Of course, too many directorships held by a given director sends a clear signal of potentially poor oversight and general bad governance. So how did we do in this case? Well, there are no widespread reports that either of the fund's two directors sat on other boards. So they each had one directorship each. Does this sound like a capacity issue to you? Me neither.

Another big issue related to capacity for some of those critical of the directorship industry is that directors should be paid more. Some argue that when directors are not paid enough, they don't take the issues seriously and they will be less involved and take on too many other positions because of the relatively low fees they are collecting for each engagement. In this case the directors were not paid anything. By being paid nothing it, as the court agreed, showed they never intended to do anything to begin with. So when a director's salary is zero, it seems that they may be inclined to do nothing and there may be some weight to the argument to paying directors more as compared with nothing at all.

Ultimately, one of the most famous takeaways from the decision in the case was the following statement regarding the role of directors: "They are not entitled to assume the posture of automatons, as these Directors did, by signing whatever documents are put in front of them by the investment manager without making enquiry or applying their minds to the matter in the issue, on the assumption that the other service providers have performed their respective roles (actual or perceived) and therefore do not need to be supervised in any way whatsoever." The reason this quote became so famous was because it succinctly outlined that directors were increasingly accountable.

The question could be asked, however: accountable to whom? As we have outlined throughout this book, investors have increased their focus on the role of the directors, but directors still have an arsenal of defenses on which to draw should problems arise. We are not arguing here that directors should be hung out to dry and left defenseless, but rather that investors should be aware they are in the post-Weavering world where there is an increased focus by directors to avoid the problems outlined in Weavering. This may seem like a win for investors, but investors should also be aware that with this increased director focus on performing fund oversight come potentially enhanced director protections. If directors have satisfied their requirements of reasonable care, skill, and diligence, they may be able to escape liability in situations where investors feel they should potentially be the ones to blame for the losses that occurred on their watch.

Case Study 3: AIJ Investment Advisors Co.—Japanese Governance Failures

AIJ Investment Advisors Co. ("AIJ") was a Japanese hedge fund manager, run by Kazuhiko Asakawa, which reportedly utilized equity and bond futures, option trades, and derivatives to produce high returns (Tabuchi, 2012). It was reported that AIJ claimed that its flagship AIM Millennium fund had returned over 241% since its inception on 2002 on Nikkei options as compared with drops of over 20% by the Japanese Topix Index (Yamazaki and Ito, 2012). Does this sound too good to be true? It certainly was, and the entire operation was, as you likely guessed, a fraud that operated as a Ponzi scheme using new investors' capital to make payments to existing investors (Osaki, 2012). Outside of a general discussion of fraud, the case also presents some interesting perspective on hedge fund governance.

As background, in early 2012 the Japanese government shut down AIJ's operation when the firm could not explain where approximately $2.62 billion in client assets had gone. AIJ's clients included many large Japanese pension funds, including Advantest, a large semiconductor equipment maker, and

Yaskawa Electric, an industrial robot maker (Tabuchi, 2012). It was reported that some funds allocated over 30% of their assets to AIJ (Hodo and Layne, 2012). Another interesting note about AIJ was that in 2009 a Japanese research service noted that AIJ had "unnaturally stable returns," although a year earlier that same research firm, Rating & Investment Information Inc., ranked AIJ number one among Japanese pension funds in a customer satisfaction survey (Inagaki et al., 2012).

Through a series of complicated transactions with affiliates and the reported use of bank accounts in the Cayman Islands, Bermuda, and Hong Kong, AIJ was able to perpetuate the scam for years (The Asahi Shimbun, 2012). The damage done by the AIJ was particularly of note since it came on the heels of the revelation the previous year of a huge corporate governance scandal in Japan where the camera maker Olympus Corp. had admitted to covering up 13 years' worth of losses (Yamazaki, 2012).

Mr. Asakawa, after first admitting his guilt and then switching his plea to not guilty at the last minute, was ultimately sentenced to 15 years in prison. Former AIJ executive Shigeko Takahashi and Hideaki Nishimura, president of AIJ subsidiary ITM Securities Co., were each sentenced to seven years in prison. In addition to the prison terms, the three defendants were also fined a total of over ¥15.6 billion (Osaki, 2013).

From a governance perspective, one of the more interesting aspects relating to AIJ were stories that came out after the scandal broke relating to the firm's reluctance to have due diligence performed on it. Effectively some investors who had been interested in allocating their assets with AIJ were rejected by the firm when they asked to perform detailed due diligence. From a due diligence perspective this would obviously be a deal killer issue that should preclude investment. What does this say about the managers' internal governance mechanisms? Why would they not want investors asking questions? In AIJ's case we know the answer was because it was a fraud. What about when other managers allow investors to perform due diligence, but draw the line with regards to transparency? If a manager allows due diligence but then cuts transparency off ahead of what other managers will give you, where as an investor do you draw the line? Does the answer change when we ask about governance issues such as fund board turnover or committee meeting minutes? If you answered yes, why would you be comfortable with less transparency in these areas?

A second interesting governance point with regards to AIJ was the institutional structure in place in Japan at the time that effectively created a perfect environment in which a fraud such as AIJ could fester. Existing laws regarding pension funds at the time in Japan did not help to promote an environment of appropriate governance controls and oversight of hedge fund investments. Japanese pension fund organizations generally maintain what can be thought of as a governing board, usually called a Board of Representatives, which is responsible for overseeing the fund's investments on a day-to-day basis. The laws concerning these boards required that all board members be composed of individuals associated with the plan, yet many plans do not have individuals with hedge fund investing experience (Horie, 2012). As such, the plans were effectively legally prohibited in certain cases from leveraging off specialized third parties to assist them with a number of functions, including ongoing due diligence and governance monitoring, which would have likely added significant value in avoiding exposure to funds such as AIJ.

While it may be easy to point the finger at Japan, as an investor do you approach due diligence, including an assessment on governance issues, any differently? For example, as we have outlined throughout this book information technology can be an area rife with governance issues. Yet most people tasked to conduct an evaluation of the governance of funds, operational due diligence (ODD) professionals, do not have information technology backgrounds. It doesn't mean they cannot do capable jobs, but that they in general may be ill-equipped in certain areas. The solutions to this would be to employ multidisciplinary ODD teams and work with third parties with special expertise. As an investor do you do this? If not, why? When a scandal such as AIJ occurs, do you reevaluate your skill sets and approach to due diligence or simply pursue the status quo in this regard?

Interestingly, an AIMA Japan and Eurekahedge survey from June 2014 highlighted in part that despite the AIJ scandal notions of governance have still not yet come to the forefront of the Japanese institutional investor mindset. Specifically, the survey found that the key factors behind Japanese investors' allocation decisions were primarily performance, risk management, and track record with governance ranking lower in importance (AIMA, 2014).

To comment on the issue I decided to speak to Mika Mukawa, a Japanese ODD professional with experience in hedge fund investing and the Japanese financial service industry. She is an ODD analyst at Colonial Consulting LLC in New York, NY, and previously worked on the hedge fund investment team in the New York–based asset management arm of one of the largest Japanese life insurers for over nine years.

Jason Scharfman:	After the AIJ scandal was revealed a widespread investigation was conducted of over 260 Japanese asset managers. Can you comment on what changes have been implemented since the AIJ scandal?
Mika Mukawa:	The Japanese Financial Services Authority ("FSA") in consultation with other Japanese regulators amended the regulations since the scandal. In particular, there was a significant focus on revising the guidelines for pension funds managed by private investment managers and increasing governance so that pension funds will make their investments only after performing proper due diligence.
Jason Scharfman:	What in particular has changed with the implementation of these new guidelines?
Mika Mukawa:	In the amended guidelines, third parties such as trusts and banks play a major role in monitoring funds' net asset value ("NAV"). Also fund managers are required to enhance disclosure of their investment strategies and auditor's report to their clients.

Jason Scharfman:	While these enhanced guidelines will likely promote more stringent oversight, this also brings up an interesting point about the Japanese hedge fund industry. Traditionally, there has been reluctance in Japan about hedge fund investing. Indeed, there are a limited number of onshore Japanese funds due to a number of reasons, including a prohibitive tax code. This in part has contributed to Japan falling behind to more prominent Asian hedge fund centers such as Hong Kong and Singapore. How do you view these regulations as balancing with Japan's increased desire to promote new hedge fund launches?
Mika Mukawa:	Yes, that's a great point. It has been rumored for a long time that the FSA had planned regulatory changes that would have lowered the hurdle to launch new funds. These new launches would likely target institutional investors, which would be a boost to the Japanese hedge fund industry. After the enhanced regulations implemented after the AIJ scandal, new barriers such as enhanced inspections for both fund managers and investors will slow this process. But I think pensioners will adjust into the environment and start investing in hedge fund since they are aware that they have to improve the performance of their funds due to the "Lost Decade" after the Japanese bubble collapsed and an ongoing "demographic crunch" that pensioners are experiencing.
Jason Scharfman:	Ultimately, then do you think the new post-AIJ regulatory environment in Japan will help pensioners in promoting governance and avoiding another AIJ scandal?
Mika Mukawa:	Yes, the new rule to improve fund transparency is a big step forward for fund governance. That being said, each pension fund still should have an ODD professional or other trustworthy third-party advisor, who is completely independent from the investment side. Most of the Japanese pension funds still have little experience in alternative fund investment, and those pension funds affected by AIJ had hired former officials from Ministry of Health, Labor and Welfare, who have no background in asset management. This is a problem. Also, ODD is not regarded as important as investment analysis in general, and it is rare to see a dedicated ODD professional in Japan while you can find dozens of them in New York City alone.
Jason Scharfman:	Yes, that seems to be a common problem not just in Japan but also globally where certain ODD professionals do not necessarily have multidisciplinary experience or in certain instances background in the area and receive on-the-job training as it were. Why do you think this is such a problem in Japan?
Mika Mukawa:	The problem for pension funds is that they need experienced professionals to perform due diligence, but it is not easy under practice widely known as "permanent employment" in Japan.
Jason Scharfman:	Does this mean that you are of the opinion that even after the AIJ scandal, there continues to be a problem with regards to the quality of professionals performing governance assessments and overall due diligence on behalf of Japanese pension funds?

(Continued)

Mika Mukawa:	The problem is that there are not many MBA programs in Japan. Instead, what happens is major companies give on-the-job training to college graduates to meet each company's needs. They train these employees as generalists who understand only the company-specific operations. Even in a large corporation, it is not surprising to see an employee who has worked as a hedge fund investment officer in a US subsidiary for a few years to be assigned to human resources department back in Tokyo headquarters when they return home. This is nothing new; it's just the way the Japanese system works. Success in their career is measured by advancement into upper management, not by their levels of achievement in specific areas of expertise such as due diligence, governance, risk management, or fraud detection. Professionals who obtained special skills during employment often leave the company to further achieve their potential in what we call "gaishikei" or foreign firms in Japan.
Jason Scharfman:	It seems that Japan is moving in the right direction in promoting new regulatory reforms, but there is still room for improvement in both the skill sets of personnel conducting the reviews and pension funds approaches to hedge fund due diligence and governance evaluations. Thank you for speaking to me about these issues.
Mika Mukawa:	My pleasure, thank you.

EXAMPLE SCENARIO: "THE SARK LARK"—ARE CERTAIN JURISDICTIONS' REGULATORY GOVERNANCE REGIMES COMPLETELY INEFFECTIVE?

Before we dive too deeply into this scenario a bit of background would likely be helpful concerning the title. For the uninitiated or those from outside the United Kingdom, you may not know what, or should we say where, exactly Sark is. For this a bit of a quick geography lesson is in order. I ask for indulgence of this diversion because, as you will see, this does relate to the subject of hedge fund governance.

Sark is located in what are known as the Channel Islands. Just to be clear the Channel Islands we are talking about here are those in the English Channel, off the French Coast. There are other places that have Channel Islands such as off Southern California that are not the subject of this discussion. The Channel Islands in the English Channel consist of two primary groups of islands that are technically so-called Crown dependencies and are known as "bailiwicks." These are the Bailiwick of Jersey and the Bailiwick of Guernsey.

Each bailiwick archipelago is made up of several islands. One of the most populated of these is Jersey, which, surprisingly enough, is in the Bailiwick of Jersey. The other three islands that make up the group of the so-called four main Channel Islands are located in the Bailiwick of Guernsey. These are the namesake island of Guernsey itself, as well as Alderney and Sark.

As is similar with many offshore island jurisdictions, there is a lack of traditional industry. As compared with more land rich jurisdictions, for example, particularly in the smaller islands, there is simply less room for farming, manufacturing, etc. As such, many of these islands saw economic opportunities to develop into what are known as offshore financial centers or OFCs. One proposed definition of an OFC is: "a country or jurisdiction that provides financial service to nonresidents on a scale that is incommensurate with the size and the financing of its domestic economy" (Zoromé, 1987).

Effectively, an OFC develops attractive legal, regulatory, and tax frameworks that encourage investors from outside the country to do business in the OFC. The form of this business is typically corporate and commercial services. As you'll know by getting this far in this book, many OFCs such as the Cayman Islands are also popular destinations for offshore hedge funds due to the tax advantages they offer. The Channel Islands collectively are another popular offshore hedge fund jurisdiction.

While we addressed the role of several popular jurisdictions in Chapter 3, as yet we haven't addressed Sark. There's a reason for that; from a hedge fund perspective, or really from the perspective of anyone but a tourist, today there isn't much to say about Sark. Looking back a few years to the 1980s, from the UK perspective at least, Sark used to be a bigger deal. Well, at least it was for what some may argue was legal tax avoidance, while others would categorize it as tax evasion. The reasons for Sark's temporary rise to prominence were loopholes in the tax laws of two aforementioned Channel Islands, Jersey and Guernsey, as well as the United Kingdom. As we have referenced, Jersey and Guernsey themselves were utilized by many UK and European companies due to their advantages. When this was combined with the use of Sark, it resulted in a controversial tax arrangement, which ultimately had modern hedge fund governance implications.

Here's an example of how this controversial tax arrangement would have worked at the time. Let's say you were a UK company or individual who wanted to shield income from your UK tax obligations. To do this you could first set up a separate Jersey or Guernsey company. But then, of course, the company would still be subject to Jersey or Guernsey taxes, and perhaps certain UK taxes by association. To lessen this already lower burden, as compared with original UK tax obligation, you would then need to take another step that involved the use of corporate directors.

Specifically, you could take advantage of a tax avoidance scheme that worked based on a loophole in the way the tax laws were written at the time. In Jersey, for example, to take full advantage of Jersey's exempt company law and its tax benefits, at the time, the management and control of the company had to be located outside of Jersey. Similar rules were also in place in Guernsey. Once these loopholes were successfully navigated, income could be earned effectively tax free with minimal, if any, tax leakage.

To facilitate this transfer of control and meet the requirement from a tax perspective, the director's meetings of the Jersey or Guernsey company as appropriate would have to be held elsewhere. Continuing our example, now with the framework of the corporate structures laid out, you then would be faced with the problem of where your nominee directors should be located. Why not a location a short boat ride away from Jersey or Guernsey, on say a loosely regulated island? Sark, of course!

If you were going to take advantage of Sark under this arrangement, then the island, as would most other offshore jurisdictions, would welcome you. That is of course as long as you boost the local economy by hiring a Sark resident to serve on your board of directors. For reference Sark, which bans transportation by cars and is noted for its old-world charm, has an estimated population of around 600 people as of 2014 (Brown, 2014).

The hiring of Sark directors was a big business for the island. In 1999, when the use of this framework was at its peak, it was estimated that the majority of the adult population of the island were in some way in the directorship business, which was also estimated to have made up 10–15% of the island's total income (Piggott, 1999).

To accomplish this goal of hiring local residents based in OFCs, in this case Sark, the concept of so-called offshore nominee directors arose. Nominee directors offered two benefits. First, from a practical perspective they would allow this tax scheme to function. Perhaps more importantly they would provide anonymity by instead putting the company under the name of the nominee directors. When trying to avoid taxes, such anonymity is often preferred of course.

Second, it was understood that they wouldn't actually take any control over the company and the associated assets, but that they would just facilitate the arrangement as a function of their Sark residency. As such, due to the effective acceptance of this king's clothes–type of arrangement, the use of Sark-based nominee directors under this structure came to be known as the so-called Sark Lark (Martin, 2006).

I should clarify that nominee directors themselves weren't necessarily illegal; it was just the way that they performed, or didn't perform, their job that were the issue in Sark. Specifically, the major problems with these Sark nominee directors were two-fold. First, it seems these nominee directors were just that, directors in name only. This is not what was, at least ostensibly, contemplated by the regulators drafting the tax code at the time. The majority of these directors were actually supposed to do something more than push paper or have the right not to sign something. Instead, it seems these were individuals based in Sark who could be thought of as fulfilling the role of legal fictions and who would merely sign paperwork to comply with technical requirements. Many of them served as paper or sham directors who had abrogated their responsibilities and had no real control, qualifications, or input into how the Jersey or Guernsey company in our example worked. This effective dereliction of duty is effectively what distinguishes a legal nominee director from an illegal one.

Second, as is the problem with most loopholes, it became overly exploited. So much so that Sark's approximately 600 residents were reported to have over

15,000 corporate directorships and some individual Stark residents had more than 1300 directorships. This is, of course, not the fault of all the people of Sark; there was clearly a demand for this arrangement, which wasn't at the time necessarily illegal in Sark itself.

Many have relegated the Sark Lark as a faint memory that no longer exists. The so-called "sham director" industry died in 1999 due in part to political pressure on the practice that resulted in subsequent law changes in Guernsey and Jersey. Also, contributing to the supposed downfall of the industry was a court case brought by the UK Department of Trade and Industry that disqualified a Sark nominee director named Philip Crowshaw who was in the *Guinness Book of World Records* for having over 3000 directorships consisting of UK, Irish, and Isle of Man directorships (Lashmar and Burrell, 1998).

Recent reports, however, have suggested that the Sark Lark still exists, but that it just relocated to other exotic locales such as Cyprus, Dubai, the British Virgin Islands, Vanuatu, Mauritius, or Nevis (Frayman, 2012). Indeed, these reports show that many of the individuals serving as nominee directors were in fact the same former Stark residents who had simply moved and keep in touch on Facebook (Ball, 2012).

Now with all this background out of the way, it may already be apparent to you the similarities between the Sark Lark and the offshore hedge fund industry. This book isn't meant to be a lesson in the intricacies of offshore tax codes or to opine on the legality of such practices. Rather, it is meant to provoke discussion on the issue as it relates to governance of hedge funds. For the purposes of our discussion one of the key lessons that we can take from the Sark Lark fiasco is as it relates to the notion of hedge fund director capacity.

While in our case Sark's nominee directors were utilized for the somewhat broad category of corporate directorships, there are definite analogies that can be made to the hedge fund industry. So, for example, is there much of a difference between a Sark nominee director serving on over 1000 corporate boards and a hedge fund director serving on over 100 boards?

As recently as 2009, an investigation by the *Financial Times* outlined that (Jones, 2011):

- A 2006 document from an international bank revealed that one Cayman individual held more than 560 board positions.
- Analysis of US regulatory filings (Form D) showed another person with over 250 directorships.

Earlier in this book we discussed notions of director capacity and some of the more recent contentious debates in this area. With recent regulatory changes and proposals of public directorship databases in locations such as the Cayman Islands, this issue will likely continue to be hotly debated. When thinking about this issue going forward, it may be useful for investors to consider that this debate is nothing new. As we demonstrated with the Sark Lark example, albeit outside the hedge fund industry, questions of director capacity have long been debated. With this perspective, the question could rightly be asked: why do investors still tolerate high-capacity directors?

Although it seems the wind is shifting toward reducing the number of directorships, in general investors should be conscious of the real-world challenges they will often be faced with. Namely outside of extreme situations of hundreds of directorships, the key question will be how many is too many. For example, does it make a difference if a director serves on 25 or 30 boards? Where is the cutoff? The Cayman Islands Monetary Authority Survey results referenced in Chapter 4 provide some perspective on opinions in this area. Recently proposed laws have sought to place more scrutiny on directors who sit on numerous boards; however, these are simply guidelines. The point here is that when seeking to evaluate these grayer areas, investors should take care to fully vet not only the actual number of directorships but also the duties involved, the directors' support staff, and the way in which they work with the hedge funds under review. If not, then as the Sark situation outlines, there is often more going on behind the story than simply considering capacity figures on face value.

REFERENCES

AIMA, 2014. Japanese Investors Planning to Maintain Hedge Fund Allocations—AIMA Japan and Eurekahedge Survey, June 25.

Ax, J., 2014. Exclusive: accountant's plea signals more possible scrutiny of Madoff son. *Reuters*, July 8.

Ball, J., 2012. Sham directors: the woman running 1,200 companies from a Caribbean rock. *The Guardian*, November 25.

Binham, C., 2014. Weavering Capital founder pleads not guilty to 16 charges. *Financial Times*, February 6.

Bowers, S., 2012. Weavering Capital founder charged with fraud. *The Guardian*, December 14.

Brown, J., 2014. A 'poisonous' paradise: MPs warn of tensions on isle of Sark. The Independent, January 15.

Croft, J., 2013. Madoff's UK operation was 'warehouse' for 'stolen money'. *Financial Times*, June 13.

Donaldson, W.H., 2003. Testimony Concerning Investor Protection Implications of Hedge Funds, Before the Senate Committee on Banking, Housing and Urban Affairs, April 10, 2003. Retrieved from: http://www.sec.gov/news/testimony/041003tswhd.htm.

Fletcher, L., 2011. Hedge fund CEO "manipulated" returns from 2003. *Reuters*, October 28.

Frayman, H., 2012. The 'Sark Lark' Britons scattered around the world. *The Guardian*, November 25.

Gordon, N., 2013. Misfeasance claims against directors of companies in liquidation. *Lexology*, December 16.

Gorman, R., 2014. Bernie Madoff revealed to have a heart attack in prison and is now suffering from stage 4 cancer. *Daily Mail*, January 2014.

Hodo, C., Layne, N., 2012. Analysis: the AIK scandal and Japan's pension time bomb. *Reuters*, March 19.

Horie, S., 2012. AIJ Scandal: Superficial and Deeper Issues Facing Japanese Pension Funds, vol. 139. Nomura Research Institute, Ltd., Tokyo, Japan.

Inagaki, K., Fukase, A., Dvorak, P., 2012. Japanese Madoff flagged. *The Wall Street Journal*, February 25.

Jones, S., 2011. Fund investors urge transparency. *Financial Times*, November 20.

Kishan, S., 2014. Woodbine capital hedge fund said to return client money. *Bloomberg*, May 27.

Lashmar, P., Burrell, I., 1998. Doors open to reveal secret world of Britain's offshore tax havens. *The Independent*, November 20.

Lattman, P., 2013. Case against Madoff Sons is dismissed in London. *DealB%k*, October 18.

Martin, D., 2006. Corporate governance: practical guidance on accountability requirements. *Thorogood Reports*, September.

Osaki, S., 2012. The AIJ Scandal and Regulation of Investment Managers, vol. 136. Nomura Research Institute, Ltd., Tokyo, Japan.

Osaki, T., 2013. AIJ Asakawa gets 15 years for huge pension fund fraud. *The Japan Times*, December 18.

Partington, R., 2013. Austrian banker testifies in U.K. Madoff trial. *The Wall Street Journal*, July 10.

Piggott, C., 1999. Stamping out the Sark Lark. *The Independent*, June 27.

Ridley, T., 2011. Sticking it to the family, Swedish style. *Cayman Financial Review*, July 17.

Sarna, J., 2010. History of Greed: Financial Fraud From Tulip Mania to Bernie Madoff. Wiley, Hoboken, NJ.

Scott, M., 2012. British authorities reopen criminal inquiry on Weavering Capital. *DealB%k*, July 9.

Sterngold, J., 2014. Madoff bankruptcy trustee files amended suit against sons. *The Wall Street Journal*, July 15.

Stevenson, A., 2014. Tech-focused hedge fund to return $2 billion to investors. *DealB%k*, April 8.

Tabuchi, H., 2012. Money fund in Japan told to halt operations. *The New York Times*, February 24.

The Asahi Shimbun, 2012. AIJ moved huge sums to Cayman Islands, Hong Kong. *The Asahi Shimbun*, February 25.

Tobin, L., 2010. Bernard Madoff's creditors sue London bosses for fraud. *London Evening Standard*, December 8.

Walton, J., Jackson, A., 2014. Madoff case: no precedent to excuse directors. *Hedge Funds Review*, May 8.

Wilkes, T., 2012. Hedge fund boss found guilty in $600 million fraud. *Reuters*, May 30.

Yamazaki, T., 2012. AIJ's Asakawa says he falsified fund performance reports. *Bloomberg*, March 27.

Yamazaki, T., Ito, K., 2012. AIJ told investors fund returned 241% since 2002 start on Nikkei options. *Bloomberg*, February 27.

Zoromé, A., 1987. Concept of offshore financial centers: in search of an operational definition. IMF Working Paper Series, International Monetary Fund.

Chapter 9

Analyzing Governance in Fund Valuations

Chapter Outline Head

INTRODUCTION TO ANALYZING GOVERNANCE IN FUND VALUATIONS

In this chapter we will focus on the relationship between governance and hedge fund valuations. To be clear by the term valuation we are not addressing valuing the hedge fund management company itself, for example, a merger or seeding arrangement. Thinking this would be understandable based on recent trends, including consolidation among hedge funds and fund of hedge funds, but it will not be our focus. Instead our discussion of valuation here will focus on governance issues surrounding valuing a hedge fund's holdings. Specifically by using the term valuation governance we are referring to the transparency, control, and oversight framework in place for hedge fund valuations.

To be clear the purpose of this chapter will be not to provide a manual by which hedge funds should value their securities. Similarly, we will not review all of the specific details regarding the way that investors can evaluate if a hedge fund is correctly determining, for example, the value of its position in Twitter stock. These topics are covered in more detail in other books (Scharfman, 2008). What we will introduce are the concepts relating to the governance process in place to provide oversight and control of fund valuations. Throughout this discussion we will also provide an overview of certain questions investors may want to consider asking hedge funds and their service providers, including directors, regarding their oversight of the valuation process. Additionally, to provide some historical perspective on this issue we will also highlight several hedge fund valuation situations that have had related governance issues.

WHAT DOES VALUATION HAVE TO DO WITH GOVERNANCE?

To take a step back for a moment you may be asking yourself, what the topic of valuation has to do with governance? If you are reading this book in order, you'll likely know that governance is more than just a policy document or the roles of the board of directors, but a broad multidisciplinary subject that is interconnected to both investment and operational factors throughout a hedge fund. Throughout this book, we have introduced the governance implications of a number of related topics ranging from information technology and conflict management to fund expense analysis and hedge fund service provider protocols. The area of valuation is not different. As we outlined above, there are certain basic operational policies and procedures that a hedge fund and their service providers such as fund administrators may implement with regards to valuation. Both the design of these initial processes and their implementation and ongoing supervision have a direct correlation with the governance framework in place. Without proper governance oversight the best valuation program in the world may fail.

HEDGE FUND VALUATION GOVERNANCE CONSIDERATIONS

Before we can analyze the concept of governance in hedge fund valuations, it makes sense to take a step back to cover some basic ground with regards to how hedge fund valuations work. We will do this by providing an overview of common considerations in analyzing internal hedge fund governance valuation mechanisms as well as the role of service providers in this regard.

For those familiar with more of the investment side of hedge fund investing, you might already be vaguely familiar with the concepts we will cover here, but may not be familiar with the mechanics of how the valuation processes work in practice. Similarly, there may be those who are relatively new to the hedge fund industry reading this book, and for those readers this introduction will be critical context. Finally, those who work in hedge fund operations or operational due diligence or who are very familiar with hedge fund valuations can skip this information, but of course a refresher never hurts and can help better frame our discussion of governance going forward.

Now with all this background out of the way let's dive into the subject of hedge fund valuation. Before talking about how a hedge fund values its position, we should talk about what it is valuing. The universe of what a hedge fund typically invests in is generally a function of what their strategy is. For example, for a long/short equity hedge fund it would likely be considered odd by root investors of that fund if it was holding illiquid positions.

Does Security Liquidity Represent Lower Governance Valuation Risk?

Broadly speaking hedge fund security types can be categorized into two primary baskets: liquid and illiquid. Simply put how liquid a security is refers to how easily the security can be bought or sold in the market. Securities with lots of liquidity (i.e., relatively easy to transact due to the large number of buyers and sellers) are thought of as hanging so-called deep markets. Large cap equities such as Google stock could be thought of as liquid stock with deep markets.

The opposite of liquid securities are simply enough called illiquid securities. As compared with liquid securities, illiquid securities have a much smaller number of buyers and sellers, and therefore are often more difficult to transact. Rather than deep markets that exist for liquid securities, illiquid securities have what are known as thinly traded markets. As an aside, to clarify we are referring to liquidity here as a function of a security's ability to be transacted in the market. This is a common and certainly valid way to consider a security's liquidity. From a valuation perspective, however, as opposed to a purely trading perspective, the market for a security also influences its value.

To clarify these points a bit consider a common hedge fund's valuation approach known as mark-to-market. As it sounds, this refers to the value of a security being determined based on some interpretation of market value. We can put aside for a moment what this "interpretation" might be (i.e., bid, ask, etc.), or who does the interpreting (i.e., administrator, hedge fund itself, third-party valuation consultant, auditor, directors, etc.), but for right now assume that the valuation comes from the market somehow. This market valuation is directly affected by a security's liquidity.

Historically, investors place a premium on liquidity. That is to say under theories such as the time value of money, liquidity has value. This is a particularly true example for hedge funds that trade frequently, such as a hedge fund trust, because theoretically there is less risk of having to wait a long time to sell, as well as less risk of finding a large number of offers (i.e., bids for prices). Others may put less of a premium on liquidity. In regards to the way in which these securities are valued, which we will address in more detail below, hedge funds themselves are traditionally more heavily involved and have more discretion in determining the value of illiquid securities as compared with liquid securities. Regulators have increasingly scrutinized the ways hedge funds implement this discretion with regards to illiquids in light of allegations of certain unscrupulous managers inflating values (Maxey, 2014).

At this point it is worth posing the question of whether you think there are any governance benefits for a fund that trades in more liquid securities as opposed to more illiquid securities. It could be argued that since prices are more readily available for liquid securities, there would be an increased likelihood of readily available comparisons, and this could facilitate easier oversight of a hedge fund's valuation mechanisms. That makes sense, doesn't it?

On the other hand, why should what a hedge fund trades matters? After all, the argument could be made that if a fund maintains detailed valuation procedures, with clearly specified parameters and appropriate governance oversight, then why should a fund be penalized for trading in illiquids? Particularly if that is consistent with its strategy? As you can imagine there are not necessarily clear-cut rules to follow here. In different situations each side of the argument may hold merit. The point here is that there is no automatic governance valuation formula that can be applied based on the fund's underlying liquidity to determine if good governance is in place. Instead, regardless of the fund's holdings investors must take measures to evaluate the specific valuation oversight and control procedures in each circumstance.

Do More Valuation Parties Represent Better Governance?

As noted above, certain securities may be easily priced by hedge funds from third-party pricing feeds. Others securities do not have liquid markets and are typically priced via broker quotes. While other securities may have very thin markets, and while certain broker quotes may be available, they are priced by the hedge fund manager. With all of this in mind, it is important to clarify the different parties besides the hedge fund managers that may be involved in providing valuation inputs or oversight. These can include the fund administrator, auditors, brokers (as noted above), and third-party valuation agents. We will address the roles of these groups in more detail, but the following question should be asked from a governance perspective: if more parties are involved, does it necessarily promote better governance?

As we have outlined above, as is the case in other areas of valuation, it is ultimately dependent on the facts and circumstances of the role of each service provider. That is to say the mere fact that a hedge fund utilizes a third-party valuation consultant should not necessarily give investors an automatic sense of comfort that appropriate valuation and governance oversight controls are in place. Although it is unheard of today for a fund not to have a third-party auditor, the same can be said with regards to brand name auditors versus less known auditors.

Furthermore, as we outlined earlier in this book the so-called *good person* problem may create a false sense of comfort with brand name service providers due to historical house view biases toward certain firms. This groupthink mentality should be avoided, particularly in the area of service provider fund valuation oversight. This is not to imply that big auditors don't do great work. After all, the question could be posed: if they were doing a bad job, then why would they have so many clients? On the other hand, just because a hedge fund works with a brand name auditor doesn't mean investors shouldn't kick the tires with regards to what these auditors are actually doing. As the Lipper example that we will discuss later in this chapter will illustrate, in some cases there may be disputes as to whether a brand name auditor was actually doing their job. The same can of course also be said of brand name administrators. For more perspective on this, you are invited to revisit the Citco and Lancer example in Chapter 4.

The bottom line is this: the more groups a hedge fund works with to conduct and provide valuation oversight, the better. Investors, however, should not automatically equate more third-party service providers with better valuation governance. It simply means there are more moving parts to evaluate when assessing valuation governance.

Does Documentation Lead to Better Governance?

As investors have increasingly focused on operational issues at hedge funds, hedge funds have responded in part by developing more internal documentation. Several years ago if you asked a hedge fund for a copy of their valuation policy, it was not uncommon to receive a reply that effectively told you something to the effect of "holdings are valued in accordance with the funds offering memorandum. This is subject to oversight by our administrator and auditors." Wow, that's super informative, isn't it? Not really. Well, maybe if you turned to the offering memorandum, it would give you better insight into not only how a fund valued their holdings but also the oversight in place. Sure that must be it! Ok, let's review a sample of the type of language you would encounter in turning to the valuation section of a fund's offering memorandum:

> *(i) In determining the value on a given date of marketable securities for which market quotations are readily available and which are available for immediate sale:*

> *(A) securities traded in non-U.S. markets shall normally be valued on the basis of the last reported closing price in its principal market, provided that if the Investment Manager in good faith determines that the last reported closing price does not reflect the fair value of any such security or if no sale occurs, such security shall be valued at the arithmetic average of the last reported "bid" and "ask" prices.*

(B) securities that are listed on a national securities exchange or quoted on NAS-DAQ shall be valued at the last sale price on the primary exchange on which such securities are traded or quoted on NASDAQ, provided that, if the Investment Manager in good faith determines that such price does not reflect the fair value of any such security, or if no sale occurs, such security shall be valued at the arithmetic average of the last "bid" and last "ask" prices;

(C) over-the-counter securities not quoted on NASDAQ shall be valued at the arithmetic average of the last reported "bid" and "ask" prices supplied by recognized quotation services or by broker dealers; and

(ii) The value of a security, the resale of which is restricted or limited, shall be appropriately discounted from market value as determined in good faith by the Investment Manager.

(iii) The amount of unrealized gain or loss on any open futures contract shall be recorded by taking the difference between the contract price as of the trade date and the settlement price reported on the primary exchange on which such contract is traded.

(iv) All margins paid or deposited in respect of futures, forward contracts, and other derivative contracts shall be reflected as accounts receivable and margins consisting of assets other than cash shall be noted as held as margins.

(v) Holdings of shares of other investment funds, if any, shall generally be calculated at the net asset value as determined by those funds.

(vi) All assets valued or denominated in a foreign currency and all liabilities and obligations payable in a foreign currency shall be converted into U.S. dollars by applying the rate of exchange determined by or under the direction of the Investment Manager as existing on the relevant date.

Did that help or is this merely valuation doggerel? Well, it was more informative than the hedge fund's original trite response, but it's also so vague as to be effectively useless. For example, this doesn't address how values are reviewed. What if there is a discrepancy between the hedge fund and third-party pricing sources? Are there limits to how much discretion a fund is allowed to take when such differences arise? Who at the fund makes the final valuation decision? How are these discrepancies documented? The list of questions could go on and on.

Over time, and after ongoing investor requests for clarity in this area, more funds developed valuation policy documents. In general, the goal of such documents is to describe in more practical terms how valuation occurs. The problem is that some funds still don't understand what investors are looking for in this regard, and just effectively copy and paste the valuation language from the fund's prospectus into a new document with a heading such as "Valuation Policy." Some documents are more practical and do help, but often they help investors in understanding the overall valuation process, including governance oversight and controls, but they do not provide detailed answers to the types of questions we outlined above.

The question should be asked, however, as to whether or not a fund has such documented policies, and if it leads to better governance with regards to valuations. Your gut reaction may be that more documentation is better. In reviewing this assessment consider the fact that the production of any additional policies doesn't change the actual valuation policies at the funds, but rather just how the fund describes these policies to investors. So if the underlying valuation processes are identical in both circumstances, is the governance with regards to the valuation processes really any different with or without the documentation?

As you can imagine the answer is, of course, it depends on both the nature of the policies and their implementation and ongoing monitoring. If a fund simply produces a voluminous valuation policy, but the oversight and controls described are poor, then what good is additional documentation describing weak valuation control practices? On the other hand, a fund with limited documentation may have excellent valuation policies, but they are just not good at communicating it to investors. The real test from a governance perspective is how well the hedge fund and its service providers implement and monitor valuations. In this instance more documentation may be representative of more well-thought-out valuation controls, but as we have outlined above this is not necessarily the case. Only by conducting detailed due diligence and collecting information on valuation oversight and controls can investors make an assessment about the quality valuation practices. It could even be argued that funds that produce investors with detailed summaries of valuation practices run the risk of lulling investors into a false sense of security with regards to valuation practices. A detailed valuation policy document from a hedge fund is a good start, but it should not be the end of an investor's review of valuation governance.

The same of course could be said for other service providers. Just because an administrator provides an investor with a detailed valuation policy or easy-to-understand description of how valuations are reviewed doesn't mean that they are actually implementing those policies with regularity. It further does not necessarily answer the questions regarding what happens when conflicts arise as well as which groups maintain discretion in certain areas. This is where due diligence comes in to fill the gap and addresses such questions. As an aside this is why increasing operational due diligence is referred to as gap-filler due diligence because it seeks to fill governance gaps such as this.

Valuation Governance by Committee?

In Chapter 5 we discussed the concept of internal hedge fund committees as governance mechanisms. An increasingly common committee at hedge funds over the last few years has been Valuation Committees. The presence of Valuation Committees is considered to have a signaling effect that there is another body in charge of overseeing valuations. As we have asked with other governance mechanisms, the question can also be raised whether such committees equate with better valuation governance.

To answer this question let us provide some background on these committees. For starters, Valuation Committees are not just for hedge funds that trade in illiquids. Even funds that trade primarily in liquid securities can maintain such committees. The work of these committees may be more straightforward, but still having the committee in place may provide additional oversight in this regard.

This brings us to our next point about Valuation Committees. They are not all created equally. One of the ways that they vary is in terms of what they actually do. Some committees provide frequent oversight over fund valuations. They may have reports prepared for them by the administrator and internal personnel that facilitate analysis of valuations. Some of the key questions these committees may consider include:

- Have there been any material deviations in valuations proposed internally by the fund and third-party sources?
- Have there been any material disagreements with the fund's administrators regarding values?
- With regards to any discrepancies why does the fund feel it is correct, and therefore the other third-party prices are not correct, with regards to these valuations?

In evaluating these types of issues, in addition to the above-referenced administrator and internal reports, Valuation Committees may have different reporting requirements. So, for example, some hedge fund Valuation Committees may require an analyst to produce a valuation memorandum only when there is a material event or change in valuation. Other Valuation Committees may require not only an analyst to update valuation memorandum for a particular position when there is a change in valuation but also that these memos be produced with regular frequency to justify current valuations.

Another consideration is how often these committees meet. Some may meet as needed, and others with a predetermined frequency such as monthly or quarterly. Additionally, there are no universal rules as to who sits on these committees or what their decision mechanisms may be. In some cases, representatives of different departments such as compliance and operations may be included on such committees, and in other cases they may not be.

In general, Valuation Committees are thought to be a signal representative of better fund governance, but this assumption should not be made by investors automatically. As we have outlined above, there are no cookie cutter rules with regards to the effectiveness, oversight, or control of these committees. Instead, investors should take care to evaluate the work of such committees to determine if they are meaningful toward promoting beneficial valuation governance.

Valuation Inquisition—Does Valuation Testing Imply Better Governance?

Another common issue that arises with regards to hedge fund valuation governance relates to valuation testing. Interestingly, it is not often the above-referenced Valuation Committee that conducts such testing, but rather other departments such as compliance or operations. The Valuations Committee, if there is one, typically reviews the results of any such testing.

It is generally thought that hedge funds that implement detailed valuation testing protocols have better governance oversight in this area. The key question is whether or not such controls are implemented effectively.

Hedge funds may conduct valuation testing in a number of ways. One common method is to back test valuations. In much the same way that an administrator would collect third-party valuation feeds to check a hedge fund's marks, this testing can be performed by an employee of the fund, such as a compliance individual. The way such a process would work would be for a compliance professional to start by reviewing the documentation surrounding the fund's adherence to its own internal valuation process. For example, if the firm's valuation policies outline that a fund is supposed to obtain three broker quotes for certain types of positions, the compliance professional would attempt to determine if appropriate documentation existed to support that three broker quotes were obtained. The next stage in testing would be for the compliance professional to reach out to brokers independently and attempt to confirm the reasonableness of prices. We will discuss some of the issues that may arise with regards to broker pricing confirmations in our example of the work of the auditor in the Lipper case below.

The testing method we have described above is simply an example. There is a wide variety of methods with regards to the scope, breadth, and frequency of testing. Some hedge funds may pursue rigorous internal testing protocols while others may not. Furthermore, some funds may enhance the effectiveness of testing by leveraging off information technology to facilitate testing while others are more manual in their approach.

If testing is appropriately implemented, it can lead to better governance, but as with all the other issues we have outlined above it cannot be said that the mere fact that a testing program is in place should imply that best practice governance in valuations is present. Once again, it is up to investors to dig into the specifics of how governance is approached with regards to valuations before making a specific determination about the practices in place at each hedge fund.

SERVICE PROVIDER VALUATION GOVERNANCE CONSIDERATIONS

Service providers can also play a critical role in implementing transparency, oversight, and controls with regards to fund valuations. To address some of the key valuation governance considerations of hedge fund service providers we will highlight several examples of ways that governance valuation questions may arise in a service provider context.

Fund Administrator Valuation Governance Considerations

In our discussion above, and throughout this text, we have discussed the role played by fund service providers in implementing and overseeing various governance-related controls throughout a hedge fund. In regards to valuation oversight, third-party administrators can prove to be a key resource for providing valuation transparency, controls, and oversight. While the goal of this text is not to explain the nuts and bolts of hedge fund administration, here we will focus on the governance implications of select administrator valuation procedures to highlight common governance questions that may arise. Similar to our other discussions of hedge fund internal governance mechanisms and even service provider governance, this discussion will not be comprehensive to all the governance issues that can be considered when reviewing the administrator's role in overseeing valuations. Rather the goal here is to introduce examples of the types of issues that investors should consider when evaluating the overall quality of hedge fund valuations, and the role played by the administrator in implementing and overseeing valuation policies.

Governance Implication of Administrator Valuation, Validation, and Verification?

If surveyed, most investors would likely agree that one of the core roles of a fund administrator is to independently value a fund's holdings. While this is perhaps oversimplifying the role of administrators a bit, the term "independently" after all is subject to interpretation, putting aside the conflicts of interests inherent in such administration relationships that may raise concerns related to the true independence of this oversight. At the end of the day this is one of the key reasons why investors insist on third-party administration for independence valuation oversight.

For liquid holdings this is a fairly straightforward and repeatable process. For example, a hedge fund purchases stock in a publicly traded liquid company, and prices it from a common third-party pricing vendor such as Reuters. The administrator would then price the security, commonly from a different source, such as Bloomberg.

As we have suggested earlier in this book the more interesting valuation questions and problems tend to arise around broker-quoted, thinly traded, and illiquid positions. So, for example, let's say a hedge fund invested in something for which there is not readily a market. There is really no limit to what these types of positions can be, and hedge funds invest in all kinds of interesting things. Perhaps a bankruptcy position or the right to acquire a drilling license. How is the administrator supposed to independently price this? Well, the answer

most times is they don't, and this has implications for the level of import investors should provide to administrators in evaluating the actual governance oversight capabilities of administrators.

Hedge Fund Validation Approaches

The majority of fund administrators don't maintain internal pricing divisions
that independently perform investment banking–style valuation of positions. As
hedge funds invest in so many unique things, many of which require specialized
industry expertise to value, it is not really economically efficient for administrators to staff up in this regard. Furthermore, hedge fund managers typically take
the position that they are the experts with regards to these types of positions,
and administrators couldn't add much to the valuation conversations. Rather,
in these cases, administrators are really just validating that the manager had
put together the appropriate paperwork to document their positions. This could
include the hedge fund manager sending the administrator internal pricing committee meeting minutes and valuation memos.

Additionally, administrators may receive copies of any third-party valuation
work, addressed in more detail below, that the hedge fund may have had performed by yet a different third-party valuation consultant. The administrators
are not really doing much with this information and they are certainly not challenging hedge fund managers in this regard. After all, remember, they are not
the experts. Instead they are simply collecting paperwork. This arrangement is
nothing new to the hedge fund industry; however, investors should be conscious
not to accept on face value a fund manager's statements that they are third-party
administered when in effect, for example, they may be only 95% administrator
valued and 5% administrator verified.

From a governance perspective, the question could be asked whether it matters if a hedge fund's holdings are 100% administrator valued as compared with
50% valued. As we have outlined above in our discussion of liquidity premiums,
the answer is that it doesn't necessarily matter. If a hedge fund's administrator
can value only 50% of the hedge fund's book, and the remaining 50% is valued
via a combination of internal oversight and third-party consultants, then this
doesn't necessarily imply poor governance in this area. If the hedge fund has a
buttoned-up valuation process that is an effective mix of internal oversight and
third-party interaction including the work of administrator's third-party valuation consultants, then this could be just as effective as a scenario with a hedge
fund that is completely third-party administered. Ultimately, as we have outlined above it depends on the initial implementation and ongoing oversight in
this area.

Considering Administrator Discretion in Valuations

Similar to other service providers involved in the fund valuation process, the
role that fund administrators play is often a conflicted one. On the one hand, an

administrator wants to convey to investors their independence in the valuation and fund NAV calculation process. On the other hand, administrators are typically hired by the fund management companies themselves, the same entities and individuals they are supposed to act independent of.

As such, when analyzing the role played by fund administrators in the valuation process, investors may find it beneficial to not only review the actual operational processes and procedures in place for typical administration services such as fund accounting and shareholder services, which would typically be conducted during the operational due diligence process, but also gauge the level of involvement and control that a fund manager exercises in this relationship.

Consider, for example, the valuation work performed by administrators. As we noted above, from a pure governance valuation analysis perspective it may not matter whether a fund is completely third-party valued by the administrator or 50% valued by the administrator. Within the percentage evaluated by the administrator, however, is the administrator merely taking values from third-party feeds and cross-referencing them with the manager? What if a discrepancy arises? Does the administrator have to select the third-party value over the fund managers or vice versa? Maybe it would be best if the administrator split the difference between the two values. Are there any rules in place that guide this process?

As you can tell by the barrage of questions, from a governance perspective this is a sometimes contentious issue that may arise. To address some of these issues, what certain investors may be unaware of is the fact that in determining the valuations of particular positions most administrators typically have a small degree of discretion. This discretion typically comes into play when an administrator attempts to price a fund's positions independently of the fund.

For example, let's say a fund manager's records indicate that a certain security, which is typically priced via broker quotes, was purchased and was worth $60.23 a share. Let's say that the administrator reaches out to other brokers independent of the fund manager and determines the price is $0.01 less than the fund manager's price, or $60.22. The administrator may have the discretion to override the fund manager's price and utilize their own price (i.e., the one they, not the manager, sourced from the brokers). Do you think such discretion is a good thing for fund governance? Perhaps it could be argued that the administrator is incentivized to keep the fund manager happy and err on the side of higher valuations? Instead, if an administrator was overly conservative and constantly chose the lower values, would this necessarily be better from a governance perspective?

Most administrators typically operate within acceptable valuation difference bands. That is a certain amount of discrepancy between the price determined by the administrator and that by the fund manager is acceptable as long as it is within predefined ranges. In many cases administrators may tell investors that they are uncomfortable disclosing the specifics of what these valuation bands may be. Do you feel such limited transparency represents a governance concern? Perhaps administrators are concerned investors may raise issues over acceptable bands that are too wide? Or instead, administrators may have liability concerns. Regardless of the reasons involved, do you think it is reasonable to expect investors to blindly trust administrators in this regard?

In most cases, the administrator's price, which is typically more conservative, is the one that is utilized. Indeed, fund administration agreements and offering memoranda may dictate as such. However, as there is discretion in the process, in practice a negotiation often occurs between the administrator and the fund manager with regards to what the final price should be. In certain cases, depending on the nature of the security, and the specifics of the administration arrangement, the fund manager may have final say over the administrator.

Understanding the way such conflicts may be resolved is critical to assessing the effectiveness of valuation governance in place. Even once the rules of engagement, so to speak, for conflict are understood, what about the ongoing monitoring that conflicts are resolved in a consistent manner? If a hedge fund or an administrator will not share the details of historical conflict resolutions between itself and administrators, do you think that this represents best practice governance transparency with regards to valuations? Do you think a hedge fund would be justified in keeping the specifics of such conflicts confidential?

Some fund managers are actively engaged with their administrators and speak to them several times a week. Others may talk to their fund administrators only at month-end when fund NAVs are being calculated. In seeking to evaluate the quality of governance management understanding not only the operational practices in place but also their ongoing implementation can add real value to the overall assessment of governance effectiveness as it relates to a hedge fund's overall valuation framework. An investor who takes the time to evaluate not only the nuts and bolts of fund administration procedures but also the degree of interaction and control exerted by a fund manager in practice may gain useful insights that other investors may not uncover during the operational due diligence process.

Has Your Hedge Fund Been Verified?

Seeking to capitalize on their existing relationships with hedge fund managers, and recognizing the desire for increased oversight by third parties, administrators have offered funds a plethora of additional services. One such service is administrator verification. This is different than both valuation and validation. Under validation administrators effectively contact the fund's custodians and prime brokers to verify that the holdings actually exist. Conceptually, this is not a very difficult service they offer. Really it's just a few extra steps for administrators since they are already interacting with the fund's prime brokers.

The thinking among hedge funds and administrators is that since investors have bought into the concept of independent administrator oversight of valuation, then wouldn't it be better to verify asset holdings as well? On the one hand, such oversight by a party other than the fund manager can't do much harm. On the other hand, such verifications result in extra fund expenses. Furthermore, investors should not take such verifications as an excuse not to conduct their own asset holding verifications.

Do you think that such a verification process does much to support the overall governance process? It could be argued that the administrator is simply moving paper around since any sort of administrator verification in this area doesn't change the facts as to whether or not a hedge fund's holdings are actually with the third parties. To take the other side of the argument, such verification services may provide an additional level of investor comfort in this area. Furthermore, the administrator may have more frequent access and transparency to custodians and prime brokers to verify holdings as compared with investors. If these verifications are properly implemented and performed, then this type of ongoing verification can provide another level of oversight with regards to asset levels, which may promote enhanced governance in this area at the hedge fund level.

Additional Comments on Administrator Valuation Governance

Administrators offer hedge funds a wide variety of services. With the effective requirement by investors of third-party administration investors may want to consider the true nature of administrator valuation versus validation efforts. During the due diligence and governance assessment processes, investors may want to focus on the internal process where a fund manager marks illiquid positions, and the subsequent oversight by the administrator to determine how truly independent the oversight actually is.

Third-Party Valuation Consultants

In certain cases a hedge fund may opt to engage a third-party valuation consultant to provide independent valuations for certain holdings. To be clear the work of these third-party valuation consultants is separate from that of the administrator. The holdings that are typically valued by third-party valuation consultants are traditionally very illiquid, and the type for which there are no broker quotes readily available. Third-party valuation consultants may interact with fund administrators, and indeed the values they produce may be utilized directly by fund administrators in calculating a fund's net asset value.

The use of such third-party valuation consultants may be representative of enhanced valuation governance oversight. As is the case with the other valuation governance mechanisms we have discussed there is a wide variety in the ways that third-party valuation is performed. In evaluating the governance oversight of such valuation consultants some key questions investors may ask could include:

- Does the hedge fund have clear rules with regards to what types of positions are valued by third-party valuation consultants? If so, what are these rules? For example, are positions of a certain size required to be valued by third parties?
- For positions that are reviewed by third-party valuation consultants, are there clear rules as to how frequently these valuations are performed? Who decided?

- What happens if the hedge fund disagrees with the work of a third-party valuation consultant? Who makes the final decision?
- If the hedge fund valuation is allowed to trump that of a third-party valuation consultant, what documentation, if any, is the hedge fund required to produce to justify its decision?
- Are third-party valuation consultants providing actual values, ranges of values, positive assurance of values, and negative assurance?

As we have outlined above, investors should understand that there are no automatic rules that imply that the use of a third-party valuation consultant implies more effective governance oversight. Before making such a determination it is up to investors to collect the facts regarding the way these consultants are utilized, and how their work figures into the overall hedge fund valuation process. Once this information has been obtained through the due diligence process, investors can then work toward making an assessment of whether such valuation consultants enhance the governance oversight and control in the valuation process.

Other Service Providers

In addition to the administrator and third-party valuation consultants other service providers can play important roles with regards to implementing effective governance in fund valuations. Among these service providers two of the more notable ones are the auditor and fund directors. We will address the role of the auditor in more detail below through the Lipper fund example. As we have outlined directors are also involved in providing valuation oversight.

Directors may be assigned a number of valuation responsibilities by a fund's offering memorandum; however, in practice much of the more practical day-to-day valuation oversight may be effectively delegated, as we have outlined earlier in this book, to other service providers and the investment manager. The following is an example of valuation language from a fund's prospectus that references the role of directors:

(i) the value of any cash on hand or on deposit, bills, demand notes, accounts receivable, prepaid expenses, cash dividends and interest declared or accrued and not yet received shall be deemed to be the full amount thereof unless the Directors shall have determined that any such deposit, bill, demand note or account receivable is not worth the full amount thereof in which event the value thereof shall be deemed to be such value as the Directors shall deem to be the reasonable value thereof;

(ii) except in the case of any interest in a unit trust, mutual fund corporation, open-ended investment company or other similar open-ended investment vehicle (a "managed fund") to which paragraph (iii) applies and subject as provided in paragraphs (iv), (v) and (vi) below, all calculations based on the value of investments quoted, listed, traded or dealt in on any stock exchange, commodities

exchange, futures exchange or over-the-counter market shall be made by reference to the last traded price (or, lacking any sales, at the mean between the last available bid and asked prices) on the principal stock exchange for such investments as at the close of business in such place on the day as of which such calculation is to be made; and where there is no stock exchange, commodities exchange, futures exchange or over-the-counter market all calculations based on the value of investments quoted by any person, firm or institution making a market in that investment (and if there shall be more than one such market maker then such particular market maker as the Directors may designate) shall be made by reference to the mean of the latest bid and asked price quoted thereon; provided always that if the Directors in their discretion consider that the prices ruling on a stock exchange other than the principal stock exchange provide in all the circumstances a fairer criterion of value in relation to any such investment, they may adopt such prices;

(iii) subject as provided in paragraphs (iv), (v) and (vi) below, the value of each interest in any managed fund which is valued as at the same day as the Company shall be the net asset value per unit, share or other interest in such managed fund calculated as at that day or, if the Directors so determine or if such managed fund is not valued as at the same day as the Company, the last published net asset value per unit, share or other interest in such managed fund (where available) or (if the same is not available) the last published redemption or bid price for such unit, share or other interest;

(iv) if no net asset value, last traded, asked, redemption, bid or offer prices or price quotations are available as provided in paragraphs (ii) or (iii) above, the value of the relevant asset shall be determined from time to time in such manner as the Directors shall determine;

(v) for the purpose of ascertaining quoted, listed, traded or market dealing prices, the Directors, the Administrator or their agents shall be entitled to use and rely upon mechanized and/or electronic systems of valuation dissemination with regard to valuation of investments of the Company and the prices provided by any such system shall be deemed to be the last traded prices for the purpose of paragraph (ii) above;

(vi) notwithstanding the foregoing, the Directors may, at their absolute discretion, permit some other method of valuation to be used if they consider that such valuation better reflects the fair value; and

(vii) any value (whether of a security or cash) otherwise than in US dollars shall be converted into US dollars at the rate (whether official or otherwise) which the Directors shall in their absolute discretion deem appropriate to the circumstances having regard, inter alia, to any premium or discount which they consider may be relevant and to costs of exchange. The term "last traded price" referred to in paragraph (ii) above, refers to the last traded price reported on the exchange for the day, commonly referred to in the market as the "settlement" or "exchange price",

and represents a price at which members of the exchange settle between them for
their outstanding positions. Where a security has not traded then the last traded
price will represent the "exchange close" price as calculated and published by
that exchange in accordance with its local rules and customs.

Similar to the sample valuation language we had outlined earlier this really
doesn't even tell us very much about the practical application of the role of
directors. As noted above, in practice the director's valuation oversight in many
cases can be similar to that of a fund's Valuation Committee in checking for reasonableness as well as any discrepancies that may arise. As we have highlighted
earlier in this book, during the 2008 financial crisis when valuations declined,
directors were placed in the position of sometimes disagreeing with managers
who were interested in maintaining precrisis valuation levels. It is in these types
of situations that directors are typically the most engaged in valuation oversight.

HISTORICAL PERSPECTIVES ON HEDGE FUND VALUATION GOVERNANCE—THE LIPPER EXAMPLE

Kenneth Lipper formerly ran a $4 billion hedge fund firm named Lipper &
Company, L.P. Mr. Lipper is an interesting man. His list of accomplishments
includes that he was a Harvard Law School graduate, he served as deputy mayor
during the Ed Koch administration in New York City, and he advised director
Oliver Stone on the film *Wall Street* and even won an Oscar himself for producing a film (Geiger, 2013). Investors in the Lipper funds reportedly included
celebrities such as Julia Roberts, Matt Lauer, and former Walt Disney CEO
Michael Eisner (Whitehouse, 2011).

In the early 2000s several of the Lipper funds began to realize significant losses. To give you a sense of the degree of the losses, it was reported that in a letter
to investors in 2002 Mr. Lipper stated that the US portfolio, Lipper Convertibles,
L.P., had declined 45% in 2001, and the internal fund had declined 10% (Colter, 2002). So what went wrong? As our discussion will outline below there are a
number of governance valuation lessons that can be learned from this situation.

Overly Concentrated Valuation Oversight

For starters it was reported that on January 14, 2002, the firm's convertible
portfolio manager Edward Strafaci, and its research director, both of whom
were involved in the security pricing process, abruptly resigned (Colter, 2002).
The timing of Mr. Strafaci's resignation was conveniently before the release of
the 2011 fund performance and valuation figures. To make a long story short in
2003 the SEC ended up charging Mr. Strafaci with manipulating the values of
four Lipper funds:

- Lipper Convertibles, L.P., f/k/a Lipco Partners, L.P.
- Lipper Convertibles Series II, L.P.

- Lipper Offshore Convertibles, L.P.
- Lipper Fixed Income Fund, L.P.

Specifically the SEC alleged that from at least 1998 to January 2002:

Strafaci did not value many of the Funds' convertible securities at or close to the prevailing market price for the security, as reflected in the current "bid" and "ask" prices for the security disseminated by major market makers or recent transactions in the security of substantial size. Nor did he price the securities at 'fair value,' setting forth the basis for that valuation in writing. Instead, he priced significant portions of the Funds' convertible securities at prices substantially higher than the prevailing market price, or the security's fair value. As a result, throughout the relevant period, the values of the Funds, and of partners' capital, were substantially overstated. *(Securities and Exchange Commission v. Edward J. Strafaci, 2003)*

In the press release related to the complaint, the SEC even put together a handy chart detailing the alleged overvaluation of funds. We have summarized this in Exhibit 9.1.

Ultimately Mr. Strafaci pled guilty for overstating the value of the funds and admitted that he had fraudulently overvalued securities in two Lipper Convertibles funds, resulting in causing losses for some investors who thought they were making money *(The New York Times, 2004)*. Mr. Strafaci was ultimately sentenced to six years in prison (Klopott and Braun, 2014). To be clear Mr. Lipper was not indicted and was never found to have participated in the scheme. Just the opposite in 2011 a New York judge cleared Lipper of any wrongdoing and approved a settlement that allowed him to recoup approximately $14 million in legal fees spent defending himself (Klopott and Braun, 2014).

Situations such as the Lipper case highlight the benefit of having multiple independent parties involved in providing oversight of valuations. As we have highlighted earlier in this chapter this could include not only multiple individuals representative of different groups within the hedge fund itself but also the

EXHIBIT 9.1 SEC Allegations of Overstatement of Value of Lipper Convertibles Funds

	Overstatement of value of Lipper Convertibles fund's convertible securities (%)	Overstatement of value of partners' capital (%)
December 31, 2000	12–14	49
June 30, 2001	13–15	44
September 30, 2001	16–19	46

Source: US SEC press release dated October 29, 2003, entitled *SEC Announced Fraud Charges Against Former Porto*.

use of third parties including administrators. It should also be noted that Lipper funds did not utilize a third-party administrator (Bloomberg, 2002). Although today such self-administration relationships virtually do not exist, lessons can still be learned from cases such as this regarding the oversight and segregation of duties with regards to fund valuations.

Allegations of Audit Oversight and Control Issue Problems

In addition to fund administrators, another service provider that can play a key role in the oversight of valuations is a fund's auditor. In the Lipper case, as can be expected, the fund's auditor PricewaterhouseCoopers ("PwC") came under scrutiny. Of note the US SEC charged Larry Stoler, a CPA and former partner at PwC, of engaging in improper professional conduct while conducting the audit of Lipper Convertibles, L.P., Lipper Convertibles Series II, L.P., and Lipper Fixed Income Fund, L.P. (Urda, 2006). To provide some perspective on the discrepancies between the PwC audits and the actual value of holdings once revalued the US SEC put together a summary of examples as summarized in Exhibit 9.2. Other allegations by the US SEC that were raised against Mr. Stoler referenced allegations of several deficiencies in the audit process including those that we will address below.

Allegations of Knowledge of Internal Control Weaknesses

One of the US SEC's allegations related to the questions of whether or not there was evidence to support the belief that Mr. Stoler suspected that the fund had poor internal controls. The US SEC allegations outlined that at the time of the

EXHIBIT 9.2 SEC Comparison of Lipper Convertibles Fund Audit Valuations and Revaluations

	Per audited financials ($)	As revalued ($)	Difference ($)
Values for Convertibles as of December 31, 2000 (in millions)			
Long positions	2297.8	2,017	280.8 (12.2%)
Partners' capital	568.7	287.9	280.8 (12.2%)
Values for Series II as of as of December 31, 2000 (in millions)			
Long positions	186.9	175.3	11.6 (6.2%)
Partners' capital	82.9	71.3	11.6 (14%)

Source: United States of America Before the Securities and Exchange Commission, February 9, 2006, Administrative Proceeding File No. 3-12179 in the Matter of Lawrence A. Stoler, CPA Respondent. Order instituting administrative cease-and-desist proceedings pursuant to Rule 102(e) of the Commission's Rules of Practice, Section 8A of the Securities Act of 1933, Section 21C of the Securities Exchange Act of 1934, and Section 203(k) of the Investment Advisers Act of 1940.

2000 audits, "Stoler knew that the Funds' internal control weaknesses called for heightened scrutiny of the valuation of their investments. The audit team had observed in prior audits that the internal controls in place with respect to valuation were inadequate and that the Funds' investments were valued by Strafaci without oversight."

The SEC also pointed out that the PwC audit work papers acknowledged this weakness by stating:

> [d]ue to the complexity of the process all pricing work is performed by the front office (Ed Strafaci with assistance from [a Fund trader].) There is no formal review of the marks external of the front office, because of a lack of technical knowledge (convertible arbitrage securities). In order to have proper segregation of duties, the pricing function should be monitored in a Middle/Back Office capacity by a part outside the front office (Product Control, Accounting). Point to be considered for including in letter to management.

Further highlighting the US SEC allegations of concerns of internal valuation weakness that may have been raised, the US SEC alleged that in the planning of the 2000 audits, Mr. Stoler approved a so-called FRISK analysis for the funds. In the proceeding against Mr. Stoler the SEC stated that, "That analysis identified the Funds' '*management governance and oversight of management*,' as a 'high risk' area, as had the FRISK analysis for the Funds' 1999 audits" (emphasis added). However, PwC never sent a management letter concerning the inadequacy of fund valuation controls.

Allegations of Knowledge and Miscalculation of Significant Valuation Discrepancies

The US SEC proceeding against Mr. Stoler also focused on comparing the work of the PwC audit team with third-party valuations. Specifically, the proceeding alleged that the comparison between the Bloomberg values obtained and the prime broker values showed that Mr. Strafaci's values for securities significantly exceeded both the prime broker values and the Bloomberg values in many cases. In particular the proceeding outlined:

> Strafaci's values for thirty-four of the forty-four convertible bonds and nineteen of the twenty convertible preferreds tested differed by 2% or more from the corresponding Bloomberg prices, with Strafaci's values being higher for all but four securities ... Had the audit team taken leverage into account it would have seen that the Bloomberg test indicated that Convertibles' partners' capital was overstated by approximately 34.4%.

To take things a step further the SEC also provided specific examples at the security level of differences between Mr. Strafaci's values, the Bloomberg price, the prime broker price, and a third-party broker confirmation price, who was referred to as Broker A in the SEC proceeding. A summary of this data is included in Exhibit 9.3.

EXHIBIT 9.3 SEC Allegations of Differences Between Strafaci's Values and the Independent Prices for These for Selected Securities Held by the Lipper Convertibles Funds

Security	Strafaci value	Bloomberg price	Prime broker price	Broker A– confirmed average*
Values for Convertibles as of December 31, 2000 (in millions)				
Chiquita $3.75	$31	$3.56	$3.56	n/a
Human Genome 5%	157	138.08	138	122.56
Human Genome 3.75%	100	83.88	84	81.06
Intermedia 144a	33	12.15	9.99	n/a
Liberty Media	90	68.08	66.50	67.37
Loral	31.22	11	12.60	n/a
MGC Comm.	35.54	7.50	7.50	n/a
United Global Comm.	39	15.88	15.88	n/a

*This represents the average of bid/ask range provided by Broker A.
Source: United States of America Before the Securities and Exchange Commission, February 9, 2006, Administrative Proceeding File No. 3-12179 in the Matter of Lawrence A. Stoler, CPA Respondent. Order instituting administrative and cease-and-desist proceedings pursuant to Rule 102(e) of the Commission's Rules of Practice, Section 8A of the Securities Act of 1933, Section 21C of the Securities Exchange Act of 1934, and Section 203(k) of the Investment Advisers Act of 1940.

Allegations of a Flawed Broker Quote Confirmation Process

During a hedge fund's valuation process, it is generally considered best practice for the fund to not solely price securities on its own, but to reach out to third parties to obtain independent prices. Some securities, such as large publicly traded companies, can be easily priced via third-party pricing sources such as the Bloomberg prices referenced above. As noted above, securities that are more thinly traded are typically priced from brokers, as opposed to from third-party pricing feeds. These are referred to as broker-quoted securities.

As part of their audit testing work of hedge fund valuations auditors may reach out to brokers to check a percentage of broker-quoted positions. In the proceeding against Mr. Stoler, the US SEC outlined that the PwC audit team did indeed perform such tests. So far so good.

Here is how the US SEC alleged it worked. Specifically, the proceedings detailed that a junior auditor sent faxes to five institutional salespeople or five broker-dealers. In the faxes the junior auditor asked the brokers to "please verify that the attached schedule of broker quotes as of 12/31/00 were [sic] provided by you to Lipper Convertibles." The problem the US SEC alleged was that this process was flawed, and therefore unreliable in several ways including:

- The referenced "attached list" was not actually provided by the broker-dealers at all but rather was prepared by the audit team itself.
- The faxes did not ask the salespeople to provide quotes for the securities or further ask them to attest to the reasonableness of the values listed on the schedule.
- The broker-dealers were asked to confirm values for a large number of securities, 54 to be exact, without regard as to whether or not they actually made markets in those securities.

Other Allegations

The US SEC also alleged that the audit of the fund's 2000 financial statements was not presented in conformity with US Generally Accepted Accounting Principles ("GAAP"). Furthermore, the SEC alleged that the audits were not conducted in accordance with Generally Accepted Accounting Standards ("GAAS") for a variety of alleged violations including a lack of professional care and a lack of supervision of those involved in the audits.

Additional Related Litigation

For reference, as is the situation in most cases when investor losses ensure, a number of lawsuits were filed including those against the fund's auditor PwC. One such case was CILP Associates LP et al. v. PricewaterhouseCoopers LLP, 2nd U.S. Circuit Court of Appeals, Nos. 11-4904, 11-4905, 11-5104, and 11-5106. Interestingly, Lipper & Co. Inc. had attempted to sue PwC, among others, for effectively not alerting the firm to the fraud being conducted by Mr. Strafaci (Hornbeck, 2013).

Ultimately a court said that these claims were blocked by a NY state law doctrine called *in pari delicto*, which prevents courts from resolving claims between two alleged wrongdoers (Matthew Serino et al. v. Kenneth Lipper et al., case number 604396/2002). It should also be noted that in 2013 an appeals court reinstated fraud claims against PwC. It was subsequently reported that Mr. Stoler, who neither admitted nor denied the allegations, agreed to be barred from practicing before the US SEC for one year (Weil, 2010).

Additional Comments on the Lipper Example

Situations such as the Lipper case did not occur in a vacuum. Unfortunately there are literally dozens, if not more, of other cases that occurred around the same time period regarding controls and oversight with respect to valuation. Two of the more notable ones include:

- Manhattan Investment Fund (1999)—Fund manager Michael Berger lost millions in bad technology stock bets resulting in approximately $400 million in losses. To cover his losses he created forged documents, including those from his clearing broker, the now defunct Bear Stearns, and issued false investor reports that showed inflated values for the fund. This helped to cover up the scam for over three years to investors, the fund's administrator (a unit of Ernst & Young's International Bermuda affiliate), and the firm's auditor (Deloitte & Touche's Bermuda affiliate) (Debaise, 2000). To make matters more interesting Mr. Berger pled guilty, jumped bail, and didn't show up for sentencing, making the FBI Most Wanted list. He was eventually captured in Austria living at his parents' house, but he wasn't extradited because of protections he enjoyed as an Austrian citizen. As an aside, Bank Austria, which had two of its directors on the board of the Manhattan Investment Fund, also had its former CEO, Gerhard Randa, investigated as part of the Madoff inquiry (*Austrian Times*, 2013).

- Beacon Hill Asset Management (2002)—A mortgage-backed securities fund that the SEC alleged manipulated the hedge fund's valuation procedures and then inflated values by 54% resulting in losses of over $300 million (U.S. Securities and Exchange Commission, 2004).

When considering these historical situations through a modern governance context it may be easy to just dismiss them all as being the result of ill-conceived and antiquated valuation oversight practices. While the overall trend of implementation of third-party administrators and enhanced oversight by an auditor continues. Third-party valuation agents and directors have certainly increased the oversight of valuations as compared with the early 2000s, but it has also made analyzing the situation more complicated. I am of the opinion that fraud can be modeled historically but not predicted with any certainty in the future. This does not mean that future frauds will not contain elements of historical frauds, but rather this is to suggest that fraud is an evolving area. Just when you think you have closed one opportunity a new one opens. To clarify, in a governance context, it does not only have to be fraud we are talking about to be detrimental. Well-intentioned, honest hedge funds can still have poor valuation practices and even worse oversight of those practices.

In analyzing hedge funds' valuation oversight, transparency, and controls not only investors should consider the most recent funds that have had valuation issues, but they may also find it useful to look back in time and see what lessons from the past can be applied today.

REFERENCES

Austrian Times, 2013. Bank Austria Admits Former CEO Being Investigated Over Madoff Fraud, February 12.

Bloomberg, 2002. The Fallen Financier, December 8.

Colter, A., 2002. Several Kenneth Lipper hedge funds are being liquidated after big losses. *The Wall Street Journal*, March 29.

Debaise, C., 2000. Hedge fund manager Michael Berger is charged with securities fraud. *The Wall Street Journal*, August 24.

Geiger, D., 2013. Ken Lipper gets back in the game. *Crain's New York Business*, April 28.

Hornbeck, E., 2013. Hedge funds can't blame PwC for collapse, judge says. *Law360*, April 26.

Klopott, F., Braun, M., 2014. Time for some problems at port authority: Lipper goes rogue. *Bloomberg*, 2014.

Maxey, D., 2014. If a security isn't trading, what is it really worth? *The Wall Street Journal*, February 4.

Scharfman, J., 2008. Hedge Fund Operational Due Diligence: Understanding the Risks. Wiley Finance, Hoboken, NJ.

Securities and Exchange Commission v. Edward J. Strafaci, 2003. http://www.sec.gov/litigation/litreleases/lr18432.htm

The New York Times, 2004. A Guilty Plea for Overstating Value of Funds, August 12.

Urda, A., 2006. SEC charges ex-PWC auditor in hedge fund scandal. *Law360*, February 10.

U.S. Securities and Exchange Commission, 2004. Litigation Release No. 18950, October 28.

Weil, J., 2010. Incite: Morgan Keegan suits leave auditor speechless, so why hasn't accounting firm PwC revisited its audits of suspect bond funds? *Investment News*, April 15.

Whitehouse, K., 2011. Ex-Koch deputy mayor Ken Lipper close to getting reputation back. *New York Post*, June 10.

Chapter 10

Field Perspectives on Governance—Interviews With Those Involved in Various Aspects of Hedge Fund Governance

Analyzing a somewhat abstract subject such as hedge fund governance can sometimes be a daunting task. As you have likely surmised by now, it's a fairly broad subject with many gray areas. As we have outlined throughout this book governance at hedge funds consists of more than just the board of directors. To understand governance you need to touch on a wide variety of disciplines ranging from the law and fund operations to various aspects of due diligence. If you want to understand fund governance, you also need to understand the different perspectives from those who work in this area including service providers that support hedge fund governance functions, and those who are tasked with analyzing governance.

While casting a broad net when analyzing governance is certainly a better approach, this is not to diminish the crucially important role of the board of directors in the overall governance equation. Understanding not only what directors do but also the tone they set can provide valuable insights into how seriously a fund takes the subject of governance.

We have covered a lot of ground so far in this book, but understanding how it all works in practice can be a different story altogether.

To facilitate a more practical application of the real-world moving parts of hedge fund governance, this chapter contains interviews with some of the leading professionals and practitioners in this space. We also thought it would be interesting to provide a regulatory perspective on trends in emerging governance jurisdictions, and therefore we have included an interview with the Malta Financial Services Authority (MFSA). The hope is that by being exposed to some of the more rigorous guidelines surrounding governance, and also hearing it straight from the horse's mouth as it were, readers will get a real-world feel of how governance can be fluid, complex, and ultimately a value-added area to focus on as part of your hedge fund investing process.

INTERVIEW WITH MS. HEATHER SMITH, CAYMAN ISLANDS MONETARY AUTHORITY

To start things off, as we have highlighted throughout this book offshore centers such as the Cayman Islands continue to play a crucial role in the area of hedge fund governance. In order to discuss trends in Cayman governance I was privileged to conduct an interview with Ms. Heather Smith (Head, Investments and Securities Division) from the Cayman Islands Monetary Authority ("CIMA" or the "Authority").

Ms. Smith was appointed Head of the Investments and Securities Division of the CIMA on June 1, 2014. In this capacity, she is responsible for the authorization and supervision of regulated hedge funds, fund administrators, and securities investment companies in the Cayman Islands, and for directing a program of continuous monitoring and inspection of licensed fund administrators and securities investment companies. Ms. Smith served as the Deputy Head of Investments and Securities from 2006 to 2014, overseeing the licensing, regulation, and supervision of mutual funds, mutual fund administrators, and entities conducting securities and investment business under the Securities Investment Business Law and the Mutual Funds Law, and ensured compliance under the Money Laundering Regulations and the Proceeds of Crime Law. Ms. Smith, who has 20 years' experience in the financial services industry, has worked with CIMA for 17 years. She holds a Bachelor of Science degree in business economics, as well as the Associate of the Securities Institute and Certified Anti-Money Laundering Specialist qualifications.

Jason Scharfman:	Historically, from the US perspective the definition of corporate governance at the hedge fund level was primarily associated with the board of offshore hedge fund vehicles such as those in the Caymans. There has been a growing acceptance that while directors are a crucial part of implementing governance, at the hedge fund level, governance oversight also encompasses the roles of the hedge fund managers themselves, service providers, and regulators such as CIMA. What role do you feel CIMA plays in promoting hedge fund governance?
Ms. Smith:	The Mutual Funds Law outlines that operators of regulated mutual funds (which includes directors, general partners, and trustees) should not act in a manner that is, or is likely to be, prejudicial to investors or creditors. As the regulator of such funds, CIMA has the responsibility of ensuring that there are adequate systems and controls in place for operators to fulfill this obligation under the Law.
Jason Scharfman:	The issue of governance at the hedge fund level has continued to gain attention from investors, hedge funds, and directors themselves. As compared with other issues, why do you think this issue continues to be so hotly debated for hedge funds with directors in the Caymans?
Ms. Smith:	As the Cayman Islands is currently the domicile of over 11,000 funds, a large number of the directors are associated with fund's resident here and, as such, the crux of the conversation would emanate from this jurisdiction. Generally, however, investors are now much more interested in the governance of their fund and are no longer content to rely solely on the fund's management. They are requiring accountability and transparency at all levels in order to gain the necessary assurance that their investment is safe.
Jason Scharfman:	In regards to the recent Cayman Islands Hedge Fund Corporate Governance Survey, a majority of respondents across all sectors of respondents indicated that they preferred a CIMA-managed public database that would divulge the number of directorships. Can you provide any guidance on CIMA's reaction to this finding and any contemplated next steps?
Ms. Smith:	The database remains under deliberation by the Authority; however, there is no affirmative time frame for implementation. The implementation of any such database would comply with the requirements of the Monetary Authority Law (2013 Revision) (the "MAL") for public consultation.
Jason Scharfman:	Additionally, in my experience many hedge fund investors and due diligence analysts feel that the disclosure of a pure number of directorships would be made more useful if the names of the actual fund boards on which directors served were also disclosed. Do you have any comment on this?
Ms. Smith:	The Authority is cognizant that the development of any database should provide information that is relevant, appropriate, and useful to the stakeholder, and that disclosures must contribute to market discipline objectives. In addition, the opportunity for public consultation provided by the MAL will allow CIMA to weigh all suggestions and recommendations from members of the public and industry on the information to be made available under any such database.

(Continued)

Jason Scharfman:	One of the key study findings relating to the assessment of corporate governance practices was a perceived weakness of Cayman directors effective management of conflicts of interest. How has CIMA approached the issue of overseeing such conflicts?
Ms. Smith:	The implementation of the Statement of Guidance (SoG) for Regulated Funds on Corporate Governance, the Directors Registration and Licensing Law (the "Law"), and accompanying regulations are all steps taken by CIMA to ensure that investors in regulated funds are aware of the Authority's expectations of the operators of such funds. In addition, the Mutual Funds Law has always required directors and other service providers of mutual funds to disclose all material information relating to the fund to their investors. In practice, CIMA expects that the management of conflicts of interest in terms of corporate governance would be disclosed to investors through the offering documents.
Jason Scharfman:	With regards to capacity limits on the number of individual directorships the majority of those surveyed (61%) responded in favor of limits based on the number of manager relationships as opposed to limits based on the absolute number of directorships (39%). Can you comment on CIMA's perspective on director capacity limits and any distinction it may draw between manager relationships and absolute directorships?
Ms. Smith:	CIMA's feedback statement on the Consultation Paper dated December 6, 2013 stated: "The Authority's stance is to monitor the effect of the Public Database and the SOG on the investment funds sector. Should the Public Database and the SOG facilitate a more consistent and comprehensive approach towards corporate governance in the sector, it would potentially negate the need for a formal limit on the number of directorships held. Although it remains to be decided, the Authority envisages allowing a two-year period to monitor the effect of the Public Database and the SOG before revisiting this topic." This remains CIMA's current position. Accordingly, the specific provisions relating to capacity in the Law have not been brought into force at this time. However, they will be brought into force at a later date. It is anticipated that if the situation arises where CIMA is contemplating directly regulating directorship numbers, CIMA will only do so after the usual industry consultation on the matter.
Jason Scharfman:	On a related note, in my experience certain hedge fund analysts and investors feel that directors are attempting to manipulate the argument when they frame the discussion in terms of manager relationships. The general position is that each fund-level directorship should be given equal time and grouping them together under the umbrella of one manager is not representative of this. Do you have any comment on this?

Ms. Smith:	CIMA is of the view that a director is equally responsible to all the entities for which they act on behalf of and that fiduciary responsibility does not allow them to consider manager relationships to the exclusion of the entity. This is in line with the common law, which holds that each incorporated company is a separate legal entity, and a director owes separate fiduciary duties to each incorporated company.
Jason Scharfman:	Some Cayman hedge fund directors who are not affiliated with the larger directorship firms have expressed concern regarding overly restrictive capacity constraints. One reason for this is that as the directorship space has become more competitive, they are facing increased pressure to reduce their fees while still effectively taking on the same liability of serving as directors. By limiting the number of directorships they feel they would have to subsequently increase their fees to balance out the limited number of boards they could serve on, which would in their perspective render them not competitive with the larger firms. What role, if any, do you feel CIMA plays in managing this conflict while balancing considerations of promoting the directorship industry as a whole?
Ms. Smith:	Please see previous response in relation to CIMA's current position on capacity limits.
Jason Scharfman:	The survey results indicated that the majority of respondents were in favor of changes in the number of directorships being reported to CIMA within the 21-day requirement of the Mutual Funds Law only after a de minimis threshold (generally 5–10) was triggered. If such a requirement was implemented, do you feel it would be CIMA's responsibility to police this or would it be self-reported?
Ms. Smith:	The Mutual Funds Law does not set a de minimis threshold and as such CIMA implementation of any such recommendations would require amendments to the Mutual Funds Law. To the extent that someone is found to be in contravention of this requirement, CIMA would take the appropriate enforcement action. In any event, the Law and the Mutual Funds Law together operate to ensure that directors notify CIMA of their appointment to mutual funds on a real-time basis, as a mutual fund cannot be registered without each director being previously licensed or registered. The act of registering a new mutual fund automatically notifies CIMA of the number of new directorships held by a particular director. Directors who fail to notify CIMA of their resignation as a director of a fund within the 21-day period provided in the Directors Registration and Licensing Law may, to the extent permitted under that Law, be subject to enforcement action. In practice, CIMA expects that directors, who now have personal responsibility to CIMA to ensure that their information is accurate, will be proactive in managing the information held by CIMA in order to be considered fit and proper.
Jason Scharfman:	The Cayman Islands recently proposed the Directors Registration and Licensing Bill (the "Bill"), to announce its intention to introduce a registration and licensing regime for directors of certain regulated entities in the Cayman Islands. Can you comment on this Bill and what CIMA hopes it will accomplish for investors and hedge fund directors in particular?

(Continued)

Ms. Smith:	The Bill has now become law, with supporting regulations outlining the process for registration or licensing. The Directors Registration and Licensing Law strengthens existing corporate governance requirements as it now closes the gap between CIMA's oversight of corporate directors and natural persons acting as directors. This law, along with the recently published Statements of Guidance for Regulated Funds on Corporate Governance, now provides much-needed clarity to the investors and industry into regulated funds of the standards expected of the operators of such funds.
Jason Scharfman:	The Bill proposes enhanced regulatory requirements for directors who hold more than 20 directorships. Can you provide some perspective on how this figure of 20 directorships was arrived at?
Ms. Smith:	CIMA's independent research, the current allocation of directorships for existing funds, and the results of the survey provided a starting point for deciding on a number. The government of the Cayman Islands is ultimately responsible for making legislative decisions.
Jason Scharfman:	Additionally, would you be able to comment on what this enhanced regulatory oversight may require?
Ms. Smith:	As a professional director, these individuals will be subject to ongoing monitoring and reporting, similar to that required of other licensees and approved persons, which includes the requirement to undergo a fitness and propriety assessment prior to licensing, the requirement to maintain adequate insurance coverage, and a review of relevant books and records by CIMA as deemed necessary. Please note that CIMA is able to conduct this review for any category of director.
Jason Scharfman:	Under the proposed Bill can you advise what sort of ongoing oversight by CIMA of fund directors is contemplated once a license may be granted to a director?
Ms. Smith:	Please see response above.
Jason Scharfman:	Some have proposed the idea of annual exams or surprise audits of directors (or directorship firms) to ensure appropriate record keeping practices, etc. Can you comment on CIMA's perspective on this?
Ms. Smith:	The Law outlines, as part of CIMA's ongoing responsibility, that it can examine, by way of scrutiny of prescribed returns, on-site inspections, or any other means determined, the affairs or business of any registered, professional, or corporate director. As such, CIMA will implement the supervisory process necessary to fulfill this requirement.
Jason Scharfman:	Jurisdictions such as Malta require that directors undergo background investigations. Is this something that may be contemplated by CIMA as part of additional director oversight? Why or why not?

Ms. Smith:	If by background investigations the reference is to an assessment to determine fitness and propriety, yes, this currently forms part of the licensing process for directors. CIMA is required to assess the honesty, integrity, and reputation; competence and capability; and financial soundness of the applicant. For both licensees and registrants, CIMA may refuse an application if there are convictions for fraud or other offences involving dishonesty; or if the applicant is the subject of an adverse finding, financial penalty, sanction, or disciplinary action by a regulator, self-regulatory organization, or a professional disciplinary body.
Jason Scharfman:	In particular Part II, clause 7(a) of the proposed Bill outlines that CIMA may refuse to register a director in the event they have "been convicted or a criminal offence involving fraud of dishonesty." To clarify is it contemplated that CIMA will be responsible for reviewing directors' history or would it be up to directors to self-disclose such a history?
Ms. Smith:	Self-disclosure is required; however, CIMA will also conduct its own independent checks of applicants for licensing. In addition, CIMA is obligated to investigate any credible information relating to any director, whether licensed or registered, that may relate to that director's history. Any director who is aware of any such convictions and fails to self-disclose will be subject to enforcement action under the Directors Registration and Licensing Law.
Jason Scharfman:	In the decision by the Grand Court of the Cayman Islands in the Weavering case, the Court outlined a series of expectations with regards to board meetings of funds such as the preparation and circulation of an agenda in advance of each meeting and that minutes should be taken at each meeting. Do you feel it is within CIMA's current responsibilities to ensure that practices such as these are followed? Or instead, do you feel it is the responsibility of investors via due diligence to ensure that such practices are followed?
Ms. Smith:	CIMA's SoG for Regulated Mutual Funds on Corporate Governance outlines that there should be a full, accurate, and clear written record of board meetings. The record should include the agenda items and circulated documents, a list of attendees present at the meeting and method of attendance (in person, via telephone, etc.), matters considered and decisions made, and any information requested and provided by service providers and advisors. CIMA will assess adherence to this SoG in its ongoing monitoring of regulated funds. Investors should also, however, conduct their own assessment of the practices of the fund into which they invest.
Jason Scharfman:	In Weavering, the Court outlined in its decision that nonexecutive directors of Cayman funds would likely rarely have the specific technical expertise to effectively monitor the sophisticated hedge fund strategies implemented in the board of funds on which they serve, nor would they be exactly expected to maintain such detailed knowledge. With this in mind, coupled with the proposed licensing requirements under the Bill, what role, if any, is it contemplated that CIMA play in evaluating directors' qualifications in this regards?

(Continued)

Ms. Smith:	A director's competence and capability, which includes an assessment of qualifications and experience, is a part of CIMA's licensing process for directors.
Jason Scharfman:	In the case of AIJ Investment Advisors Co. ("AIJ"), it was reported that AIJ transferred large sums of corporate pension assets it manages to a fund in the Cayman Islands and then moved the money to the Hong Kong account of a major European bank. Can you comment on this?
Ms. Smith:	Section 50 of the MAL prohibits CIMA from disclosing the affairs of a licensee. In practice, any information that CIMA may make available about any licensee is published on our website.
Jason Scharfman:	If you are unable to comment on AIJ specifically, can you comment on what changes, if any, CIMA has implemented since the AIJ scandal was revealed to prevent similar occurrences going forward?
Ms. Smith:	As CIMA is prohibited from disclosing the affairs of its licensees other than in the information made available on the website, CIMA is not in a position to respond to this question.
Jason Scharfman:	In recent years after cases such as Madoff in particular, there has been a transition away from service providers whose primary business was in other areas, such as fund administrators, offering directorship services. Instead this role has now been largely filled by professional directorship firms. Do you feel that this specialization has been an improvement in promoting best practice governance in the Caymans?
Ms. Smith:	CIMA supports the trend by industry to put in place the persons best suited for and with the ability to focus on the very important role that a director plays. Any enhancements to governance practices resulting from this are of welcomed benefit to the industry and regulatory regime.
Jason Scharfman:	Can you briefly summarize from a regulatory perspective what advantages the Cayman Islands offers to hedge funds and investors as compared with other Caribbean jurisdictions such as the British Virgin Islands?
Ms. Smith:	Without making a comparison to any other jurisdiction, the Cayman Islands has continued to attract hedge funds and investors, and financial services business in general, due to several factors. These include a fully developed companies law, an English-based legal system, and a regulatory and professional infrastructure capable of implementing large and complex international business transactions. CIMA conducts ongoing review of the regulatory regime for funds and other regulated entities to ensure that it maintains the right balance between requiring compliance with international standards for all registrants/licensees and enabling the economic growth of the Islands and entities resident here.
Jason Scharfman:	Can you comment on CIMA's perspective on the increased popularity of hedge funds establishing reinsurers in the Caymans?

Ms. Smith:	The business partnership between hedge funds and reinsurance operations is nothing new in the global arena, with hedge funds choosing to invest indirectly into the (re)insurance markets through Insurance-Linked Securities ("ILS") structures or by buying equity in the holding companies operating reinsurance business. However, with traditional asset classes not producing the high double-digit returns that were once possible prior to the global economic crisis in 2008, asset managers have responded by setting up their own reinsurance operations to try to achieve substantial returns, and also attract larger investments from institutional investors such as pension funds. With the Cayman Islands being the leading jurisdiction for hedge funds domiciliation and the second largest jurisdiction for offshore (re)insurance operations, it is well positioned to build on its expertise to be the domicile of choice for the emerging hedge fund–backed reinsurers. The Cayman Islands has the necessary expertise and regulatory framework to ensure such hedge fund–backed reinsurance operations are managed to protect the financial interests of all stakeholders, including policyholders and investors alike.
Jason Scharfman:	In particular, how do you respond to the governance concerns that in many cases the assets of these reinsurers are managed by the investment adviser of the hedge funds that establish them? The particular concerns that have been raised are that there are minimal capital requirements, minimal disclosure requirements, and no strict regulation on how these companies invest their money. With this in mind, what steps has CIMA taken to promote good governance in this hedge fund and associated reinsurer companies framework?
Ms. Smith:	Whether it's a traditional arrangement or a hedge fund–backed operation, (re)insurance operations are regulated as risk-bearing entities with the right level of supervision to ensure that they have put in place appropriate risk mitigation controls, including capital in excess of risk-based minimum capital requirements as a buffer against unforeseen events such as higher than expected (re)insurance claims. In addition, all risk-bearing (re)insurance licensees of CIMA are required to get their investment strategies/policies preapproved by CIMA and to abide by these guidelines to ensure that they do not make excessively risky investments that could blow up.
Jason Scharfman:	With regards to director liability and solvency, does CIMA have any comment or perspective on minimum levels and types of insurance, such as Directors and Officers or Errors and Omissions, that they would advise it would be best practice for directors to obtain? If not, do you feel it is best left for the market (i.e., investors and hedge funds) to dictate this?
Ms. Smith:	The Directors Registration and Licensing Law outlines that a professional and corporate director "… shall at all times be covered by insurance with an insurer, to cover loss arising from claims in respect of civil liability incurred in connection with the business of the (professional or corporate) director, in an amount which is a minimum aggregate cover of one million dollars and a minimum cover of one million dollars for each and every claim."

(Continued)

Jason Scharfman:	Can you provide some perspective on how CIMA works with other regulators such as the US SEC to promote good governance practices in hedge funds?
Ms. Smith:	CIMA has entered into 54 memoranda of understanding with a variety of international regulators, including the US SEC and the (former) UK FSA, now the FCA. These MOUs have strengthened the Authority's international relationships and have promoted international cooperation in monitoring and investigating good corporate governance. In addition, the Authority is an active member of IOSCO and as such a signatory of the multilateral memorandum of understanding, which currently has 124 countries as signatories.
Jason Scharfman:	In light of the regulatory challenges posed by AIFMD, and concerns relating to offshore funds remaining domiciled in non-EU jurisdictions, some hedge funds have transitioned from the Caymans to EU jurisdictions such as Malta. Would you be able to comment on whether such concerns by hedge fund managers are well founded?
Ms. Smith:	CIMA has been engaged from the onset in active discussions with ESMA relating to the AIFMD and its requirements. In 2013, CIMA signed cooperation agreements with 27 EU member states, thus enabling the provision of mutual assistance regarding the supervision of managers of alternative investment funds who operate on a cross-border basis in these jurisdictions. There are continued discussions with the remaining member states in this regard, as well as an active ongoing review by CIMA of its regulatory regime for securities investment business.
Jason Scharfman:	After the passage of Dodd–Frank the US SEC revamped its whistleblower system to facilitate ease of reporting and expediting of financial rewards to whistleblowers. The Cayman Islands recently proposed the Protected Disclosures Bill 2014 that would provide enhanced protections to whistleblowers. Although the impetus behind this law primarily relates to cases of civil servants not coming forward, can you comment if you feel enhanced whistleblower protections and rewards, as it relates to the Cayman hedge fund industry, would be contemplated or beneficial to promoting good governance in the Cayman hedge fund industry?
Ms. Smith:	Amendments to the legislative regime of the Cayman Islands, including "whistleblowing" by civil servants, fall under the Cayman Islands government.
Jason Scharfman:	Can you comment on what trends you see in governance in the Caymans going forward?
Ms. Smith:	The increase in investors' engagement in ensuring that a sound corporate governance structure is in place for entities in which they invest will continue, and the presence of independent directors on fund boards will continue, with a heightened move toward a fully independent board.

INTERVIEW WITH MARK COOK AND GEOFF RUDDICK (INTERNATIONAL MANAGEMENT SERVICES LTD.)

Fund directors play critical roles in implementing the overall governance structures in place at hedge funds. Throughout this book we have discussed the various duties of board members in detail. While such discussions are informative, to gain some direct perspective on the role of director, I conducted an interview with two leaders in the fund directorship space: Mark Cook, B.Com, B.Econ, CA, Acc.Dir., and Geoff Ruddick CA, CFA, FICA, Acc.Dir.

Mr. Ruddick is a resident of the Cayman Islands, is a Canadian Chartered Accountant, a member of the Institute of Chartered Financial Analysts, a member and fellow of the International Compliance Association, and a founding member of the Cayman Islands Directors Association, and holds the Accredited Director designation granted by the Institute of Chartered Secretaries of Canada. Mr. Cook is also a Cayman Islands resident, is an Australian Chartered Accountant, a member of the Cayman Islands Society of Professional Accountants, and a founding member of the Cayman Islands Directors Association, and holds the Accredited Director designation granted by the Institute of Chartered Secretaries of Canada. Both Mr. Cook and Mr. Ruddick serve as directors on the boards of alternative investment funds and special-purpose vehicles.

Jason Scharfman:	What has been IMS role in the development of the Cayman directorship industry?
Mark Cook and Geoff Ruddick:	IMS is the longest established Cayman Islands firm providing directorship services, having been incorporated in 1974. It has helped shape the directorship industry by always having provided highly experienced professionals as fund fiduciaries. Our model is such that the individual directors who are appointed to the fund board are the primary points of contact for dealing with all fund-related matters. Paul Harris, the Chairman of IMS, was also responsible for the creation of the Cayman Islands Directors Association.
Jason Scharfman:	Can you please provide a general summary of what you feel to be the key duties of a director?
Mark Cook and Geoff Ruddick:	The directors' primary objective should be that fund investors are being provided with the investment opportunity that they have signed up for. The directors' oversight should focus on the investment manager delivering the investment strategy as outlined in the offering document and appropriately dealing with any conflicts between the investment manager and the fund as well as conflicts between investors. In some cases, this may involve sufficient disclosure in the offering document.
Jason Scharfman:	How do you define governance at the hedge fund level?

(Continued)

Mark Cook and Geoff Ruddick:	A Cayman Islands fund director's role involves providing oversight of the fund's activities, as conducted by other fund service providers, primarily the investment manager and administrator. The directors should work with the investment manager and administrator, as well as the auditor and legal counsel, to minimize the risk of the fund's activities being conducted inappropriately.
Jason Scharfman:	How has the role of directors evolved over time? What role has technology played in this?
Mark Cook and Geoff Ruddick:	Directors in the current environment are required to be more active and vigilant as a general rule. Efforts made to verify information provided by the manager, especially in sensitive cases, are ever increasing. Technology has enabled directors to obtain and analyze a significant amount of financial information on an ongoing basis.
Jason Scharfman:	Can you provide your perspectives on how you feel hedge funds should think of directors?
Mark Cook and Geoff Ruddick:	Managers and investors should consider the benefits of experienced and qualified fund directors who sit on multiple fund boards, as these directors are well placed to observe and shape industry trends and best practices. Fund directors provided by IMS are well placed in this regard, having a wealth of relevant experience coupled with ongoing involvement with quality fund managers. Investors should feel as though they can engage with the board more frequently and should set out expectations if they have particular thoughts, for example, on frequency of board meetings and agenda items to be discussed at those meetings or particular powers, decisions, and oversight that should ultimately rest with the directors rather than being delegated to the manager or administrator.
Jason Scharfman:	What due diligence do you feel hedge funds should perform before hiring directors? Do most hedge funds do a good job at this?
Mark Cook and Geoff Ruddick:	Fund managers (as the parties most commonly selecting directors) should consider the director's professional background with particular focus on how long the director has actually served as a director on fund boards or worked in the corporate governance field, particularly in the hedge fund industry. This should also be understood in the context of other business interests or day-to-day responsibilities the director may have. The level of due diligence conducted varies widely with some taking a sophisticated approach and others focusing on a single aspect (e.g., price or affiliation with other service providers).
Jason Scharfman:	Can you provide a perspective on how investors should think about and evaluate directors?
Mark Cook and Geoff Ruddick:	As above and additionally, investors should be able to engage more freely with fund managers to suggest directors for appointment to fund boards.

Jason Scharfman:	Can you provide a summary of how as a director you interact with other fund service providers (i.e., auditor, administrator, law firms, etc.)?
Mark Cook and Geoff Ruddick:	The most frequent interaction occurs with the investment manager and this will be by e-mail, by telephone, or in person, at either our offices or the investment manager's offices. We periodically obtain reports and confirmations from the administrator in order to verify that the fund is being operated in accordance with its governing documents. Interaction with the auditor occurs at least annually in relation to the fund's financial statements and on an ad hoc basis where there are accounting or valuation issues that require board involvement. Consultation with lawyers occurs in relation to the preparation and update of fund documents and for advice in relation to contentious issues.
Jason Scharfman:	Can you provide a summary of how you think about director liability and insurance coverage?
Mark Cook and Geoff Ruddick:	It's unexpected that an independent director is going to conduct fraud. Therefore, the benefit and protection of D&O insurance is to fund the directors' defense of legal actions in cases where the fund's assets (that the directors would usually have access to under the fund's articles of association) are not accessible, for example, where the assets are illiquid.
Jason Scharfman:	What changes, if any, have occurred in the directorship space in the aftermath of cases such as Weavering case and AIJ?
Mark Cook and Geoff Ruddick:	For the majority of professional director firms, it has been business as usual as many were already aware of the responsibilities associated with the role and the types of issues arising. Perhaps, Weavering has simply added weight to the argument that independent directors should actually be independent and be engaged more frequently.
Jason Scharfman:	Can you provide your perspective of directors serving on multiple fund boards, including the self-imposed cap model of IMS and directorship database disclosure proposals?
Mark Cook and Geoff Ruddick:	In our view, directors serving on a reasonable number of fund boards should be desirable as it evidences the director's ongoing knowledge of the industry. It could be argued that a director sitting on too few boards would find it difficult to keep abreast of developing industry trends. Of course, if a director is appointed to so many boards that they are unable to personally deal with the issues arising and oversight required, our view is that that particular director has exceeded their capacity. Additional responsibilities beyond their fund board appointments (e.g., other business interests, internal management responsibilities) should also be taken into consideration in determining capacity.
Jason Scharfman:	Can you provide your perspective on the regulation of directors including perspectives on self-regulation versus the role of financial regulators such as CIMA?

(Continued)

Mark Cook and Geoff Ruddick:	Given the breadth of fund structures, strategies, and managers, prescriptive regulation would more likely than not hinder the proper governance of funds. Directors should be allowed to exercise their professional judgment in carrying out their duties and regulation should be focused on excluding and/or sanctioning bad actors. Fund stakeholders should be able to take comfort that a fund director is regulated by either a self-governing body or a regulator.
Jason Scharfman:	Can you provide an overview of what you feel to be some of the challenges directors face in valuation oversight including side pockets, illiquids, etc.?
Mark Cook and Geoff Ruddick:	Where board involvement is required, the primary difficulty in this regard is obtaining independent, specialist input into the valuation. The manager is often best placed to determine the current value of side pockets and illiquid positions, but it is not usually easy to verify that value. The director's role is more likely to involve obtaining confirmation from the administrator and auditor that they are comfortable with the valuation attributed, than to actually determine the value. Provided a side pocket is structured properly and its use is appropriately disclosed in the offering document, it should overcome the valuation issues associated with illiquid positions.
Jason Scharfman:	Can you provide a summary of the duties of a director when a fund goes into liquidation? During the 2008 crisis do you feel many directors handled subsequent liquidations appropriately? What mistakes were made? Lessons learned?
Mark Cook and Geoff Ruddick:	The directors' duties when a fund goes into liquidation essentially require ensuring assets are realized, creditors are paid, contracts and other commitments are terminated, and the balance of funds is paid to investors. The precise responsibilities will depend on the point in time during the process that the liquidator is appointed. Once a liquidator has been appointed, the directors' powers cease. The 2008 crisis was atypical in that many securities, across many markets and geographies, suffered a crisis of liquidity at the same time. In a general sense, many directors and managers handled the situation appropriately in that assets were not sold at fire-sale prices simply to achieve liquidity and in many cases gates and suspensions operated precisely as they should have given the circumstances. One point highlighted by the 2008 crisis that is still relevant for fund directors is the ongoing need to critically assess the information provided by the fund managers especially as it relates to the liquidity/illiquidity of certain positions and the carrying value of investments with limited liquidity.
Jason Scharfman:	Can you provide some perspective on how directors approach the management of conflicts of interest?

Mark Cook and Geoff Ruddick:	An acute awareness of the conflicts of interest that exist is a helpful starting point. Beyond the often nominal fee that independent directors are paid, the directors do not typically have a vested interest in the fund structure. This enables conflicts to be addressed on an objective basis. Obviously, there are myriad conflicts that may exist depending on the particular circumstances, but these broadly fall into three categories—first, between the fund and the manager; second, between subsets of investors; and third, between service providers to the fund.
Jason Scharfman:	In a master–feeder complex what is your perspective on the role of the master fund board in trumping the board of the offshore fund? Doesn't this effectively render the offshore vehicle powerless?
Mark Cook and Geoff Ruddick:	In a master–feeder structure the master fund is the vehicle where the fund's investment strategy is conducted, but the master fund has typically two investors (onshore and offshore feeder funds) and the offshore fund has only a single investment but many investors. For a stand-alone corporate fund, the investment strategy and investor base interface in the same vehicle. Fund directors should make the distinction between the vehicles in a master–feeder structure and be engaged at both levels. In our view, having an independent board at the feeder fund level and not at the master fund level is a missed opportunity for good corporate governance.
Jason Scharfman:	Some investors, particularly operational due diligence (ODD) professionals, have taken a skeptical view toward the actual oversight and enforcement abilities of directors. Can you respond to these criticisms?
Mark Cook and Geoff Ruddick:	Increased dialogue between investors and fund directors would help close the perceived gap between investor expectations and the activities actually being taken by the fund directors. There will inevitably be instances where investors may say that board oversight is lacking (perhaps due to a lack of awareness of what a particular board does on an ongoing basis) but very few instances where investors will say what steps they would have expected the fund board to take. Of course, this is not to suggest that in some situations fund boards were lacking in oversight or enforcement. Our directors are typically active in providing oversight, but this level of activity is not commonly reported to fund investors.
Jason Scharfman:	What trends in governance and directorships do you see going forward?
Mark Cook and Geoff Ruddick:	There will be better communication between fund boards, the administrators, and auditors in order to regularly verify the activities undertaken by the investment manager. There will also be increased interaction between investors and fund directors as more investors realize that independent, professional fund directors generally are focused on protecting investor interests under all circumstances. There will also be an increased demand for the specialist skills provided by professional directors to onshore fund vehicles that have not historically had an independent governance voice.

INTERVIEW WITH GEORGE BASHFORTH OF APPLEBY TRUST (CAYMAN) LTD.

As we have highlighted throughout this book directors play a critical role in the implementation of hedge fund governance. While we have discussed the general role and duties of directors earlier in this book, as we highlighted above, there is no better source on this issue than to hear directly from a director. To that end, I interviewed George Bashforth, Head of Directorship Services at Appleby Trust (Cayman) Ltd. in Grand Cayman.

At Appleby George Bashforth works on a wide range of investment fund products, including multi-manager funds, hedge funds, private equity funds' insurance structures, and CLOs. He is a member of the Cayman Islands Directors Association, and he also holds the Accredited Director designation from Chartered Secretaries Canada.

Jason Scharfman:	Can you please provide a background of Appleby and overview of the directorship services offered as it relates to hedge fund governance?
George Bashforth:	Appleby is one of the world's largest providers of offshore legal and fiduciary services. We employ around 800 people, and we operate from 12 offices around the globe. Appleby's Fiduciary group provides offshore management services to funds, high-net-worth individuals, private companies, and global corporations. Our directorship capabilities allow us to offer the full spectrum of fund governance services from our team of specialist in-house independent professional directors, all of whom are senior employees with over 15 years' financial services experience, both onshore and offshore. They have experience working with hedge funds, private equity, and structured finance vehicles and the expertise necessary to enhance governance requirements to safeguard the interests of investors. Uniquely, we can also offer industry professionals with specific investment and risk management experience through our network of external independent directors. These external industry professionals have all held senior investment and/or risk management roles and are available to be appointed independently or alongside our in-house independent professional directors.
Jason Scharfman:	Can you please provide a general summary of what you feel to be the key duties of a director?
George Bashforth:	All fund directors should have a detailed understanding of the fund industry and appreciate the risks relevant to a particular fund and its structure, etc. In a typical fund the majority of the day-to-day duties are generally outsourced to other service providers, but nevertheless all of the directors of the fund should have a good understanding of all functions such as fund administration, accounting, investment management, etc., so that they can review and analyze the performance and potential risk of each service provider.

Directors have a number of technical requirements outlined in the law and fund documents as well as more general best practice requirements. Specifically, I would outline the key duties of a Cayman Islands fund director as follows:

- Act honestly and in good faith at all times
- Operate with due skill, care, and diligence
- Exercise independent judgment, always acting in the best interests of the fund, taking into consideration the interests of its investors as a whole
- Make full and relevant enquiries when issues are raised on matters within scope of the board and be satisfied that appropriate and timely course of action is being taken
- Communicate adequate information to all investors that it is properly able to disclose
- Ensure sufficient capacity to oversee and supervise each fund where he/she acts
- Review and ensure that constitutional and offering documentation complies with Cayman Law
- Ensure investment strategy and conflicts of interest are clearly described in the PPM
- Appoint and remove service providers and terms of contracts, and ensure CIMA and investors are notified of any changes
- Retain ultimate responsibility for any delegated functions
- Review all service provider contracts to ensure roles and responsibilities are clearly defined
- Ensure that all service providers are performing in accordance with respective contracts
- Perform annual review of service providers

At Appleby it should be noted that for each fund engagement all of our directors:

- Review all documentation including, but not limited to, the Articles of Association, the Offering Document, the Investment Management Agreement, the Fund Administration Agreement, and any Prime Brokerage/Custody Agreements so as to fully understand the fund's investment strategy and operation
- Conduct due diligence on all service providers to the fund
- Obtain the net asset value (NAV) as calculated by the fund administrator to enable them to track the performance of the fund
- Hold regular board meetings, ideally quarterly, to discuss performance and any issues that may have arisen in the prior period. Additional board meetings may be necessary to discuss issues that occur outside of this schedule
- Discuss the audit and any issues that may have arisen on an annual basis, prior to approving the financial statements, with the auditor, investment manager, and fund administrator present

(Continued)

Jason Scharfman:	How do you define governance at the hedge fund level?
George Bashforth:	Governance as it relates to the fund board is the framework of rules and practices by which a board of directors ensures accountability, fairness, and transparency to a fund and its investors. For a fund, the voting majority of this board should be independent of the investment manager. To ensure a board is being operated fairly and equitably, board members should limit the number of appointments they have to an appropriate level and the boards should be composed of persons with a wide range of skills (accounting, legal, risk, investment management, etc.).
Jason Scharfman:	Can you provide an overview of what you feel to be the different duties and responsibilities of directors' role in regards to governance oversight?
George Bashforth:	A director's duty is to ensure corporate governance mechanisms are in place. Also in the Cayman Islands the duty of the director to act in the best interests of the fund is rooted in long-standing principles of English common law and equity. The duties of a director fall into two broad groups: the duties of loyalty, honesty, and good faith; and the duties of care, skill, and diligence (known as fiduciary duties). In practice, corporate governance for a fund requires the board of directors to be in close consultation with the investment manager and the other service providers to the fund.
	Directors of funds are ultimately responsible for overseeing and supervising the activities of the fund. They should regularly monitor and take steps to ensure that the fund and its service providers are conducting the affairs of the fund in compliance with the fund's defined investment criteria, investment strategy, and restrictions as well as with all applicable laws, regulations, and other rules. Directors should receive regular reporting from the investment manager and service providers to ensure they are able to make informed decisions and to adequately oversee and supervise the fund.
Jason Scharfman:	Can you provide a summary of the ways in which you feel CIMA works to promote director regulation and how you feel they promote hedge fund governance?
George Bashforth:	First, there is the CIMA SoG. The SoG applies to investment funds regulated under the Mutual Funds Law of the Cayman Islands (Funds). The SoG sets out best practice and lays down minimum standards for governing bodies of Funds on the topic of corporate governance.
	The SoG does not impose a strict or all-encompassing code of conduct on governing bodies or operators of Funds. Rather it establishes an overall framework for good corporate governance within which Funds should operate. I should mention that the SoG is not a prescriptive or exhaustive guide. It sets out the key corporate governance principles related to the governing body of a fund and its operators.

	Specifically, the SoG covers the following areas and gives guidance on them: oversight function, conflicts of interest, governing body meetings, and operator duties and documentation. Second, we can look to the new law that the Cayman Islands government approved on June 4, 2014—the Cayman Islands Directors Registration and Licensing Law 2014 (Law). This Law requires all directors of funds regulated under the previous Mutual Funds Law (2013 Revision), and directors of companies listed as "excluded persons" under the Securities and Investments Business Law (2011), to register with CIMA within three months. Under the Law, directors are now subject to regulation and inspection by CIMA and will be expected to undertake their roles in an appropriate manner, applying sound governance practices with the aim, at a minimum, of complying with the standards detailed in CIMA's SoG. The Law also requires directors to consider their personal capacity before taking on new mandates.
Jason Scharfman:	Can you provide your perspective of directors serving on multiple fund boards and directorship database disclosure proposals?
George Bashforth:	Many factors impact the number of directorships a person can hold, such as the sophistication and size of the back-office of the professional director. I believe the number of board appointments should be disclosed [including the number of active portfolios for any Segregated Portfolio Companies (SPCs)] along with the number of manager relationships. While there are arguments that not all funds are the same, full transparency about the number of boards a professional director sits on would enhance the reputation of the Cayman Islands as a financial services jurisdiction. I also support the proposal for a directorship database as this will allow market forces to dictate the standards of the sector and also assist investors with their due diligence and verification of the fund. This will allow interested parties to review how many directorships individual directors hold. What this final database will look like and timing of its release are still to be determined but I predict that such a database in some form will happen shortly.
Jason Scharfman:	What due diligence do you feel hedge funds should perform before hiring directors?
George Bashforth:	It is imperative that hedge funds conduct ample due diligence on professional directors before hiring them. They will be starting a long-term relationship with this individual, and the firm they work for. It's worth them investing some time into evaluating the relationship before diving in head first. To start hedge funds should seek to obtain confirmation that the director has an unblemished character. As part of this they should ensure that they are not subject to any current litigation or regulatory investigations and historically have not been. This would include that the director does not have any past adverse findings by a court, regulatory body, or any adverse media coverage.

(Continued)

	Next hedge funds should also review the experience of the professional director including a curriculum vitae (CV) review. Some questions to ask include: • What specific experience do they have and what skills do they bring to the role? • How many years have they spent working in the industry? • Where did they work prior to becoming a professional director? • What is the particular professional director's educational experience? • Do they hold any professional licenses? It is also important to ask questions about their other current directorships: • How many boards do they currently sit on? • What do they feel their capacity is to handle additional new directorship positions? How did they reach this figure? • What types of strategies do these other funds follow? • Do they serve on any boards where investor gates have been imposed or any suspensions are in place and generally if they are pending, or being restructured? • If so, what issues were raised and how were they resolved? • In general, can they provide the hedge fund manager with a sense of context regarding those other relationships? After obtaining this background information, hedge funds should also find out how the relationship between the professional director and the other board members and the investment will work in practice. Some questions I would ask in this regard include obtaining details on: • Current workflow; any policy and procedures manual • How they go about discharging their fiduciary duties in practice? • How they are remunerated—is it linked to how many boards they are on? • Do they have any relationships that are responsible for a significant amount of their income/time? It is also important to understand the level of sophistication and size of the back-office infrastructure and support systems available to the director at their firm. Many of these items are similar to what an investor would look for at a hedge fund itself during an ODD review. Investment managers should investigate the details of the directors' operational support infrastructure, information technology systems in place, compliance oversight, and support and disaster recovery capabilities, to name a few areas. Finally, I would add that it is vitally important for hedge funds to not only collect all of this information on background but also actually interview directors on these issues to get an in-person sense of the individual. At Appleby, we always invite our potential hedge fund clients to visit us onsite.
Jason Scharfman:	Following up on that point, in my experience it is becoming more common for directors to be tasked with not just more questions from a hedge fund that might be hiring them, but after a director is hired directors are also receiving more inquiries from investors conducting due diligence on the directors themselves. As you know, several years ago this was not the case. Can you comment on trends you have seen with regards to this?

George Bashforth:	Yes certainly. We have definitely seen an uptick in this regard. More investors are asking more questions and this takes directors more time to respond to these reviews. At Appleby we have experience in dealing with investment consultants, institutional investors, and their ODD and legal teams. In particular, more recently, since the financial crisis and especially post-Weavering, it has become commonplace for directors to be interviewed and questioned on the fund operations and governance by these teams. Our approach, which has met with positive reviews and feedback, is based on: • Transparency about the number of fund boards each director sits on and the number of investment manager relationships that make up those appointments • Our requirement to have regular board meetings, ideally quarterly, although for some strategies semiannual may be sufficient • Face-to-face meetings with our clients where possible to ensure not all meetings are conducted over the phone
Jason Scharfman:	On a related note, can you provide a perspective on how investors should think about and evaluate directors?
George Bashforth:	There are many independent professional director service providers based in the Cayman Islands, including us at Appleby Trust (Cayman) Ltd., who are able to provide professional independent directors and corporate secretarial services for investment funds. When deciding on the makeup of a board of directors of a fund, a promoter should consider the following: • What other interests a director has in the structure of the fund and its advisers? A connected person (e.g., a principal of the investment manager) may want to consider either not sitting on the board or making sure that they are in a minority position. This reduces potential conflicts of interest. • A director should have sufficient and relevant knowledge and experience to carry out their duties as a director. How does the director meet this standard? • A director should have sufficient time to carry out those duties and that should be reflected in their remuneration. Is the director not charging enough or too much compared with their peers? This could signal red flags with regards to a number of issues including capacity, sophistication, and scalability. • While there is no requirement to be able to understand the granular details of the trading strategies of the fund, a director does need to have a proper understanding of financial statements and be able to review balance sheets and reports provided. Do they have the background and experience to facilitate this analysis? A director who is also a member of the investment manager is likely to be held to a higher standard on the basis of their particular skills with regards to the investment strategies being employed by the investment manager on behalf of the fund. • It is up to directors to acquire and maintain sufficient knowledge to enable them to carry out the role. Directors should use the advisers of the fund, such as legal counsel, to provide advice on any areas of which they are unsure.

(Continued)

	• Even if directors are also employees or principals of the investment manager or any other connected party, their director duties remain unchanged. They should ensure that they are wearing the right "hat" when turning their minds to the fund's affairs and be aware of actual and potential conflicts of interest.
Jason Scharfman:	This last point you highlighted is a very important one that often gets overlooked. The problem of course is, as you pointed out, ensuring that there are enough checks and balances in place to ensure that these individuals who may be in multiple roles remember to wear the correct "hat" as appropriate to the decisions they are undertaking at the time. On a related note, can you provide a summary of how as a director you interact with other fund service providers (i.e., auditor, administrator, law firms, etc.)?
George Bashforth:	Interaction with service providers is somewhat determined by the "life cycle" of the fund and which phase the fund is currently in. The life cycle of a fund can be split into four distinct phases: establishment, ordinary course of business, crisis management, and wind down.
	Establishment:
	• Directors must satisfy themselves as to the overall structure of the fund and the terms of service provider contracts. In particular those relating to the determination of NAV, remuneration, indemnification, and limitation of liability are reasonable and consistent with industry standards and to the extent that they are not, there are specific reasons for the divergence. Where a fund structure or service provider agreement is not standard, then this would definitely be a matter for disclosure in the offering document.
	• Directors should find out what service providers will and will not be doing for the fund, and ensure that delegation and the division of responsibilities is appropriate. For example, the directors should ensure that responsibility for calculating NAV, anti-money laundering compliance, maintaining accounts, preparing management accounts, and preparing financial statements is split appropriately between the investment manager and the fund administrator.
	• As a practical matter, the role of professional directors is slightly different in that they won't be expected to be involved in detailed negotiations with service providers. However, it would be sensible for a director to ask, before any agreements are signed, the investment manager or whoever is undertaking negotiations to inform the counterparties that the independent directors will want to review and in due course approve them and may have comments or questions before doing so.

- Directors are responsible for the contents of the offering document of the fund. As such they should ensure that the offering document is accurate and not misleading on launch and on an ongoing basis. In the case of a Cayman Islands–registered mutual fund, they should be satisfied that the offering document describes the equity interests in all material respects and provides such information as is necessary for an investor to make an informed decision as to whether or not to purchase the equity interests. Directors can no longer be passive. They cannot simply rely on the fact that the document has been prepared by reputable advisers, but should enquire as to what sort of verification exercise has been undertaken in relation to various aspects of the document and satisfy themselves that it has been properly done.
- If the appointment of a service provider is approved in resolutions, for example, the auditor, the directors should make sure that the appointment actually happens and ask to see a copy of the appointment letter and have the ability to review the same. For example, an auditor will be appointed annually and if the making of this appointment has been delegated to the investment manager, the directors should ensure that the terms are consistent with industry practice.
- If an item has been delegated to a single director to approve, for example, a final draft of an agreement or the final draft of the offering document, the directors should ensure that there is a process in place to circulate final documents to all of the board members and consider noting this as having been done at a subsequent meeting.
- At the establishment stage, when considering their duties to act in the best interests of the fund, the directors should be thinking about potential investors and raising capital.

Ordinary course of business:

- The directors perform a high-level supervisory role. The very nature of an offshore fund means that directors are nonexecutive and the investment management, administration, and accounting functions are delegated to third parties. This is acceptable but in the words of the judge in Weavering, "they are not entitled to assume the posture of automatons." As mentioned earlier, direction can no longer be passive. Simply to sit back after delegation of a role to a service provider and assume it is being done properly is not acceptable and would breach the SoG. Directors are not absolved from performing their duties and must supervise the discharge of any delegated functions.
- Directors should hold regular board meetings. Board meetings should be held sufficiently frequently so that the board is able to carry out its role effectively. The frequency of meetings will depend on the nature of the fund and the circumstances. If market or other conditions require it, directors should consider if an extraordinary meeting is necessary (see "crisis management" below).

(Continued)

- Agendas and underlying documents should be circulated before formal meetings with sufficient time for review of both. An agenda should reflect input from the investment manager, administrator, directors, and any other relevant party.

- Directors should not approve resolutions or board minutes that refer to documents that they have not reviewed or discussions that have not been had.

- Detailed board minutes as maintained in the fund's minute books should be kept for all board meetings that are held. These should fairly and accurately record the matters that were considered and the decisions that were made. Discussions do not need to be recorded in detail, but should be summarized, at least to the extent necessary to record the basis on which the decisions were made.

- Directors should keep evidence of enquiries made to service providers, such as e-mails or records of telephone conversations that take place outside of board meetings.

- Directors should ensure that a minute book is kept and that copies (at least) are sent to Cayman Islands legal counsel and the registered office in the Cayman Islands. For funds or directors based in some jurisdictions, to have the minute book offshore might be important from a tax perspective to avoid the fund's management being brought "onshore."

- If using written resolutions for significant decisions, the directors should ensure that these detail the scope of enquiry made in relation to a particular issue rather than simply "noting" that something has been done. For example, if the investment manager has provided reports or detailed advice, the directors should provide a summary of the review that they have carried out and, if necessary, a summary of the advice and append a copy of any reports.

- Directors are responsible for ensuring that the financial statements of the fund give a true and fair view of the fund's state of affairs at the end of the year. This is not altered by any delegation of account preparation to the administrator or the investment manager.

- As directors may be required to provide a letter of representation to the auditors, they should review the accounts and may wish to seek similar representations from those to whom they have delegated powers (and consider including this as an obligation in the relevant service contract).

- The board should require regular reporting from the investment manager to ensure that investments of the fund continue to be made within the relevant investment parameters and restrictions set out in the offering document and the investment management agreement. This should be done at least at every board meeting and possibly more frequently, for example, in line with subscription and redemption frequency.

- The board should ask the investment manager to provide copies of management accounts at least as frequently as subscription and redemption frequency if not monthly.
- The board should ask questions of all service providers and require reports and documents to be provided regularly or in special circumstances. For example, the board should require the administrator to regularly update the board by either report or attendance at a board meeting as to, among other things, AML compliance, changes in pricing sources, pricing problems, and deviation from standard procedures.
- In addition to regular management or other accounts and reports, the board should also ask for copies of all documentation that is sent to investors or regulators by the investment manager or the administrator.
- Directors should find out how the audit is carried out and what the timing is. All Cayman Islands–registered funds have at least six months from their financial year-end to finalize their audited financial statements and to file them with the CIMA. Directors should ensure that they are provided with the draft of financial statements in plenty of time to review them and ask any relevant questions. For a fund of funds, for example, this is particularly important because it might not be possible to finalize the audit until very late in the six-month period.
- Side letters—although these are common, if the fund is a party undertaking to carry out certain actions, then the directors should review and ultimately approve them and be comfortable with their terms from a commercial perspective. For example, if the side letter imposes extra investment restrictions, can these be carried out and does agreeing to these impact on the rest of the strategy as reported to investors? It is not enough to simply know that legally they can be entered into by the fund. If the investment manager has been given delegated authority to negotiate and execute side letters on behalf of the fund, this should form part of the regular reporting to the board and the scope of such authority should be agreed.

Crisis management:

Throughout the life cycle of the fund, directors should be proactive in ensuring that the investment manager is providing information to the board. In addition to standard regular reporting requirements, the directors should be asking the investment manager and the other service providers whether there is anything that should be brought to the attention of the board. A nonexhaustive list of the types of things that would fall under this heading is:

- If there is any actual, pending, or threatened litigation against the fund
- If there are any disputes with investors or counterparties that would fall short of actual litigation

	• Are there any conflicts of interest that need to be disclosed/managed • If redemption requests are likely to have a considerable impact on any dealing day • If accepting subscriptions in respect of ERISA/pension assets is likely to have an impact on current investors • If market or other conditions are having or are likely to have a material impact on the trading strategies of the fund • If there is any significant counterparty risk for over-the-counter transactions • If there are large redemptions, which could destabilize/affect the liquidity or cash flow of the fund • If there is any move away from the investment strategy or restrictions set out in the relevant offering documents • If there is any reduction in the investment manager's holding in the fund—skin in the game • If there are any actual or impending material changes of staff at the investment manager (e.g., triggering key man events) or any other service provider
Jason Scharfman:	Following up on that last point, the 2008 financial crisis was a real-world test in crisis management for many directors. How has the environment changed with regards to oversight since that time?
George Bashforth:	Yes, when a fund finds itself in difficulties, the directors cannot sit back and assume that other service providers, and in particular the investment manager, will rescue the fund without significant oversight from the directors. In Weavering, the judge stated that the actions of the directors in the circumstances following the collapse of Lehman Brothers in September 2008 provided "the most compelling evidence that they never intended to perform their duties as directors." A good starting point of reference is the Alternative Investment Management Association ("AIMA") Guide that sets out primary heads of responsibility for the board of directors of an offshore fund. I have found this serves as a useful work list for any director to consider.
Jason Scharfman:	Can you provide your perspective on the regulation of directors including perspectives on self-regulation versus the role of financial regulators such as CIMA?
George Bashforth:	A key strength of the Cayman investment fund industry is the supervisory framework that allows market forces and investors' demand to drive the function of the market. This allows stakeholders in investment funds to structure them in a manner that meets investment needs. So I think the current framework, as recently updated, strikes an effective balance.
Jason Scharfman:	Can you provide some perspective on how directors approach the management of conflicts of interest?

George Bashforth:	The consideration and management of conflicts of interest is a key duty of the board of directors. The best means of managing conflicts of interest at the fund level would be a majority or a fully independent board. The board would demonstrate an awareness of conflicts by having a written conflicts policy and procedures designed to address such conflicts of interest. For example, Cross Trades and Principal Transactions. Trading between two affiliated funds or between a fund and a manager for their own account must be closely monitored as there is risk that trades will be executed at off-market rates. A conflicts policy can detail how such trades can be managed and priced so that no one side is disadvantaged. We at Appleby provide a Conflicts Review/Independent Investment Professional service for a number of our clients to additionally provide investor consent to these trades and so comply with Section 206(3) of the Investment Advisors Act.
Jason Scharfman:	In a master–feeder complex what is your perspective on the role of the master fund board in trumping the board of the offshore fund? Doesn't this effectively render the offshore vehicle powerless?
George Bashforth:	In a master–feeder structure, from a governance perspective, until recently the main focus of investors, fund professionals, and promoters was on the feeder fund level. However, where are the assets once the "fund" is up and running? A typical Cayman Islands fund structure may involve a Cayman Islands feeder company, an onshore feeder (which may be a Delaware limited liability company), and a Cayman Islands master fund, which may be either a company or a limited partnership. The promoter may put in place an independent board of directors on the offshore feeder but in most cases, the promoter serves as the general partner or managing member of the onshore feeder. Which approach is taken at the master fund level? If the master fund is also a Cayman Islands company, then invariably the same board will sit at the master fund level. So far, so good, as far as governance at the asset level is concerned. But what if the master fund is a partnership? Traditionally, the general partner of the offshore master partnership has almost always been the investment manager or a special-purpose company under the control of the investment manager. The fact that there may be a board of directors at the offshore feeder level, who are wholly independent or contain a majority of independent directors, will be used as a selling point. The offering memorandum will say that the feeders will invest all or substantially all of their assets in the master. However, at the offshore level, once assets are invested into the master fund, independent governance may be lost at asset level in the event an offshore partnership vehicle is used.

	Realistically what can the directors of the offshore feeder do? The memorandum says that the directors have appointed the manager to carry out the primary investment objective of the fund, which is to invest in the master fund. So the manager directs investment in the master fund. What control does the board of the feeder then have over the activities of the general partner of the master fund or the investment manager providing services to the master fund? Legally? None. In an effort to address this mismatch, institutional investors and director service providers alike are now insisting that the same independent governance model run through the entire fund structure. As noted above, if the master fund is also a Cayman Islands company, that is easy to achieve. However, where the master fund is a limited partnership, some legal gymnastics are required. Structures that have begun to be used at the master fund level include the following: • The sole general partner of the master fund is a Cayman Islands company whose board mirrors the board of directors of the offshore feeder. • A secondary "governance" general partner of that fund is incorporated as a Cayman Islands company. This company is a second general partner, which sits alongside the manager's general partner vehicle and whose responsibilities are clearly delineated in the master fund limited partnership agreement with a focus on governance. • Special limited partners of the master fund who are party to the limited partnership agreement have the benefit of limited liability but also have a role on an advisory board that focuses on governance. • A simple advisory board with veto powers. In addition to adding independent governance at asset level, we have seen secondary "governance" general partners provide the same services at the onshore feeder level. This way governance practices that are instituted at the offshore feeder level can legally and from an enforcement perspective be baked into the fund structure in such a way as to give real teeth to the independent directors.
Jason Scharfman:	Do you have any final thoughts on trends in the directorship space going forward?
George Bashforth:	The judgment in Weavering has shown that good corporate governance is no less important for an offshore fund than for a company listed on a major stock exchange. Directors must strive to ensure that their role does not become a "tick-box" passive function and that they are fulfilling their high-level supervisory role in a manner that is consistent with the expectations of the investors in funds and complies with the SoG.

	Going forward, this decision may require some independent director service providers to reevaluate aspects of their business models and standard practices. While any changes made may have an impact on fees, investors and investment managers should welcome these changes as a positive development. Given the enhanced focus of investors on protection mechanisms such as an experienced and professional independent board, we could well see a concerted trend for funds increasingly to employ the services of independent directors who do meet these standards, especially in a market where fund-raising, for many, remains challenging.
Jason Scharfman:	Thank you for taking the time to conduct this interview. As you pointed out, the directorship role involves many aspects of both legal technicalities and practical application of those rules, particularly during crisis management situations as you highlighted.
George Bashforth:	Yes, and as recent and proposed changes in the Cayman Islands show, it's an industry that is still evolving. It was my pleasure to speak with you.

INTERVIEW WITH INGRID PIERCE OF WALKERS GLOBAL

As we have highlighted throughout this book, much of the discussion surrounding hedge fund governance is focused around the role of offshore fund directors. While these individuals certainly serve a key governance function, all too often the role of other service providers can be minimized. This includes many key service providers such as fund legal counsel that can not only perform critical functions for hedge funds themselves but also provide guidance to directors.

To discuss the role legal counsel plays in fund governance, and to provide an on-the-ground perspective of Cayman governance trends, I was fortunate to interview a leading legal practitioner in the Caymans, Ingrid Pierce, Managing Partner from Walkers. Ms. Pierce is based in Walkers Cayman Islands office where she also heads the Investment Funds Group. She has over 20 years' experience in advising fiduciaries and represents major institutions, fund managers, directors, and trustees in all aspects of investment funds, including structuring and ongoing operations. She advises on directors' duties and responsibilities, indemnities, confidentiality laws, and issues related to electronic communication.

Jason Scharfman:	Among investors and ODD professionals over the past few years we have seen an increased interest in governance issues across hedge funds. This has been accompanied by an increased focus on directors. Yet beyond the role of directors, what exactly constitutes governance remains a subjective question depending on who you speak to. One of the premises of this book is that in order to understand and evaluate hedge fund governance, you must incorporate more than just a review of the directors. Coming from both the Cayman and fund counsel perspectives, what are your thoughts on this?
Ingrid Pierce:	I agree with your premise that governance is wider than just the board of directors and that's clear from the way in which industry participants, experts, and regulators are talking about governance. We're seeing that in Cayman in particular. The CIMA issued a SoG for Regulated Mutual Funds at the beginning of this year entitled *Corporate Governance*, and one of its objectives is to deal with the oversight, direction, and management of regulated funds. To clarify although they are called "mutual funds" under the Cayman Islands Mutual Funds Law, they are really just open-ended hedge funds. The purpose of the SoG is to give the governing body of the fund and its operators some guidance on the expectations for sound and prudential governance. It covers a myriad of issues, and although the directors are primarily responsible for implementing the Guidance, they aren't the only players in the piece. So I would agree with what you say that governance involves more than just the directors; it's all the players in the hedge fund who participate in the operation, management, and control of it who have a role to play in what governance means today.
Jason Scharfman:	With this broad governance perspective in mind, it seems there are misunderstandings among investors in particular surrounding how directors, investment managers, and fund legal counsel interact. Can you provide some perspective on what role counsel plays in this framework? Where do you feel counsel adds more value, in supporting directors to tick the boxes from a compliance perspective, with regards to both fund formation and any ongoing filings, or instead focusing on having more of an ongoing dialogue with the investment manager and directors?
Ingrid Pierce:	It's the latter really. Most investment fund lawyers, and certainly those with an appreciable share of the market in this space, will tell you that their role in both the structuring and establishment of the fund is just the beginning. It's fair to say that our initial contact will be with the investment manager of the soon to be formed but not yet hatched fund. It's not until the director selection process has taken part that we will have direct contact with the proposed directors in relation to that specific fund.

	Their role is obviously key at that point, although that is just the beginning. Once the fund has been formed and all of the parties have signed off on the fund documents, as you know from your experience, it really is a case of what happens next? Of course, it is the lawyers' job to make sure that the documents are properly drafted and filed in time, but that really is just the tip of the iceberg because once the fund has formed and has been launched, that is really where the hard work begins. Some of that work is undertaken by the investment manager and other players in the piece, and the directors have a key ongoing role. Lawyers are called upon more or less frequently depending on the activity of the fund. This is a distinction you might notice between onshore counsel and offshore counsel. Onshore counsel is very often counsel to the investment manager. Offshore counsel, on the other hand and of course there are variations and exceptions to this, typically is counsel to the fund. The role of offshore counsel on a longer-term basis is to provide advice to the fund on regulatory compliance, market practice, and general ongoing activity during the life of the fund. Where counsel has been asked to advise on something, even as simple as preparing a set of board resolutions, counsel's role is to ensure that proper steps are taken to document the decisions that are taken. We often have input on not just whether the decision to be taken is within the legal parameters of what is permitted by the fund documents but also whether all the parties have been properly consulted and whether they understand the ramifications of the exercise of their discretion. Of course, the directors understand what they are doing; it is just that we are often called upon to advise on not only whether something is technically permitted but also whether it is typically done in the market, whether it is commercial and can be said to be in the best interest of investors. While lawyers are not ultimately making those decisions, they are often quite closely involved in advising the fund on the issues.
Jason Scharfman:	This last point you highlighted regarding how law firms provide advice on fund decisions is an interesting one. Regardless of the service provider, whether you look at legal counsel, such as an administrator or a director one of the big issues that makes discussions of governance between investors and fund managers so contentious is the question of whose interests service providers ultimately represent, the fund or investors. As you know the answer to this question can often be a nuanced one. Taking legal counsel as an example, your responsibility may be to the fund, as fund counsel, but you interact with the investment manager and directors, and hardly ever with the investors themselves. This can put you in a bit of an interesting position because you may be advocating for a group that you have limited interaction with. How do you resolve this?

(Continued)

Ingrid Pierce:	Well, that's often true. Unless we are retained specifically by an investor to advise on a particular matter, which does happen from time to time, as fund counsel our responsibility is not to any one investor but to the fund. But you're right; counsel often find themselves in an interesting position, although one which I think enables them to be fairly objective. On the one side, you'll have the input from the investment manager. On the other side, you'll have the input from the directors on their view as directors of the fund, and we can take the more neutral position as fund counsel to say this is what you are permitted to do, this is what is market, these are the considerations you need to think about, and these are your fiduciary responsibilities in exercising your discretion. So I think it does enable us to take a more objective approach.
Jason Scharfman:	Following up on that, beyond structuring of the initial fund itself, could you provide examples of these types of issues and situations that you are asked to provide guidance on?
Ingrid Pierce:	A typical example is where an investor-related issue crops up. Counsel's role is not to advise on the investment itself, but it may be, for example, that there is a liquidity issue and the manager is looking to provide a preference to a particular investor. I don't mean a preference that the investor is not entitled to; rather a preference that is within the power of the manager or the board to give. In this scenario we may be asked to review the relevant document (e.g., side letter) and advise on the ability of the fund to enter into it. One governance-related question we typically consider is: who are the right parties? Is this really within the manager's remit or is it something that should be entered into by the directors? That is very often a classic example of where we are asked to advise. Sometimes the directors have not been brought into the loop, and we will advise if the board needs to make the decision, and what is permissible. We will often be involved in discussions about whether the proposed activity is appropriate in the circumstances; for example, are other investors prejudiced? So that is a fairly typical, if not overly exciting, example. The sort of ongoing activity we get involved in.
Jason Scharfman:	This raises another interesting point, and a challenge that certain directors have mentioned to me, that the directors' visibility into certain issues may be effectively limited to some extent at the discretion of the manager. This is perhaps counterintuitive to the way many investors perceive the role of the board, where many investors may reasonably pose the question, "Well isn't the board seeing everything?" What you are highlighting here is legal counsel's role in raising certain issues to the level of board review. As you outline, the board may have the ability to review these issues proactively, but in practice certain issues or decisions may not be brought to their attention until after the fact in some cases. Can you provide further context on this?

Ingrid Pierce:	I see one of the jobs of fund counsel is to ask those questions. It may be imperative because the decision is legally required to be a board decision and not a manager's decision. Alternatively, it may simply be a question of judgment, namely, that it is a decision that could be made by the manager but, nevertheless, the directors ought to be informed about it.
Jason Scharfman:	In this instance then, counsel seems to play an important role beyond the simply technical application of fund rules. With regards to what items should be brought to the board, it seems counsel can be a facilitator of the oversight role of the board in some respects. Regardless of the route taken, once issues are brought to the board can you provide some perspective on what happens if the directors and counsel should disagree on certain issues? I am curious; does the board frequently challenge counsel on issues that are not merely technical applications of the fund rules?
Ingrid Pierce:	It doesn't happen that often. More often than not the board is looking for guidance and is pleased that counsel is available to give advice even if it is not necessarily the advice that the board is looking for. Of course, if any of these issues affect the directors' position and they need advice in a personal capacity as directors, then we always advise them to get their own independent advice. One of the more unusual examples is where there is actually a disagreement between the parties. For example, there may be a disagreement between the directors and an investor, or there may be a disagreement between the directors and the manager. It is not always a highly contentious situation, although it might be a potentially contentious situation. That's obviously more interesting for us in terms of the work that we do and also it brings sharply into focus our role as fund counsel.
Jason Scharfman:	In those types of situations, to give an example, the manager may say I want to dissolve. The board on the other hand may say that is too hasty. Will then counsel come and advise and lay out the options as well as arguments for and against such an issue?
Ingrid Pierce:	Yes exactly, or to give you another example let's say the fund is holding a lot of illiquid assets. Let's also say that some of those assets are already in side pockets and the manager has been managing those assets for a while, and there is a question mark about whether or not those assets should be realized immediately and the proceeds returned to investors. There then may be a disagreement because the manager may consider that they should hold those assets for longer because they can get more value out of them down the road, and they are the experts on that question. On the other hand, the directors might not be happy that investors are being charged the same level of management fees during that period.
Jason Scharfman:	In those types of cases, when push ultimately comes to shove, what happens? Do directors typically force the issue and does it ultimately go to litigation? What do you typically see in those types of situations?

Ingrid Pierce:	More often than not we find that managers and directors do end up reaching agreement, even if they start off in different places. They typically end up resolving matters in a way that has the best interests of investors in mind. In my experience, that is what most people want to do and our experience is pretty positive in that regard. That being said, there are outliers. In an extreme case, there can come a point where the directors actually have to say, "No, this is not right." We have been involved in matters where the directors have had to terminate the investment manager or put the fund into provisional liquidation. These are drastic steps that may be required if the circumstances dictate.
Jason Scharfman:	That's an interesting point to highlight as well because it seems the presumption in many cases is that any sort of liquidations would be primarily investor, and not director, driven. On a related note how do you view counsel's role in advising directors and managers on jurisdictional issues? As you know, hedge fund investing is increasingly global in scope. Directors are not acting as counsel, and may not have legal backgrounds or necessarily be familiar with all the intricacies of the laws of the jurisdictions in which they practice. From a governance perspective, what role do you see played by counsel in advising on agreements or issues that cross jurisdictions?
Ingrid Pierce:	This is where working with co-counsel is invaluable! We have an international practice and so we often see funds where the manager is from one jurisdiction, the directors from another, and the fund is operating in multiple jurisdictions with investors all over the world. Further complicating matters, service provider agreements may be covered by the laws of different jurisdictions and sometimes agreements provide that one clause is governed by the laws of one jurisdiction and the rest of the agreement is governed by the laws of another. So there are lots of interesting international law questions that we are asked to consider. We will work with counsel qualified and experienced in the relevant jurisdictions to give specific advice on these sorts of issues.
Jason Scharfman:	To change topics, one of the points I wanted to also discuss was how the environment in the Caymans has changed since the Weavering and AIJ cases. Specifically, with regards to the environment before these events where directors may have perhaps been a bit more standoffish with counsel and less concerned about personal liability as opposed to today where they may take more of a sense of comfort to know that counsel has been actively involved. What are your thoughts on this?

Ingrid Pierce:	They do ask for counsel's input. In general terms, directors are more conscious of the level of scrutiny they are under and so there is more awareness of the need to engage in a full debate over any issues and, if appropriate, record that debate.
	As an example, the SoG that I referred to earlier that talks about the directors' responsibilities in supervising service providers and regularly monitoring them. It seems to me that although directors were generally doing those things, they now have a road map to follow if they need it. In some cases they may need to point to the regulatory guidance to highlight why they are taking certain actions. In effect they can say: not only do we think this is the right thing to do but we are also mandated by the regulator to do it.
Jason Scharfman:	Yes, that's what we see at Corgentum Consulting as well in interviewing directors directly as part of our due diligence. Regardless of any concerns of additional liability it seems that this has fostered a more receptive environment for directors, as all the parties including managers understand the need to be more involved. To that point, it seems that there is a trend post-Weavering of certain fund managers seeking to have directors more engaged than they used to be. In certain instances, managers are willing to pay more to directors for this increased involvement.
	For example, at Corgentum we see some United States–based funds with Cayman offshore vehicles where the managers want more frequent meetings with directors, including in-person meetings and even on-site visits with the managers at their US offices. While that's more the exception, we also see an increased focus from managers, as you pointed out, in wanting more documentation of director meeting minutes. In some cases, however, the fund managers want this increased director involvement but they don't necessarily want to pay commensurate fee increases. Have you seen that as well?
Ingrid Pierce:	Yes, well everybody wants more for less. In my view, in the current regulatory climate it is inevitable that as the cost of doing business increases all fees must rise, and that the fees of directors are no exception. The directors are also demanding greater remuneration for having to do more. For example, the requirement to have two board meetings a year may mean an increased requirement to travel and spend time dedicated to preparing for more meetings. For other funds this poses no extra burden on them and a number of our institutional clients schedule quarterly board meetings for every fund, so it just depends.
	In any event, now that the managers are more conscious of the SoG some managers are requesting in-person meetings. So there is more time being taken to actually conduct those meetings, particularly if directors have to travel to do those meetings, and so in my mind it is only natural that directors' fees are going to have to increase. We've certainly seen that in the market generally.

Jason Scharfman:	Related to that notion of how involved directors will be, putting fees aside. At Corgentum Consulting we see different approaches that funds take to selecting the actual directors. As counsel, do you often get asked to recommend directors or directorship firms to funds that are starting up that may ask for your advice, or instead does counsel try to take a more neutral approach?
Ingrid Pierce:	We are asked to make recommendations all the time and sometimes this advice is sought by either managers who are looking to make a change from existing directors or start-up managers of new funds. For the latter group, they may have had some exposure to directors based on their experience at another fund, but they are really looking for broad input. In my experience, both of these groups usually have plenty of people they can ask for their views. Whether they are colleagues or former colleagues or other industry professionals whom they can speak to, and we are another sound check for them.
	I would not expect them to rely solely on counsel; they will ask the administrator and other service providers. We certainly speak with the investment manager about different independent director firms and also our experience of working with the individuals as opposed to the firms themselves. You can have a firm that has 50 people, but at the end of the day you've got to be happy with the person appointed and the directors need to be comfortable with each other.
	The approach of nonexecutive independent directors varies tremendously in terms of nature of the work done, the level of the fees charged, and their particular background experience.
	So we see our role as being more of a facilitator. We'll listen to what clients want and we'll ask questions. Sometimes we sit in on interviews with prospective directors, which is also insightful.
	For example, a manager/director may prefer a director with an audit background or an investment manager background or a legal background and we can help them with their research. So, we're certainly not making any selections on behalf of anybody, nor can we say that a particular director is going to be the right director for a particular fund, but we can give some examples of a director's experience.
	Are they part of a big firm that has a lot of infrastructure or are they part of a smaller firm? Does that matter? As you know, there are so many questions around this, and each fund will view the answers to those questions differently.
Jason Scharfman:	In my experience part of the weight given to the decision depends of course on the manager, and it also depends on how vocal the fund's investors are on the issue. An up and running manager may not revisit the issue until they get a very large or smaller vocal investor who expresses an opinion or concerns about the issue. Particularly, if an established fund has had directors for a long time and investors start asking questions about the directors. Or alternatively, if an existing manager is launching a new fund, they may view it as an opportunity to have a fresh person in the director role.

Ingrid Pierce:	Right, we've also had clients, and this happens a fair bit with new managers, where they have a seed investor or a large founding investor who will ask about the identity of proposed service providers, including the directors. This investor may indicate to the manager that they have a list of suggested providers or individuals who may or may not be acceptable. That is not the norm, but it does happen with increasing regularity and that's great; it makes the manager's life a lot easier.
Jason Scharfman:	Exactly, they know who their investors like. Another issue that I've seen certain investors focus on is the role of the board of the master fund in master–feeder complexes. Where the master board can effectively trump, in some cases, the offshore board. As you know, the master board has traditionally received a lot less scrutiny from investors, and has historically consisted of a single individual such as the Chief Investment Officer or lead Portfolio Manager of the hedge fund. I'm curious how you view that sort of relationship from a structuring perspective these days. At Corgentum Consulting, we've seen certain investors not only focus more on identifying who is on that board but also, in much more limited cases, attempt to diversify the master board. Are you seeing people trying to diversify the master board or raise concerns around this issue?
Ingrid Pierce:	Yes, that's consistent with what we've seen. I would make just a couple of points to make on this issue. The first is that for Cayman-registered feeder funds, the master funds now have to be registered with CIMA, so master funds are also regulated. Where we have a corporate master–feeder, in the overwhelming majority of those cases the master fund will have the same board as the feeder fund. So if there are independent directors on the feeder fund, they will also be on the master fund. Where there is a difference is if the master fund is an exempted limited partnership and, therefore, its general partner may be an entity that is affiliated with the investment manager. That's where there may be no (or limited) independent oversight of the master fund board.
Jason Scharfman:	A common arrangement like this we come across is where you have a Delaware general partner.
Ingrid Pierce:	Yes, exactly. So I think it's important to make the distinction because it is not all master funds that fall into this bucket. That being said, we have definitely seen questions from certain large institutional investors about the level of oversight of a master fund. We have seen a few cases where an independent, and I'm going to call it "board" in the loose sense because it's not really a board, oversight committee or advisory board will be brought in at the master fund level to assist with some independent oversight.
Jason Scharfman:	And in those cases, and I understand it's a smaller majority, are you seeing a matching to the offshore board or is it just a different group of people?

(Continued)

Ingrid Pierce:	It depends. Where it is a matching of the offshore board, we have seen the independent directors on the offshore board feeder being placed on the advisory board of the master fund. We've also seen a case where one major institutional client put an advisory board in place across all of its funds. This board is composed of highly experienced, independent experts in the industry from around the globe. I would caution against making a generalized statement about whether that is an effective mechanism of introducing oversight because it clearly depends on the parameters, the scope of that board's authority, and whether or not they have an ability to veto particular matters. They may simply have power to resolve conflicts like a typical advisory board, or they may have the power to deal with liquidity issues and suspensions. The latter is very powerful, but that is not always the case.
Jason Scharfman:	What are your thoughts on the changing regulatory environment in the Caymans as it relates to directors? How do you view fund counsel's role as changing going forward? Also, what impact do you feel the new Cayman licensing requirements will have?
Ingrid Pierce:	I actually think the new licensing requirements are a good thing. If you really drill down to the essence of what this is all about, it's making sure that the regulator has more information about the operators of a regulated entity. Of course, they should have that information. I really can't see why it would be considered to be controversial. The only issue for those who are required to register is that they have another step to take; they have more ongoing compliance and they have more annual reporting. So it just adds to the ever increasing list of regulatory compliance requirements.
Jason Scharfman:	One of the arguments against the director licensing requirements is that this is simply the first step on a slippery slope, whereby Cayman regulators will use this as an entry point in moving toward further oversight of directors. Certain directors, particularly smaller directorship firms, have expressed concerns to me that this will lead to realization of controversial director database proposals detailing to the public, for example, how many boards different directors sit on. What are your thoughts on this?
Ingrid Pierce:	CIMA is clearly contemplating whether to have a publicly available database of information. What's also clear from the law is that they will have the ability to examine the capacity of any director who sits on a regulated entity, and to determine whether or not the director has sufficient capacity to carry out their duties as a director. That part of the law is not yet in force, but it is included in the law and so it seems to me that some level of regulation about those provisions will be forthcoming.

Jason Scharfman:	Following up on the issue of capacity, in its recent corporate governance survey CIMA seemed to be looking for guidance from the market with regards to how many directorships were appropriate. The survey data suggested a potential disconnect between what numbers of directorships investors, managers, and directors thought appropriate. It seems based on the new regulations, both enacted and those contemplated, that CIMA has settled around 20 directorships as being the level above which more or less scrutiny by the regulator may be applied. What do you think about the issue of director capacity?
Ingrid Pierce:	It's a perennial question about whether an individual's capacity to do his or her job is something that can be objectively determined or if it's a subjective question and I suppose it's both. So much depends on the nature and requirement of each fund. But, of course, when you get to a certain level, it becomes harder to say, "Of course I can do 95 identical jobs at the same time."
Jason Scharfman:	Exactly; yes when you talk to some directorships firms, they argue they can handle more capacity than others through more efficient procedures, enhanced use of technology, increased integration with legal counsel, etc. Outside of certain extreme levels, depending on who you talk to, specific numbers relating to director capacity can be a subjective question. One of the other questions I wanted to ask you was that outside of the Caymans and particularly in Europe, the regulatory oversight of directors and reporting requirements can differ. Some have suggested that other jurisdictions may provide enhanced director oversight and that managers may switch jurisdictions related to the perception of this enhanced oversight. Additionally, some have pointed to the practical marketing implications some jurisdictions may offer related to recent AIFMD considerations of offering funds in Europe. What trends have you seen in this area?
Ingrid Pierce:	We haven't seen a significant number of managers redomiciling. We have seen some of our clients setting up European funds precisely because they want to be able to offer into Europe through a European fund, and they don't want to have to re-register their Cayman product. So we've seen some of that. All Cayman-regulated funds have to file audited financial statements and if you are a licensed director under the new CIMA regime, then you have to provide a lot of background information when you complete a personal questionnaire. There is a fit and proper test for anyone who is licensed by CIMA. So I think CIMA is doing perfectly well, and that the Cayman product, for what it offers to the market that it caters to, has a good balance of regulation and investor protection coupled with the freedom to set up and make private offerings.

(Continued)

Jason Scharfman:	Finally, what other trends or challenges do you see in fund governance going forward?
Ingrid Pierce:	I think there are going to be even more challenges for new start-ups not just to launch but also to maintain their existence given the number of regulatory requirements, the cost of procuring the right level of advice, and the general cost of doing business. All of this makes the barriers to entry higher and higher. In the final analysis, the costs have to be borne by someone, so it becomes more costly for the investment manager and for the investors too.
Jason Scharfman:	This has been a very interesting discussion. I think your comments highlight the often overlooked role played by fund counsel in the governance process and in supporting the work of directors. Many investors would likely stand to benefit not only by speaking to fund managers and directors but also by taking more time to speak to fund counsel during the preinvestment and ongoing due diligence processes for further insights on governance. Thank you very much for your time.
Ingrid Pierce:	My pleasure, thank you.

INTERVIEW WITH PROFESSOR JOE BANNISTER AND DR. CHRIS BUTTIGIEG OF THE MALTA FINANCIAL SERVICES AUTHORITY

Due to the continued popularity of the Cayman Islands as a jurisdiction for offshore hedge funds, I have taken care throughout this book to highlight particular governance considerations for the Caymans including the recent role of the CIMA in governance oversight, and specific guidance and laws effecting Cayman directors.

It would be a mistake, however, to approach the subject of hedge fund governance with a singular focus on the Caymans. Around the globe in many of the major financial centers where hedge funds are popular, there are requirements for boards of directors to be present as well. One of these offshore jurisdictions that have grown in popularity in recent years is Malta. To gain some perspective on Malta's approach to governance and the role of Maltese directors, I was afforded with the opportunity to interview two key professionals from the MFSA. Professor Joe Bannister is the Chairman of the MFSA, and Dr. Chris Buttigieg is the Deputy Director within the Securities and Markets Supervision Unit of the MFSA.

Jason Scharfman:	Can you please provide some perspective as to why in your opinion Malta has become an attractive destination for hedge fund managers? What role has the MFSA played in this increased popularity?

Professor Bannister and Dr. Buttigieg:	Malta's development as a jurisdiction of choice for international financial services is the result of 20 years of diligent work and focus by the financial industry. This was triggered by government policy in the early 1990s to develop Malta into a financial services center. The MFSA is one of the key contributors to Malta's success in this field. The MFSA's approach to regulation and supervision focuses on achieving investor interests and ensuring the stability of the financial system, while applying a certain degree of flexibility to allow the financial operators to continue developing their business. These are in our view the key factors that have made Malta an attractive jurisdiction for fund managers. Since the financial crisis, investors have become more interested in the level of regulation in the jurisdiction where a fund is domiciled. The regulation in Malta provides for the necessary transparency requirements even at the level of the fund to ensure that investors are fully informed of the activity undertaken by the fund manager. Moreover, Malta's legislative framework implements the European Union directives and regulations that, in the aftermath of the financial crisis, have been reformed to ensure a higher degree of investor protection and systemic stability. The European dimension is a key factor that has made Malta a jurisdiction of choice for fund managers who wish to operate at a European-wide level.
Jason Scharfman:	On a related note, why do you feel that some hedge funds from other traditional offshore non-EU jurisdictions such as the Cayman Islands, British Virgin Islands, and Switzerland have transitioned to Malta? Similarly, do you feel that AIFMD will ultimately serve to promote Malta over other non-EU jurisdiction?
Professor Bannister and Dr. Buttigieg:	The adoption of a European framework for the regulation of alternative fund managers was necessary to strengthen investor confidence in the financial system and the fund industry. We were fully supportive of the reform to the European regulatory and supervisory framework post the financial crisis as we knew that this would have Europe better placed as a financial region. Nonetheless, we were, and still are, concerned about certain European approach to regulation that may result in over-regulation, which completely disregards the principle of proportionality. Proportionality is a fundamental principle of the European treaties, which require that regulation and supervision must be limited to what is necessary to achieve the objectives of regulation. The redomiciliation of hedge funds from traditional offshore non-EU jurisdictions to Malta has arisen primarily on the back of the EU passport that will allow cross-border marketing of funds. Furthermore, the new regulatory framework that emerged from the financial crisis, including the AIFMD, has strengthened the investor protection and financial stability framework in Malta. As a consequence, Malta has become a more serious contender for international financial business. This has attracted significant business from serious players in the market. However, it has also put off players who are not willing to update their policies and procedures to come in line with the more robust regulatory requirements applicable in terms of the directive. Some of these players have decided to move their operations to off-shore jurisdictions.

(Continued)

Jason Scharfman:	Can you comment on the greater popularity of the Professional Investor Funds ("PIF") structures among Maltese funds as opposed to UCITS funds? From a regulatory perspective, is one structure subject to more or less oversight?
Professor Bannister and Dr. Buttigieg:	Both retail (UCITS) and PIF are subject to rigorous oversight by the MFSA to ensure that they are carrying out their business activity in line with regulatory requirements. The extent of regulation and oversight is, however, different given the unique features of these types of funds. Retail funds are subject to more detailed ongoing investor protection obligations such as the imposition of strict investment restrictions and eligible assets. On the other hand, the regulation of PIF focuses on inter alia transparency with investors and does not make specific restrictions on the investment of the portfolio of the fund. The supervision of both types of funds is conducted through on-site and off-site supervision of the fund and the service providers. The intensity of supervision is, however, much more substantial in the case of retail funds.
Jason Scharfman:	Malta seems to have been ahead of its time in embracing the promotion of fund oversight and transparency both ahead of joining the EU and before the passage of AIFMD. Can you comment on what role the MFSA has played in promoting this fund scrutiny and oversight?
Professor Bannister and Dr. Buttigieg:	The policy on Malta's financial center has always been that all operators established in Malta should be subject to the licensing requirement and that on an ongoing basis they should be subject to appropriate governance, prudential, conduct of business, and transparency requirements. The Authority has since 2002 been vested with the role of ensuring that government policy in this area is achieved in the most efficient and effective way possible. This also applies to the fund's business. In this regard, Malta applies a policy that a fund should not be allowed to operate in Malta unless it has obtained the required authorization and is subject to adequate supervision.
Jason Scharfman:	How does the MFSA view its role in promoting and overseeing governance at the fund level?
Professor Bannister and Dr. Buttigieg:	Robust governance structures are fundamental for the proper conduct of business of a licensed entity. We have over the years been putting more focus on governance to ensure that funds are run properly. Last year we issued a handbook on corporate governance for directors of investment companies and collective investment schemes. The MFSA considers the role of directors to be vital for the proper operation of an investment fund. The manual has the purpose of guiding directors in the fulfillment of their duties. MFSA also monitors compliance with the governance requirements. This is being carried out through on-site inspections at the offices of licensed entities. These visits focus on governance, compliance, and risk management. During these visits the MFSA supervisors obtain a good understanding on how licensed entities operate and identify the entity's main governance weaknesses. Recommendations on how to address these weaknesses are made to licensed entities after the inspection.

Jason Scharfman:	How does the MFSA view the role of Maltese-based service providers such as law firms, custodians, and auditors in promoting fund governance?
Professor Bannister and Dr. Buttigieg:	The custodian and the auditors fulfill a *quasi*-supervisory role. The custodian monitors the activity of the manager to verify that the asset management of the fund is being undertaken in terms of law, the constitutional documents of the fund, and in the best interest of investors. Auditors have the role of verifying that the financial statements of the fund give a true and fair view. As part of their checks, the auditors also prepare a management letter that has the purpose of identifying the weaknesses in the controls of the fund including the entity's governance structures. The custodian and the auditors discuss their findings with the directors and also make recommendations for the strengthening of the overall governance of the scheme. In our view the *quasi*-supervisory role of custodians and auditors is fundamental for promoting the sound governance of investment schemes established in Malta. Law firms in Malta have a very active role in preparing the structure and setup of funds that apply for authorization and therefore have an important role in promoting fund governance during the time when the fund is being established. In particular, by ensuring that the fund has proper technical and competent directors and senior officers on board and that adequate governance procedures have been put in place. A number of law firms also provide compliance and adviser services to collective investment schemes and this helps in promoting sound fund governance.
Jason Scharfman:	How has the MFSA worked with the hedge fund industry to promote better governance practices?
Professor Bannister and Dr. Buttigieg:	Issues relating to governance are raised both at application stage and on an ongoing basis. In this connection, the MFSA maintains ongoing contact with licensed entities and through its monitoring processes it has managed to identify issues in the governance of funds. These have been addressed in the MFSA corporate governance manual for directors of investment companies and collective investment schemes. However, the monitoring of governance arrangements is an ongoing process and in this regard the MFSA is keeping an open eye to developments in the industry, and how these may have an impact on the overall corporate governance of licensed entities. From time to time our monitoring may suggest that further guidance is required. In such instances the MFSA may decide to publish circulars providing additional guidance to the industry.
Jason Scharfman:	Can you provide background on why Maltese funds need hedge fund directors from both a technical and a practical perspective?

(Continued)

Professor Bannister and Dr. Buttigieg:	The *raison d'être* for requiring persons who are technically competent and practical on boards is that of ensuring that the board has the required skills to carry out its functions effectively. In Malta an entity that is applying for a collective investment scheme license is subject to the "fit and proper" test. This test aims at ensuring that the company is managed by persons who are honest, competent, and solvent and that ab initio and on an ongoing basis the fund's business is conducted professionally and in the best interest of the fund and the investors. It also seeks to ensure that a proper compliance culture is maintained. All these factors put together are essential to achieve adequate fund governance.
Jason Scharfman:	The Companies Act of Malta (e.g., Article 136A of Chapter 386) outlines that "A director of a company shall be bound to act honest and in good faith in the best interest of the company." This implies that directors owe a primary duty to the funds that hire them and not shareholders (even if appointed by them). How should investors think of the role of the MFSA in helping them to mitigate potential conflicts surrounding these director duties?
Professor Bannister and Dr. Buttigieg:	The directors owe a primary duty to act in the best interests of the fund that is tantamount to the best interest of investors. The conflict of interest may however arise when special arrangements are entered into with specific shareholders through side letters, as the best interest of such shareholders may conflict with the other shareholders. However, to address this specific conflict the regulatory framework requires that the content of side letters should be disclosed to other investors so that the investors are aware that they may be subject to a different treatment.
Jason Scharfman:	What measures does the MFSA take to police further duties of a director as outlined under Article 136A such as the prohibitions in directors engaging in self-dealing, no conflicts (Article 143)? For example, how would the MFSA know if a director was engaged in self-dealing? Is detecting these types of situations proactively the primary role of the MFSA or shareholders in funds?
Professor Bannister and Dr. Buttigieg:	The director owes a standard of care to the company in line with bonus pater familias and they would not be expected to take any action that would be harmful to the company and its shareholders. That said, MFSA rules and guidance cater for conflicts of interests and how these should be managed. The rules contain extensive provisions to ensure that the interests of investors are duly safeguarded.
Jason Scharfman:	Other jurisdictions such as the Cayman Islands have recently proposed creating a database that discloses more detail regarding fund directors including the number of different boards they serve on. What is the MFSA's perspective on these types of disclosures? Does the MFSA feel the number of directors should be subject to hard capacity limits?

Professor Bannister and Dr. Buttigieg:	Malta applies a full transparency policy with regards to the activity of locally registered companies. In this regard, all information on company directorships is readily available online from the database of the Registry of Companies. This includes information on the directors who serve on the board of licensed collective investment schemes. In approving a director, the MFSA takes into account the applicants' existing directorships. In particular, we need to be satisfied that the applicant has sufficient time to fulfill their responsibilities.
Jason Scharfman:	How does the MFSA feel it empowers investors with the transparency and information to conduct their own due diligence on funds managers and directors? Do you feel that investors should rely on the oversight of the MFSA prior to investing, or instead be more hands with hedge funds to complement the oversight of the MFSA?
Professor Bannister and Dr. Buttigieg:	The regulatory framework in Malta requires transparency with investors through the offering memorandum, the annual financial statements that must be provided to investors, and the obligation to notify investors, and in certain instances also obtain their consent, for any major changes to the governance structure of the fund. The financial crisis has demonstrated the importance of investor activism. The MFSA has always encouraged professional investors to minimize reliance and be active in the monitoring of the activity of the funds with which they have placed their assets. This is consistent with the message of the European institutions that have adopted regulation that aims at reducing reliance, particularly on credit rating agencies, and that require institutional investors to be more active in the risk management of their portfolio.
Jason Scharfman:	The US SEC and the UK FCA in recent years have taken an active interest in policing hedge fund securities laws violations in areas including insider trading, conflicts of interest, and information security. How has the MFSA approached these issues? Are there any issues that the MFSA views as being particular enforcement or oversight priorities going forward?
Professor Bannister and Dr. Buttigieg:	Enforcement action may result from the Authority's monitoring of licensed entities. However, every regulator has its own supervisory priorities depending on the risks to financial market integrity and investor protection, which are identified in the particular jurisdiction. In recent years the MFSA has focused on the application of leverage restrictions by managers of property funds and product misselling of professional financial products to retail investors. The Authority took regulatory action against licensed entities, including fund managers and custodians of collective investment schemes, for breaches of regulatory requirements relating to conduct of business. In line with the Authority policy on transparency with the market, the enforcement action taken by the MFSA is made public on the MFSA website http://www.mfsa.com.mt/pages/AdministrativeMeasuresPenalties.aspx. The industry is therefore aware that we are keeping an eye on the manner in which they operate and our appetite for enforcement action. In this regard, the main operators are constantly developing their compliance functions and procedures in order not to be found lacking.

(Continued)

Jason Scharfman:	Do you feel that enhanced regulations throughout the EU such as AIFMD have assisted in promoting better governance at the hedge fund level or have simply placed additional compliance burdens on funds? Why or why not?
Professor Bannister and Dr. Buttigieg:	The introduction of the AIFMD was important to strengthen market confidence in the alternative investment fund industry. The directive regulates the governance structure of the funds through requirements such as the appointment of a depositary to safekeep the assets of the fund and to monitor the manager. Moreover, the AIFMD also seeks to ensure that the fund is managed in a way that is in the best interest of investors.
	There are, however, instances where in our view the requirements in the directive have gone beyond what is necessary to achieve the investor protection and systemic stability objectives of regulation. For example, the fund is required to appoint a depositary established in the same member state of the fund. The jurisdictional restriction on depositary business limits the jurisdictional choice for promoters of investor funds, restricts the choice of depositaries, and lessens the competition within the depositary industry. Moreover, the requirement goes against the internal market objectives set in the treaty and the directive.
	As a result of AIFMD and UCITS V there is significant harmonization of depositary services. It is therefore incorrect and unreasonable that a depositary passport has not been provided for in the directive. In the EU, harmonization is not implemented for harmonization's sake but for the purpose of allowing an internal market to be established and operate properly. This has not been the case for depositaries where extensive harmonization has been applied without the benefit of a passport. It is surprising that the jurisdictional restriction on depositaries has never been challenged at the level of the European Courts.
Jason Scharfman:	There have been some historical criticisms that Malta did not have sufficient personnel with experience in providing operations support or regulatory oversight of more complex hedge fund strategies. How has this situation changed over time? Has the MFSA increased the expertise of its personnel or resources over time?
Professor Bannister and Dr. Buttigieg:	In a dynamic and growing financial center human resources will always be an issue. The MFSA together with the University of Malta is however contributing to the process that will strengthen the technical expertise and resources in this field. The Authority has an educational program in place to attract young scholars to the financial industry. Moreover, the University of Malta has reinforced its courses in fields that are relevant to financial services. Over 400 students graduate each year in a discipline that is relevant to this field of business. Most of these students also get further training overseas.

	The MFSA continuously increases its staff complement. Moreover, we are constantly providing staff with training opportunities in Malta and abroad. We also have a substantial budget for staff wanting to pursue further studies. Furthermore, there are various institutes in Malta that provide specialized training in fields relating to finance, including the MFSA's training arm, the Malta International Training Centre (MITC). The MITC provides various courses, including at diploma level, in specialized fields such as governance, compliance, and risk management.
Jason Scharfman:	The MFSA has promoted itself as conducting extensive due diligence before granting licenses to funds. Can you provide an overview of this process? What ongoing due diligence is performed? Can you provide examples of situations in which licenses have been denied?
Professor Bannister and Dr. Buttigieg:	The MFSA may grant a license to operate as a financial service provider only if it is satisfied that an applicant will be in a position to comply with regulation. In this regard, as already mentioned, the Authority is required to apply the "fit and proper" test that an applicant who is granted a license must continue to satisfy on an ongoing basis. To assess compliance with the fit and proper test, the MFSA requires persons to complete a personal questionnaire form containing relevant details about the person's knowledge and experience in the relevant investment field and their post conduct of business. The information is verified through various enquiries with relevant parties to ensure that the proposed directors and officers are fit and proper persons to carry out the functions required of them. Furthermore, in the case of a collective investment scheme, the Authority would also undertake due diligence checks on the proposed service providers. The MFSA reserves the right to refuse a license if a party involved with the proposed applicant is deemed not to be fit and proper.
Jason Scharfman:	Similarly, Malta requires background checks on fund owners and directors. Other jurisdictions do not have these requirements. What do the background checks cover, and why does the MFSA feel these are important?
Professor Bannister and Dr. Buttigieg:	The MFSA carries out extensive due diligence checks on the proposed officials of a collective investment scheme to ensure that only honest, competent, and solvent persons have access to Malta's financial center. To verify the competence and solvency of the proposed individual, background checks are carried out with inter alia past employers and bankers. A police conduct certificate is normally also required in order to verify the person's integrity. The process aims at weeding out the bad apples in the market, thereby ensuring proper market integrity. This process has made Malta an even more attractive jurisdiction of choice for international financial services, as diligent promoters take jurisdictional reputation very seriously.

(Continued)

Jason Scharfman:	The MFSA requires that funds produce audited annual financial statements. What oversight or analysis does the MFSA perform on these statements?
Professor Bannister and Dr. Buttigieg:	The analysis of the financial statements of a collective investment scheme is conducted in order to allow the MFSA to understand the manner in which the activity of the scheme is being carried out. The extent of our review depends on a risk-based approach adopted by the Authority. A high degree of attention is made on the review of documentation submitted by retail schemes.
Jason Scharfman:	On a related note, the MFSA has a reputation as being an approachable regulator that offers a relative fast time to market for licensing in Europe. How does the MFSA balance this desire to be helpful and expedite licensing with the goals of rigorous fund manager due diligence and oversight?
Professor Bannister and Dr. Buttigieg:	Being approachable and efficient is not synonymous with inaction when this is required. As indicated in other sections of this interview, the MFSA has a thorough due diligence process in place. Moreover, we monitor on a continuous basis the activity of financial entities licensed in Malta. We also take enforcement action when this is necessary.
Jason Scharfman:	What impact, if any, have cases such as Weavering case and the AIJ fraud in the Cayman Islands had on the way the MFSA approaches notion of director oversight and liability?
Professor Bannister and Dr. Buttigieg:	The Weavering case was one of the triggers for the development of guidance on corporate governance for directors of investment companies and collective investment schemes issued by the Authority last year. The MFSA has always taken a serious approach to director oversight. The guidance codifies what the MFSA expects from directors of collective investment schemes, which is normally tested during on-site inspections. With regards to standards of liability, this is a test for the Courts to assess and to determine the level of liability as set out by law.

Clarification of Terms Used in This Interview

For those unfamiliar with some of the legal terminology used in this interview, it may be helpful to review the following clarifications:

- Ab initio is Latin for "from the beginning" (*Black's Law Dictionary*, 2004). The term is often used in legal discussions and for the purposes of interpreting the comments in this interview for those without a legal background, the term ab initio is used to outline that one of the purposes of fund directors in Malta is to provide the above-referenced oversight both initially (i.e., ab initio) and on an ongoing basis.

- Bonus pater familias is Latin for "good family father" (*Black's Law Dictionary*, 2004). The term has roots in Roman law and is commonly used under British law to effectively convey the equivalent of a normal, prudent man standard of care (Faure, 2003). Sometimes an associated term diligens paterfamilias is also utilized to refer to a "careful head of a family" (Adolf, 1953). For the purposes of clarifying the interview comments for those without a legal background, the term bonus pater familias is used to outline that directors are effectively held to a standard of that of how a prudent person, or in this case director, would be expected to act. When it comes, for example, to a court analyzing the activities of the directors, when, for example, litigation ensues, this standard along with a host of other factors likely including fund indemnification provisions, among other considerations, would be typically employed.

INTERVIEW WITH ADAM COHEN OF PERELLA WEINBERG PARTNERS

To gain further perspective on how hedge fund allocators and ODD professionals in particular view the topic of governance, I decided to call upon another leading ODD practitioner, Adam Cohen.

Adam Cohen serves as Head of Operational Due Diligence for Perella Weinberg Partner's Agility platform, a provider of outsourced investment solutions. Perella Weinberg Partners is a leading independent, financial services firm that provides advisory and asset management services to a broad, global client base.

The Agility platform was created to provide outsourced investment solutions for clients. Serving as a client's Outsourced Investment Team, Agility offers customized investment programs that meet clients' individual needs. The Agility Team has extensive experience and executes a disciplined due diligence process to identify and invest with top managers across asset classes. Agility was named "2014 Outsourced CIO of the Year" by *Institutional Investor*, a leading financial publication.

Jason Scharfman:	In the hedge fund space, governance is becoming an increasingly broad topic. As an ODD professional how do you think about governance at hedge funds?
Adam Cohen:	Corporate governance could be viewed as a theme that runs across multiple areas of an ODD review. Therefore, taking a broad view of governance is likely prudent. The hedge fund industry does not appear to have reached the point where, from an ODD perspective, one can currently confine one's assessment of governance to matters pertaining only to a fund's board of directors.

(Continued)

	While examining the composition, qualifications, and responsibilities of a board can certainly yield information useful to ODD analysis, some funds—particularly onshore funds in the United States—are unlikely to have boards of directors at present.
	Additionally, some argue that, for those funds with boards, there are limitations to independent directors' authority, and that a lack of physical proximity to the fund's operations (particularly in the case of directors residing offshore) can be detrimental to their level of knowledge of a manager and a fund's operations. Furthermore, there are others who believe that independent directors' level of knowledge of a manager and its fund's operations can vary with the number of directorships held by a director.
	In addition to a fund's board of directors, I therefore think about governance in the context of the investment manager's internal systems, policies, and procedures relating to its operational and compliance infrastructure. In assessing these areas, it is important to examine the investment manager's human resources to ascertain how effectively it can implement and maintain the firm's policies and procedures.
	Over the past few years, we have seen significant growth in the use of third-party compliance consulting firms in the alternative investment industry. Some hedge fund managers retain these consulting firms to not only assist with the development, maintenance, and monitoring of compliance policies and procedures but also conduct "mock audits," which help assess the manager's readiness for an SEC review.
	Given the growth in this area, developing knowledge of these consulting firms and the services that they offer to managers is worthwhile. Some may argue that the refinement that has taken place in some of these consultants' service offerings over the years is beneficial from an overall governance perspective to the managers who retain them.
Jason Scharfman:	On a related note, it seems in recent years the task of evaluating fund governance has fallen to the ODD function (as opposed to the investment due diligence function). Why do you think this is so?
Adam Cohen:	Evaluating fund governance appears to be evolving to become the responsibility of the ODD function as, over time, governance has broadened into matters that have traditionally been a part of the ODD review. This is particularly true in the area of investment manager and fund internal compliance infrastructure. Additionally, many ODD professionals have prior firsthand experience in areas that may aid the evaluation of governance, including hedge fund operations and administration, and leveraging this experience in the overall due diligence process could be beneficial.
Jason Scharfman:	How do you feel governance at hedge funds differs from other alternative asset classes such as private equity? Do you feel one group gets more leeway from investors in this regard?

Adam Cohen:	Using a broad definition of governance, one could make the argument that the hedge fund industry has historically been ahead of private equity in some respects. A contributing factor to this argument would be that a higher number of hedge fund managers voluntarily registered as investment advisers with the SEC in the years prior to 2012, when SEC registration became mandatory for many hedge fund and private equity investment managers. SEC registration has arguably contributed toward managers formalizing certain aspects of their firm's operations, particularly in the area of compliance. However, an argument could also be made that the widespread use of advisory boards in the private equity industry has positively impacted private equity fund governance. Advisory boards generally consist of representatives from a fund's limited partner, and convene on an annual or more frequent basis. While the scope and degree of advisory boards' responsibilities vary in accordance with a fund's organizational documents, it is not uncommon for matters relating to conflicts of interest and valuation of the fund's portfolio to require referral to the advisory board. However, not all private equity funds have advisory boards, and some may argue that the advisory board's role is limited in the overall scope of a fund's governance. Over the past few years, a trend has emerged where investors seem to be intensifying their ODD efforts with respect to private equity. If this continues, we may see governance in the private equity industry receiving more attention from investors than it has historically.
Jason Scharfman:	Do you think ODD groups in general are doing an acceptable job of evaluating governance? Do you feel the investment analysts should play more of an active role in this regard?
Adam Cohen:	For reasons already mentioned, it makes sense that ODD analysts are more involved in assessing governance than investment analysts. However, I also believe that there is room for improvement in ODD assessments related to certain areas of governance, most notably the board of directors. Given the wide range of topics that an ODD review can encompass, including the role that ODD typically plays in examining a number of fund counterparties (such as prime brokers, administrators, and auditors), and that not all funds will have boards of directors, it is not surprising that this area has not received more ODD scrutiny in the past.
Jason Scharfman:	Turning to the board of directors, can you provide an overview of what due diligence you feel investors ought to be doing on directors?
Adam Cohen:	For those funds with a board of directors, a basic starting point for conducting ODD could be to identify the fund's directors and their responsibilities, determine the composition of the board of directors, and examine directors whose names appear most frequently in one's manager coverage universe.

(Continued)

	I have generally found that independent directors, and the firms for which they work, will provide information about their background and services, on request. Several may have prepared written materials that they are willing to share, and may be willing to make themselves available for phone or in-person meetings. Additionally, there has been a healthy debate on a number of issues relating to fund directors in various industry forums over the past few years. Several of these debates remain unresolved, and I therefore think that investors and ODD professionals should make an effort to remain abreast of developments in these debates, as they will inform best practices going forward.
Jason Scharfman:	One of the things ODD professionals are typically tasked with evaluating is fund fees. What are your thoughts on directorship fees?
Adam Cohen:	Investors express a range of opinions on this point. Investors more focused on cost control by the fund may want to see fewer directors, at a lower cost, particularly if their view is that the board of directors' role is not as important in overall fund governance as that of other components of the fund's governance infrastructure. Other investors, particularly those who feel that the fund's board is an important component of governance and that some independent directors may currently be overburdened by having taken on too many directorships, have taken a philosophical view that directors' fees should increase on a relative basis over time. These investors feel that this would enable independent directors to take on fewer directorships and therefore devote more time to their directorship duties on a per fund basis.
Jason Scharfman:	Do you think that there should be a database where offshore jurisdictions should force directors to disclose their board memberships to investors? Why or why not?
Adam Cohen:	There are two sides to this argument, and I think it remains to be seen which side ultimately prevails. There are some, largely among the ODD community, who see this as a positive development. Others, largely from the offshore directorship community, are not in favor of public disclosure as hedge funds are private investment vehicles. While a publicly accessible database of this sort would probably provide additional insight to investors, particularly as to the number of funds for which an individual acts as director, in recent years efforts have been made to develop this information from existing sources, including Form ADV filings. It is important to note that investors can ask directors for the number of boards on which they serve, which directors may be willing to provide.
Jason Scharfman:	We've covered some interesting topics related to the expanded focus on governance in the hedge fund space and the key role ODD plays in this effort. It's always interesting to hear perspective from people with practical, on-the-ground experience keeping their eyes on hedge funds in this area.
Adam Cohen:	My pleasure, happy to discuss. As I've outlined it definitely appears to be an area that more investors and ODD professionals are focusing on.

INTERVIEW WITH LOUIS RODRIGUEZ (OPERATIONAL DUE DILIGENCE PROFESSIONAL)

From the investors' perspective all too often the roles of fund directors are commonly viewed as being more operational in nature as opposed to investment related. That being said of course it depends on the circumstance of the particular issues directors are tasked with evaluating. For example, in regards to the director's review of a fund manager's valuations of positions, some investors may argue that this has a lot more to do with the investment side of a hedge fund's house than its operational side.

Putting these types of issues aside, and of course there is room for debate on both sides of the issue, most investors generally agree that the actual nuts and bolts of directors' common duties are rooted in more of an operational context as opposed to a purely investment one. We can make this statement with some confidence perhaps, because the task of evaluating the directorship function typically falls not to investment analysts, but to an investor's ODD functions.

To gain some perspective on the role ODD plays in evaluating directors I thought it would be interesting for readers to conduct an interview with an ODD industry veteran, Louis Rodriguez. Mr. Rodriguez currently serves as Head of Operational Due Diligence for a multibillion dollar alternative asset manager based in New York. He has 20 years of experience in the financial industry, half of that dedicated to performing ODD on hundreds of hedge funds globally.

Jason Scharfman:	From an ODD perspective, how do you define fund governance? Do you feel that governance can simply be equated to the board of directors or instead does it involve anything else such as fund controls and best practices?
Louis Rodriguez:	I view governance holistically. "Fund" governance may be just that, the fiduciary and governance responsibilities of certain individuals assigned as directors. However, the concept of "governance" to me is much broader. It encompasses fund governance as well as a manager's concept and implementation of best practices. Along with this is a desire on behalf of the manager to have a keen interest in third-party oversight, and that can be by a board of directors, advisory panel, extended service provider involvement, third-party certifications (SSAE 16, operational certifications), etc. When I conduct ODD, we are looking to see whether a manager approaches, and can demonstrate, governance from this holistic perspective and implement best practices or instead just ineffectively "outsource" governance to directors.
Jason Scharfman:	What is your perspective on the role and responsibilities of fund directors?

(Continued)

Louis Rodriguez:	The board of directors should make sure that the fund manager's fiduciary responsibility to its investors prevails above all else. The fund board is intended to provide an independent level of oversight of the manager, and to ensure that policies and procedures and appropriate management are taking place. Although the board is retained by the manager, they are paid by the fund. They should keep the best interest of the fund investors in mind always. As an investor I view the director's role should be to challenge a manager and question things that may not make sense or seem appropriate.
Jason Scharfman:	On a related note, when you conduct ODD on hedge funds, what are the elements of fund governance that you feel hedge funds in general are poor at executing?
Louis Rodriguez:	I believe transparency is one area that is still poor. Managers are often not overly communicative about the role and responsibilities of a fund board. While there has been some level of improvement over the years, I think most investment managers also do a poor job of using their board directors as a resource. Many directors have diverse and extensive levels of experience that can add tremendous value. The perception, at least somewhat, is that fund governance is a necessary evil.
Jason Scharfman:	That's a great point. In my ODD experience, I find some managers underutilize directors as well. Outside of the fund directors themselves, what role do you feel service providers such as administrators or auditors play in implementing good governance practices at funds?
Louis Rodriguez:	Yes, service providers other than directors, especially the administrator and auditor, also play key roles in the life of a fund. My sense is that over the last five to six years there has been much more communication and transparency between these other service providers and fund board members. Most boards have final sign-off on the audited financial statements. Many directors I have spoken with will contact the auditor with questions or comments. Additionally, more fund administrators are producing transparency and risk reports that are consumed by both directors and investors. By being available to a board of directors and producing more information and reporting, they are fostering good, independent governance.
Jason Scharfman:	Not just analyzing the role of the director themselves but also the interaction between directors and service provider is something that can get overlooked by investors during the ODD process, so that's a great point. As you know, conducting an ODD review is a document-intensive process. What governance lessons do you think investors can learn from the quality of a hedge fund's documentation?

Louis Rodriguez:	I believe that if a manager's documentation is well prepared, transparent, and comprehensive for investors, then they are probably taking the same approach with their fund directors. If a manager is serious about doing the right thing by investors, then odds are they take the concept of fund governance seriously as well. The more transparent a manager is (which can be ascertained by the quality of documents), the more likely they take governance seriously and adhere to industry best practices.
Jason Scharfman:	Following up on that point, going beyond the documents what due diligence, if any, do you currently conduct on fund directors? Can you comment on what documentation investors can and should collect from directorship firms?
Louis Rodriguez:	Admittedly it has been difficult to arrive at a one-size-fits-all approach to performing due diligence on fund directors. What makes this difficult is that a board is most often composed of different, unrelated individuals who may reside in different geographic locations. It becomes difficult to reach out to these directors and triangulate or reconcile what the board does as a cohesive unit. I like to see an independent board with at least three members, with only one member having affiliation with the fund manager. I also like to see varying levels of experience in the industry. I do not want to see blood-related or married individuals. During the ODD process, I will ask to see board minutes during due diligence meetings. I will also question the directors in detail about their role, responsibilities, working arrangements, experience, and involvement in other board memberships. If the board works on behalf of a professional governance firm, it can also sometimes make it easier to perform additional due diligence as needed.
Jason Scharfman:	Ultimately, do you think hedge funds care about what their directors have to say?
Louis Rodriguez:	This is obviously a difficult question. I try to gage a manager's seriousness of the governance role when conducting an on-site interview. Some make it obvious that they care about governance, are transparent about it, and view their directors as a resource. Others have made it painfully clear, without actually saying so, that governance is a necessary burden that they do not take too seriously. It may be a 50/50 split. Some do care while others do not.
Jason Scharfman:	Yes, it's interesting to see how some managers still are resistant in this area. Often times hedge funds will promote directors to investors as providing independent oversight of funds. Do you feel directors can ultimately do much to protect the interests of investors? If so, what are your thoughts on the relatively limited interaction between investors and directors?

(Continued)

Louis Rodriguez:	I think it boils down to a matter of timing. If something is going wrong at a management firm, the directors may know about it before investors, but perhaps it is too late. I think there is little directors can do on a proactive, preemptive manner. Obviously this depends on the situation. However, directors still add value when something wrong does happen. The value may come when things are already in a bad state, but, nevertheless, the directors can do some of the following things that help the interest of investors: declare the management company incapable of managing assets, force an orderly wind down of the fund, restrict redemptions, ensure proper oversight by service providers, ensure proper valuation of investments, etc. Clearly this depends on the director's mandate and their willingness to enforce such actions. I highly doubt that directors are in a position to be proactive enough to detect fraud, determine if poor investment decisions are being made, etc. I am a strong proponent that directors should be proactive in another way. They should publish letters to investors describing what they have done and perhaps make attestations that, as far as they know, everything is going ok at the manager. Some managers have been more accommodating and have had directors meet with select investors for lunch meetings, etc. We should see more of this.
Jason Scharfman:	Some investors, and ODD professionals in particular, are very critical of the legitimacy of the role of board of directors of offshore funds. Do you think these criticisms are well founded?
Louis Rodriguez:	I think the criticism is well founded, to a degree, for the reasons I previously alluded to. There is a clear lack of consistency around the rules for board membership and responsibilities. The model for long-only mutual funds is somewhat clearer in this regard. Hedge fund governance is still up to the individual managers to decide how they wish to establish the mandate and what role the directors will play. There is an obvious conflict of interest here. Until the model is fixed, and perhaps that means determination and stipulation by regulators, governance will continue to remain weak in hedge funds.
Jason Scharfman:	If a hedge fund's offshore vehicle is not established in the Caymans, does that raise governance yellow or red flags from an ODD perspective?
Louis Rodriguez:	To a degree, yes. It is well known and understood that some jurisdictions, such as the Cayman Islands and Ireland, have better governance regimes than others. Luckily, it is rare to find uncommon jurisdictions being used by fund managers because it does raise red flags.
Jason Scharfman:	On a related note, what do you think of the new CIMA licensing requirements for directors? From an investor's perspective, some have argued that this is more of a marketing move by the Caymans than anything else while others feel it is a step toward more substantial oversight; what are your thoughts on this? Also, what impact do you think will change the directorship industry going forward? As an ODD person do you think these licensing requirements will ultimately give you better information to make decisions about directors or not?

Louis Rodriguez:	I really don't think this is a marketing move. I think CIMA is trying to make a genuine effort to improve fund governance, especially since they are a bastion of fund registration and governance. But there are still some gaps. Unfortunately the registration and licensing law does not provide for a qualifications requirement, but perhaps that is difficult to implement. And, not all three of the director types will be regulated by CIMA. Nevertheless, I think this is a step in the right direction, and will perhaps spur other jurisdictions to follow suit. Perhaps this could be the biggest impact. As an ODD professional, this new mandate will add some level of comfort. However, it still does not address what responsibilities these directors will have to investors. If we saw CIMA mandate a comprehensive list of expectations, requirements, and responsibilities, that would have gone a long way.
Jason Scharfman:	From an ODD perspective, how do you think about professional directorship firms versus independent freelance directors?
Louis Rodriguez:	I think professional directorship firms have gotten a bad rap lately. I think these firms do add value and most directors here have good backgrounds and reputations. The added advantage is that they probably sit on the boards of many funds; therefore, they have more perspective into the industry and what other managers are doing. Of course, there is the concern that they may sit on many boards, thereby diluting their value. However, I think this is also misunderstood. Freelance directors can also be good, but it depends on the individual. We should hope to see someone who is familiar with the industry and has the requisite background and experience. This is not always the case. At least at a professional firm you know they are hired with the proper credentials. Also, a professional firm has the firm and individual reputational risk at stake. This puts their skin more in the game.
Jason Scharfman:	Do you think that offshore jurisdictions should force directors to disclose their board memberships to investors? Why or why not?
Louis Rodriguez:	I think they should be disclosed. I don't see what the big secret is here. Obviously this would tell investors a great deal including: • How many boards they sit on • The types of funds (which would be telling about the experience they have across different strategies, etc.) • How much time it would take to handle the workload However, even more telling would be a requirement to disclose all of the fund boards that they have sat on in the past and no longer belong to! As an investor I am interested more in why did a director step down, or instead was he or she asked to leave? We never really know the reasons behind these actions. Also, how many board memberships has he/she declined, and why?

(Continued)

Jason Scharfman:	Do you think there is any value to conducting background investigations on fund directors?
Louis Rodriguez:	I think there is a value. However, it is a difficult and cost-prohibitive exercise. The value is that you are essentially checking on the decision-making capability of the manager to retain qualified board members. Although the chance is remote, there is a possibility that these directors may one day determine the status and condition of your investment. The more due diligence you can perform, the better. However, given the cost involved, among other things, there is a clear cost–benefit analysis that must be decided upon by investors. This is clearly a difficult one.
Jason Scharfman:	How can you tell if a director is qualified to perform their job?
Louis Rodriguez:	Unfortunately many ODD professionals still do not run background checks and rely on the biography or CV of the director and what a manager tells us. Additionally, many investors also do not interview directors. Instead, they focus more on the manager. If I can determine that a manager is serious about governance and takes the role of the director as one of importance, then that can get you part of the way there in trusting that the manager is retaining well-qualified directors. Within the industry you tend to see many of the same director names and know of their reputation. This helps as well.
Jason Scharfman:	Yes, it seems to be a resource issue for some investors and others, as you suggested, focus more heavily on the manager. Turning to the hedge funds themselves now, do you feel many hedge funds perform any sort of due diligence on the directors before they hire them, or do most of them just hire big firms, or perhaps whoever their lawyer tells them to hire?
Louis Rodriguez:	I think the latter used to be the case. However, after Madoff and the events of the past four to six years, I think governance is taken a little bit more seriously. I think many managers now pay attention to the real qualifications and value-add of prospective directors. I would say that smaller managers probably care more because they tend to view the directors as a resource. Larger, institutional firms that have been around for a long time probably care a bit less. It goes back to the attitude of the manager and how seriously they take governance. Non-US managers probably tend to care more as well.
Jason Scharfman:	There have been some directorship firms that have tried to provide other services such as operations consulting to hedge funds. Do you think this can add any value?
Louis Rodriguez:	I must admit that I have not seen much of this from directorship firms. However, I would think it would add little value as managers depend on their administrators. The administrators do this for a living and know the strategies, instruments, fund accounting, etc., better than anyone else. I don't think directorship firms would have the day-to-day expertise to help here.

Jason Scharfman:	In much the same way the directorship space is in flux, it seems investors' and ODD professionals' attitudes toward directors also continue to change over time. Thank you for taking the time to conduct this interview.
Louis Rodriguez:	It was nice to speak to you. As you know ODD professionals are left to evaluate directors and governance at the hedge fund as a whole, so it's interesting to discuss the different and sometimes contentious aspects of this area.

PERSPECTIVES ON TRANSPARENCY: ADDITIONAL INTERVIEW COMMENTS

Some directorship firms understandably, and similar to many hedge funds, don't like to talk about what it is exactly they do. Well, that should be clarified; they are fine with talking about it to their clients (i.e., hedge funds), and their client's clients (i.e., investors in said hedge funds). Yet, they are surprisingly shy when certain questions are asked of them. An example of this is a story I once heard about a well-known hedge fund director who was speaking on a panel at a hedge fund conference in Europe.

During the panel this director reportedly made comments on how issues such as capacity were managed by their team in part by the scalability of the firm's model as well as strong internal procedures, and a well-developed information technology infrastructure. When time came for questions to be asked, one of the people in the audience asked the director: how many boards in particular they sat on? The director responded with a standard party line answer but this was not enough for the inquisitor. Rather, the person in the audience followed up again and asked the director if he would specifically disclose how many boards he sat on. The director once again reportedly politely refused. The investor reportedly once again pushed the issue asking the director why he was so guarded surrounding the number of directorships if in fact, throwing the director's claims back at them, it wasn't a real issue and indeed it was a scalable process. The director at this point told the investor to stop asking questions, and threatened to walk out on the conference if he didn't. The investor then dropped the issue, but had still made their point.

This is but one of many such stories circulating regarding interesting interactions investors have had with directors. Not immune, I'm sure directors and hedge fund managers have equally interesting stories about investors and ODD professionals in particular. And certainly there are less confrontational ways to approach the issue. Regardless of the truth of such stories, I think they highlight an interesting contradiction inherent in the directorship industry itself relating to what information certain directors are comfortable sharing.

Furthermore, some directors, it seems, perhaps are a bit gun shy due to enhanced regulatory oversight in many jurisdictions, and are tepid in their response to the media when what they may deem to be somewhat controversial issues, such as director capacity, come about. In practice, these issues don't need to be that controversial at all, especially when a logical frank discussion is had about them. Certainly reasonable people can disagree, but why not let your opinion be heard and understood?

It seems such reticence is also the case for certain groups when books such as this start calling for interviews. Not all directors are like this and this doesn't mean that a director who was, for example, not interviewed in this book is in any way less than an excellent director. On the contrary, not everyone who is good at what they do needs to go on record about it. Furthermore, if you're good at what you do, you're likely very busy, and schedules don't always afford conducting an interview.

On the other hand, it seems a bit ironic that an industry that builds itself as a cornerstone of maintaining transparent oversight on funds continues to be itself lacking in an overwhelming transparent response in this area. Indeed it's a bit reminiscent of the secrecy many offshore jurisdictions once prided themselves on. Regardless, as you read these interviews some may be thinking, "Oh I can't believe so and so wasn't interviewed." Well, it's really not sour grapes on my part; if people don't want to be interviewed, no harm, no foul. But believe me I tried. I approached what I believed to be a good representation of directors, directorship firms, and regulators from key hedge fund jurisdictions around the world. Some initially agreed to participate, but thought the better of it once I outlined some of the aforementioned "controversial" issues. As I mentioned the goal was not to be confrontational or ruffle feathers, but merely understand how different groups approached these issues for information purposes.

The reason I bother to explain the above is not to harangue any one individual or group, but rather to commend those who do participate in interviews, conferences, conduct research, and the like in this area. Ultimately, this type of information helps everyone become better investors, directors, and hedge fund managers, and promotes further discussions on governance.

REFERENCES

Adolf, B., 1953, Encyclopedic Dictionary of Roman Law. In: Transactions of the American Philosophical Society, vol. 43, part 2. The American Philosophical Society, Philadelphia.

Garner, B.A., 2004. Black's Law Dictionary (Editor-in-Chief). Thomson West.

Faure, M., 2003. Tort liability in France: an introductory economic analysis. In : Deffains, B., Kirat, T., (Eds.), Law and Economics in Civil Law Countries, The Economics of Legal Relationships. Routledge, Amsterdam, The Netherlands.

Chapter 11

Good Governance in Bad Situations: Understanding Governance During Fund Turmoil and Liquidations

Chapter Outline Head

INTRODUCTION

Throughout this book we have discussed a wide variety of topics related to hedge fund governance. Our discussion has outlined a number of governance pitfalls that investors and funds must be cautious of. We also highlighted a number of historical governance failures such as the Weavering case. Often once a fund fails, that seems to be the end of the story. Articles are written. Some people come out of the woodwork wagging their fingers and disapprovingly shaking their heads with "I told you so," claiming they knew there were problems at the fund the whole time, but pretty much that's the end of it. Isn't it? Well, it might be for observers at least. As we have outlined earlier in this text, often for those unfortunate investors who lost money with poorly run hedge funds, this result is years of expensive litigation that may not yield any recovery.

In some cases, there is no fraud involved, merely that hedge funds make poor investment bets or the market turns and they decide to close up shop. Regardless of the motivations for the decision, for better or worse once a fund has decided to close its doors, or is forced to, time does not stop. Service providers, including directors, can still be actively involved in assisting in the process of shutting down the fund. This process is sometimes called a fund wind down or liquidation. Often times when these liquidations occur, there are multiple competing interests involved, some of which may be polar opposites, including those of fund manager and investors. Also influencing the liquidation process may be various lawsuits and regulatory inquiries. In this chapter we will introduce this situation and outline some governance considerations that come into play during the fund liquidation process. For clarification, as we have stated in the other chapters the aim here is not to provide a legal manual by which to teach litigators and investors how to work through a fund wind down; rather we will focus on the governance issues that arise during such turmoil and liquidations. To start the process off, it will first be useful to provide some historical background on fund closures.

BACKGROUND ON FUND LIQUIDATIONS

Hedge funds can decide to close for a variety of reasons. To clarify the term "close" often takes on a special meaning for a hedge fund. In Chapter 5 we provided a review of the terminology related to fund closures, as well as discussing governance implications of fund closures. For reference we will include a brief summary of the terminology here as it will clarify our discussion.

A hedge fund seeking to raise capital, once it has reached a particular capacity limit, may temporarily stop accepting capital; as we outlined earlier in this book, this is commonly known as a so-called "soft" close. The term "soft" close generally indicates the fund may accept capital again at some point in the future, but currently will not. The term "hard" close, on the other hand, is often used by a hedge fund to signal that it is not accepting any new capital. Of course, as is shared commonly between the hedge fund industry and the English language, there are exceptions. As any investor in a hedge fund will likely be familiar with, and indeed private equity as well, the terms "soft" and "hard" close are often marketing terms. A fund could very well be soft closed, but if an investor is willing to write a large enough check, poof, magically it is reopened. Also, a so-called "hard" closed fund or strategy could reopen in the future if the opportunity set changes significantly, for example. The types of hedge fund opening and closing we have just outlined are not the type of hedge fund closures we will be discussing in this chapter.

Rather we will be covering the more literal interpretation of the term close, when a hedge fund actually shuts down and ceases to operate. This could be the closure of a particular fund strategy, while others continue to operate, or the effective shutdown of an entire fund management company and its assumed funds.

IS A CLOSURE AND A LIQUIDATOR THE SAME THING?

To clarify a bit of terminology we must first classify the difference between the closing of a fund and a liquidator. The two terms are not necessarily synonymous, or at least that is to say that closures and liquidators do not need to happen at the same time.

For the purposes of this discussion, and perhaps to better clarify the distinction in terminology here, we will talk about a fund closure as the point in time that the hedge fund makes the decision to cease trading for the purpose of continuing as an ongoing enterprise. While I know that this may be a bit of a long and awkward definition, however, the words were chosen carefully here. You'll notice we didn't say the point at which a hedge fund stops trading entirely, nor did we say at the point at which the hedge fund ceases to be profitable. With that in mind, let us consider the term liquidation in this context. For our purposes here we can think of a hedge fund liquidation as the process of selling off a hedge fund's assets with the ultimate goal of returning capital to investors. You'll notice here we did not say returning capital quickly or profitability to investors. These are often some of the most contentious points surrounding hedge fund liquidators.

COMMON REASONS HEDGE FUNDS CLOSE

Hedge fund closures may come about for a variety of reasons. In this section we will outline three typical situations where these come about.

Death by Boredom

The first is the most common reason many hedge funds close, death by boredom. This concept refers to the fact that particularly among nascent hedge funds, survival largely depends not only on how well a fund's investments actually perform but also on how much new capital the fund can attract. Many new launches cannot overcome these initial fund-raising hurdles and subsequently put themselves out of business because of a lack of ability to raise new capital. What happens is that the business no longer becomes profitable or capitally effective to continue to operate. The manager then effectively decides to shut down.

Key Person Events

The second reason a hedge fund may liquidate is because of a so-called key man, sometimes called a key person, event. A key person event generally refers to a situation where key personnel of the fund die, become incapacitated, or are generally uninvolved with the fund for an extended period of time. For reference we discussed these key person events in more detail in Chapter 7. When a key person event occurs, some hedge fund's offering documents contain key person clauses. These clauses provide for a number of features including special redemption rights as well as fund liquidation provisions. Here is an example of how the language from a key person clause may read:

> *The Fund will undertake to liquidate portfolio positions in a commercially reasonable manner, to the extent necessary in order to meet any such redemption requests. To ensure that the liquidation of portfolio positions under such circumstances does not adversely affect non-redeeming Shareholders, no time*

period has been set within which all such redemption requests must be satisfied. Until such redemption requests are satisfied, the redeeming Shareholders will remain subject to the risks of the Fund's portfolio.

Let's unpack this clause a bit. First, you could imagine how the term "commercially reasonable manner" can be up for debate. As an investor if you want or even need your capital sooner rather than later, then commercially reasonable may be immediately. The example key person clause here anticipates such an objection and that's why it clarifies that "no time period has been set" for the liquidation. Do you think that investors, perhaps a pension fund who needs to meet obligations, should be put in this situation?

On the other hand, it could be argued that since the key person event wasn't expected to happen, the investors otherwise would have had the capital locked up in the fund anyway. This could be true, but it could also be true that they were past any potentially required lockup periods, and were planning on submitting a redemption at the next redemption window, such as at the end of the next quarter. Now these investors are lumped alongside everyone else and locked out of the early redemption pool as it were.

We can also consider investors less in need of the capital who may want the time frame to be extended so that higher prices may be obtained for the positions. Assuming there is not enough capital to meet redemption requests, do you think that from a governance perspective some investors should have the right to force liquidations to meet their requests for capital? Is it fair to lock their capital up in a fund that no longer has the key person they entrusted it with to manage it?

To look at the other side of the coin couldn't it be argued that providing some investors with partial liquidation rights could do more harm than good to the remaining fund investors? There is no clear-cut answer here, and it obviously depends on which side of the argument you are coming from. In reviewing such key person clauses, however, investors may want to consider what position they will actually be in should a key person event occur, and perhaps seek to preplan accordingly such as special redemption rights via a side letter in the event a key person event should occur.

Death by Drowning—Underwater Hedge Funds

The third common reason a hedge fund may typically close is because they become what is known as "underwater." This term may be familiar to the readers of the book related to the mortgage crisis. In that context, a borrower (i.e., person typically living in the home) ends up owing more on the house (i.e., the remaining mortgage balance) than what the house is worth (i.e., market value). In these situations many homeowners seek to renegotiate with banks, commonly called a refinance arrangement or refi, while others simply decide to walk away from their home. Others are trapped in limbo between foreclosure and paying off a mortgage for more than the home is worth. They still live in the homes, but they are stuck between a rock and a hard place.

So what does this have to do with hedge funds? Well, a lot actually. Continuing the matter there, a common feature of many hedge funds is something known as the high-water mark. In general, a high-water mark can be thought of as cumulative loss account that effectively ensures that a fund manager will not earn a performance fee when they have demonstrated negative performance as compared with prior period (Stowell, 2010). This is of course a generic definition as high-water marks can come in many different modified high-water mark varieties.

If a hedge fund becomes too deep underwater and has no prospect of digging, or perhaps it should be bailing, itself out from the hole it has dug itself into, then, similar to the underwater homeowner, some hedge fund managers may simply decide the best course of action is to give up. From the hedge fund manager's perspective, after closing up shop they may simply wait a while and then launch a new fund, which is not plagued by being underwater. This gives a fresh start to the new manager, unfortunately not for the investors in the former hedge fund who are left holding the bag. This scenario is not some big hedge fund industry secret, but rather as we have noted above merely the ability of a hedge fund manager to bail out when underwater. By the way, generally, hedge fund managers are perfectly within their rights according to fund documents to do this.

To pause for a moment, the question could be asked as to whether or not you believe it is in the best interest of investors from a governance perspective to allow such underwater escape clauses? On the one hand, does it really do investors any good to have a manager who is not financially incentivized to continue to perform? You can imagine how sometimes the hole they dig themselves in can seem too deep to dig out of. On the other hand, if the manager can just throw in the towel, outside of any reputational damage, then in such situations are the incentives too perverse to really promote investors' best interests? It could be argued that it would benefit investors more if the ultimate decision for such liquidations was the result of a more democratic approach, such as an investor vote, as opposed to letting the manager completely hold the reins.

Ah, but smart hedge fund attorneys have anticipated situations such as this. Typically fund offering documents contain clauses entitled something to the effect of "Variation of Rights." These sections explain the circumstances by which investor's rights in hedge fund shares (i.e., their investment in the fund) may be changed or varied. Here is an example of such a clause:

*The rights attaching to any class of Shares (unless otherwise provided by the terms of issue of the Shares of that class) may, **whether or not the Fund is being wound up**, be varied with the consent in writing of the holders of not less than two-thirds of the issued Shares of that class, or with the sanction of a resolution passed by a majority of two-thirds of the votes cast at a separate meeting of the holders of the Shares of that class.*

To be fair there are mechanisms, in our example a two-thirds vote, to pass certain resolutions, but you'll notice that there are no special circumstances for fund wind downs, which are referred to as wind ups in the example. Regardless of what you call it, do you think that it represents good governance from the investor's perspective to create a situation where in the special circumstance of a fund wind down it should be business as usual? You could argue that the clause is there in plain sight for all investors, and if they don't like it, they can either not invest or try to change the clause. In practice, many investors, particularly small ones, don't focus on details such as this.

Returning to our underwater discussion, this is not to suggest that investors should micromanage the hedge fund manager on a day-to-day basis, but in these types of special circumstances such as a fund closure, which results in being underwater, perhaps the use of governance mechanisms that put more power back in the hands of investors would add value to the overall relationship between themselves and the fund manager. This is not to suggest the manager should continue to work for what some may deem as "for free" while they attempt to bail out from being underwater. Instead perhaps in exchange for enhanced voting power over such situations, investors would be willing to give the fund manager some form of compensation, which could be thought of as reduced advance on future performance fees earned.

As an aside, it's debatable whether these managers are working "for free." They had the opportunity to make money and they blew it. Being a hedge fund manager is not a salaried position; you eat what you kill. In this case, they were bad hunters. Is it unreasonable for them to share some of the blame and go a little hungry? This is obviously up for debate. This proposal here is by no means perfect and would likely result in neither investors nor fund managers being completely happy, but ultimately this may be the sign of a good compromise. By working together both sides may still be better off than simply forcing the situation and walking away. Such situations could also be preplanned for, and we will address liquidation preplanning later in this chapter.

Death by Assassination? Forced Hedge Fund Liquidations

Another big reason hedge funds close is when they are forced to close. This forced closure is typically not the type of force we alluded to for the reasons above (i.e., boredom or underwater). Now, if we were to classify these types of hedge fund closures discussed above, we could say that they share elements of both manager volunteerism (i.e., a desire by themselves) and social pressure (i.e., I don't want a bad reputation, so I'll just start fresh). Forced hedge fund closures, on the other hand, are completely different animals altogether. These are closures of funds that are effectively taken out of the hands of the fund manager. These forced closures commonly come in two primary forms. The first such form of forced liquidation is what we will refer to as obligation-related liquidations.

Obligation-Related Liquidations

If you page through a hedge fund's offering prospectus, likely somewhere deep within the document, you may find language related to hedge fund financing arrangements. These financing arrangements are common in hedge funds, and the language in the offering document typically addresses such financing in the context of the use of a fund's leverage. In this financing language block you may also come across language that clarifies what happens if a hedge fund cannot meet its financing obligations. Here is a sample of such a clause:

The fund could be forced to liquidate its portfolio on short notice to meet its financing obligations. The forced liquidation of all or a portion of the fund's portfolio at distressed prices could result in significant losses to the fund.

Does this scenario sound familiar? Now certainly it wouldn't be in the interests of investors for a hedge fund in which they were invested to not meet their financing obligations. The fund manager also likely has little to gain from proceeding with a fire sale of positions in order to meet obligations. Putting these considerations aside, let's return to the governance implications of the liquidation control mechanism and rights in this case. What clauses like these outline is that the fund manager, to meet the fund's financing obligations, effectively has discretion to liquidate and investors don't really have much to say about when or how they do it. As we outlined above, certainly it's in everyone's interest to meet current financing obligations coming due (i.e., the fund receives a call from a prime broker), but what about anticipated ones?

Based on clauses such as this and other offering memorandums that are replete, fund managers could argue that they were "forced" to liquidate to meet these anticipated future obligations. Why would a manager do this? Well, let's say they've locked in great performance for the quarter, but they want to hedge their future obligations as it were and make sure they don't give back too much in performance if the cost of leverage widely varies. Couldn't a situation arise where the so-called old leverage they purchase has now become too expensive based on whatever is going on in their portfolios, and now they would prefer to play it safe and set aside capital to meet these expenses?

This whole scenario may be a moot point altogether because this would likely be viewed not as a forced liquidation at all but merely the standard course of fund management. Regardless of how you classify it, some investors may not agree with this approach to meet anticipated financing obligations. For the purposes of our discussion here, one of the questions to consider would be: should investors be consulted before any such financing liquidations occur? Or to take it a step further, should they have rights to perhaps exercise a vote with regards to the timing of such financing liquidations? Putting investors aside, what about the fund board voting on or approving such liquidations? Should the amount or timing of the liquidations matter? Of course, investors, or even directors, may not be experts in this area, which is why they hire the fund manager to begin with, but when significant losses from liquidations could result, do you think it represents best practice governance, which is the control and oversight framework from their perspective, if they do not even have a say?

Investor-Driven Liquidations

The second common form of forced liquidations is investor-driven liquidations. These investor-driven liquidations typically occur at odds with hedge fund manager and therefore are forced. To be fair, all such types of liquidations may not necessarily be investor driven. As was highlighted in the interview contained in Chapter 10, in some cases directors may take the initiative and initiate liquidation proceedings ahead of investors. Outside of the liquidation situations we described, why would the directors or investors want to force a manager to liquidate? Before addressing this issue we should first explain about a phenomenon that has begun to grow in popularity after the 2008 financial crisis known as zombie funds.

The Role of Zombie Funds in Liquidations

Lately around the hedge fund water cooler you may have heard increasing talk of zombies. It's not a reference to the zombie craze that has increasingly become popular around the world through movies such as *World War Z*; instead people are discussing the rise of so-called zombie funds. Zombie funds are effectively funds that are living dead. In much the same way that the underwater homeowners we referenced earlier in our discussion were in limbo, so too are zombie fund investors. A zombie fund is effectively a fund that should have been liquidated, but is still up and running.

They are called zombies because these funds are effectively the living dead. They are still functioning, but they are so underwater that they have no real prospects of ever coming back to life as it were and becoming profitable for the manager again. You might be asking why investors don't just pull the plug and put the zombie out of its misery? Well, many of them may be locked up (i.e., unable to redeem their capital for a predefined period of time) and simply can't take their money out. What about the manager? Can they be merciful and kill the zombie? It depends; some managers may feel they can get above water. Others may not be so sure, but they don't want to be associated with the stink of failure. Others are not so bothered by this and instead are content. Zombie funds are not just a hedge fund industry problem. Industry data suggest that almost 1200 private equity funds, representing over $100 billion, can be classified as inactive zombie funds that are poor performers and have little hope of raising more money (Hutchinson, 2013).

In the shadow of investors looking to dump their interests in zombie funds, a booming secondary funds industry has grown up. A secondary refers to a hedge fund investor effectively selling their interest in the zombie fund to another investor at a discount. To simplify matters, it could be thought of as buying a bankruptcy claim. To clarify a secondary does not need necessarily need to be an interest in a zombie fund. It could also be an interest in a well-functioning hedge fund that an investor, for liquidity or other reasons, simply wants to exit. Based on hedge fund terms such as lockups, an investor may not be able to simply submit a redemption request, and could therefore look to the secondary market to exit the position at a discount.

One of the key issues for zombie funds is that the assets in the fund are not being actively managed, but the investment manager is still collecting fees. Hedge fund increasingly came under scrutiny for running zombie funds during the aftermath of the 2008 financial crisis. In those situations many funds' assets were significantly reduced in value. Rather than sell the assets, closing the funds and recouping what they could, many smart hedge fund managers turned into tough litigators. Why should they close the funds when they can continue to collect fees on capital that they don't really have to manage?

Now the hedge fund managers may raise the argument that they are really protecting the investors by holding the assets until they can obtain a more favorable price. A 2014 report outlined that according to research by HFR, 904 hedge funds, close to 1/10th of all hedge funds tracked by the research firm, liquidated and are now "arguing with the investors over valuations for those lingering illiquid assets" (McCrum, 2014). Generally, according to the fund's legal documents hedge fund managers have enough discretion to do this. If you, or the fund directors, don't like it, then you can sue them in an attempt to force liquidation, and also shut off the ongoing leech like drip of fees that slowly drain investor's capital.

Do you think this represents a good governance mechanism that the fund managers should have what in some cases may seem like absolute executive discretion over matters such as this? From a governance perspective do you think it represents best practice that fund manager should be able to do this? As we outlined with several of the scenarios we discussed above, the ability to do this may have been stated in the fund's offering documents and shame on investors for not believing it could happen. Part of the problem, however, is that investors don't often like to believe that such situations may ever occur when they set out investing in a fund.

Non-Zombie Forced Liquidation

Now that we have an understanding of the problems investors in zombie funds face, we can now return to our original questions of why investors would be motivated to force a fund to liquidate. The zombie fund scenario is obviously a good example of this. Could there be any other reasons as to why such forced liquidations may be sought outside of a zombie scenario?

Perhaps this is best demonstrated by an example. Consider a hedge fund that pre-2008 invested in a number of different securities including equities, bonds, futures, CDs, CCOs, SMPs, futures, and repos, among others. It has a diverse portfolio. To take things further let us also say, for the purposes of our example, the manager also had afforded investors in the fund the chance to participate in a less liquid opportunity than the rest of the fairly liquid portfolio. Let's say this was a security related to private equity–style investment in the equity of a privately held company, a portion of a tranche of financing related to a fleet of airplanes, and even an exotic security related to a gambling license in Vietnam. This might sound fantastic, but hedge funds can and do invest in all kinds of things, both plain vanilla and exotic. These less liquid alternatives afforded to investors in the existing liquid fund via a structure known as a side pocket. A side pocket is effectively a tool that allows a fund manager to segregate certain types of holdings from others. Traditionally, assets that are in a side pocket have different and generally longer liquidity profiles, compared with the remaining pooled fund. Sometimes these may be called synthetic side pockets depending on the bells and whistles that are involved.

Now let's say the economy around 2008 makes a significant direction shift, as it did, and now once liquid positions are altogether illiquid, or at least less liquid than they once were. So now the hedge fund has a portfolio of previously liquid valuable securities sitting on the books with an unrealized loss. What can they do? Well, they have several options. First, the fund could simply sell the securities and realize a loss. While investors may be unhappy with this option, the matter would be concluded. Another option for the manager would be to effectively remove the existing less liquid investments from the pool and place them in another side pocket, effectively performing a liquidity bisect on the portfolio. One bucket would be the illiquid side pocket in which all the illiquid losers would live. The second bucket would be where the remaining more liquid securities would remain. To clarify the second liquid remaining bucket would be the existing pooled hedge fund vehicle the investors had originally subscribed to.

Another option would be for a hedge fund manager to decide to hold the securities. It should be noted this could generally be accomplished if the positions were placed in a side pocket or not. The manager may feel that selling the securities in the market now at a large discount may not be in the best interest of the fund. How nice of them to think of the investors! Of course, we are being a bit tongue and cheek here.

The manager of course is also considering the economic impact to themselves in this regard. If they lose money for investors, they do not earn a performance fee. As noted with the zombie fund scenario the manager will continue to collect management fees while arguably treading water until some undetermined point in the future when the manager's expectations of valuation and the market's fair value align. This of course does not sit well with everyone, and here the rubber really starts to hit the road in terms of the use of governance mechanisms in this area.

In these types of situations investors may attempt to force the hedge fund to liquidate the side pockets. It may be a difficult fight due to all the protections afforded to the manager, but these types of situations do arise. In certain cases, the investors may try to work things out with the manager or negotiate a solution. If that doesn't work, the investors, or as noted above the directors, may indeed initiate proceedings in an attempt to force liquidation. Preplanning for such events can greatly enhance everyone's understanding of the situation. Indeed, it may also present an opportunity for investors to negotiate for better rights in such situations, and enhance the quality of their positions should these types of liquidation situations arise.

GOVERNANCE PERSPECTIVES ON LIQUIDATIONS

As you likely have surmised by now, when a hedge fund closes shop and liquidates, it can be a contentious situation to say the least. From a governance perspective, the questions of who has control in the situation can often be the determining factor as to who walks away from the situation feeling they weren't completely taken to the cleaners. Transparency and oversight into the process by investors and directors can also prove to be a valuable governance mechanism in these situations. In addition to the points we have outlined above, in this section we will discuss some of the governance considerations surrounding liquidations.

Do Liquidators Promote Good Governance?

When a hedge fund goes into liquidation, typically the court will appoint a liquidator to wind down the funds by selling off assets and facilitating investor redemptions. Hedge fund's offering memoranda will often reference the role of liquidators with language such as "If the Company shall be wound up the liquidator shall apply the asset of the Company in such manner and order as he thinks fit in satisfaction of creditor's claims."

In certain cases the hedge fund manager may not want the fund to be liquidated and may sue the funds seeking to block the liquidation. This was the case when a bankrupt hedge fund named Fletcher International Ltd. sued some of its own Cayman Islands–based funds to block the liquidator, Ernst & Young, from selling the fund's assets (Schneider and Kary, 2012).

The question could be posed as to whether from the perspective of investors if they are better off with the liquidator or not? Of course, liquidators get paid by funds, as they rightly should, to perform their job, which may decrease the amount investors recover after expenses. However, others may argue that liquidators serve useful roles. For example, without the liquidator the hedge fund may hold onto the assets for much longer and investors would have to continue to pay fees (i.e., zombie fund situations). As their name implies liquidators liquidate and can facilitate an expedited return of capital to investors.

From a governance perspective, investors should understand the potential control they could be forced to turn over to liquidators. Investors should also consider more broadly the general role and powers of liquidators in the event of a fund shutdown.

Evaluating Hedge Fund Preplanning Efforts

So far in this chapter we have primarily addressed what happens after a fund closes and liquidation may ensure. We have not addressed, however, the concept of liquidation preplanning by hedge funds.

Hedge funds have a number of mechanisms by which they can direct through preplanning the way a fund will terminate. To be clear these liquidation mechanisms may not only be via language or clauses contained in fund offering memorandum, but in choosing the fund structure itself, certain structures may be easier to wind down than others (Harris, 2009). Some regulators have proposed concepts similar to living wills be created for funds and banks to plan for such eventualities before they happen (Saunders, 2010).

Of course, if left to their own devices, a hedge fund manager will understandably structure the liquidation mechanisms more in their favor as compared with investor's interests. While such preplanning efforts may have taken place before an investor even shows up to invest in a hedge fund, this does not mean that investors should ignore their presence or absence. Investors should take measures during the overall due diligence and governance assessment process to understand any framework that may be in place for liquidations. Specifically, they should consider if any liquidation preplanning represents their interest appropriately? If not, can they do anything to change the situation perhaps via a side letter? Additionally, even if they cannot change the situation, would they have appropriate transparency into the liquidation process? Have they discussed with directors their potential role in any liquidations? For example, have the directors dealt with liquidations before? While preplanning may add clarity to hedge fund liquidation, investors should take measures to vet preplanning procedures to ensure that not just the fund manager's interests are protected.

CONCLUSION

In this chapter we highlighted common governance considerations that arise when hedge funds experience turmoil and may eventually liquidate. As we highlighted at the beginning of this chapter, our discussion here was not meant to be a detailed walkthrough of the fund liquidation process, but rather to provide examples of the key governance issues that may arise in these situations. The hedge fund liquidation is fraught with a wide variety of other issues we did not address in this chapter.

One example is considerations for managers in determining the priority of redemption payments during liquidation. Another example includes interaction between the relationship between bankruptcy laws and investor redemptions during fund closures. One example of this was the unusual lawsuit filed by investors in the case of a hedge fund named Ritchie Capital Management LLC (US SEC, 2008). In that case, three investors pursuing claims of $46 million against the firm's Ritchie Multi-Strategy Global Trading Ltd. fund filed an involuntary Chapter 11 bankruptcy action in an attempt to force the fund into bankruptcy

(Harris, 2008). Ultimately the bankruptcy court dismissed the investors' case, in part because it found that they were financially sophisticated and not creditors of the fund according to the law (Feldman and Dudanowicz, 2009).

We also did not address in detail the role of other hedge fund service providers, besides fund directors, such as fund administrators and auditors in the liquidation process. For example, as part of the liquidation process funds will typically provide final audited financial statements to investors. There may also be considerations such as when a hedge fund manager liquidates one fund and rolls the assets over to another fund. Additionally, there are also a number of manual processes that we did not describe, such as a United States–based hedge fund filing so-called Articles of Cancellation in Delaware.

Fund liquidation is a broad concept that presents a number of legal and operational conflicts for funds, service providers, and investors. Although such considerations may be far from investors' minds when they initially subscribe to a fund, as we have highlighted throughout this chapter when a hedge fund experiences turmoil and faces liquidation, understanding the governance framework in place can add real value.

REFERENCES

Feldman, M., Dudanowicz, J., 2009. Hedge Fund Liquidations. New York Law Journal, March 2.

Harris, A., 2008. Hedge Funds Holding Up Investors Face Involuntary Bankruptcy. Bloomberg, February 19.

Harris, J., 2009. Setting up for the wind down: closing a hedge fund. Hedge Funds Review, November 11.

Hutchinson, C., 2013. More than $100 billion trapped in 'zombie funds:' industry data. Reuters, June 13.

McCrum, D., 2014. Zombie hordes thrive, await further hedge fund corpses. Financial Times, March 25.

Saunders, D., 2010. Q+A with Alistair Darling, British Chancellor of the Exchequer. The Globe and Mail, February 4.

Schneider, J., Kary, T., 2012. Fletcher Sues to Block Cayman Liquidation of Hedge Fund. Bloomberg, July 5.

Stowell, D., 2010. An Introduction to Investment Banks, Hedge Funds, and Private Equity. Academic Press, San Diego, California.

US SEC, 2008. Chicago-area hedge fund advisor to pay $40 million in settlement. February 5. http://www.sec.gov/news/press/2008/2008-10.htm

Chapter 12

Trends and Future Developments

INTRODUCTION

Governance is not set in stone. Rather it is an evolving area of hedge fund due diligence and investing that is subject to change. This change is driven by several different parties. As we have outlined throughout this book, investors are increasingly focusing on governance-related aspects of hedge funds with the most notable example being the recent trends of increasing focus on fund directors. Hedge funds themselves, largely in response to the investor focus in this area, have similarly paid more attention in recent years to governance-related issues including the role of fund boards. As we have outlined earlier in this book, other parties such as regulators have also increasingly focused on implementing laws that promote further governance. In this chapter we will contemplate the future of hedge fund governance and discuss trends in the space going forward. As investors of all sizes continue to increase their hedge fund allocations, continuing to monitor governance trends will be essential to effectively navigate the increasingly complex hedge fund universe.

THE DILIGENCE GOVERNANCE CORRELATION

Earlier in this book we outlined that in recent years, there has been an increasing amount of attention paid to operational due diligence (ODD). This has resulted in investors allocating more resources in this area including increased personnel devoted to this function. As this area has become increasingly complex more hedge fund investors have begun to work with specialized ODD consultants. My firm, Corgentum Consulting, LLC, is an example of such a firm that conducts institutional-level, deep-dive reviews of hedge funds as well as other types of funds on behalf of investors. Increasingly, due to the increasing scope of ODD reviews firms such as Corgentum have also continued to provide direct support to ODD analysts.

Along with this increased focus on ODD has come an increased focus on analyzing fund governance. As more resources are dedicated toward ODD it is likely that we will continue to see a continued positive correlation between increased ODD efforts and the focus on hedge fund governance. This *diligence governance correlation* will not likely solely be a resource issue. That is, the sole factor fueling this increased focus will not simply be that as more resources are dedicated toward ODD, more investors will cover difference.

Additionally, the increased strength of the diligence governance correlation will likely be a result of the changing definition of governance we have also mentioned throughout this book. We will address this trend in more detail below; however, for our purposes here the point we are attempting to highlight relates to the expanding scope of governance as it relates to due diligence. Therefore, we will likely continue to see not only that will more resources be dedicated toward hedge fund ODD, but that the scope of the governance concerns that they are tasked to evaluate will increase as well.

CONTINUED EXPANSION OF THE DEFINITION OF HEDGE FUND GOVERNANCE

The definition of governance has expanded beyond simply the board of directors. As we outlined above, and throughout this text, this definition has expanded to encompass all areas of a hedge fund. In particular, there is an increasing acceptance that governance is best thought of as an overlay of transparency, oversight, and controls to the underlying operational and investment standards and functions of a hedge fund. Furthermore, investors are increasingly grouping considerations of fund terms including fees, high-water mark provisions, and liquidity under the governance heading. It should also be noted that this definition applies regardless of fund structure. That is to say that just because an investor is invested with a hedge fund via a separately managed account as compared with a pooled fund the interest in governance has continued to remain. This is despite prior arguments made by some in the industry that separate account structures are effectively free of operational and governance risk, and therefore these items should not be considerations.

Additionally, the definition of these governance protocols is not limited to just the hedge fund itself, but to service providers other than directors including auditors, administrators, legal counsel, information technology consultants, compliance consultants, and third-party valuation agents. As more research is done in this area combined with the continued investor focus on governance, it is likely that the definition of governance will continue to expand and become even further refined over time.

INCREASED IMPLEMENTATION OF BOARDS WHERE THEY ARE NOT MANDATED BY LAW

Hedge funds with investment vehicles domiciled in certain jurisdictions such as Delaware in the United States are not mandated to have a board of directors, but from the perspective of an investor wouldn't such board be a good thing to promote governance oversight? Why do we need offshore boards but not onshore boards? Well, the answer likely depends who you ask, but increasingly investors are asking such questions and hedge funds are listening. This has resulted in increased popularity of advisory boards. We discussed the role of these advisory boards in Chapter 7. For reference, advisory boards, which are sometimes referred to as qualified boards, do not necessarily focus solely on the domestic board, but instead advise the whole hedge fund organization on a wide range of issues and can even provide additional support to offshore boards.

A key difference between advisory boards and offshore fund boards is that these advisory boards do not typically maintain any actual authority to do anything other than advise. What happens, for example, if the advisory board and the offshore board have conflicting opinions? From a purely legal perspective it is likely that the offshore board would trump the advisory board, but the question could be asked if the advisory board should be given more authority over offshore boards in certain circumstances. It could also be pointed out that such conflicts may actually be a good thing to promote governance because they show conflicting opinions, which may suggest enhanced oversight.

Despite such questions, and the fact that the use of these boards is not widespread, we anticipate that the use of advisory boards will continue going forward. Particularly supporting this trend will be the increased attention paid by investors to governance in conjunction with increased due diligence. This increased focus will put increased pressure on funds to demonstrate enhanced governance oversight and controls. While the use of such boards is still nascent, investors should consider whether such boards are simply marketing constructs to feign onshore governance or instead offer any real value.

REGULATORY DATABASE MANAGEMENT
OF BOARD OF DIRECTORS

Associated with the continued interest in governance has come an increased focus on fund directors, particularly those on the boards of offshore funds. As we outlined in Chapter 2 the role of these directors is a controversial one to say the least. One of the more contentious issues, as we have pointed out in earlier chapters, is related to the concept of investor capacity.

Complicating matters further has been the obfuscation of specific capacity figures among directors. Some have proposed publicly searchable databases of such directorships. At least investors would then be provided with this information, so they would be more empowered to make their own assessment as to whether a director sitting on a certain number of boards was too many for their comfort. Of course, there would then be questions as to whether enough specifics would be provided to be meaningful. An example of this would be the discussion we outlined earlier in this book in Chapter 4 relating to the number of director fund manager relationships as compared with their actual board positions.

Certain directors understandably do not like the concept of such disclosures. One of the objections voiced is common to the objections that always tend to crop up when a new type of hedge fund quantitative transparency is required. Namely that the numbers will be misleading. As we outlined in Chapter 4, and putting extreme cases aside, analyzing director capacity should incorporate a great deal more than simply a number. Despite the continued investor interest in this area, at present it doesn't seem as if such a database will be available any time soon. Recent reports suggest that a publicly accessible directorship database in places like the Cayman Islands have been relegated to the distant future (COO Connect, 2014). Indeed the interview comments contained in Chapter 10 with Ms. Smith from the Cayman Islands Monetary Authority suggested as much as well.

It is a likely trend, however, that eventually such a database produced by regulators will be made available and searchable for investors. This would of course present a number of further questions. As outlined above, one question would be if the database contained the number of individual directorship or relationships. Additionally, who would be responsible for making sure the database was accurate and up to date? Would it be the responsibility of directors to self-report? Would it enhance the quality of reporting of hedge fund managers themselves if they were forced to have more skin in the game and be responsible for updating such reporting? Additionally, less of a practical concern is what about the potential situations where a director serves on boards in multiple jurisdictions? What about situations where a director may serve on a so-called advisory board that is effectively a consulting relationship for the fund? It is unlikely that these would be captured by the database.

As these questions highlight, it is likely that any public data solution once implemented will be imperfect at best. This is not necessarily the fault of the regulators who may be seeking to balance transparency with other regulation needs as well as the practical needs of the directorship industry. Instead, our goal here is to highlight that even once investors are provided with a so-called official number from a database there is a great deal more due diligence that can be performed. By asking additional questions to evaluate the unique circumstance of each situation, rather than simply focusing on numbers, investors will likely be able to make a much better informed evaluation of a director. Investors have already begun to ask more questions of directors in this regard, and as more resources are dedicated to ODD, we are hopeful that this trend will continue going forward.

INCREASED REGULATORY SCRUTINY AND PROSECUTION OF GOVERNANCE-RELATED ISSUES

Along with the increased regulatory focus on increased data disclosures of governance-related data there will likely be an enhanced focus on regulating and prosecuting governance-related issues. One of the more recent examples of this is the focus on insider trading. Some may argue that these are purely compliance or legal issues, but aren't the failures in compliance departments that lead to such insider trading cases really also part and parcel of a poor internal control and oversight framework?

For reference we discussed the relationship between hedge fund insider trading cases and governance in Chapter 3. It is anticipated that as the compliance environment for hedge funds becomes increasingly complex, and better-resourced regulators continue to focus on governance-related areas such as this, the number of prosecutions will also similarly increase. In places like the United States in particular we see the increased use of advanced surveillance technology and interagency coordination between the US Securities and Exchange Commission and traditional law enforcement agencies such as the Federal Bureau of Investigation ("FBI"). A recent example of this were the reports of a 2014 inquiry relating to allegations of insider tipping by hedge fund manager Carl Icahn relating to two companies, Dean Food and Clorox Co. (Pulliam and Rothfeld, 2014). As this book is being written there are also reports of inquiries by the US House Ways and Means Committee relating to allegations that a top staff member illegally passed tips to dozens of hedge funds that resulted in insider trading in the shares of health insurance company Humana Inc. (Hurtado, 2014).

As there unfortunately continues to be allegations of misconduct by fund managers in this area, we anticipate that regulators and prosecutors will continue to focus on these areas. As we noted above, while problems such as hedge fund insider trading may be rooted in areas such as compliance, they are also representative of poor operational control and oversight that is squarely in the wheelhouse of governance oversight.

INCREASED DIRECTOR REPORTING BUT
NOT NECESSARILY MEANINGFUL TRANSPARENCY

Consider the following. You're an investor in two different hedge funds. One fund shares answers to any question you may have about the fund's directors and that's it. The other not only answers your questions but also provides you with detailed reporting that includes a summary of the minutes of the fund's most board meeting. Which one gives you more meaningful governance information? I know it's not fair; this is a trick question.

Well, of course, the second fund that provides the additional reporting provides you with more reporting. More reporting generally leads to enhanced transparency standards that among other things can be a key element of a good governance program. The problem is, would such reporting be very meaningful? Perhaps, however, if the reporting were overly summarized or too technical, it may not be useful for investors. What about if a hedge fund offered you an annual certification or formal director declaration that the fund was being run in accordance with the prospectus? Some have proposed this idea in seeking to make incoming investors feel more comfortable (COO Connect, 2014). In reality it's really just a marketing ploy.

As a hedge fund investor would such a certificate make you feel better? Of course, the more things in writing you get, the bigger the file you can compile. More paper generally makes investors feel better, but once again is this very meaningful? Said another way, can you learn more about the governance in place at a fund if you receive a director certification as opposed to not receiving one? Three points of note with regards to proposals such as this. First, as we have outlined throughout this book, investors shouldn't sit on their hands waiting for directors to be proactive with them. It just won't happen. Second, if the fund was not operating in conjunction with its prospectus, and the directors knew it, wouldn't the director have the obligation to take action? As such, waiting around for an all's clear piece of paper at year end wouldn't seem to add much value at all. Finally, would this director certification come with any enhanced acceptance of director liability? Probably not.

There is nothing wrong with enhanced director reporting; the key is whether such reporting will be meaningful to investors seeking to make governance assessments. Recognizing the flaws in proposed director-driven certifications or summarized reporting, going forward, it is likely that investors will continue to press proactively for meaningful investor-focused reporting on the role of directors.

Outside of proposed databases detailing the number of directorships a director may hold across multiple firms and funds, it is likely that going forward the types of information investors will increasingly be asking for will focus on the director-specific relationship with a particular hedge fund management firm and fund under review. This information will likely include enhanced details of the actual decisions made by directors, enhanced details regarding directors' meeting frequency, and participation. Such reporting will likely provide much more meaningful insights to investors than a simple certification. Wouldn't it be nice if in the same way that hedge fund managers produce investor update letters, the directors would produce similar letters summarizing their activities, and areas of concern for funds going forward? Of course, while we like to see such a trend take hold, it is likely more of a wish than a reality in the short term.

THE FUTURE RISE AND FALL OF ANNUAL GOVERNANCE MEETINGS ("AGMs")

Continuing our discussion of trends related to director transparency we should also discuss a phenomenon that has been discussed of late and proposed by some in the directorship industry known as AGMs (COO Connect, 2014). Effectively AGMs refer to a concept whereby investors could meet with directors on an annual basis to question directors. Putting valid concerns relating to confidentiality aside, would such meetings add value? Certainly investors may learn a thing or two about the funds and the ongoing duties of directors. So yes, that would be valuable, but should meetings such as this be a substitute for director due diligence and analysis? Certainly not.

To understand AGM proposals, we should consider a similar phenomenon that took place in the ODD field. As investors continued to focus more on fund operations and conduct more ODD meetings, increasingly funds spent more and more time dealing with the subject. To head off the issue, some funds started to have what were effectively ODD days for their investors. At these meetings the funds would provide an update on key fund operational functions and have senior leaders in these areas give presentations. Investors would then have the opportunity to ask questions. Some funds still hold these meetings today. It's not necessarily a bad thing, and once again such meetings can be informative, but you can imagine how investors would not necessarily receive the level of detail or access from such meetings as they would from hands-on ongoing ODD monitoring. While initially popular, investors increasingly grew to accept this and virtually no ODD groups rely on such meetings to supplant their own due diligence efforts. As such, the funds end up spending more time and effort dedicated to ODD because in addition to all the meetings they were having before now they have an ODD day to boot. This has led to a general scaling back of such events.

We anticipate the same will likely be true for AGMs, if such proposals even get off the ground. In light of enhanced regulatory oversight of directors through recent changes in laws in places such as the Cayman Islands, it is likely that in the short term investors and hedge funds will be distracted enough not to pursue director AGMs. Even if such meetings were to happen, it is likely that investors will quickly realize that they are not a substitute for ongoing director monitoring and we predict that any previous popularity would wane. While increased opportunities to engage with funds and directors in particular on governance issues should always be welcomed by investors, it is unlikely that AGMs will be a viable option anytime in the future.

INCREASED FOCUS ON DIRECTOR DISCLOSURES TO INVESTORS

The debate about proposals such as director AGMs is grounded in the increased desire for investor information and transparency regarding the role of directors and fund governance in general. As part of this process, investors are increasingly engaging more with directors during the due diligence process. As can be imagined some investors are more focused on this area than others. Among those investors some may be conducting more detailed inquiries as opposed to others.

Consider a fund director who is sitting on the board of a hedge fund. Let's say he receives a general inquiry from an investor regarding his relationship with the fund. He responds by outlining that he has a good relationship with them and sends over some promotional material from his firm that provides a high-level overview of the general directorship services offered. The investor is seemingly satisfied by this and the director never hears from them again. Now let's say a different investor in the same fund calls upon this director. This investor is a lot more aggressive and asks a wide variety of questions including if there is anything bad or concerning going on at the fund that the investor should know about? Of course, the director wants to seem responsive and transparent, but can they even legally answer this question? Should they defer to the fund or just keep mum? If they truly work for the fund, and not any individual investor, couldn't it be argued that they might be disadvantaging the fund by making such disclosures selectively, as opposed to sharing information on any current concerns regarding ongoings or disputes with all fund investors and not just the ones who ask the better questions?

Let's assume that the director does answer the question, but tells the investor there is nothing to worry about. The fund subsequently blows up and the investor sues everyone including the fund directors. Can this investor claim increased reliance on the director's statements? Even if they legally can't argue reliance from a technical perspective, should an investor be able to rely on such statements practically? Maybe there are problems going on in other areas of the fund that the director wasn't privy to. Another question to consider is whether the director is keeping track of what information he is telling to different investors. Are they even required to under the laws of different offshore jurisdictions? For example, let's say a lawsuit does ensue; wouldn't it be helpful for the directorship firm's lawyer seeking to defend them to have a record of all material sent and conversations with directors? Furthermore, from a practical standpoint wouldn't it be helpful for the hedge fund to know which investors are calling up and asking questions? Does the hedge fund have protocols in place with directorship firms to monitor such communication?

We anticipate that these types of issues will likely continue to come to the forefront for directors and hedge funds. As more investors begin to engage with directors during initial and ongoing due diligence, it is likely that there will be an increased trend of focusing around tightening up this communication and disclosures. Ultimately investors, hedge funds, and directors will need to find a balance between enhanced disclosures, and running afoul of the types of issues we outlined above. Additionally, it is likely that investors will continue to focus more on the way in which the directorship firm's infrastructure is in place, and seek to support oversight of any guidelines that may be in place for engaging with investors.

INCREASED FOCUS OF DIRECTOR CONFLICT MANAGEMENT

To date the bulk of the investor focus on evaluating the role of fund directors has been in regards to their duties at specific funds that investors are evaluating. As part of this analysis investors have broadened their scope a bit to look to a director's other relationships with different hedge funds from primarily a capacity perspective.

One issue that has not received much attention is the conflicts of interest that may arise as a result of the positions held by directors in multiple funds. Let's highlight what we are referring to by way of example.

Consider a director who sits on multiple hedge fund boards. During the course of his duties on the board of one fund, let's call it Fund A, the director learns that Fund A is going to be firing the fund's current administrator because they are unhappy with the quality of service provided by the firm. The director supports the decision to terminate the current administrator, which we can call AdminCo., and believes that based on his experience with the anticipated replacement administrator the decision will be a benefit to the fund. To continue our example, as we noted above, this director sits on multiple boards including another fund, which we can call Fund B.

At a recent Fund B board meeting the director learns that Fund B is also unhappy with the fund's current administrator, which we will call Admin2. The director further inquires with the fund manager which administrator is anticipated to be hired as a replacement. Wouldn't you know it, the fund manager recently received a very competitive pricing proposal from AdminCo. Remember this was the administrator that Fund A is going to be firing. What happens next?

Should the director say something? Do they have an obligation to? Are they legally allowed to? Obviously directors are hired for their experience and a more experienced director is thought to be more qualified; however, this presents a situation where a director may not be able to use all of their experience, or should we say knowledge to bear. After all don't they owe obligations of confidentiality to each of the funds? Perhaps sharing the knowledge that Fund A is firing AdminCo. with Fund B would be detrimental to Fund A even if it would benefit Fund B. Often times they can offer their opinion or share information without technically violating the rules. This could involve speaking in generalities so they can get their point across without saying so directly or having funds read between the lines.

As a follow-up question, who is policing the director's conduct in this regard? Of course, directors may be members of local director organizations that have codes of conduct, and such conduct may even be illegal, but who's actually enforcing it? After all, if you were Fund B in the scenario above, you wouldn't necessarily want illegal information, but of course it would be beneficial to get as much legal information as you could on the inside scoop as it were on information such as this. You see how such multiple roles could present the potential for conflicts?

Let's take it a step further. Hedge funds do not change administrators often. What if a director sits on the boards of two funds with similar strategies, such as two event-driven funds? Let's say as part of their portfolio certain large positions overlap among the funds. What if one fund is long a certain position and the other is short the same position? Most would likely argue that it's not the director's job to raise any questions in this regard among the difference in opinion among the funds as long as both of them are complying with their respective guidelines.

We are not judging the director's role in this case; that's the way the directorship system works and it's perfectly acceptable for a director to sit on both boards in such a situation. You do however see how a situation may arise where a director may, even inadvertently, let some information slip out? Once again, we are not saying such information leaking would be appropriate, or even legal, but the point is that the potential for a conflict is there. Who is policing this conflict? For example, let's say a director just blurts out the information and tells the fund that is long about the short position by the other fund in the same security. Is the long fund now conflicted out of trading of this position? Do they have a duty to alert the other fund? You see how these could be complicated questions to address. Perhaps the fund that is long may not want to deal with them and agree to pretend with the director that it never happened to keep everyone's life simple. We are not saying that this necessarily occurs in the real world, but it certainly has the potential to and that can pose a governance risk.

As investors continue to expand their focus on fund governance oversight and conflict management in particular, it is likely that issues such as those contemplated by the scenarios will likely come under increased scrutiny by both investors and regulators. This increased focus will likely accompany enhanced director disclosure and transparency requirements, as we highlighted earlier in this chapter, as well as further regulatory surveillance of comparison of the activities of different funds on which the same directors may sit.

GLOBAL GOVERNANCE CODES—A SELF-REGULATORY PIPE DREAM?

Every few years in the hedge fund industry it seems a new code or proclamation comes out that provides guidance in this area or that from one of the many hedge fund industry lobby organizations. While such guidance is certainly commendable, in recent years prior to the enacting of laws such as Dodd–Frank in the United States, much of this guidance has been focused on promoting self-regulation of the hedge fund industry. In more recent years now that the regulatory shoe has dropped so to speak, the focus has understandably been on advocating for lighter regulation. Of course, it could be argued that some of these proposals support what could be more practical or well-reasoned regulations and to be fair some of them do not.

The area of fund governance has been no different. Some have proposed code of conduct by which hedge funds should prescribe to. Of course, these codes would be completely voluntary and enforced on a self-regulatory basis. Similar to the objections we raised relating to director certifications, such codes are rife with potential problems. Some examples of the types of questions that come about with such expansive industry-wide governance codes could include:

- Would such high-level codes provide any real enforcement of governance controls or simply be so overly high level in nature as to be useless?
- How could a universal code be broad and vague enough to apply to all funds, yet provide enough specificity to give investors any comfort of appropriate governance controls and oversight?
- Who would make sure the hedge fund is complying with the codes? The hedge fund itself?
- Would there be a requirement for third-party audits of code compliance to be performed?
- What happens if a hedge fund violates the codes? Do they simply have to disclose it?
- What if a hedge fund signed up for such a code, violated it, and then simply dropped the code altogether? Would they be required to disclose this?
- Would it just be funds that would be required to sign up for such codes? Why not fund's service providers such as directors and administrators as well?

As you can see there are more questions than answers relating to such code proposals. Once again, with enhanced focus on regulatory oversight of hedge funds and directors of late, it seems that the calls for proposals may have largely been muted by regulators.

FURTHER BROADENING OF SCOPE OF DIRECTOR SERVICES

As we have noted several times throughout this book the world of compliance and regulations has become increasingly complex on a global scale in recent years. As a result hedge funds now have a number of new regulations to comply with. As part of this many funds have enhanced regulatory reporting requirements as well. These regulatory requirements coupled with increased investor demands for institutional operational quality operations have made launching a hedge fund today more expensive than ever before.

Seeking to capitalize on their existing relationships with hedge funds, we anticipate an increased trend of directorship firms seeking to offer more services to hedge funds. These services will likely run the gamut from nonregulatory services to regulatory related ones. We have already seen the early stages of this trend with directorship firms assisting funds in some cases with nonregulatory services such as the aforementioned advisory boards. In regards to regulatory services directorship firms have begun to offer services for regulatory compliance and reporting to deal with regulations such as the Alternative Investment Fund Managers Directive ("AIFMD"), EU passporting, and the Foreign Accounting Tax Compliance Act ("FATCA") including appointing so-called FATCA responsible officers.

As we outlined earlier in this book this expansion of existing service provider relationships is nothing new. Administrators increasingly have sought to expand upon their existing hedge fund relationships to offer services traditionally offered by other service providers such as US SEC Form PF reporting. Similarly hedge fund law firms are increasingly engaged in the traditional work of compliance consultants and vice versa. This is a logical step for many directorship firms seeking to generate additional revenues from an increasingly crowded director marketplace.

Questions arise whether the use of such providers is necessarily beneficial for investors due to both the increased fees and the potential for conflicts that may arise. As we discussed in Chapter 4, when different service providers compete for the same business and are still required to work for each other, it can create potential conflicts of interest. This is particularly true when these service providers delegate duties to each other and effectively rely on the work of one another. You see how there could be a potential conflict when, for example, a directorship firm was competing for the business that they now have to rely on someone else for. Despite these potential conflicts, we anticipate this trend will continue as hedge funds continue to focus on enhancing operational redundancies and leverage off service providers.

REFERENCES

COO Connect, 2014. Publicly accessible CIMA database of directors still a long way off. *COO Connect*, July 3.

COO Connect, 2014. GAIM Ops Cayman: hedge funds urged to hold AGMs. *COO Connect*, April 10.

Hurtado, P., 2014. SEC Says House Insider Probe Involves 44 Funds, Entities. *Bloomberg*, July 18.

Pulliam, S., Rothfeld, M., 2014. FBI, SEC probe trading of Carl Icahn, Bill Walter, Phil Mickelson, Wall Street Journal. May 30.

Index